HIGH COURT CASE SUMMARIES

TORT LAW

Keyed to Franklin, Rabin and Green's
Casebook on Tort Law,
8th Edition

THOMSON

WEST

Mat #40537676

© West, a Thomson business, 2001
© 2006 Thomson/West
      610 Opperman Drive
      P.O. Box 64526
      St. Paul, MN 55164–0526
      1–800–328–9352

Printed in the United States of America

ISBN–13: 978–0–314–17266–2
ISBN–10: 0–314–17266–1

 TEXT IS PRINTED ON 10% POST CONSUMER RECYCLED PAPER

Table of Contents

Page

CHAPTER ONE.   Introduction to Tort Liability 1
Hammontree v. Jenner 3
Christensen v. Swenson et al. 5
Roessler v. Novak 9

CHAPTER TWO.   The Negligence Principle 11
Brown v. Kendall 15
Adams v. Bullock 17
United States v. Carroll Towing Co. 19
Bethel v. New York City Transit Authority 21
Baltimore & Ohio Railroad Co. v. Goodman 23
Pokora v. Wabash Railway Co. 25
Andrews v. United Airlines, Inc. 27
Trimarco v. Klein 29
Martin v. Herzog 31
Tedla v. Ellman 33
Negri v. Stop and Shop, Inc. 35
Gordon v. American Museum of Natural History 37
Byrne v. Boadle 39
McDougald v. Perry 41
Ybarra v. Spangard 43
Sheeley v. Memorial Hospital 47
States v. Lourdes Hospital 49
Matthies v. Mastromonaco 51

CHAPTER THREE.   The Duty Requirement: Physical Injuries 53
Harper v. Herman 57
Farwell v. Keaton 59
Randi W. v. Muroc Joint Unified School District 61
Tarasoff v. Regents of University of California 65
Uhr v. East Greenbush Central School District 69
Strauss v. Belle Realty Co. 71
Reynolds v. Hicks 73
Vince v. Wilson 75
Carter v. Kinney 77
Heins v. Webster County 79
Posecai v. Wal-Mart Stores, Inc. 81
Broadbent v. Broadbent 83
Riss v. City of New York 85
Lauer v. City of New York 87
Friedman v. State of New York 89
Cope v. Scott 91

CHAPTER FOUR.   The Duty Requirement: Nonphysical Harm 95
Falzone v. Busch 97
Metro-North Commuter Railroad Company v. Buckley 99
Gammon v. Osteopathic Hospital of Maine, Inc. 101
Portee v. Jaffee 103
Johnson v. Jamaica Hospital 105
Nycal Corporation v. KPMG Peat Marwick LLP 107
532 Madison Avenue Gourmet Foods, Inc. v. Finlandia Center, Inc. 109
Emerson v. Magendantz 111

CHAPTER FIVE.   Causation 113
Stubbs v. City of Rochester 115
Zuchowicz v. United States 117
Alberts v. Schultz 119
Summers v. Tice 121

	Page
Hymowitz v. Eli Lilly & Co.	123
Benn v. Thomas	127
Overseas Tankship (U.K.) Ltd. v. Morts Dock & Engineering Co., Ltd. (The Wagon Mound)	129
Doe v. Manheimer	131
Palsgraf v. Long Island R.R. Co.	133

CHAPTER SIX. Defenses — **135**

Fritts v. McKinne	137
Dalury v. S-K-I, Ltd.	139
Murphy v. Steeplechase Amusement Co.	141
Davenport v. Cotton Hope Plantation Horizontal Property Regime	143
Levandoski v. Cone	145
Geier v. American Honda Motor Company, Inc., et al.	147

CHAPTER SEVEN. Strict Liability — **149**

Fletcher v. Rylands	151
Rylands v. Fletcher	153
Sullivan v. Dunham	155
Indiana Harbor Belt R.R. Co. v. American Cyanamid Co.	157

CHAPTER EIGHT. Liability for Defective Products — **159**

MacPherson v. Buick Motor Co.	161
Escola v. Coca Cola Bottling Co. of Fresno	163
Soule v. General Motors Corporation	165
Camacho v. Honda Motor Co., Ltd.	167
Hood v. Ryobi America Corporation	171
Edwards v. Basel Pharmaceuticals	173
Vassallo v. Baxter Healthcare Corporation	175
General Motors Corporation v. Sanchez	177
Jones v. Ryobi, Ltd.	179
Liriano v. Hobart Corp.	181
Royer v. Catholic Medical Center	183
East River Steamship Corp. v. Transamerica Delaval Inc.	185

CHAPTER NINE. Trespass and Nuisance — **187**

Martin v. Reynolds Metals Co.	189
Boomer v. Atlantic Cement Co., Inc.	193

CHAPTER TEN. Damages and Insurance — **195**

Seffert v. Los Angeles Transit Lines	197
McDougald v. Garber	199
Arambula v. Wells	203
Taylor v. Superior Court	205
State Farm Mutual Automobile Insurance Co. v. Campbell	209
Frost v. Porter Leasing Corp.	213
Lalomia v. Bankers & Shippers Ins. Co.	215
Pavia v. State Farm Mutual Automobile Ins. Co.	217

CHAPTER TWELVE. Intentional Harm — **219**

Garratt v. Dailey	221
Picard v. Barry Pontiac-Buick, Inc.	223
Wishnatsky v. Huey	225
Lopez v. Winchell's Donut House	227
Womack v. Eldridge	231
McDermott v. Reynolds	233
Hustler Magazine v. Falwell	235
Hart v. Geysel	237
Courvoisier v. Raymond	239
Katko v. Briney	243
Vincent v. Lake Erie Transportation Co.	247
Wilson v. Layne	249

CHAPTER THIRTEEN. Defamation — **253**

Romaine v. Kallinger	255
Matherson v. Marchello	257
Matherson v. Marchello	259
Liberman v. Gelstein	261

Page

Liberman v. Gelstein 263
Medico v. Time, Inc. 265
Burnett v. National Enquirer, Inc. 267
Carafano v. Metrosplash.com, Inc. 269
New York Times Co. v. Sullivan 271
Gertz v. Robert Welch, Inc. 273
Wells v. Liddy 277
Milkovich v. Lorain Journal Co. 281
Flamm v. American Association of University Women 283
Khawar v. Globe International, Inc. 285

CHAPTER FOURTEEN.   Protecting Privacy **287**
Haynes v. Alfred A. Knopf, Inc. 289
The Florida Star v. B.J.F. 291
Humphers v. First Interstate Bank of Oregon 295
Cantrell v. Forest City Publishing Co. 297
Nader v. General Motors Corp. 299
Galella v. Onassis 303
Desnick v. American Broadcasting Companies, Inc. 305
Shulman v. Group W Productions Inc., et al. 307
Bartnicki v. Vopper 311
Zacchini v. Scripps-Howard Broadcasting Co. 313
Winter v. DC Comics 317

CHAPTER FIFTEEN.   Intentional Economic Harm **319**
Ollerman v. O'Rourke Co., Inc. 321
Imperial Ice Co. v. Rossier 325
Della Penna v. Toyota Motor Sales, U.S.A., Inc. 327
All-Tech Telecom, Inc. v. Amway Corporation 331

*

Alphabetical Table of Cases

Adams v. Bullock, 227 N.Y. 208, 125 N.E. 93 (N.Y.1919), 17

Alberts v. Schultz, 126 N.M. 807, 975 P.2d 1279 (N.M.1999), 119

All–Tech Telecom, Inc. v. Amway Corp., 174 F.3d 862 (7th Cir.1999), 331

Andrews v. United Airlines, Inc., 24 F.3d 39 (9th Cir.1994), 27

Arambula v. Wells, 85 Cal.Rptr.2d 584 (Cal.App. 4 Dist.1999), 203

Baltimore & Ohio Railroad Co. v. Goodman, 275 U.S. 66, 48 S.Ct. 24, 72 L.Ed. 167 (1927), 23

Bartnicki v. Vopper, 532 U.S. 514, 121 S.Ct. 1753, 149 L.Ed.2d 787 (2001), 311

Benn v. Thomas, 512 N.W.2d 537 (Iowa 1994), 127

Bethel v. New York City Transit Authority, 681 N.Y.S.2d 201, 703 N.E.2d 1214 (N.Y.1998), 21

Boomer v. Atlantic Cement Co., 309 N.Y.S.2d 312, 257 N.E.2d 870 (N.Y.1970), 193

Broadbent v. Broadbent, 184 Ariz. 74, 907 P.2d 43 (Ariz. 1995), 83

Brown v. Kendall, 60 Mass. 292 (Mass.1850), 15

Burnett v. National Enquirer, Inc., 144 Cal.App.3d 991, 193 Cal.Rptr. 206 (Cal.App. 2 Dist.1983), 267

Byrne v. Boadle, 1863 WL 6189 (Unknown Court—UK 1863), 39

Camacho v. Honda Motor Co., Ltd., 741 P.2d 1240 (Colo. 1987), 167

Cantrell v. Forest City Publishing Co., 419 U.S. 245, 95 S.Ct. 465, 42 L.Ed.2d 419 (1974), 297

Carafano v. Metrosplash.com. Inc., 339 F.3d 1119 (9th Cir. 2003), 269

Carroll Towing Co., United States v., 159 F.2d 169 (2nd Cir.1947), 19

Carter v. Kinney, 896 S.W.2d 926 (Mo.1995), 77

Christensen v. Swenson, 874 P.2d 125 (Utah 1994), 5

Cope v. Scott, 45 F.3d 445, 310 U.S.App.D.C. 144 (D.C.Cir. 1995), 91

Courvoisier v. Raymond, 23 Colo. 113, 47 P. 284 (Colo.1896), 239

Dalury v. S–K–I, Ltd., 164 Vt. 329, 670 A.2d 795 (Vt.1995), 139

Davenport v. Cotton Hope Plantation Horizontal Property Regime, 333 S.C. 71, 508 S.E.2d 565 (S.C.1998), 143

Della Penna v. Toyota Motor Sales, U.S.A., Inc., 45 Cal. Rptr.2d 436, 902 P.2d 740 (Cal.1995), 327

Desnick v. American Broadcasting Companies, Inc., 44 F.3d 1345 (7th Cir.1995), 305

Doe v. Manheimer, 212 Conn. 748, 563 A.2d 699 (Conn.1989), 131

East River Steamship Corp. v. Transamerica Delaval, Inc., 476 U.S. 858, 106 S.Ct. 2295, 90 L.Ed.2d 865 (1986), 185

Edwards v. Basel Pharmaceuticals, 933 P.2d 298 (Okla.1997), 173

Emerson v. Magendantz, 689 A.2d 409 (R.I.1997), 111

Escola v. Coca Cola Bottling Co. of Fresno, 24 Cal.2d 453, 150 P.2d 436 (Cal.1944), 163

Falzone v. Busch, 45 N.J. 559, 214 A.2d 12 (N.J.1965), 97

Farwell v. Keaton, 396 Mich. 281, 240 N.W.2d 217 (Mich. 1976), 59

532 Madison Avenue Gourmet Foods, Inc. v. Finlandia Center, Inc., 727 N.Y.S.2d 49, 750 N.E.2d 1097 (N.Y.2001), 109

Flamm v. American Association of University Women, 201 F.3d 144 (2nd Cir.2000), 283

Fletcher v. Rylands, 1866 WL 8245 (Ex Chamber 1866), 151

Florida Star v. B.J.F., 491 U.S. 524, 109 S.Ct. 2603, 105 L.Ed.2d 443 (1989), 291

Friedman v. State of New York, 502 N.Y.S.2d 669, 493 N.E.2d 893 (N.Y.1986), 89

Fritts v. McKinne, 934 P.2d 371 (Okla.Civ.App. Div. 2 1996), 137

Frost v. Porter Leasing Corp., 386 Mass. 425, 436 N.E.2d 387 (Mass.1982), 213

Galella v. Onassis, 487 F.2d 986 (2nd Cir.1973), 303

Gammon v. Osteopathic Hospital of Maine, Inc., 534 A.2d 1282 (Me.1987), 101

Garratt v. Dailey, 46 Wash.2d 197, 279 P.2d 1091 (Wash. 1955), 221

Geier v. American Honda Motor Co., Inc., 529 U.S. 861, 120 S.Ct. 1913, 146 L.Ed.2d 914 (2000), 147

General Motors Corp. v. Sanchez, 997 S.W.2d 584 (Tex.1999), 177

Gertz v. Robert Welch, Inc., 418 U.S. 323, 94 S.Ct. 2997, 41 L.Ed.2d 789 (1974), 273

Gordon v. American Museum of Natural History, 501 N.Y.S.2d 646, 492 N.E.2d 774 (N.Y.1986), 37

Hammontree v. Jenner, 20 Cal.App.3d 528, 97 Cal.Rptr. 739 (Cal.App. 2 Dist.1971), 3

Harper v. Herman, 499 N.W.2d 472 (Minn.1993), 57

Hart v. Geysel, 159 Wash. 632, 294 P. 570 (Wash.1930), 237

Haynes v. Alfred A. Knopf, Inc., 8 F.3d 1222 (7th Cir.1993), 289

Heins v. Webster County, 250 Neb. 750, 552 N.W.2d 51 (Neb.1996), 79

Hood v. Ryobi America Corp., 181 F.3d 608 (4th Cir.1999), 171

Humphers v. First Interstate Bank of Oregon, 298 Or. 706, 696 P.2d 527 (Or.1985), 295

Hustler Magazine v. Falwell, 485 U.S. 46, 108 S.Ct. 876, 99 L.Ed.2d 41 (1988), 235

Hymowitz v. Eli Lilly and Co., 541 N.Y.S.2d 941, 539 N.E.2d 1069 (N.Y.1989), 123

Imperial Ice Co. v. Rossier, 18 Cal.2d 33, 112 P.2d 631 (Cal.1941), 325

Indiana Harbor Belt R.R. Co. v. American Cyanamid Co., 916 F.2d 1174 (7th Cir.1990), 157

Johnson v. Jamaica Hospital, 478 N.Y.S.2d 838, 467 N.E.2d 502 (N.Y.1984), 105

Jones v. Ryobi, Ltd., 37 F.3d 423 (8th Cir.1994), 179

Katko v. Briney, 183 N.W.2d 657 (Iowa 1971), 243

Khawar v. Globe International, Inc., 79 Cal.Rptr.2d 178, 965 P.2d 696 (Cal.1998), 285

Lalomia v. Bankers & Shippers Ins. Co., 35 A.D.2d 114, 312 N.Y.S.2d 1018 (N.Y.A.D. 2 Dept.1970), 215

Lauer v. City of New York, 711 N.Y.S.2d 112, 733 N.E.2d 184 (N.Y.2000), 87

Levandoski v. Cone, 267 Conn. 651, 841 A.2d 208 (Conn. 2004), 145

Liberman v. Gelstein, 590 N.Y.S.2d 857, 605 N.E.2d 344 (N.Y.1992), 261, 263

Liriano v. Hobart Corp., 677 N.Y.S.2d 764, 700 N.E.2d 303 (N.Y.1998), 181

Lopez v. Winchell's Donut House, 126 Ill.App.3d 46, 81 Ill. Dec. 507, 466 N.E.2d 1309 (Ill.App. 1 Dist.1984), 227

MacPherson v. Buick Motor Co., 217 N.Y. 382, 111 N.E. 1050 (N.Y.1916), 161
Martin v. Herzog, 228 N.Y. 164, 126 N.E. 814 (N.Y.1920), 31
Martin v. Reynolds Metals Co., 221 Or. 86, 342 P.2d 790 (Or.1959), 189
Matherson v. Marchello, 100 A.D.2d 233, 473 N.Y.S.2d 998 (N.Y.A.D. 2 Dept.1984), 257, 259
Matthies v. Mastromonaco, 160 N.J. 26, 733 A.2d 456 (N.J. 1999), 51
McDermott v. Reynolds, 260 Va. 98, 530 S.E.2d 902 (Va. 2000), 233
McDougald v. Garber, 538 N.Y.S.2d 937, 536 N.E.2d 372 (N.Y.1989), 199
McDougald v. Perry, 716 So.2d 783 (Fla.1998), 41
Medico v. Time, Inc., 643 F.2d 134 (3rd Cir.1981), 265
Metro–North Commuter Railroad Co. v. Buckley, 521 U.S. 424, 117 S.Ct. 2113, 138 L.Ed.2d 560 (1997), 99
Milkovich v. Lorain Journal Co., 497 U.S. 1, 110 S.Ct. 2695, 111 L.Ed.2d 1 (1990), 281
Murphy v. Steeplechase Amusement Co., 250 N.Y. 479, 166 N.E. 173 (N.Y.1929), 141

Nader v. General Motors Corp., 307 N.Y.S.2d 647, 255 N.E.2d 765 (N.Y.1970), 299
Negri v. Stop and Shop, Inc., 491 N.Y.S.2d 151, 480 N.E.2d 740 (N.Y.1985), 35
New York Times Co. v. Sullivan, 376 U.S. 254, 84 S.Ct. 710, 11 L.Ed.2d 686 (1964), 271
Nycal Corporation v. KPMG Peat Marwick LLP, 426 Mass. 491, 688 N.E.2d 1368 (Mass.1998), 107

Ollerman v. O'Rourke Co., Inc., 94 Wis.2d 17, 288 N.W.2d 95 (Wis.1980), 321
Overseas Tankship (U.K.) Ltd. v. Morts Dock & Engineering Co., Ltd. (The Wagon Mound), [1961] A.C. 388 (Privy Council, 1961), 129

Palsgraf v. Long Island R.R. Co., 248 N.Y. 339, 162 N.E. 99 (N.Y.1928), 133
Pavia v. State Farm Mutual Automobile Insurance Co., 605 N.Y.S.2d 208, 626 N.E.2d 24 (N.Y.1993), 217
Picard v. Barry Pontiac–Buick, Inc., 654 A.2d 690 (R.I.1995), 223
Pokora v. Wabash Railway Co., 292 U.S. 98, 54 S.Ct. 580, 78 L.Ed. 1149 (1934), 25
Portee v. Jaffee, 84 N.J. 88, 417 A.2d 521 (N.J.1980), 103
Posecai v. Wal–Mart Stores, Inc., 752 So.2d 762 (La.1999), 81

Randi W. v. Muroc Joint Unified School District, 60 Cal. Rptr.2d 263, 929 P.2d 582 (Cal.1997), 61
Reynolds v. Hicks, 134 Wash.2d 491, 951 P.2d 761 (Wash. 1998), 73
Riss v. City of New York, 293 N.Y.S.2d 897, 240 N.E.2d 860 (N.Y.1968), 85
Roessler v. Novak, 858 So.2d 1158 (Fla.App. 2 Dist.2003), 9

Romaine v. Kallinger, 109 N.J. 282, 537 A.2d 284 (N.J.1988), 255
Royer v. Catholic Medical Center, 144 N.H. 330, 741 A.2d 74 (N.H.1999), 183
Rylands v. Fletcher, 1868 WL 9885 (HL 1868), 153

Seffert v. Los Angeles Transit Lines, 56 Cal.2d 498, 15 Cal.Rptr. 161, 364 P.2d 337 (Cal.1961), 197
Sheeley v. Memorial Hospital, 710 A.2d 161 (R.I.1998), 47
Shulman v. Group W Productions, Inc., 74 Cal.Rptr.2d 843, 955 P.2d 469 (Cal.1998), 307
Soule v. General Motors Corp., 34 Cal.Rptr.2d 607, 882 P.2d 298 (Cal.1994), 165
State Farm Mutual Automobile Insurance Co. v. Campbell, 538 U.S. 408, 123 S.Ct. 1513, 155 L.Ed.2d 585 (2003), 209
States v. Lourdes Hospital, 762 N.Y.S.2d 1, 792 N.E.2d 151 (N.Y.2003), 49
Strauss v. Belle Realty Co., 492 N.Y.S.2d 555, 482 N.E.2d 34 (N.Y.1985), 71
Stubbs v. City of Rochester, 226 N.Y. 516, 124 N.E. 137 (N.Y.1919), 115
Sullivan v. Dunham, 161 N.Y. 290, 55 N.E. 923 (N.Y.1900), 155
Summers v. Tice, 33 Cal.2d 80, 199 P.2d 1 (Cal.1948), 121

Tarasoff v. Regents of University of California, 131 Cal.Rptr. 14, 551 P.2d 334 (Cal.1976), 65
Taylor v. Superior Court, 157 Cal.Rptr. 693, 598 P.2d 854 (Cal.1979), 205
Tedla v. Ellman, 280 N.Y. 124, 19 N.E.2d 987 (N.Y.1939), 33
Trimarco v. Klein, 451 N.Y.S.2d 52, 436 N.E.2d 502 (N.Y. 1982), 29

Uhr v. East Greenbush Central School District, 698 N.Y.S.2d 609, 720 N.E.2d 886 (N.Y.1999), 69
United States v. _____ (see opposing party)

Vassallo v. Baxter Healthcare Corp., 428 Mass. 1, 696 N.E.2d 909 (Mass.1998), 175
Vince v. Wilson, 151 Vt. 425, 561 A.2d 103 (Vt.1989), 75
Vincent v. Lake Erie Transportation Co., 109 Minn. 456, 124 N.W. 221 (Minn.1910), 247

Wells v. Liddy, 186 F.3d 505 (4th Cir.1999), 277
Wilson v. Layne, 526 U.S. 603, 119 S.Ct. 1692, 143 L.Ed.2d 818 (1999), 249
Winter v. DC Comics, 134 Cal.Rptr.2d 634, 69 P.3d 473 (Cal.2003), 317
Wishnatsky v. Huey, 584 N.W.2d 859 (N.D.App.1998), 225
Womack v. Eldridge, 215 Va. 338, 210 S.E.2d 145 (Va.1974), 231

Ybarra v. Spangard, 25 Cal.2d 486, 154 P.2d 687 (Cal.1944), 43

Zacchini v. Scripps–Howard Broadcasting Co., 433 U.S. 562, 97 S.Ct. 2849, 53 L.Ed.2d 965 (1977), 313
Zuchowicz v. United States, 140 F.3d 381 (2nd Cir.1998), 117

CHAPTER ONE

Introduction to Tort Liability

Hammontree v. Jenner

Instant Facts: An epileptic suffered a seizure while driving his car and crashed through the wall of a shop, damaging the shop and injuring the shop owner.

Black Letter Rule: The liability of a driver, suddenly stricken by an illness rendering him unconscious, for injury resulting from an accident occurring during that time must rest on principles of negligence, and not absolute liability.

Christensen v. Swenson et al.

Instant Facts: A woman's employer was sued after the employee hit a motorcyclist with her car while she was going to get her lunch during a break.

Black Letter Rule: Summary judgment is inappropriate when reasonable minds could differ as to whether the defendant was acting within or outside the scope of her employment when an accident occurred.

Roessler v. Novak

Instant Facts: Roessler (P) claimed that his complications were caused by Lichtenstein's (D) misreading of an x-ray, and the Hospital (D) claimed that Lichtenstein (D) was an independent contractor.

Black Letter Rule: A principal may be held liable for the acts of an agent if the principal permits the appearance of authority in the agent.

Hammontree v. Jenner

(*Injured Shop Owner*) v. (*Epileptic Driver*)

20 Cal.App.3d 528, 97 Cal.Rptr. 739 (1971)

THE DOCTRINE OF STRICT LIABILITY DOES NOT APPLY TO AUTOMOBILE DRIVERS

■ **INSTANT FACTS** An epileptic suffered a seizure while driving his car and crashed through the wall of a shop, damaging the shop and injuring the shop owner.

■ **BLACK LETTER RULE** The liability of a driver, suddenly stricken by an illness rendering him unconscious, for injury resulting from an accident occurring during that time must rest on principles of negligence, and not absolute liability.

■ **PROCEDURAL BASIS**

Appeal from a jury verdict in favor of the defendant.

■ **FACTS**

Jenner (D) was driving home from work when he became unconscious during an epileptic seizure and lost control of his car [oops!]. His car then crashed through the wall of Hammontree's (P) bicycle shop, struck Hammontree (P) and caused personal injuries and damage to the shop. Jenner (D) claimed that his last recollection before the accident was leaving a stop light, and that he could recall nothing more until after the accident when he was being taken out of his car in Hammontree's (P) shop. Jenner (D) testified that he has a medical history of epilepsy, and that he was on medication which controlled his seizures. Eleven or twelve years before the accident, the Department of Motor Vehicles was advised that Jenner (D) was an epileptic and placed him on probation under which he had to report to a doctor every six months. Four years later, his probation was changed to a once-a-year report. His doctor testified that he believed it was safe for Jenner (D) to drive. [Messed that one up, didn't he?] Hammontree (P) contends that the trial court erred in refusing to grant her motion for summary judgment on the issue of liability and motion for a directed verdict on the pleadings. Hammontree (P) also contends that the trial court committed prejudicial error in refusing to give a jury instruction on absolute liability.

■ **ISSUE**

Does the doctrine of strict liability apply to automobile drivers?

■ **DECISION AND RATIONALE**

(Lillie, J.) No. Under the present state of the law found in appellate authorities, the trial judge properly refused the instruction Hammontree (P) requested. The prior cases generally held that the liability of a driver, suddenly stricken by an illness rendering him unconscious, for injury resulting from an accident occurring during that time rests on principles of negligence. However, in this case, Hammontree (P) withdrew her claim of negligence and, after both parties rested and before jury argument, objected to the giving of any instructions on negligence electing to stand solely on the theory of absolute liability. We decline to superimpose absolute liability upon drivers under the circumstances here. To invoke a rule of strict liability on users of the streets and highways, without also establishing in substantial detail how the new rule should operate would only contribute confusion to the automobile accident problem.

Settlement and claims adjustment procedures would become chaotic until the new rules were worked out on a case-by-case basis, and the hardships of delayed compensation would be seriously intensified. Only the Legislature, if it deems it wise to do so, can avoid such difficulties by enacting a comprehensive plan for the compensation of automobile accident victims in place of or in addition to the law of negligence. The judgment is affirmed.

Analysis:

Hammontree (P) drew a parallel between this case and products liability cases, arguing that only the driver affected by a physical condition that could suddenly render him unconscious, and who is aware of that condition, can anticipate the hazards and foresee the dangers involved in his operation of an automobile. Thus, Hammontree (P) argued, the liability of those who by reason of seizure or heart failure or some other physical condition lose the ability to safely operate and control an automobile resulting in injury to an innocent person should be predicated on strict liability. While this argument is logical, the court declined to accept it instead of leaving it up to the Legislature to make a change. Note that Jenner (D) took the position that he was not at fault, that he had no means of anticipating the attack, and that the accident was an act of God.

■ CASE VOCABULARY

ABSOLUTE LIABILITY: Responsibility without fault or negligence.

DIRECTED VERDICT: The trial judge's entry of a verdict without allowing the jury to consider the evidence because, as a matter of law, there can only be one verdict.

PREJUDICIAL ERROR: An error which substantially affects the party's legal rights or obligations, or which affects the final results of the trial.

RES IPSA LOQUITUR: A rule of evidence whereby negligence of the alleged wrongdoer may be inferred from the mere fact that the accident happened.

SUMMARY JUDGMENT: A procedural device available for prompt and expeditious disposition of a controversy without a trial when there is no dispute as to either material facts, or if only a question of law is involved.

Christensen v. Swenson et al.

(*Injured Motorcyclist*) v. (*Car Driver*)
874 P.2d 125 (Utah 1994)

WHETHER AN EMPLOYEE IS ACTING WITHIN THE SCOPE OF HER EMPLOYMENT IS ORDINARILY A QUESTION OF FACT FOR THE JURY'S DETERMINATION

■ **INSTANT FACTS** A woman's employer was sued after the employee hit a motorcyclist with her car while she was going to get her lunch during a break.

■ **BLACK LETTER RULE** Summary judgment is inappropriate when reasonable minds could differ as to whether the defendant was acting within or outside the scope of her employment when an accident occurred.

■ **PROCEDURAL BASIS**

Appeal from the court of appeals' affirmance of the trial court's grant of summary judgment in favor of the defendant.

■ **FACTS**

Swenson (D), a Burns (D) employee, was guarding a gate at a steel plant. Guards worked eight-hour continuous shifts, with no scheduled breaks. However, employees were permitted to take ten- to fifteen-minute unscheduled lunch and restroom breaks. Whether the guards brought their lunches or ordered from a café directly across the street from the plant, they were expected to eat at their posts [such task-masters!]. On the day of the accident, Swenson (D) noticed a lull in the traffic at the gate and decided to get a cup of soup from the café across the street. She phoned in her order, and then drove her car to the café. She intended to pick up the soup and return to the gate to eat at her post. On her return trip, however, she collided with Christensen's (P) motorcycle in a public intersection just outside the plant. Several people were injured. When suit was brought against Swenson (D) and Burns (D), claiming that Swenson (D) had driven negligently, Burns (D) moved for summary judgment on the ground that Swenson (D) was not its employee nor acting in the scope of her employment at the time of the accident. The trial court granted the motion and the court of appeals affirmed.

■ **ISSUE**

Did the court err in granting summary judgment on the grounds that the defendant was not acting in the scope of her employment at the time of the accident?

■ **DECISION AND RATIONALE**

(Durham, J.) Yes. Summary judgment is appropriate when the record indicates that there is no genuine as to any material fact and the moving party is entitled to judgment as a matter of law. We view all relevant facts and all inferences arising from those facts in the light most favorable to the party opposing the motion. Acts falling within the scope of employment are those acts which are so closely connected with what the servant is employed to do, and so fairly and reasonably incidental to it, that they may be regarded as methods, even though quite improper ones, of carrying out the objectives of employment. There are three criteria helpful in determining whether an employee is acting within or outside the scope of her employment. First, the employee's conduct must be of the general kind the employee is hired to perform. Second, the employee's conduct must occur substantially within the hours and ordinary spatial boundaries of the employment. Finally, the employees conduct must be motivated, at least in part, by the purpose of serving the employer's interest. The court of appeals held that Swenson (D) was not substantially within the ordinary spatial boundaries of the employment because the accident did not occur on Plant property. The court of appeals did not address the first and third criteria, however, and our review of the record indicates that reasonable minds could differ on all three criteria. Thus, to avoid a second summary judgment on remand, we address all three of the criteria. The first criterion requires the employee to be doing the employer's business and the duties assigned by the employer, as opposed to being wholly involved in a personal endeavor. Reasonable minds could differ as to whether Swenson (D) was involved with Burns' (D) business when she was involved in the traffic accident. We base this conclusion on two disputed issues of material fact. Swenson (D) argues that the short distance to the café was within the area Burns (D) sought to protect. Burns' (D) contrary position is supported by the deposition of another security guard who stated that he considered lunch trips to the café to be entirely personal in nature. A second material issue of fact remains as to whether Burns (D) tacitly sanctioned the practice of obtaining lunch from the café. The record indicates that Burns (D) was aware that its employees occasionally traveled to the café during the unscheduled breaks but had never disciplined them for it. Thus, reasonable minds could differ as to whether Burns (D) tacitly sanctioned, or at least contemplated, that its guards would go to the café for food. With respect to the second criterion, we find that reasonable minds might differ as to whether Swenson (D) was substantially within the ordinary spatial boundaries of the employment. While it is true that Swenson (D) was not on Plant property when the accident occurred, she was attempting to obtain lunch during her ten- to fifteen-minute break. Finally, applying the third criterion to the facts of this case, poses the question of whether Swenson's (D) trip to the café was motivated, at least in part, by the purpose of serving Burns' (D) interest. Again, reasonable minds might differ on this question, as two Burns (D) employees testified that employee breaks benefit both the employee and the employer. Employees must eat and use the restroom, and employers receive the corresponding benefit of productive, satisfied employees. Additionally, given the continuous-shift nature of the job, the break policy obviously placed a premium on speed and efficiency. In this respect, reasonable minds might conclude that Swenson's (D) conduct was motivated, at least in part, by the purpose of serving Burns' (D) interest. In sum, we hold that reasonable minds could differ as to whether Swenson (D) was acting within or outside the scope of her employment when she collided with Christensen's (P) motorcycle. Thus, summary judgment is inappropriate. We reverse and remand for further proceedings.

Analysis:

Under the doctrine of respondeat superior, employers are vicariously liable for torts committed by employees acting within the scope of their employment. Thus, Christensen (P) sued both Swenson (D) and Burns (D), as Swenson's (D) employer at the time of the accident. In reality, the plaintiff is looking for "deeper pockets," with the hope of recovering the highest possible money award. The problem here is in deciding whether Swenson (D) was actually "working" at the time of the accident so that Burns (D) could also be held accountable. Whether an employee is acting within the scope of her employment is ordinarily a question of fact that must be submitted to the jury whenever reasonable minds could differ as to the answer. However, when the employee's activity is so clearly within or outside the scope of employment that reasonable minds cannot differ, the court may decide the issue as a matter of law.

■ CASE VOCABULARY

REMAND: The act of an appellate court when it sends a case back to the trial court and orders further action.

RESPONDEAT SUPERIOR: A doctrine whereby employers are vicariously liable for torts committed by employees acting within the scope of their employment.

SCOPE OF EMPLOYMENT: Acts which are so closely connected with what the servant is employed to do, and so fairly and reasonably incidental to it, that they may be regarded as methods, even though quite improper ones, of carrying out the objectives of employment.

VICARIOUS LIABILITY: The imposition of liability on one person for the actionable conduct of another, based solely on the relationship between the two persons.

Roessler v. Novak

(Patient) v. *(Physician)*

858 So.2d 1158 (Fla. Dist. Ct. App. 2003)

APPARENT AGENCY MAY RESULT IN VICARIOUS LIABILITY

Yes, I'm a radiologist. And yes I work at the hospital. And yes I'm the only choice the hospital offers. But why would you think I work for the hospital?

stus.com

■ **INSTANT FACTS** Roessler (P) claimed that his complications were caused by Lichtenstein's (D) misreading of an x-ray, and the Hospital (D) claimed that Lichtenstein (D) was an independent contractor.

■ **BLACK LETTER RULE** A principal may be held liable for the acts of an agent if the principal permits the appearance of authority in the agent.

■ **PROCEDURAL BASIS**

Appeal from an order granting summary judgment to the Hospital (D).

■ **FACTS**

Roessler (P) was admitted to Sarasota Memorial Hospital (Hospital) (D). While in the Hospital (D), Lichtenstein (D), a radiologist, took and read scans of Roessler's (P) abdomen. The scans were taken in the radiology department of the Hospital (D). After the scans were read, surgery was performed on Roessler (P). Serious complications developed after the surgery.

Roessler (P) claimed that Lichtenstein (D) misinterpreted the scans and was negligent in making his diagnosis. The Hospital (D) claimed that it was not liable for Lichtenstein's (D) alleged negligence, since he was not an employee of the Hospital (D), but was an employee of an independent entity, SMH Radiology (D). SMH (D) was the exclusive provider of radiology services to the Hospital (D), and its only offices were on the grounds of the Hospital (D).

■ **ISSUE**

Could the Hospital (D) be held vicariously liable for the negligence of Lichtenstein (D), even though he was not an employee of the Hospital (D)?

■ **DECISION AND RATIONALE**

(Salcines, J.) Yes. A principal may be held liable for the acts of an agent if the principal permits the appearance of authority in the agent. Agency is often based on an express agreement, but a principal may also be liable to a third party for acts that are within the agent's apparent authority. Apparent agency exists when there is a representation by the purported principal, a third party relies on that representation, and the third party changes his or her position in reliance on the representation. A party should be estopped from denying an agent's authority if that party permitted the appearance of authority, thereby justifying another's reliance on that appearance of authority.

The Hospital (D) and SMH (D) entered into an independent contractor agreement, with the expectation that vicarious liability would not attach to the Hospital (D) for any negligent acts of the physicians employed by SMH (D). Such an agreement will not prevent a hospital from being held vicariously liable if the physicians act with the apparent authority of the hospital. The question of a physician's apparent authority to act for a hospital is often a question of fact for the jury.

The Hospital (D) argued on appeal that Roessler (P) never spoke to Lichtenstein (D), so there could have been no reliance on any representations. The crucial question is not what transpired between Lichtenstein (D) and Roessler (P), but instead, what representations were made by the Hospital (D), the purported agent, that would have led Roessler (P) to rely on it to provide radiological services. Reversed and remanded.

■ CONCURRENCE

(Altenbernd, C.J.) The doctrine of apparent agency does not work well in a complex environment, such as a hospital, in which many interrelated independent contractors work side-by-side. Patients, medical professionals, risk managers, and insurers all need to have predictable rules to set out the parameters of vicarious liability.

It is arguable that hospitals should have a nondelegable duty to provide adequate care to patients. Ordinarily, the choice of which independent contractor to use belongs to the hospital, not the patient. Medical economics would work better if the general rule made hospitals vicariously liable for the activities that go on in the hospital.

Analysis:

There are many reasons a hospital might choose to use independent contractors to provide medical services. For example, several different hospitals in an area maybe able to use the services of one group of physicians, thus saving the costs of hiring, equipping, and administering the physicians themselves. From the evidence set out in the majority's opinion, however, the contractor arrangement here seems like nothing more than an attempt to avoid liability. If nothing else, the name of the practice—SMH Radiology (D), which performs services exclusively for Sarasota Memorial Hospital (D)— is strong evidence that the contractor arrangement was not a real contractor arrangement, but just a cover for an employment relationship.

■ CASE VOCABULARY

INDEPENDENT CONTRACTOR: One who is hired to undertake a specific project but who is left free to do the assigned work and to choose the method for accomplishing it. Unlike an employee, an independent contractor who commits a wrong while carrying out the work does not create liability for the one who did the hiring.

SUMMARY JUDGMENT: A judgment granted on a claim about which there is no genuine issue of material fact and upon which the movant is entitled to prevail as a matter of law. This procedural device allows the speedy disposition of a controversy without the need for trial. Fed. R. Civ. P. 56.

CHAPTER TWO

The Negligence Principle

Brown v. Kendall

Instant Facts: The defendant accidentally hit the plaintiff in the eye with a stick as he was trying to separate two fighting dogs.

Black Letter Rule: The burden of proof is on the plaintiff to establish facts which are essential to enable him to recover.

Adams v. Bullock

Instant Facts: A child was shocked and burned when a wire he was swinging over the side of a bridge contacted the trolley wire running below.

Black Letter Rule: Ordinary caution does not involve forethought of extraordinary peril.

United States v. Carroll Towing Co.

Instant Facts: A barge, without a bargee on broad broke adrift, was carried by wind into a tanker whose propeller broke a hole in barge's bottom, and barge lost its cargo and sank.

Black Letter Rule: Absence a reasonable excuse, barge owner's failure to take reasonable steps to prevent unreasonable risk of barge breaking away in busy wartime harbor by manning barge with bargee is negligence.

Bethel v. New York City Transit Authority

Instant Facts: A man was injured when a wheelchair seat on a bus collapsed under him only eleven days after repairs had been made to the seat.

Black Letter Rule: A common carrier is subject to the same duty of care as any other potential tortfeasor reasonable care under all of the circumstances of the particular case.

Baltimore & Ohio Railroad Co. v. Goodman

Instant Facts: A man was hit and killed by a train as he crossed the tracks in his truck.

Black Letter Rule: If a driver crossing a railroad track relies upon not hearing a train or any signal, and takes no further precaution he does so at his own risk and will be responsible for his actions.

Pokora v. Wabash Railway Co.

Instant Facts: A man was hit by a train as he crossed the railroad tracks because his vision of the tracks was blocked by other train cars.

Black Letter Rule: The question was for the jury whether reasonable caution forbade the driver from going forward across the tracks in reliance on the sense of hearing, unaided by that of sight.

Andrews v. United Airlines, Inc.

Instant Facts: A woman was injured when a briefcase fell on her from the overhead compartment of an airplane.

Black Letter Rule: Since a jury could make a rational decision either way on the record presented, summary judgment is inappropriate.

Trimarco v. Klein

Instant Facts: A man was badly cut in the defendant's apartment building when he fell through a glass shower door which was not made of shatterproof glass, as was the custom.

Black Letter Rule: When proof of a customary practice is coupled with a showing that it was ignored and that this departure was a proximate cause of the accident, it may serve to establish liability.

Martin v. Herzog

Instant Facts: The Martins (P) were driving a buggy without lights at night when they were struck by Herzog's (D) automobile, which was traveling on the wrong side of the road.

Black Letter Rule: The unexcused omission of statutory signals is negligence in itself.

Tedla v. Ellman

Instant Facts: Two pedestrians were hit from behind by a car as they walked along the side of a roadway on the incorrect side (as defined by statute) of the route.

Black Letter Rule: A pedestrian is at fault if he fails without good reason to observe the statutory rule of conduct.

Negri v. Stop and Shop, Inc.

Instant Facts: Negri (P) slipped and fell in a grocery store on broken and spilled jars of baby food which the store (D) had failed to clean up.

Black Letter Rule: Plaintiff having made out a prima facie case, it was error to dismiss the complaint.

Gordon v. American Museum of Natural History

Instant Facts: A man sued after he slipped and fell on a piece of paper, which he claims came from a Museum (D) concession.

Black Letter Rule: To constitute constructive notice, a defect must be visible and apparent and it must exist for a sufficient length of time prior to the accident to permit the defendant's employees to discover and remedy it.

Byrne v. Boadle

Instant Facts: A man was injured when a barrel of flour fell out of a window and hit him.

Black Letter Rule: If a person passing along the road is injured by something falling upon him, the accident alone is prima facie evidence of negligence, and if there is any state of facts to rebut the presumption of negligence, the defendant must prove them.

McDougald v. Perry

Instant Facts: A spare tire bounced from under a trailer injuring the driver following the trailer.

Black Letter Rule: Res ipsa loquitur provides an inference of negligence when the accident is the type that does not occur without negligence and the defendant is in control of the circumstances.

Ybarra v. Spangard

Instant Facts: A man lost the use of his arm due to an injury which occurred while he was unconscious and receiving medical treatment for another ailment.

Black Letter Rule: Where a plaintiff receives unusual injuries while unconscious and in the course of medical treatment, all those defendants who had any control over his body or the instrumentalities which might have caused the injuries may properly be called upon to meet the inference of negligence by giving an explanation of their conduct.

Sheeley v. Memorial Hospital

Instant Facts: Sheeley (P) sued her doctor and the hospital after she developed complications at the episiotomy incision site after giving birth.

Black Letter Rule: A physician is under a duty to use the degree of care and skill that is expected of a reasonably competent practitioner in the same class to which he or she belongs, acting in the same or similar circumstances.

States v. Lourdes Hospital

Instant Facts: While undergoing surgery for the removal of an ovarian cyst, States's (P) arm was injured, allegedly due to Lourdes Hospital's (D) negligence in administering anesthesia.

Black Letter Rule: The doctrine of res ipsa loquitur permits a factfinder to draw an inference of negligence when the injury-causing event is of a kind that ordinarily does not occur absent negligence.

Matthies v. Mastromonaco

Instant Facts: Matthies' (P) doctor (D) treated her broken hip with bed rest instead of surgery, without consulting with her about her options, and she never walked again.

Black Letter Rule: To obtain a patient's informed consent to one of several alternative courses of treatment, the physician should explain medically reasonable invasive and noninvasive alternatives, including the risks and likely outcomes of those alternatives, even when the chosen course is noninvasive.

Brown v. Kendall

(Victim of a Poke in the Eye) v. *(Stick-Wielding Eye Poker)*

6 Cush. (60 Mass.) 292 (1850)

THE PLAINTIFF MUST PROVE AS PART OF HIS CASE EITHER THAT THE INTENTION WAS UNLAWFUL OR THAT THE DEFENDANT WAS AT FAULT IN ORDER TO RECOVER

■ **INSTANT FACTS** The defendant accidentally hit the plaintiff in the eye with a stick as he was trying to separate two fighting dogs.

■ **BLACK LETTER RULE** The burden of proof is on the plaintiff to establish facts which are essential to enable him to recover.

■ **FACTS**

Two dogs, belonging to Brown (P) and Kendall (D), respectively, were fighting. Kendall (D) picked up a four foot long stick and began to beat the dogs in order to separate them. During the course of the struggle, Kendall (D) inadvertently hit Brown (P) in the eye with the stick, causing severe injury [Hence the proverbial poke in the eye with a sharp stick?]. This action of trespass for assault and battery was originally brought against Kendall (D), however he died pending the suit and his executrix was summoned in. The court instructed the jury that Kendall (D) had to prove his duty of care.

■ **ISSUE**

Did the court err in instructing the jury that the burden of proof as to the duty of care was on the defendant?

■ **DECISION AND RATIONALE**

(Shaw, C.J.) Yes. This case proceeds on the assumption that the damage sustained by Brown (P) from Kendall's (D) stick was inadvertent and unintentional. The case involves the question how far, and under what qualifications, the party by whose unconscious act the damage was done is responsible for it. We use the term "unintentional" rather than involuntary because in some cases it is stated that the act of holding and using a weapon or instrument, the movement of which is the immediate cause of hurt to another, is a voluntary act, although its particular effect in hitting and hurting another is not within the purpose or intention of the party doing the act. Dicta in past cases has stated that when one receives injury from the direct act of another, trespass will lie. But we think that this is said in reference to the question whether trespass and not case will lie. We think that the proper rule is that the plaintiff must come prepared with evidence to show either that the intention was unlawful, or that the defendant was at fault. If the injury was unavoidable, and the conduct of the defendant was free from blame, he will not be liable. We have no doubt that Kendall's (D) act in attempting to part the fighting dogs, one of which was his own, was a lawful and proper act, which he could so by safe and proper means. If in doing this act, using due care and all proper precautions necessary to the exigency of the case to avoid injury to others, he raised his stick and accidentally hit Brown (P) in the eye, this was the result of a pure accident, or was involuntary and unavoidable, and therefore the action would not lie. The court instructed the jury that if it was not a necessary act, and Kendall (D) was not duty bound to part the dogs, but might with propriety interfere or not as he chose, Kendall (D) was responsible for the consequences of the blow, unless it appeared that he was in the exercise of extraordinary care, so that the accident was inevitable. This is to be taken in connection with the charge given afterwards, that if the jury believed that the act of interference in the fight was unnecessary, then the burden of proving extraordinary care on Kendall's (D) part, or want of ordinary care on Brown's (P) part, was on Kendall (D). We are of the opinion that these directions were not conformable to law. If the act of hitting Brown (P) was unintentional on Kendall's (D) part, and done in the doing of a lawful act, then Kendall (D) was not liable unless it was done with the want of exercise of due care, adapted to the exigency of the case. Therefore, such want of due care becomes part of Brown's (P) case, and the burden of proof was on Brown (P) to establish it. The charge to the jury placing the burden of proof on Kendall (D) was incorrect. Those facts which are essential to the plaintiff's case must be proved by the plaintiff. If it appears that Kendall (D) was doing a lawful act and unintentionally hit and hurt Brown (P), then unless it also appears to the satisfaction of the jury that Kendall (D) is chargeable with fault, negligence, carelessness, or want of prudence, Brown (P) fails to sustain the burden of proof and is not entitled to recover. New trial ordered.

Analysis:

If, in the course of a lawful act, an accident occurs, no action can be supported for an injury arising therefrom. To this effect, if both the plaintiff and defendant at the time of the blow were using ordinary care, or if at that time both the plaintiff and the defendant were not using ordinary care, then the plaintiff could not recover. What constitutes ordinary care will vary with the circumstances of cases. In general, it means that kind and degree of care that prudent and cautious men would use, such as is required by the exigency of the case, and such as is necessary to guard against probable danger. To qualify as accidental, the incident must be such that the defendant could not have avoided it by the use of the kind and degree of care necessary to the exigency under the circumstances in which he was placed.

■ CASE VOCABULARY

BILL OF EXCEPTIONS: A formal statement in writing of the objections taken by a party during the course of a trial to the decisions, rulings, or instructions of the trial judge.

DICTA: Opinions of a judge which do not embody the resolution or determination of the specific case before the court, and are not binding in subsequent cases as legal precedent.

DUE CARE: That care which an ordinarily prudent person would have exercised under the same or similar circumstances.

EXECUTRIX: A woman appointed by a testator to carry out the directions and requests in his will, and to dispose of the property according to his testamentary provisions.

TRESPASS VI ET ARMIS: Literally, "with force and arms"; common-law action for damages for injury committed by the defendant with direct and immediate force or violence against the plaintiff or his property.

Adams v. Bullock

(Burned Little Boy) v. *(Trolley Operator)*
227 N.Y. 208, 125 N.E. 93 (1919)

ONE IS NOT GUILTY OF NEGLIGENCE WHEN ONE FAILS TO FORESEE THE UNUSUAL AND REMOTE CONDUCT OF OTHERS

■ **INSTANT FACTS** A child was shocked and burned when a wne lie was swinging over the side of a bridge contacted the trolley wire running below.

■ **BLACK LETTER RULE** Ordinary caution does not involve forethought of extraordinary peril.

■ **PROCEDURAL BASIS**

Appeal from the Appellate Division's affirmance of the trial court's verdict in favor of the plaintiff.

■ **FACTS**

Bullock (D) runs a trolley line which employs the overhead wire system. At one point, the road is overpassed by a railroad bridge Pedestrians often use the bridge as a shortcut between streets, and children play on it. Adams (P), a twelve-year-old boy, was crossing the bndge swinging a wire about eight feet long. In swinging it, he brought it in contact with the trolley wire, which ran about four and three quarters feet beneath the bridge. Adams (P) was shocked and burned when the wires came together. The trial court found in favor of Adams (P), and the Appellate Division affirmed This appeal followed.

[margin: 4 feet / n ¾ inches]

■ **ISSUE**

Was the defendant negligent in (not) taking special measures *of* precaution to guard the trolley wires?

■ **DECISION AND RATIONALE**

(Cardozo, J.) No. We think the verdict cannot stand. Bullock (D), in using an overhead trolley, was in the lawful exercise of its franchise. Therefore, negligence cannot be imputed to it because it used that system and not another. There was, of course, a (duty) to adopt all reasonable precautions to minimize the resulting perils, however there is no evidence that this duty was ignored. The trolley wire was placed so that no one standing on, or leaning over, the bridge could reach it. Only some extraordinary casualty, not fairly within the are of ordinary contemplation, could make it a thing of danger. There was no amount of vigilance, however alert (aside from the gift of prophecy), that could have predicted such an accident. Ordinary caution does not involve the forethought of extraordinary peril. To have averted the possibility of this accident and others like it, Bullock (D) would have had to abandon the overhead system, and put the wires underground. Neither its power nor its duty to make the change is shown, and as such the judgment should be reversed.

Analysis:

This accident in this case was not within the range of prudent foresight and, as such, Bullock (D) could not be held liable for negligence. Negligence is the doing of something that a reasonably prudent person would not do, or the failure to do something that a reasonably prudent person would do, under circumstances similar to those shown by the evidence. It is the failure to use ordinary or reasonable care. In this case, it cannot be said that Bullock (D) did not use reasonable care in elevating the trolley wire. It seems that, at the point along the trolley route, a mischievous or careless child might touch the wire with a metal pole or fling another wire across it. No accident like that had occurred before, and no custom had been ignored.

■ CASE VOCABULARY

NEGLIGENCE: The doing of something which a reasonably prudent person would not do, or the failure to do something which a reasonably prudent person would do, under circumstances similar to those shown by the evidence.

United States v. Carroll Towing Co.

(*Party in Admiralty*) v. (*Tug Boat Towing Company*)

159 F.2d 169 (2d Cir. 1947)

UNITED STATES COURT OF APPEALS FINDS THAT BARGE OWNER AND ITS EMPLOYEES WERE NEGLIGENT WHEN BARGEE WAS ABSENT WHEN BARGE BROKE ADRIFT, LOST HER CARGO, AND SANK

■ **INSTANT FACTS** A barge, without a bargee on board broke adrift, was carried by wind into a tanker whose propeller broke a hole in barge's bottom, and barge lost its cargo and sank.

■ **BLACK LETTER RULE** Absent a reasonable excuse, barge owner's failure to take reasonable steps to prevent unreasonable risk of barge breaking away in busy wartime harbor by manning barge with bargee is negligence.

■ **PROCEDURAL BASIS**

Proceedings in admiralty.

■ **FACTS**

A barge broke adrift from a tugboat that the (Carroll) Towing Co. (Carroll) (D) operated. Upon breaking adrift, the wind and tide carried the barge against a tanker. The tanker's propeller broke a hole in the barge. As a result, the barge lost its cargo of flour and sank. The trial court found that the owners and operators of the tugboat assigned to the barge were liable for the damages to the barge and then considered if the absence of a bargee on board the barge at the time of the incident reduced the recovery of the owner of the barge.

■ **ISSUE**

Whether absence a reasonable excuse, barge owner's failure to take reasonable steps to prevent unreasonable risk of barge breaking away in busy wartime harbor by manning barge with bargee is negligence?

■ **DECISION AND RATIONALE**

(Hand, J.) Yes. Absence a reasonable excuse, barge owner's failure to take reasonable steps to prevent the unreasonable risk of the barge breaking away in the harbor by manning a barge with a bargee is negligence. There is no general rule to determine when the absence of a bargee will make the owner of a barge liable for damages to other vessels. Under certain circumstances, any vessel may break free from her mooring and become a menace to other vessels. Therefore, the duty of a vessel's owner depends upon the probability (P) that the vessel will break free, the gravity of the resulting injury (L) if she does break free, and the burden (B) of adequate precautions to prevent her from breaking free or mitigating damages if she does break free. If the burden of adequate precautions is less than the product of the probability that a vessel will break free and the gravity of the resulting injury if she does (B < PL), liability would attach under the appropriate circumstances. Whether a barge will break from her fast and cause damage depends on circumstances such as stormy weather and busy harbor conditions. However, a barge is not a bargee's prison. In the instant case, the bargee left the barge at 5:00 PM on January 3rd. The barge broke away at 2:00 PM on the following day. The bargee was absent, without excuse, from 5:00 PM on January 3rd to 2 00 PM the following day. The bargee's absence occurred in January when the days are short. Further, the incident of the instant case occurred in the full tide of war activity when barges are constantly drilled in an out. Given the weather conditions and the busy nature of the harbor, this court holds that it is reasonable to require a barge owner to have a bargee on board during the working hours of daylight, unless there is a reasonable excuse for the bargee's absence.

Analysis:

Judge Hand recognized the traditional idea that a weighing of risks and utilities was necessary. The burden of precaution in Judge Hand's formula includes any cost the defendant might have to incur to make things safe enough, but it also includes costs that would be inflicted upon others or upon society at large. Here, the burden or precaution was simple: the increased or marginal cost to the defendant of keeping a bargee on board twenty-four hours a day. Thinking about costs and benefits in terms of the Carroll Towing formula, a judge or juror can compare benefits with costs because they have now been put on a common scale. One,, of the most important functions of the formula may be to direct lawyers to helpful kinds of evidence. Plaintiffs' lawyers may claim that the defendant failed to use a cheaper means of achieving safety. For instance, a plaintiff's lawyer might try to prove that the defendant could have avoided the breakaway in *Carroll Towing* by making a one-time capital investment in better tie-down technology that would be far less costly than either the full-time bargee or the potential harm from breakaways. Although probability is used to discount the damage when the point is to determine the defendant's negligence, probability is not used to reduce the plaintiff's actual recovery.

Something wrong with using π & Δ.

Here, (Analysis) π - Carroll

Δ - Conners

Bethel v. New York City Transit Authority

(Injured Bus Passenger) v. *(Bus Operator)*

92 N.Y.2d 348, 703 N.E.2d 1214, 681 N.Y.S.2d 201 (1998)

THERE IS NO STRATIFICATION OF DEGREES OF CARE AS A MATTER OF LAW, RATHER, THERE ARE ONLY DIFFERENT AMOUNTS OF CARE AS A MATTER OF FACT

Not problem with wheelchair lift
but with wheelchair accessible seat.

■ **INSTANT FACTS** A man was injured when a wheelchair seat on a bus collapsed under him only eleven days after repairs had been made to the seat.

■ **BLACK LETTER RULE** A common carrier is subject to the same duty of care as any other potential tortfeasor—reasonable care under all of the circumstances of the particular case.

■ **PROCEDURAL BASIS**

Appeal from the Appellate Division's affirmance of the trial court's jury verdict in favor of the plaintiff.

■ **FACTS**

Bethel (P) was injured on the Transit Authority's (D) bus when the wheelchair accessible seat collapsed under him. Bethel could not prove that the Transit Authority (D) actually knew of a defect, but relied on a theory of constructive notice evidenced by a repair record of the bus containing two notations that, 11 days before the accident, repairs were made to a "Lift Wheelchair." Bethel (P) contends that these repairs were to the seat in question, and that a prior inspection during those repairs would have revealed the defect causing the seat to collapse. The court charged the jury that, as a common carrier, the bus company (D) had a duty to use the highest degree of care that human prudence and foresight can suggest in the maintenance of its vehicles and equipment for the safety of its passengers. On the issue of constructive notice, arising out of the earlier inspection and repair, the trial court submitted the question of whether considering the duty of care that is imposed on common carriers with respect to this equipment, a reasonable inspection would have led to the discovery of the condition and its repair before the accident. The jury found for Bethel (P) on the constructive notice theory and the Appellate Division affirmed without addressing the issue of standard of care. The court of appeals concluded that the instruction was the dispositive issue on appeal.

■ **ISSUE**

Should a duty of highest care continue to be applied, as a matter of law, to common carriers?

■ **DECISION AND RATIONALE**

(Levine, J.) No. The duty of common carriers to exercise the highest degree of care was widely adopted at the advent of the age of steam railroads in 19th century America. Their primitive safety features resulted in a phenomenal growth in railroad accident injuries and with them, an explosion in personal injury litigation, significantly affecting the American tort system. In this century, however, through technological advances and intense governmental regulation, public conveyances have become at least as safe as private modes of travel. The objective, reasonable person standard in basic traditional negligence theory necessarily takes into account the circumstances with which the actor was actually confronted when the accident occurred, including the reasonably perceivable risk and gravity of harm to others and any special relationship of dependency between the victim and the actor. It is our opinion that the single, reasonable person standard is sufficiently flexible by itself to permit courts and juries fully to take into account the ultrahazardous nature of a tortfeasor's activity. We therefore conclude that the rule of a common carrier's duty of extraordinary care is no longer viable. Rather, a common carrier is subject to the same duty of care as any other potential tortfeasor—reasonable care under all of the circumstances of the particular case. Here, because the jury was specifically charged that the defendant carrier was required to exercise the highest degree of care that human prudence and foresight can suggest in connection with the issue of its constructive notice of the defective seat, the error cannot be deemed merely harmless. The case was remanded for a new trial.

Analysis:

The whole theory of negligence presupposes some uniform standard of behavior, yet the infinite variety of situations that arise make it impossible to fix definite rules in advance for all conceivable human conduct. The standard of conduct that the community demands must be an external and objective one, rather than the individual judgment, good or bad, of the particular actor. The courts have dealt with this very difficult problem by creating a fictional person, the "reasonable person of ordinary prudence." The reasonable person standard allows sufficient flexibility to allow for all of the particular circumstances of the case that may reasonably affect the conduct.

■ **CASE VOCABULARY**

CONSTRUCTIVE NOTICE: Such notice as is implied or imputed by law, usually on the basis that the information is a part of a public record or file.

Baltimore & Ohio Railroad Co. v. Goodman

(*Train Operator*) v. (*Driver Hit by Train*)
275 U.S. 66, 48 S.Ct. 24, 72 L.Ed. 167 (1927)

IF A DRIVER CANNOT BE SURE WHETHER A TRAIN IS DANGEROUSLY NEAR HE MUST STOP AND GET OUT OF HIS VEHICLE

■ **INSTANT FACTS** A man was hit and killed by a train as he crossed the tracks in his truck.

■ **BLACK LETTER RULE** If a driver crossing a railroad track relies upon not hearing a train or any signal, and takes no further precaution he does so at his own risk and will be responsible for his actions.

■ **PROCEDURAL BASIS**

Appeal from the Court of Appeals' affirmance of the trial court's judgment for the plaintiff.

■ **FACTS**

Goodman (P) was driving a truck when he was hit and killed by a train [look both ways!]. This suit was brought by his widow and administratrix, who is claiming that Goodman (P) "had no practical view" of the train. The Railroad (D) claims that Goodman's (P) own negligence caused his death. At the trial, the Railroad (D) asked the Court to direct a verdict for it, but the Court refused, and entered judgment for Goodman (P). The Court of Appeals affirmed, and this appeal followed.

■ **ISSUE**

Did the lower court err in assigning responsibility to the Railroad (D) for Goodman's (P) death as a result of being hit by a train?

■ **DECISION AND RATIONALE**

(Holmes, J.) Yes. When a man goes across a railroad track, he knows that he will be killed if a train comes along before he is clear of the track. He knows that he must stop for the train, and that the train will not stop for him. In such circumstances, it seems to us that if a driver cannot be sure otherwise whether a train is dangerously near, he must stop and get out of his vehicle. It seems to us that if he relies upon not hearing a train or any signal, and takes no further precaution he does so at his own risk and will be responsible for his actions. It was Goodman's (P) own fault that he did not reduce his speed earlier and come to a stop. Judgment reversed.

Analysis:

The question of due care is generally left to the jury. However, when the standard is clear, the Court here believed it should be laid down once and for all. Obviously, when a person comes to a train crossing, he will often not be required to do more than stop and look. But common sense and prudence dictates that whatever is necessary to determine whether a train is approaching must be done. If a person does not take these precautions, he will be responsible for his own death. The Court's statement that one must actually stop and get out of his vehicle has been a fertile source of controversy.

■ CASE VOCABULARY

ADMINISTRATRIX: A woman appointed by the court to administer the assets and liabilities of a decedent.

Pokora v. Wabash Railway Co.

(Driver Hit by Train) v. *(Railroad)*

292 U.S. 98, 54 S.Ct. 580, 78 L.Ed. 1149 (1934)

EXTRAORDINARY SITUATIONS MAY NOT WISELY OR FAIRLY BE SUBJECTED TO LEGAL TESTS THAT ARE FITTING FOR THE COMMONPLACE OR NORMAL

■ **INSTANT FACTS** A man was hit by a train as he crossed the railroad tracks because his vision of the tracks was blocked by other train cars.

■ **BLACK LETTER RULE** The question was for the jury whether reasonable caution forbade the driver from going forward across the tracks in reliance on the sense of hearing, unaided by that of sight.

■ **PROCEDURAL BASIS**

Appeal from the court of appeals' affirmance of the trial court's grant of a directed verdict for the defendant.

■ **FACTS**

Pokora (P) was driving his truck across four railroad tracks owned by Wabash Railway (D). A string of boxcars sitting on the tracks cut off Pokora's (P) view. However, as he moved past that track he heard no bell or whistle. As he reached the main track, he was struck by a train coming at 25–30 miles per hour. The evidence showed that Pokora (P) had no view of the track until the train was so near that his escape had been cut off [never saw it coming]. Relying on *Goodman* [driver crossing railroad track is responsible if he is hit by a train], the court of appeals upheld a directed verdict for the railroad (D).

■ **ISSUE**

Did the court err in taking the case from the jury and directing a verdict in favor of the plaintiff? *defendant*

■ **DECISION AND RATIONALE**

(Cardozo, J.) Yes. In such circumstances, the question, we think, was for the jury as to whether reasonable caution forbade Pokora's (P) going forward in reliance on the sense of hearing, unaided by that of sight. There is no doubt that he had a duty to look along the track from the driver's seat of his truck, if looking would have warned him of the danger. This does not mean, however, if his vision was cut off by obstacles, that continuing on would be negligence. Pokora (P) used the faculties available to one in his position. A jury, but not the court, might say that with his faculties thus limited, he should have found some other means of assuring his safety before crossing. The crossing was, however, a frequently used one, and there was a line of cars behind him, ready to follow. To some extent, at least, there was assurance in the thought that Wabash Railway (D) would not run its train without sounding a bell or whistle. The argument is made, however, that our decision in *Goodman* is a barrier in Pokora's (P) path. There is no doubt that the opinion in that case is correct in its result. Goodman had a clear space within which the train was plainly visible. With that opportunity, Goodman fell short of the legal standard of duty established for a traveler when he failed to look and see. This was decisive of the case, but the court did not stop there. It unnecessarily added the remark that the driver must stop and get out of his vehicle. This, however, is an uncommon and sometimes dangerous practice which, in some situations would be futile in any event. The opinion in *Goodman* has been a source of confusion in the federal courts to the extent that it imposes a standard for application by the judge, and has had only wavering support in the courts of the states. We limit it accordingly. The judgment should be reversed and the cause remanded for further proceedings.

Analysis:

The Court here is chastising itself for some remarks made in the *Goodman* case. If a driver leaves his vehicle when he nears obstructed railroad tracks, he will learn nothing by getting out about the perils that exist. By the time he returns to the vehicle and sets it in motion, the hidden train might be upon him. A train traveling at a speed of thirty miles per hour will cover a quarter of a mile in thirty seconds. Instead of helping himself by getting out, he might do better by proceeding with all his faculties alert. Additionally, while a traveler looks in one direction, a train might be approaching from the other. The courts must be cautious in framing standards of behavior that amount to rules of law. What is suitable conduct is ordinarily left to the judgment of the jury.

■ CASE VOCABULARY

DIRECTED VERDICT: In a case in which the party with the burden of proof has failed to present a prima facie case for jury consideration, the trial judge may order the entry of a verdict without allowing the jury to consider it because, as a matter of law, there can be only one such verdict.

PRIMA FACIE CASE: A case which has proceeded upon sufficient proof to that stage where it will support a finding if evidence to the contrary is disregarded.

Andrews v. United Airlines, Inc.

(Airplane Passenger) v. *(Airline)*

24 F.3d 39 (9th Cir. 1994)

COMMON CARRIERS OWE BOTH A DUTY OF UTMOST CARE AND THE VIGILENCE OF A VERY CAUTIOUS PERSON TOWARDS ITS PASSENGERS

■ **INSTANT FACTS** A woman was injured when a briefcase fell on her from the overhead compartment of an airplane.

■ **BLACK LETTER RULE** Since a jury could make a rational decision either way on the record presented, summary judgment is inappropriate.

■ **PROCEDURAL BASIS**

Appeal from the district court's dismissal of the plaintiff's suit on summary judgment.

■ **FACTS**

Andrews (P) was a passenger on a United Airlines (D) flight. After the plane had arrived at the gate, a briefcase fell from an overhead compartment [bonk!] and seriously injured Andrews (P). No one knows who opened the compartment, or what caused the briefcase to fall, and Andrews (P) doesn't claim that airline personnel were involved in stowing the object or opening the bin. Her claim, rather, is that the injury was foreseeable and the airline (D) didn't prevent it. The district court dismissed the suit on summary judgment, and this Court reviews de novo.

■ **ISSUE**

Do the facts of this case present a triable issue of fact?

■ **DECISION AND RATIONALE**

(Kozinski, C.J.) Yes. To show that United (D) did not satisfy its duty of care toward its passengers, Andrews (P) presented the testimony of two witnesses. United's (D) Manager of Inflight Safety disclosed that the airline had received 135 reports of items falling from overhead bins. As a result of these incidents, United (D) decided to add a warning to its arrival announcements that passengers should use caution in opening the overhead bins because items may have shifted during flight. Andrews' (P) second witness was a safety and human factors expert, who testified that United's (D) announcement was ineffective because passengers could not see objects poised to fall until it was too late to prevent it. He also testified that United (D) could have taken additional steps to prevent the hazard, such as retrofitting its overhead bins with baggage nets. United (D) argues that Andews (P) presented too little proof to satisfy her burden. United (D) says 135 incidents are trivial when spread over the millions of passengers traveling each year. Indeed, United (D) sees the low incidence of injuries as proof that the safety measures suggested by Andrews' (P) expert would not merit the additional cost and inconvenience to airline passengers. It is a close question, but we conclude that Andrews (P) has made a sufficient case to overcome summary judgment. The case turns on whether the hazard is serious enough to warrant more than a warning. Jurors, many of whom will have been airline passengers, will be well equipped to decide whether United (D) had a duty to do more than warn passengers about the possibility of falling baggage. A reasonable jury might conclude United (D) should have done more; it might also find that United (D) did enough. Either decision would be rational on the record presented to the district court which, of course, means that summary judgment was not appropriate.   Reversed and remanded.

Analysis:

United (D), as a common carrier, owes both a duty of utmost care and the vigilance of a very cautious person towards its passengers.   Though United (D) is responsible for even the slightest negligence and is required to do all that care, vigilance, and foresight require under all the circumstances, it is not an insurer of its passengers' safety.   The degree of care and diligence that it must exercise is only such as can reasonably be exercised consistent with the practical operation of its business.   Given the heightened duty of a common carrier, even a small risk of serious injury to passengers may form the basis of liability if that risk could be easily eliminated.   Thus, a jury could reasonably find that United (D) failed to do all it reasonably could have done under the circumstances here.   As such, the court was correct in holding that summary judgment was not appropriate.

■ CASE VOCABULARY

DIVERSITY ACTION: A cause of action between citizens of different states, which brings it under the jurisdiction of the federal courts.

REVIEW DE NOVO: Hearing the matter anew, as if for the first time, the same as if no decision had been previously rendered.

SUMMARY JUDGMENT: Procedural device available for a prompt and expeditious disposition of a controversy without a trial when there is no dispute as to material facts, or if only a question of law is involved.

Trimarco v. Klein

(Injured Tenant) v. *(Landlord)*

56 N.Y.2d 98, 436 N.E.2d 502, 451 N.Y.S.2d 52 (1982)

CUSTOM AND USAGE MAY BE USED TO PROVE THAT ONE CHARGED WITH NEGLIGENCE HAS FALLEN BELOW THE REQUIRED STANDARD

■ **INSTANT FACTS** A man was badly cut in the defendant's apartment building when he fell through a glass shower door which was not made of shatterproof glass, as was the custom.

■ **BLACK LETTER RULE** When proof of a customary practice is coupled with a showing that it was ignored and that this departure was a proximate cause of the accident, it may serve to establish liability.

■ **PROCEDURAL BASIS**

An appeal from the appellate division's reversal of the jury's award for the plaintiff, and its dismissal of the plaintiff's case.

■ **FACTS**

Trimarco (P) was cut very badly when he fell through the glass door that enclosed his shower in Klein's (D) apartment building. The door turned out to be ordinary thin glass that looked like the tempered glass that Trimarco (P) thought it was. The building had been built, and the shower installed, in 1953. Trimarco (P) presented expert evidence that at least since the 1950s a practice of using shatterproof glass in bathroom enclosures had come into common use, so that by 1976, the date of the accident, the glass door no longer conformed to accepted safety standards. Klein's (D) agent admitted that it was customary for landlords who had to install glass for shower enclosures to do so with "some material such as plastic or safety glass." The jury awarded Trimarco (P) damages, however a divided appellate division reversed the judgment and dismissed the case.

■ **ISSUE**

Do customary safeguards establish a standard of care?

■ **DECISION AND RATIONALE**

(Fuchsberg, J.) Yes. The appellate court held that even if there was a custom and usage at the time to substitute shatterproof glass, and even if that was a better and safer method of enclosing showers, there was no common-law duty on Klein (D) to replace the glass unless prior notice of the danger had come to Klein (D) either from Trimarco (P) or by reason of a similar accident on the building. Since Trimarco (P) made no such showing, the appellate division majority reversed and dismissed the case. We think that this rule is wrong. It has been held, and we believe it to be true, that when proof of an accepted practice is accompanied by evidence that the defendant conformed to it, this may establish due care. Contrariwise, when proof of a customary practice is coupled with a showing that it was ignored and that this departure was a proximate cause of the accident, it may serve to establish liability. However, it is not to be assumed that customary practice and usage need be universal. It suffices that it be fairly well defined and in the same calling or business so that the actor may be charged with knowledge of it or negligent ignorance. Once its existence is credited, a common practice or usage is still not necessarily a conclusive or even compelling test of negligence. Before it can be, the jury must be satisfied with its reasonableness, just as the jury must be satisfied with the reasonableness of the behavior which adhered to the custom or the unreasonableness of that which did not. So measured, the case Trimarco (P) presented was enough to send it to the jury and to sustain the verdict reached. The expert testimony, the admissions of Klein's (D) manager, the evidence of how replacements were handled by the industry, and other evidence presented, easily filled that bill. Moreover, it was also for the jury to decide whether, at the point in time when the accident occurred, the cost and availability of safety glass and the custom to use it for shower enclosures had transformed what once may have been considered a safe part of the apartment into one which no longer could be so regarded. It was for the jurors to determine whether or not the evidence in this case does establish a general custom or practice. [The court reversed the dismissal but ordered a new trial because the trial judge had erroneously admitted certain evidence that had hurt the defense.]

Analysis:

The probative power of custom and usage is described differently by various authorities, but all agree on its importance. Chief among the rationales offered is, of course, the fact that it reflects the judgment, experience, and conduct of many. Support for its relevance and reliability comes too from the direct bearing it has on feasibility, for its focus is on the practicality of a precaution in actual operation and the readiness with which it can be employed. The question in each instance is whether it meets the test of reasonableness. As Holmes's classic statement expresses, "[w]hat usually is done may be evidence of what ought to be done, but what ought to be done is fixed by a standard of reasonable prudence, whether it usually is complied with or not." *Texas & Pacific Ry. Co. v. Behymer.*

■ CASE VOCABULARY

PROXIMATE CAUSE: That which, in a natural and continuous sequence, unbroken by any efficient intervening cause, produces injury, and without which the result would not have occurred.

Martin v. Herzog

(Injured Buggy Passenger) v. *(Automobile Driver)*
228 N.Y. 164, 126 N.E. 814 (1920)

JURORS HAVE NO RIGHT TO IGNORE STATUTORY LAWS

■ **INSTANT FACTS** The Martins (P) were driving a buggy without lights at night when they were struck by Herzog's (D) automobile, which was traveling on the wrong side of the road.

■ **BLACK LETTER RULE** The unexcused omission of statutory signals is negligence in itself.

■ **PROCEDURAL BASIS**

Appeal from the Appellate Division's reversal of the jury's finding for the plaintiff.

■ **FACTS**

Mrs. Martin (P) and her husband were driving in a buggy at night, when they were struck by Herzog's (D) automobile coming in the opposite direction. They were thrown to the ground, and Mr. Martin was killed [no seatbelts back then]. At the point of the collision, Herzog's (D) car was rounding a curve in the road when it suddenly came upon the buggy, emerging from the gloom. Herzog (D) was charged with negligence in that he did not keep to the right of the center of the highway in violation of a statute. Negligence was also charged against Mr. Martin (P) for traveling without lights, also a statutory violation. There were no defects with Herzog's (D) car, nor was he speeding. The case against him rests solely on his divergence from his lane of traffic. The jury found Herzog (D) to blame, and Mr. Martin (P) blameless. The Appellate Division reversed, and ordered a new trial.

■ **ISSUE**

Is the violation of a statute requiring lights negligence as a matter of law?

■ **DECISION AND RATIONALE**

(Cardozo, J.) Yes. We agree with the Appellate Division that the charge to the jury was erroneous and misleading. In the body of the charge the trial judge said that the jury could consider the absence of light in determining whether Mr. Martin (P) was guilty of contributory negligence in failing to have a light on the buggy as provided by law. He went on to say that the absence of light does not necessarily make Mr. Martin (P) negligent, but that it is a fact for the jury's consideration. Herzog (D) requested a ruling that the absence of a light on Martin's (P) buggy was prima facie evidence of contributory negligence. This request was denied. We think, however, that the unexcused omission of the statutory signals is more than just some evidence of negligence. It *is* negligence in itself. That, we think, is now the established rule in this state. We are persuaded that the tendency of the charge and of all the rulings following it, was to minimize unduly, in the minds of the triers of the facts, the gravity of Mr. Martin's (P) fault. Errors may not be ignored as unsubstantial when they tend to such an outcome. A statute designed for the protection of human life is not to be brushed aside as a form of words, its commands reduced to the level of cautions, and the duty to obey attenuated into an option to conform. The order of the Appellate Division should be affirmed, and judgment absolute directed on the stipulation in favor of Herzog (D), with costs in all courts.

Analysis:

This case involves the admitted violation of a statute intended for the protection of travelers on the highway, yet the jurors were instructed in effect that they were at liberty to treat the omission of lights either as innocent or as culpable. Jurors have no power by which they may relax the duty that one traveler on the highway owes under a statute to another. The omission of the lights was a wrong, and being wholly unexcused was also negligent.

■ CASE VOCABULARY

CONTRIBUTORY NEGLIGENCE: Conduct by a plaintiff which is below the standard to which he is legally required to conform for his own protection and which is a contributing cause which cooperates with the negligence of the defendant in causing the plaintiff's harm.

INTESTATE: A person who has died without a will.

STIPULATION: An agreement or admission made in a judicial proceeding by the parties or their attorneys.

Tedla v. Ellman

(Injured Pedestrians) v. *(Automobile Driver)*

280 N.Y. 124, 19 N.E.2d 987 (1939)

VIOLATION OF A STATUTE IS NOT AUTOMATICALLY CONSIDERED NEGLIGENCE IF THERE IS A GOOD REASON TO DEPART FROM THE DICTATES OF THE STATUTE

■ **INSTANT FACTS** Two pedestrians were hit from behind by a car as they walked along the side of a roadway on the incorrect side (as defined by statute) of the route.

■ **BLACK LETTER RULE** A pedestrian is at fault if he fails without good reason to observe the statutory rule of conduct.

■ **PROCEDURAL BASIS**

Appeal from the appellate division's affirmance of the trial judge's judgment in favor of the plaintiff.

■ **FACTS**

The Tedlas (P) were brother and sister junk collectors. They were walking eastward along a major route with their baby carriages filled with junk. There were no sidewalks, and they could not use the grass center strip because the carriage wheels would have gotten stuck in the soft ground. There was a statute stating that pedestrians walking on the paved portion of a roadway must keep to the left of the center line (walk facing the oncoming traffic). The traffic on the night in question was much heavier on the westbound side of the roadway, and there were very few cars headed east, so the Tedlas (P) chose to travel on the edge of the eastbound lane (in violation of the statute). The two were hit from behind by Ellman's (D) car, and the trial judge entered judgment in the Tedlas (P) favor. The appellate court affirmed, and Ellman (D) appealed, claiming that the Tedlas (P) were contributorily negligent as a matter of law.

■ **ISSUE**

Is a violation of a statute always negligence?

■ **DECISION AND RATIONALE**

(Lehman, J.) No. Negligence is the failure to exercise the care required by law. Where a statute defines the standard of care and the safeguards required to meet a recognized danger, then, as we have said, no other measure may be applied in determining whether a person has carried out the duty of care imposed by law. Failure to observe the standard imposed by statute is negligence, as a matter of law. On the other hand, where a statutory general rule of conduct fixes no definite standard of care which would under all circumstances tend to protect life, limb, or property, but merely codifies or supplements a common-law rule which has always been subject to limitations and exceptions, then the statute, in the absence of clear language to the contrary, should not be construed as intended to wipe out the limitations and exceptions which judicial decisions have attached to the common-law duty. Neither should it be construed as an inflexible command that the general rule of conduct intended to prevent accidents must be followed even under conditions when observance might cause accidents. We may assume reasonably that the Legislature directed pedestrians to keep to the left of the center of the road because that would cause them to face traffic approaching in that lane and would enable them to care for their own safety better than if the traffic approached them from the rear. We cannot assume reasonably that the Legislature intended that a statute enacted for the preservation of the life and limb of pedestrians must be observed when observance would subject them to more imminent danger. Even under that construction of the statute, a pedestrian is, of course, at fault if he fails without good reason to observe the statutory rule of conduct. The general duty is established by the statute, and deviation from it without good cause is a wrong and the wrongdoer is responsible for the damages resulting from his wrong. In each action, the judgment should be affirmed, with costs.

Analysis:

The statute in this case is of a different nature than that in *Martin*, which required the use of lights on a vehicle driven at night. It does not prescribe additional safeguards that pedestrians must provide for the preservation of life or limb or property, nor does it impose upon pedestrians a higher standard of care. What the statute does provide is rules of the road to be observed by pedestrians and vehicles, so that all who use the road may know how they and others should proceed, at least under usual circumstances. A general rule of conduct—and specifically a rule of the road—may accomplish its intended purpose under usual conditions, but when the unusual occurs, strict observance may defeat the purpose of the rule and produce catastrophic results.

Negri v. Stop and Shop, Inc.

(Injured Shopper) v. *(Store)*

65 N.Y.2d 625, 480 N.E.2d 740, 491 N.Y.S.2d 151 (1985)

WHEN THE PLAINTIFF HAS MADE OUT A PRIMA FACIE CASE, IT WOULD BE ERROR TO DISMISS THE COMPLAINT

■ **INSTANT FACTS** Negri (P) slipped and fell in a grocery store on broken and spilled jars of baby food which the store (D) had failed to clean up.

■ **BLACK LETTER RULE** Plaintiff having made out a prima facie case, it was error to dismiss the complaint.

■ **PROCEDURAL BASIS**

Appeal from the Appellate Division's reversal of the trial court's judgment for the plaintiff, and dismissal of the complaint.

■ **FACTS**

While shopping at the Stop and Shop (D), Negri (P) fell backward and hit her head directly on the floor where broken jars of baby food lay. A witness in the immediate vicinity of the accident did not hear any jars break during the 15 or 20 minutes prior to the accident. Some evidence showed that the aisle had not been cleaned or inspected for somewhere between 50 minutes and two hours prior to the accident. The record also contains some evidence tending to show that Stop and Shop (D) had constructive notice of the dangerous condition. After a verdict for Negri (P) in the trial court, the Appellate Division reversed and dismissed the complaint.

■ **ISSUE**

Does an Appellate Court err in dismissing a complaint after the plaintiff has made out a prima facie case?

■ **DECISION AND RATIONALE**

(Justice Not Stated) Yes. Viewing the evidence in a light most favorable to Negri (P), it cannot be said as a matter of law that the circumstantial evidence was insufficient to permit the jury to draw the necessary inference that a slippery condition was created by jars of baby food which had fallen and broken a sufficient length of time prior to the accident to permit Stop and Shop's (D) employees to discover and remedy the condition. Negri's (P) having made out a prima facie case, it was error to dismiss the complaint. If the jury verdict be deemed by the Appellate Division to be against the weight of the evidence, that court's power is limited to ordering a new trial. The order of the Appellate Court is reversed, with costs, and remitted to that court for consideration of the facts.

Analysis:

Because of the testimony that the jars did not fall or break within the previous twenty minutes and that the aisle had not been inspected for at least fifty minutes prior to the accident, the store had constructive notice of the dangerous condition. While it may not actually have known of the spill, enough time had elapsed that it should have been discovered and corrected by store employees. This evidence established a prima facie case of the store's negligence. That is, if taken as true, the evidence tends to show that the store (D) could be found to have been negligent, so a dismissal was indeed improper.

Gordon v. American Museum of Natural History

(Injured Museum Patron) v. *(Museum)*

67 N.Y.2d 836, 492 N.E.2d 774, 501 N.Y.S.2d 646 (1986)

A DEFECT MUST BE NOTICEABLE AND HAVE EXISTED FOR SOME PERIOD OF TIME BEFORE A DEFENDANT CAN BE CHARGED WITH CONSTRUCTIVE NOTICE

■ **INSTANT FACTS** A man sued after he slipped and fell on a piece of paper, which he claims came from a Museum (D) concession.

■ **BLACK LETTER RULE** To constitute constructive notice, a defect must be visible and apparent and it must exist for a sufficient length of time prior to the accident to permit the defendant's employees to discover and remedy it.

■ **PROCEDURAL BASIS**

Appeal from the Appellate Division's affirmance of the jury's finding against the defendant.

■ **FACTS**

Gordon (P) slipped on a piece of white, waxy paper as he was coming down the steps from a Museum (D). He contends that he didn't see the paper until he was in midair [at which point he was flying without wings]. He alleged that this piece of paper came from a concession vendor which the Museum (D) contracted to have present near the museum entrance. Gordon (P) also claims that the Museum (D) was negligent insofar as its employees failed to discover and remove the paper before he fell on it. The case was submitted to the jury on the theory that the Museum (D) had either actual or constructive notice of the dangerous condition presented by the paper on the steps. The jury found against the Museum (D) on the issue of liability, and a divided Appellate Division affirmed and granted the Museum (D) leave to appeal on a certified question.

■ **ISSUE**

Did the trial court err in allowing the case to go to the jury on a theory of actual or constructive notice?

■ **DECISION AND RATIONALE**

(Not Stated) Yes. There is no evidence in the record that the Museum (D) had actual notice of the paper and the case should not have gone to the jury on that theory. To constitute constructive notice, a defect must be visible and apparent and it must exist for a sufficient length of time prior to the accident to permit the defendant's employees to discover and remedy it. The record contains no evidence that anyone, including Gordon (P), observed the piece of paper prior to the accident. Nor did he describe the paper as being dirty or worn, which would have provided some indication that it had been present for some period of time. Thus, on the evidence presented, the piece of paper that caused Gordon's (P) fall could have been deposited there only minutes or seconds before the accident. Any other conclusion would be pure speculation. The defect in Gordon's (P) case here is not an inability to prove the causation element in his fall, but the lack of evidence establishing constructive notice of the particular condition that caused his fall. The order of the Appellate Division should be reversed, with costs, and the complaint dismissed.

Analysis:

Contrary to Gordon's (P) contentions, neither a general awareness that litter or some other dangerous condition may be present, nor the fact that Gordon (P) observed other papers on the steps approximately ten minutes before his fall, is legally sufficient to charge the Museum (D) with constructive notice of the paper he slipped on. A prima facie case is only made when a plaintiff has established that the fall was a natural and probable consequence of the conditions present. In *Negri*, the plaintiff was able to establish that the condition had existed for a sufficient period of time for the store employees to have discovered and rectified the danger. In this case, there was absolutely no evidence tending to show that the Museum (D) employees could or should have discovered the piece of paper that Gordon (P) slipped on. Thus, constructive notice was not established, and the case should not have been submitted to the jury.

■ **CASE VOCABULARY**

CERTIFIED QUESTION: A question of law which has been submitted to a higher court for appellate review.

Byrne v. Boadle

(Injured Passerby) v. *(Flour Dealer)*

2 H. & C. 722, 159 Eng.Rep. 299 (1863)

NEGLIGENCE CAN ARISE FROM THE FACT OF AN ACCIDENT

■ **INSTANT FACTS** A man was injured when a barrel of flour fell out of a window and hit him.

■ **BLACK LETTER RULE** If a person passing along the road is injured by something falling upon him, the accident alone is prima facie evidence of negligence, and if there is any state of facts to rebut the presumption of negligence, the defendant must prove them.

■ **PROCEDURAL BASIS**

Appeal from the Assessor's nonsuit of the plaintiff after a jury award in his favor.

■ **FACTS**

Byrne (P) was walking down the sidewalk when he was struck by a barrel of flour which had fallen from a high window in Boadle's (D) shop [he should have been on the lookout]. He was knocked down and injured. The jury found in favor of Byrne (P), and assessed £50 in damages. The Assessor nonsuited Byrne (P), however. Counsel for the plaintiff obtained a rule nisi to enter the verdict for the plaintiff, on the ground that the Assessor erred in ruling that there was no evidence of negligence on Boadle's (D) part.

■ **ISSUE**

When the defendant has the exclusive control of the instrumentality which causes an accident and must have been negligent for the accident to occur, can the burden of proof shift to the defendant?

■ **DECISION AND RATIONALE**

(Pollock, C.B.) Yes. There are many accidents from which no presumption of negligence can arise, but it would be wrong to lay down as a rule that in no case can a presumption of negligence arise from the fact of an accident. It is the duty of persons who keep barrels in a warehouse to take care that they do not roll out, and such a case would, beyond all doubt, afford prima facie evidence of negligence. A barrel could not roll out of a warehouse without some negligence, and to say that a plaintiff who is injured by it must call witnesses to prove negligence seems preposterous. If a person passing along the road is injured by something falling upon him, the accident alone is prima facie evidence of negligence, and if there is any state of facts to rebut the presumption of negligence, the defendant must prove them. Reversed.

Analysis:

This case introductes *res ipsa loquitur,* "the thing ~~stands~~ *speaks* for itself." The barrel that fell on Byrne (P) was in the custody of Boadle's (D) business and thus, the court held, was his responsibility. Additionally, Boadle (D) was responsible for the acts of his servants who had physical control over the barrel. The fact that the barrel fell was itself prima facie evidence of negligence, for a barrel could not possibly fall out of a window unless someone was somehow negligent. As such, if there are any facts inconsistent with negligence, it is for the defendant to prove them.

■ CASE VOCABULARY

NONSUIT: Name of a judgment given against the plaintiff when he is unable to prove his case.

RULE NISI: A rule which will become final *unless* cause can be shown against it.

McDougald v. Perry

(Injured) v. *(Trailer Puller)*
716 So.2d 783 (Fla. 1998)

THE DOCTRINE OF RES IPSA LOQUITUR IS ALIVE AND WELL

■ **INSTANT FACTS** A spare tire bounced from under a trailer injuring the driver following the trailer.

■ **BLACK LETTER RULE** Res ipsa loquitur provides an inference of negligence when the accident is the type that does not occur without negligence and the defendant is in control of the circumstances.

■ **PROCEDURAL BASIS**

Appeal from reversal of trial court's instruction on res ipsa loquitur.

■ **FACTS**

McDougald (P) was driving behind a tractor-trailer driven by Perry (D). As Perry (D) drove over some railroad tracks, a large spare tire came out of its cradle underneath the trailer and fell to the ground. As the trailer drove over the spare tire, it bounced up and into the windshield of McDougald's (P) Jeep. The spare tire was secured in its cradle by a chain wrapped around the tire. The chain was attached to the body of the trailer by a nut and bolt. Perry (D) testified at trial that he inspected the chain, but admitted he did not check every link in the chain.

■ **ISSUE**

Is it proper to assert that a particular accident could not have occurred in the absence of some negligence?

■ **DECISION AND RATIONALE**

(Wells, J.) Yes. The trial court correctly instructed the jury on the doctrine of res ipsa loquitur. Res ipsa loquitur is a Latin phrase meaning "the thing speaks for itself." It is a rule of evidence that permits, but does not require, an inference of negligence in certain circumstances. It can provide an injured plaintiff with an inference of negligence where there is no direct proof of negligence. Here, McDougald (P) must show that the instrumentality causing the injury was under Perry's (D) exclusive control, and that the accident is one that would not ordinarily occur without the negligence of the one in control. An injury alone does not ordinarily indicate negligence. There are many types of accidents which occur without the fault of anyone. However, in rare instances, an injury can be such that it would not occur without negligence. Expert testimony is not necessary to establish that this is the type of accident that does not occur absent some negligence. In many cases, common knowledge is sufficient to make this showing. Furthermore, McDougald (P) does not have to eliminate all other possible causes of the accident. He merely has to show that on the whole it is more likely than not that there was negligence associated with the cause of the accident. Therefore, we conclude that the spare tire escaping from the trailer is the type of accident, as a matter of general knowledge, that would not occur but for the lack of reasonable care by the person who had control of the tire. Reversed and remanded with directions to reinstate the jury's verdict in favor of McDougald (P).

■ CONCURRENCE

(Anstead, J.) I write separately to note that an old appellate opinion written in 1863 is still useful today. The case of Byrne v. Boadle involved a barrel falling from a window of the defendant's flour business and striking plaintiff. The court applied res ipsa loquitur and found that such an accident does not occur without negligence. The court noted that it would be impossible for the plaintiff to ascertain the exact cause of the accident. The fact of the barrel falling is prima facie evidence of negligence, and it is for the defendant to prove otherwise. We cannot improve upon this explanation today. The common law tradition is alive and well.

Analysis:

Res ipsa loquitur is a useful tool for plaintiffs when they cannot prove exactly what what caused the accident. Another type of case where res ipsa loquitur is used is airplane accidents in good weather. In the present case, note that Perry (D) argued res ipsa loquitur was not proper because McDougald (P) failed to produce any expert testimony that this was the type of accident that does not occur without negligence. The court rejected this finding that it was a matter of common knowledge. Is this really the case? What other causes, besides Perry's (D) negligence, might have caused the accident? What about a manufacturing defect in the chain or a design defect of the tire cradle? It probably would not be fair to McDougald (P) to require him to rule out all of these other possible causes.

Ybarra v. Spangard

(*Injured Patient*) v. (*Doctors*)

25 Cal.2d 486, 154 P.2d 687 (1944)

RES IPSA LOQUITUR MAY BE INVOKED IN CASES OF INJURY FROM MEDICAL TREATMENT

■ **INSTANT FACTS** A man lost the use of his arm due to an injury which occurred while he was unconscious and receiving medical treatment for another ailment.

■ **BLACK LETTER RULE** Where a plaintiff receives unusual injuries while unconscious and in the course of medical treatment, all those defendants who had any control over his body or the instrumentalities which might have caused the injuries may properly be called upon to meet the inference of negligence by giving an explanation of their conduct.

■ **PROCEDURAL BASIS**

Appeal from the trial court's entry of nonsuit judgments as to all defendants.

■ **FACTS**

Ybarra (P) was diagnosed with appendicitis by Dr. Tilley (D), and made arrangements for an appendectomy to be performed by Dr. Spangard (D) at a hospital owned and managed by Dr. Swift (D), Ybarra (P) was wheeled into the operating room by a nurse whom he believed to be Gisler (D). Dr. Reser (D), the anesthetist, adjusted Ybarra (P) on the operating table, laying him back against two hard objects at the top of his shoulders, about an inch below his neck. Reser (D) then administered the anesthetic and Ybarra (P) lost consciousness. When he awoke the following morning, he was in his hospital room attended by Nurse Thompson (D). Ybarra (P) testified that prior to the operation he had never had any pain in, or injury to, his right arm or shoulder, but that when he awakened, he felt a sharp pain half way between his neck and shoulder. He complained to his nurse and to Tilley (D) [talk about a pain in the neck!], who gave him diathermy treatments while he remained in the hospital. The pain did not cease, but spread down his arm and grew worse. He was unable to use his arm and developed paralysis and atrophy of the muscles. He received further treatments from Tilley (D) for about six months. Ybarra (P) consulted another physician, Dr. Clark, who took X-rays. Clark said that Ybarra's (P) condition was due to trauma or injury due to pressure or strain, applied between his right shoulder and neck. Dr. Garduno also examined Ybarra (P), and said that the injury was a paralysis of traumatic origin.

■ **ISSUE**

Did the trial court err in holding that the doctrine of res ipsa loquitur could not be invoked against several defendants and instrumentalities?

■ **DECISION AND RATIONALE**

(Gibson, C.J.) Yes. Ybarra's (P) theory is that the foregoing evidence presents a proper case for the application of the doctrine of res ipsa loquitur, and that the inference of negligence arising therefrom makes the granting of a nonsuit improper. The Doctors' (D) main defense may be briefly stated in two propositions: (1) that where there are several defendants, and there is a division of responsibility in the

---

use of an instrumentality causing the injury, and the injury might have resulted from the separate act of either one of two or more persons, the rule of res ipsa loquitur cannot be invoked against any one of them; and (2) that where there are several instrumentalities, and no showing is made as to which caused the injury or as to the particular defendant in control of it, the doctrine cannot apply. We are satisfied, however, that these objections are not well taken in the circumstances of this case. The present case is of a type which comes within the reason and spirit of the doctrine more fully perhaps than any other. It is difficult to see how the doctrine can, with any justification, be so restricted in its statement as to become inapplicable to a patient who submits himself to the care and custody of doctors and nurses, is rendered unconscious, and receives some injury from instrumentalities used in his treatment. Without the aid of the doctrine, a patient who received permanent injuries of a serious nature which are obviously the result of someone's negligence, would be entirely unable to recover unless the doctors and nurses in attendance voluntarily chose to disclose the identity of the negligent person and the facts establishing liability. If this were the state of the law of negligence, the courts, to avoid gross injustice, would be forced to invoke the principles of absolute liability, irrespective of negligence, in actions by persons suffering injuries during the course of treatment under anesthesia. But we think this juncture has not yet been reached, and that the doctrine of res ipsa loquitur is properly applicable to the case before us. The argument of the Doctors (D) is simply that Ybarra (P) has not shown an injury caused by an instrumentality under a defendant's control, because he has not shown which of the several instrumentalities that he came in contact with while in the hospital caused the injury. They also argue that Ybarra (P) has not shown that any one defendant or his servants had exclusive control over any particular instrumentality. They contend that in view of the nature of the injury, the number of defendants and the different functions performed by each, they could not all be liable for the wrong, if any. We do not believe that either the number or relationship of the defendants alone determines whether the doctrine of res ipsa loquitur applies. Every defendant in whose custody the plaintiff was placed for any period was bound to exercise ordinary care to see that no unnecessary harm came to him and each would be liable for failure in this regard. Any defendant who negligently injured him, and any defendant charged with his care who so neglected him as to allow injury to occur, would be liable. It may appear at the trial that, consistent with the principles outlined above, one or more defendants will be found liable and others absolved, but this should not preclude the application of the rule of res ipsa loquitur. The control, at one time or another, of one or more of the various instrumentalities which might have harmed Ybarra (P) was in the hands of every defendant or of his employees or temporary servants. This, we think, places upon them the burden of initial explanation. Ybarra (P) was rendered unconscious for the purpose of undergoing surgical treatment by the defendants; it is manifestly unreasonable for them to insist that he identify any one of them as the person who did the alleged negligent act. The other aspect of this case which the Doctors (D) so strongly emphasize is that Ybarra (P) has not identified the instrumentality any more than he has the particular guilty defendant. However, we believe that it should be enough that Ybarra (P) can show injury resulting from an external force applied while he lay unconscious in the hospital; this is as clear a case of identification of the instrumentality as he may ever be able to make. We do not at this time undertake to state the extent to which the reasoning of this case may be applied to other situations in which the doctrine of res ipsa loquitur is invoked. We merely hold that where a plaintiff receives unusual injuries while unconscious and in the course of medical treatment, all those defendants who had any control over his body or the instrumentalities which might have caused the injuries may properly be called upon to meet the inference of negligence by giving an explanation of their conduct. The judgment is reversed.

Analysis:

The doctrine of res ipsa loquitur has three conditions: (1) the accident must be of a kind that ordinarily does not occur in the absence of someone's negligence; (2) it must be caused by an agency or instrumentality within the exclusive control of the defendant; and (3) it must not have been due to any voluntary action or contribution on the part of the plaintiff. There is, however, some uncertainty as to the extent to which res ipsa loquitur may be invoked in cases of injury from medical treatment. This is in part due to the tendency, in some decisions, to lay undue emphasis on the limitations of the doctrine, and to give too little attention to its basic underlying purpose. The result has been that a simple, understandable rule of circumstantial evidence, with a sound background of common sense and human experience, has occasionally been transformed into a rigid legal formula, which arbitrarily precludes its application in many cases where it is most needed. It would be patently unfair if the law were to deny an individual, clearly entitled to damages, satisfaction merely because he is unaware of facts that are solely within the knowledge of the party who should, in all justice, pay them.

■ CASE VOCABULARY

RES IPSA LOQUITUR: Rebuttable presumption or inference that the defendant was negligent, which arises upon proof that the instrumentality causing injury was in the defendant's exclusive control, and that the accident was one which ordinarily does not happen in the absence of negligence.

RESPONDEAT SUPERIOR: A doctrine which holds that the master is liable in certain cases for the wrongful acts of his servant, and a principal for those of his agent.

Sheeley v. Memorial Hospital

(Injured Patient) v. (Hospital)
710 A.2d 161 (R.I. 1998)

THE STANDARD OF CARE FOR MEDICAL PROFESSIONALS IS THAT OF A REASONABLY COMPETENT PROFESSIONAL IN THE SAME FIELD (REGARDLESS OF WHERE THE DEFENDANT IS PRACTICING)

NOT TONIGHT, HONEY, I HAVE COMPLICATIONS FROM THE SURGERY!

■ **INSTANT FACTS** Sheeley (P) sued her doctor and the hospital after she developed complications at the episiotomy incision site after giving birth.

■ **BLACK LETTER RULE** A physician is under a duty to use the degree of care and skill that is expected of a reasonably competent practitioner in the same class to which he or she belongs, acting in the same or similar circumstances.

■ **PROCEDURAL BASIS**

Appeal from the trial court's grant of the defendant's motion for a directed verdict.

■ **FACTS**

When Sheeley (P) gave birth, Dr. Ryder (D), a second-year family practice resident, performed an episiotomy, which involves cutting into the mother's perineum to facilitate the birth and then stitching the incision after the birth. Sheeley (P) developed complications at the site of this surgery and sued Dr. Ryder (D) and the hospital (D). At the trial on the malpractice action, Sheeley (P) sought to introduce the expert testimony of Dr. Leslie, a board certified OB/GYN. Dr. Leslie planned to testify about Dr. Ryder's alleged malpractice and the applicable standard of care as it relates to the performance of an episiotomy. The Hospital (D) objected and filed a motion in limine to exclude the testimony, arguing that Dr. Leslie, as an OB/GYN, was not qualified to testify against a family practice resident who was performing obstetric and gynecological care. Relying on *Soares v. Vestal*, the Hospital (D) maintained that a testifying expert was required to be in the same medical field as the defendant physician. Agreeing that *Soares* was determinative, the trial justice granted the Hospital's (D) motion. Sheeley (P) did not have any other experts prepared to testify, nor was she able to procure one within the two-day period allowed by the trial justice. Consequently, the Hospital's (D) motion for a directed verdict was granted.

■ **ISSUE**

Must a physician expert witness in a medical malpractice case practice in the same field and same community as the defendant?

■ **DECISION AND RATIONALE**

(Goldberg, J.) No. The determination of the competency of an expert witness to testify is within the discretion of the trial justice. This court will not disturb that decision in the absence of clear error or abuse. In fairness to the trial justice, we note that in making her determination with respect to the admissibility of the expert's testimony, she was without the benefit of our decisions in *Marshall v. Medical Associates of Rhode Island, Inc.,* and more importantly *Buja v. Morningstar,* which have distinguished *Soares* and limited its holding to situations in which the physician-expert lacks knowledge, skill, experience, or education in the same medical field as the alleged malpractice. Nevertheless, after a review of these cases, we find it clear that the trial justice did in fact abuse her discretion and commit reversible error in excluding the testimony of Dr. Leslie. In view of this, there can be little doubt that we must reverse the decision of the trial justice and remand the case for a new trial. For over three-quarters of a century, this court has subscribed to the principle that when a physician undertakes to treat or diagnose a patient, he or she is under a duty to exercise the same degree of diligence and skill which is commonly possessed by other members of the profession who are engaged in the same type of practice in similar localities having due regard for the state of scientific knowledge at the time of treatment. This "similar locality" rule is a somewhat expanded version of the "strict locality" rule, which requires that the expert testifying be from the same community as the defendant. The rationale underlying the development of the "strict locality" rule was a recognition that opportunities, experience, and conditions may differ between densely and sparsely populated communities. This court is of the opinion that whatever geographical impediments may previously have justified the need for a "similar locality" analysis are no longer applicable in view of the present-day realities of the medical profession. Accordingly, we join the growing number of jurisdictions that have repudiated the "same or similar" communities test in favor of a national standard and hold that a physician is under a duty to use the degree of care and skill that is expected of a reasonably competent practitioner in the same class to which he or she belongs, acting in the same or similar circumstances. In this case, the alleged malpractice occurred in the field of obstetrics and involved a procedure and attendant standard of care that has remained constant for over thirty years. Dr. Leslie, as a board certified OB/GYN with over thirty years of experience, and a clinical professor of obstetrics and gynecology at a major hospital, is undoubtedly qualified to testify regarding the appropriate standard of care. The case is remanded to the lower court for a new trial.

Analysis:

In a medical malpractice case, expert testimony is essential in proving the standard of care applicable to the defendant, unless the lack of care is so obvious as to be within the layman's common knowledge. Any doctor with knowledge of or familiarity with the procedure, acquired through experience, observation, association, or education, is competent to testify concerning the requisite standard of care and whether the care in any given case deviated from that standard. The resources available to a physician, his or her specific area of practice, and the length of time he or she has been practicing are all issues that should be considered by the trial judge in making a decision regarding the qualification of an expert. No one factor, however, should be determinative. Furthermore, except in extreme cases, a witness who has obtained board certification in a particular specialty related to the procedure in question, especially when that board certification reflects a national standard of training and qualification, should be presumptively qualified to render an opinion.

■ CASE VOCABULARY

EPISIOTOMY: Surgical cutting of the vaginal opening to avoid the tearing of tissues in childbirth.

MOTION IN LIMINE: A pretrial motion requesting the court to prohibit opposing counsel from referring to, or offering evidence on a particular matter.

States v. Lourdes Hospital

(*Patient*) v. (*Hospital*)

100 N.Y.2d 208, 792 N.E.2d 151, 762 N.Y.S.2d 1 (2003)

EXPERT MEDICAL TESTIMONY MAY BE INTRODUCED ON RES IPSA LOQUITUR

■ **INSTANT FACTS** While undergoing surgery for the removal of an ovarian cyst, States's (P) arm was injured, allegedly due to Lourdes Hospital's (D) negligence in administering anesthesia.

■ **BLACK LETTER RULE** The doctrine of res ipsa loquitor permits a factfinder to draw an inference of negligence when the injury-causing event is of a kind that ordinarily does not occur absent negligence.

■ **PROCEDURAL BASIS**

On appeal to review a decision of the New York Appellate Division reversing a trial court denial of summary judgment.

■ **FACTS**

States (P) successfully underwent surgery at Lourdes Hospital (D) to remove an ovarian cyst. Before the procedure, States's (P) arm was placed on a board, rotated, and connected to an IV tube. States (P) complained of pain and discomfort, but there were no complications during surgery. Upon awakening from anesthesia, States (P) complained of increasing pain in her arm and shoulder and suffered arm injuries. States (P) sued the hospital for medical malpractice. At the close of discovery, the defendant moved for summary judgment based on a lack of direct evidence of negligence by the anesthesiologist. States (P) responded that, despite the absence of direct evidence, expert medical testimony can establish that her injuries would not have occurred absent negligence, invoking res ipsa loquitur. The motion for summary judgment was denied, but the New York Appellate Division reversed, holding that the injury was not of the kind about which a jury could draw upon its common experience and knowledge to establish an inference of negligence. States (P) appealed.

■ **ISSUE**

May expert medical testimony be introduced to a jury to establish the likelihood that the injury would not have occurred absent negligence?

■ **DECISION AND RATIONALE**

(Ciparick, J.) Yes. When appropriate, the doctrine of res ipsa loquitur permits a factfinder to draw an inference of negligence by the fact that an injury occurred. To establish res ipsa loquitur, the plaintiff must prove not only that the injury would not occur absent negligence, but also that the injury was caused by an agent or instrumentality exclusively in the defendant's control and that the plaintiff contributed to the injury in no way. Once these three elements are established, a factfinder may infer the defendant's negligence.

Addressing the first element, the defendant contends that the jury may only rely on its common everyday experiences to determine whether the injury would occur absent negligence. The plaintiff counters that expert medical testimony may be offered to inform the jury's decision. Restatement of Torts § 328D supports the plaintiff's position. Under the Restatement, the jury may consider the issue

---

through not only its common knowledge, but also through evidence offered by the parties, including expert testimony in matters requiring specialized knowledge. Expert testimony reliably establishes the probability that negligence occurred to the same extent that layperson knowledge establishes matters of common understanding. Expert testimony is offered for the purpose of educating and assisting the jury, but the ultimate inference must be drawn by the jury on the basis of its understanding of the case. The burden remains on the plaintiff to establish the elements of res ipsa loquitur and prove the defendant's liability, albeit by reasonable inference. Because the plaintiff is free to offer expert medical testimony in support of its theory, summary judgment was appropriately denied. Reversed.

■ Analysis:

As the case properly reflects, the doctrine of res ipsa loquitur permits an inference that negligence occurred. Many courts, however, state that res ipsa loquitur creates a presumption of negligence. While that may be the law in some jurisdictions, courts often mistakenly interchange the inference of negligence and the presumption of negligence standards. The distinction actually is not subtle. With an inference, a jury is permitted to conclude that negligence occurred, while with a presumption, the jury is compelled to find negligence absent rebuttable evidence offered by the defendant.

■ CASE VOCABULARY:

INFERENCE: A conclusion reached by considering other facts and deducing a logical consequence from them.

NEGLIGENCE: The failure to exercise the standard of care that a reasonably prudent person would have exercised in a similar situation; any conduct that falls below the legal standard established to protect others against unreasonable risk of harm, except for conduct that is intentionally, wantonly, or willfully disregardful of others' rights.

PRESUMPTION: A legal inference or assumption that a fact exists, based on the known or proven existence of some other fact or group of facts. A presumption shifts the burden of production or persuasion to the opposing party, who can then attempt to overcome the presumption.

RES IPSA LOQUITUR: The doctrine providing that, in some circumstances, the mere fact of an accident's occurrence raises an inference of negligence so as to establish a prima facie case.

Matthies v. Mastromonaco

(Elderly Woman with Broken Hip) v. *(Doctor)*

160 N.J. 26, 733 A.2d 456 (1999)

IN INFORMED CONSENT ANALYSIS, THE DECISIVE FACTOR IS NOT WHETHER A TREATMENT ALTERNATIVE IS INVASIVE OR NONINVASIVE, BUT WHETHER THE PHYSICIAN ADEQUATELY PRESENTS THE MATERIAL FACTS SO THAT THE PATIENT CAN MAKE AN INFORMED DECISION

■ **INSTANT FACTS** Matthies' (P) doctor (D) treated her broken hip with bed rest instead of surgery, without consulting with her about her options, and she never walked again.

■ **BLACK LETTER RULE** To obtain a patient's informed consent to one of several alternative courses of treatment, the physician should explain medically reasonable invasive and noninvasive alternatives, including the risks and likely outcomes of those alternatives, even when the chosen course is noninvasive.

■ **PROCEDURAL BASIS**

Appeal from the Appellate Division's reversal of the jury's finding in favor of the defendant.

■ **FACTS**

Matthies (P) was 81 years old when she fell in her apartment and broke her right hip. When she was discovered two days later, she was transported to emergency care. Dr. Mastromonaco (D) reviewed Matthies' (P) medical history, condition, and X-rays. He decided against pinning her hip, a procedure that would have involved the insertion of four steel screws. Instead, he prescribed bed rest rather than surgery. Dr. Mastromonaco (D) reached that decision for several reasons. Matthies (P) was elderly, frail, and in a weakened condition. Surgery involving the installation of screws would be risky. Second, Matthies suffered from osteoporosis, which led Dr. Mastromonaco (D) to conclude that her bones were too porous to hold the screws. He anticipated that the screws would probably loosen, causing severe pain, and necessitating a partial or total hip replacement. Third, Matthies (P) had suffered a stroke earlier, which had left her partially paralyzed on her right side. Consequently, she wore a brace and essentially used her right leg as a post while propelling herself with her left leg. Before her fall, Matthies (P) had maintained an independent lifestyle. She is now confined to a nursing home. Matthies' (P) expert, Dr. Sicherman, a board-certified orthopedic surgeon, testified that under the circumstances, bed rest was an inappropriate treatment. In fact, due to the bed rest without traction, Matthies' (P) femur displaced, and she has never regained the ability to walk. Even Dr. Mastromonaco's (D) expert, Dr. Rochelle, admitted that pinning Matthies' (P) hip would have decreased the risk of displacement. He nonetheless agreed with Dr. Mastromonaco (D) that Matthies' (P) bones were probably too brittle to withstand insertion of the pins. Dr. Mastromonaco's (D) goal in conservatively treating Matthies (P) was to help her "get through this with the least complication as possible and to maintain a lifestyle conducive to her disability." Matthies (P) asserts that she would not have consented to bed rest if Dr. Mastromonaco (D) had told her of the probable effect of the treatment on the quality of her life. There was conflicting evidence as to whether Dr. Mastromonaco (D) consulted either with Matthies (P) or her family about the possibility of surgery.

■ ISSUE

(1) Does the doctrine of informed consent require a physician to obtain the patient's consent before implementing a nonsurgical course of treatment, and (2) must a physician, in addition to discussing with the patient treatment alternatives that the physician recommends, discuss medically reasonable alternative courses of treatment that the physician does not recommend?

■ DECISION AND RATIONALE

(Pollock, J.) Yes. In informed consent analysis, the decisive factor is not whether a treatment alternative is invasive or noninvasive, but whether the physician adequately presents the material facts so that the patient can make an informed decision. That conclusion does not imply that a physician must explain in detail all treatment options in every case. The standard obligates the physician to disclose only that information material to a reasonable patient's informed decision. Physicians thus remain obligated to inform patients of medically reasonable treatment alternatives and their attendant probable risks and outcomes. Otherwise, the patient, in selecting one alternative rather than another, cannot make a decision that is informed. A physician may select a method of treatment that is medically reasonable, but not the one that the patient would have selected if informed of alternative methods. Like the deviation from a standard of care, the physician's failure to obtain informed consent is a form of medical negligence. Physicians may neither impose their values on their patients nor substitute their level of risk aversion for that of their patients. One patient may prefer to undergo a potentially risky procedure, such as surgery, to enjoy a better quality of life. Another patient may choose a more conservative course of treatment to secure reduced risk at the cost of a diminished lifestyle. The choice is not for the physician, but the patient in consultation with the physician. By not telling the patient of all medically reasonable alternatives, the physician breaches the patient's right to make an informed choice. The physician's duty to inform the patient of alternatives is especially important when the alternatives are mutually exclusive. If, as a practical matter, the choice of one alternative precludes the choice of others, or even if it increases appreciably the risks attendant on the other alternatives, the patient's need for relevant information is critical. That need intensifies when the choice turns not so much on purely medical considerations as on the choice of one lifestyle or set of values over another. The issue of informed consent often intertwines with that of medical malpractice. Because of the interrelationship between the malpractice and informed consent issues in the present case, the jury should consider both issues at the retrial. The judgment of the Appellate Division is affirmed.

Analysis:

Choosing among medically reasonable alternatives is a shared responsibility of physicians and patients. To discharge their responsibilities, patients should provide their physicians with the information necessary for them to make diagnoses and determine courses of treatment. Physicians, in turn, have a duty to evaluate the relevant information and disclose all courses of treatment that are medically reasonable under the circumstances. Generally, a physician will recommend a course of treatment. As a practical matter, a patient often decides to adopt the physician's recommendation. Still, the ultimate decision is for the patient. For consent to be informed, the patient must know not only of alternatives that the physician recommends, but of medically reasonable alternatives that the physician does not recommend. In sum, physicians do not adequately discharge their responsibility by disclosing only treatment alternatives that they recommend.

■ CASE VOCABULARY

INFORMED CONSENT: A person's agreement to allow something to happen (such as surgery) that is based on a full disclosure of facts needed to make the decision intelligently.

CHAPTER THREE

The Duty Requirement: Physical Injuries

Harper v. Herman

Instant Facts: A man sues a boat owner when during an outing on Lake Minnetonka the man dove head first into three feet of water and was paralyzed.

Black Letter Rule: A boat owner hosting a social gathering on his boat is under no legal duty to warn his guests that the water is too shallow for diving because the boat owner's relationship with his guests does not fall into one of the discrete categories that have been acknowledged as giving rise to such a duty.

Farwell v. Keaton

Instant Facts: A man sues his son's friend when the son died of severe head injuries after he and his friend got into a fight and the friend, after making an initial effort to revive the son, abandoned him in a car in his grandparents' driveway.

Black Letter Rule: When an individual comes to the aid of another, he is subject to the duty to take no action that would leave the victim worse off than before; and friends spending time together socially are under the affirmative obligation to come to each other's aid in an emergency.

Randi W. v. Muroc Joint Unified School District

Instant Facts: A vice principal's last four employers provided his new employer with glowing recommendations of his character and fitness without disclosing that complaints of sexual misconduct had been filed against him, and when he sexually assaulted one of his students, she sued.

Black Letter Rule: An employer has the duty to use reasonable care in recommending a former employee without disclosing material negative information that would relate to his fitness for the job.

Tarasoff v. Regents of University of California

Instant Facts: A murdered woman's parents sued the University (D) because therapists employed there failed to warn their daughter of death threats made towards her by a patient.

Black Letter Rule: Once a therapist does in fact determine, or under applicable professional standards reasonably should have determined, that a patient poses serious danger of violence to others, he bears a duty to exercise reasonable care to protect the foreseeable victim of that danger.

Uhr v. East Greenbush Central School District

Instant Facts: A family sues the school district when, in violation of state law, the school failed to test their daughter for scoliosis with the result that her illness progressed undetected.

Black Letter Rule: A court will not infer a private right of action under a statute unless the plaintiff is a member of the class the statute was intended to benefit; recognizing a private right of action would promote the legislative purpose; and recognizing a private right of action would be consistent with the legislative scheme.

Strauss v. Belle Realty Co.

Instant Facts: A man sues his landlord and the electric company after he fell down a flight of stairs in his apartment building during a blackout.

Black Letter Rule: A public utility does not owe a duty of care to those who do not have a contractual relationship with it.

Reynolds v. Hicks

Instant Facts: The under-age nephew of the groom was served alcohol at a wedding reception and when he caused a car accident on his way home, the injured driver sued the bride and groom.

Black Letter Rule: A social host that supplies a minor with alcohol does not owe a duty of care to third persons.

Vince v. Wilson

Instant Facts: After getting into a car accident with a drunk, unlicensed driver, the injured passenger sues the dealership that sold the car to the drunk driver and the woman that paid for the car.

Black Letter Rule: The doctrine of negligent entrustment, under which liability arises out of the combined negligence of the incompetent driver and the person that sold him the car, is applied to anyone who sells, lends, leases, or gives a car to an incompetent driver, as well as anyone who finances a car for an incompetent driver.

Carter v. Kinney

Instant Facts: A man sues the host of a weekly Bible study group after he slipped and fell in the host's icy driveway.

Black Letter Rule: A guest at a weekly social gathering in a private home is not an invitee, but rather a licensee; and the homeowner is not subject to the elevated duty of care owed to persons entering his property in order to do business with him.

Heins v. Webster County

Instant Facts: A man sues a county hospital after he slipped and fell on hospital property while visiting his daughter, a nurse.

Black Letter Rule: Nebraska courts will no longer apply the common-law distinction between invitees and licensees; instead, landowners will owe a duty of reasonable care to all lawful visitors.

Posecai v. Wal–Mart Stores, Inc.

Instant Facts: A woman sues Sam's Club for negligence after she is mugged in the store's parking lot.

Black Letter Rule: Businesses have the duty to exercise reasonable care to protect their patrons from the reasonably foreseeable criminal actions of third persons.

Broadbent v. Broadbent

Instant Facts: A father, acting as his son's conservator, sues the child's mother for negligence after the son was severely injured due to the mother's negligent supervision while he was swimming in her backyard pool.

Black Letter Rule: A parent is no longer immune from tort liability toward his child solely by virtue of the parental relationship.

Riss v. City of New York

Instant Facts: Riss (P) sued City (D) for negligence due to the police failing to provide protection from attacker who had previously threatened her on numerous occasions.

Black Letter Rule: A municipality is not liable for failure to provide special police protection to a member of the public who was repeatedly threatened with personal harm and eventually suffered injuries for lack of protection.

Lauer v. City of New York

Instant Facts: A man sues the city medical examiner when he was investigated for the murder of his son after the medical examiner mistakenly reported the death as a homicide and then failed to correct his error as soon as he found out about it.

Black Letter Rule: A member of the public can recover from a municipality when the ministerial negligence of one of its employees causes injury in breach of a duty the employee owes to the injured party.

Friedman v. State of New York

Instant Facts: A woman sues the New York Department of Transportation after she got into a head-on collision on a state highway with no protective median barrier separating lanes of traffic.

Black Letter Rule: When the government decides to take action to remedy a dangerous condition, it may be held liable when it fails to do so in a reasonable time.

Cope v. Scott

Instant Facts: A man sues the National Parks Service after getting into a car accident on a poorly maintained roadway with no warning signs.

Black Letter Rule: A federal agency's decision not to maintain a roadway is discretionary and immune from suit under the Federal Tort Claims Act; however, its decision not to post warning signs, although discretionary, is not immune from suit because it is not a decision that is fraught with public policy considerations.

Harper v. Herman

(*Diver*) v. (*Boat Owner*)

499 N.W.2d 472 (Minn. 1993)

BOAT OWNER HAS NO DUTY TO WARN GUESTS WHEN THE WATER AROUND THE BOAT IS TOO SHALLOW TO DIVE INTO

WE SHOULD HAVE TOLD HIM THE WATER IS TOO SHALLOW FOR DIVING!

■ **INSTANT FACTS** A man sues a boat owner when during an outing on Lake Minnetonka the man dove head first into three feet of water and was paralyzed.

■ **BLACK LETTER RULE** A boat owner hosting a social gathering on his boat is under no legal duty to warn his guests that the water is too shallow for diving because the boat owner's relationship with his guests does not fall into one of the discrete categories that have been acknowledged as giving rise to such a duty.

■ PROCEDURAL BASIS

Appeal to the Supreme Court of Minnesota of an appellate court ruling denying summary judgment for the defendant in a negligence suit for damages.

■ FACTS

Jeffrey Harper (P), age 20, was one of four guests on board Theodor Herman's (D) boat. Cindy Alberg Palmer, another of Herman's (D) guests, had invited Harper (P) along on the sailing outing on Lake Minnetonka. Herman (D) and Harper (P) did not know each other before the outing. Herman (D) was an experienced boat owner and had spent hundreds of hours sailing on Lake Minnetonka. Herman (D) considered himself to be in charge of the boat and its passengers. Harper (P) was an experienced swimmer, but had no training in diving. During the outing, Herman's (D) guests decided to go swimming and Herman (D) headed toward Big Island, a popular recreation spot that Herman (D) knew well. Harper (P) had been to Big Island once before. Herman (D) positioned the boat in an area where the water was shallow enough that his guests could use the boat's ladder to enter the water, but deep enough so that they could swim. Harper (P) asked Herman (D) if he was "going in" and when Herman (D) said "yes," Harper (P) dove into the water without warning. Because the water was only two or three feet deep at the spot where Harper (P) dove, Harper (P) hit the bottom of the lake head first, broke his spinal cord, and became a quadriplegic. Harper (P) sued Herman (D), claiming that Herman (D) owed him a duty to warn him that the water was too shallow for diving. The trial court granted Herman's (D) motion for summary judgment, but the court of appeals reversed, holding that Herman (D) did have a duty to warn Harper (P) that the water around the boat was too shallow for diving.

■ ISSUE

Does a boat owner that is hosting a social gathering on his boat have a duty to warn his guests that the water around the boat is too shallow to dive into?

■ DECISION AND RATIONALE

(Page, J.) No. Harper (P) argues that Herman (D) owed him a duty of care because Herman (D) was an experienced boat owner whereas Harper (P) was a relatively inexperienced swimmer and diver. This court has held in previous cases that the affirmative duty to act to prevent injury only arises when a special relationship exists between the parties. Even if Herman (D) should have known that Harper (P) needed protection, Harper (P) must still prove that a special relationship existed that gave rise to an affirmative duty to act. Harper (P) argues that the special relationship arose when Herman (D) allowed an inexperienced diver on his boat. However, under the Restatement rule, a special relationship is only found on the part of common carriers, innkeepers, owners of land held open to the public, and persons that have custody over another individual under such circumstances that the individual is deprived of normal opportunities of self-protection. Harper (P) is not able to show that Herman (D) had custody of him under such circumstances that he was deprived of normal opportunities for self-protection. Harper (P) has not shown that he was particularly vulnerable or otherwise lacked the ability to protect himself, nor has he shown that Herman (D) had considerable power over his welfare. Additionally, Harper (P) has made no allegation that he expected any protection from Herman (D). The court of appeals ruled in Harper's (P) favor because it found that Herman (D) knew that the water was dangerously shallow and under Minnesota case law, actual knowledge of a dangerous condition imposes a special duty to take affirmative action. However, actual knowledge without a special relationship giving rise to a duty to provide protection is not sufficient to establish liability for negligence. Finally, under the Restatement, there are certain dangers, such as those posed by fire and water, that can be appreciated by any child. If a child can be expected to appreciate the danger of diving into water, so can a 20-year-old adult.

Analysis:

If a duty to warn had been found in the *Harper* case, how might Herman (D) have complied with that duty? Would he have been required to ask all of his guests if they were experienced swimmers and divers before inviting them on board? What if the decision to go swimming was spontaneous? Would Herman (D) have been required to give an oral warning to each guest? Would he be required to make sure that each guest fully understood his warning before they dove into the water? Perhaps because an affirmative duty is so difficult to impose, the Minnesota Supreme Court in *Harper* has chosen to take a categorical approach to the Good Samaritan question. Certain relationships give rise to a duty to warn: relationships involving a guest's paying a host to use the recreational facilities he owns and relationships involving an individual's being placed in a situation where he has no ability to protect himself. There is no duty to warn if the plaintiff cannot show that his relationship with the defendant fell into one of these narrow categories. This result may not be the moral one, but it does avoid a multitude of difficult legal questions.

■ CASE VOCABULARY

ARGUENDO: For argument's sake

Farwell v. Keaton

(Father of the Friend Who Was Injured) v. *(Friend Who Ran Away)*

396 Mich. 281, 240 N.W.2d 217 (1976)

FRIENDS SPENDING TIME TOGETHER SOCIALLY ARE REQUIRED TO COME TO EACH OTHER'S AID IN AN EMERGENCY

HE HAS BEEN BEATEN UNCONSCIOUS, AND I CAN'T HELP HIM!

■ **INSTANT FACTS** A man sues his son's friend when the son died of severe head injuries after he and his friend got into a fight and the friend, after making an initial effort to revive the son, abandoned him in a car in his grandparents' driveway.

■ **BLACK LETTER RULE** When an individual comes to the aid of another, he is subject to the duty to take no action that would leave the victim worse off than before; and friends spending time together socially are under the affirmative obligation to come to each other's aid in an emergency.

■ **PROCEDURAL BASIS**

Appeal to the Supreme Court of Michigan of a jury verdict for the plaintiff in a wrongful death action for damages.

■ **FACTS**

On the evening of August 26, 1966, David Siegrist (D) and Richard Farwell returned a car that Siegrist (D) had borrowed from a friend. While they waited for Siegrist's (D) friend, they drank some beer. Two girls walked by and Siegrist (D) and Farwell tried to talk to them. Eventually, they followed the girls to a drive-in restaurant down the street. The girls complained to their friends that Siegrist (D) and Farwell were following them, and a group of boys chased Siegrist (D) and Farwell down the street. Although Siegrist (D) was unharmed, Farwell was severely beaten. Siegrist (D) applied ice to Farwell's head and then drove Farwell around for about two hours. At some point during the drive, Farwell climbed into the back seat of the car and fell asleep. At midnight, Siegrist (D) drove to Farwell's grandparents' house. He tried to wake Farwell up, but was unable to and eventually left. Farwell's grandparents found him in the car the next morning and took him to the hospital. He died three days later of an epidural hematoma. Farwell's father (P) sued Siegrist (D) for wrongful death, contending that if Siegrist (D) had taken Farwell to the hospital or notified someone of Farwell's condition, Farwell would not have died. A neurosurgeon testified at trial that if an individual in Farwell's condition had been taken to the hospital within half an hour of losing consciousness, he would have had an 85 to 88 percent chance of recovery. The jury awarded Farwell's father (P) $15,000 in damages. The Court of Appeals reversed the jury verdict, finding that Siegrist (D) had assumed no duty to obtain medical treatment for Farwell.

■ **ISSUE**

In a situation where an individual attempts to aid an injured victim, does a duty to take affirmative action arise where the individual and the victim were friends spending time together socially?

■ **DECISION AND RATIONALE**

(Levin, J.) Yes. Every person is subject to the legal duty to avoid any affirmative actions that could worsen a situation involving a person in distress. In a case such as this one, where the existence of a duty of care is a question of fact for the jury to answer, the jury must first determine whether the defendant tried to help the victim. If he did, the defendant is required to act as a reasonable person. Farwell's father (P) presented ample evidence that Siegrist (D) owed a legal duty to Farwell, Siegrist (D) knew Farwell had been in a fight, he applied an ice pack to Farwell's head, and while he was driving Farwell climbed into the back of the car and fell asleep. Siegrist (D) also attempted to wake Farwell up, and was unsuccessful. Siegrist (D) argues that he owed no duty to Farwell because he did not have a special relationship with Farwell that would give rise to such a duty. However, courts will find a duty where reasonable men would agree that one exists. Farwell and Siegrist (D) were spending time together socially. The understanding that if one companion is in danger the other will help him if by doing so he won't put himself in danger is implicit in any social undertaking, and to find that Siegrist (D) did not have the duty to seek medical attention or tell someone about Farwell's condition after he had been badly beaten and was laying unconscious in Siegrist's (D) car would be "shocking to humanitarian considerations." In this case, the social nature of Siegrist's (D) undertaking with Farwell gave rise to a special relationship. Siegrist (D) had an affirmative duty to come to Farwell's aid.

■ DISSENT

(Fitzgerald, J.) The majority holds that the personal relationship between Farwell and Siegrist (D) gave rise to a special relationship that established a legal duty to obtain assistance. There is no legal authority to support this holding, and if the court wants to extend the concept of special relationships based on social policy considerations, the appropriate place to start would be with "co-adventurers," not social companions. Co-adventurers are people who embark on a dangerous activity together with the understanding that they are dependent on each other for their safety. There is no evidence in this case that Farwell relied upon Siegrist (D) for any assistance.

Analysis:

The *Farwell* court has created a new category of special relationship: friends. Under the *Farwell* court's approach, because society recognizes that friends engaged in a common social activity are dependent on each other for their safety and have a moral duty to come to each other's aid in a emergency, friends also have a legal duty to come to each other's aid. The *Farwell* court also finds that Siegrist (D) had a duty toward Farwell on the ground that Siegrist (D) voluntarily attempted to assist Farwell. Once an individual voluntarily comes to the aid of another, he is subject to a reasonable standard of care. Establishing a duty of care for people that voluntarily come to aid others in an emergency does turn a moral obligation into a legal one, but it also creates a problem. A volunteer that is inexperienced in emergency assistance may actually make a victim's situation worse while thinking that he is helping. Later on, the victim may sue the volunteer for damages. Fear of being sued may actually turn the duty of care into a disincentive for potential Good Samaritans.

■ CASE VOCABULARY

PROXIMATE CAUSE: The predominant cause from which an injury follows in a natural, direct, and unbroken way.

Randi W. v. Muroc Joint Unified School District

(Student) v. *(School District)*

14 Cal.4th 1066, 929 P.2d 582, 60 Cal.Rptr.2d 263 (1997)

EMPLOYERS CAN BE HELD LIABLE FOR FAILING TO DISCLOSE MATERIAL NEGATIVE INFORMATION WHEN GIVING JOB REFERENCES

■ **INSTANT FACTS** A vice principal's last four employers provided his new employer with glowing recommendations of his character and fitness without disclosing that complaints of sexual misconduct had been filed against him, and when he sexually assaulted one of his students, she sued.

■ **BLACK LETTER RULE** An employer has the duty to use reasonable care in recommending a former employee without disclosing material negative information that would relate to his fitness for the job.

■ **PROCEDURAL BASIS**

Appeal to the Supreme Court of California of appellate court's reversal of trial court's granting of defendant's demurrers in a negligence action for damages.

■ **FACTS**

Robert Gadams, a school vice principal, sexually assaulted a 13-year-old student, Randi W. (P). The Livingston school district, Gadams' employer, had hired Gadams after receiving glowing recommendations from the four school districts (D), including the Muroc Joint Unified School District, that had employed him in the past. But none of the recommendations mentioned that charges or complaints of sexual misconduct and impropriety had been filed against Gadams while he had been working for those districts. Randi W. (P) sued the districts (D) for negligent misrepresentation, fraud, and negligence per se. The trial court granted the districts' (D) demurrers to all three claims, but the court of appeals reversed.

■ **ISSUE**

Can an employer be held liable for failing to use reasonable care in recommending a former employee to another employer without disclosing material information that would relate to the former employee's fitness for the job?

■ **DECISION AND RATIONALE**

(Chin, A.J.) Yes. Although a recommending employer is usually not accountable to a third party for its failure to disclose negative information about a former employee, a court can impose liability in cases such as this one, where the recommendation letter amounts to affirmative misrepresentation. Randi W. (P) may proceed with the claims based on negligent misrepresentation and fraud, but may not proceed on the negligence per se claim because the districts' (D) failure to report the charges against Gadams to the authorities in violation of state law does not, as a matter of law, constitute negligence per se. In order to determine whether Randi W. (P) can proceed on the negligent misrepresentation and fraud claims, the court will examine whether Randi W. (P) has sufficiently pleaded that the districts (D) owed her a duty of care, that they breached that duty by making misrepresentations, and that the Livingston school district's reliance on the districts' (D) misrepresentations was the proximate cause of Randi W.'s (P) injury. Randi W. (P) is not arguing that a special relationship existed between her and the districts (D), but instead is presenting an issue of first impression. She wants the court to determine that an entity that intentionally or negligently provides false information to another entity owes a duty to a third party, despite the fact that the third party never received the false information and had no relationship with the entity providing it. In California, the general rule is that everyone is subject to the duty to use ordinary care to prevent others from being injured by his conduct. In determining whether to impose liability here, the court will examine factors including foreseeability and causality, moral blame, availability of insurance or alternative courses of conduct, and public policy considerations. First, the assault on Randi W. (P) was reasonably foreseeable because the districts (D) could have foreseen that the Livingston district would not have hired Gadams without their recommendations and could have foreseen that Gadams would molest a Livingston student. Second, the question of moral blame depends on the evidence presented at trial, but it can be argued that the districts' (D) recommending Gadams to the Livingston district without disclosing past charges of sexual misconduct was morally blameworthy. Third, standard liability insurance will cover the negligent misrepresentation claim, but not the fraud claim. And the districts (D) had available alternative courses of conduct to protect themselves from liability. They could have disclosed the relevant facts in their recommendations, or written "no comment" letters that merely stated basic employment dates and details without providing any representations as to Gadams' character or fitness. Liability may not be imposed for mere failure to act, unless a special relationship exists that gives rise to such a duty. Fourth, public policy clearly recognizes the importance of preventing future harm and preventing child abuse. This policy outweighs the one advanced by the districts (D)—that requiring this type of disclosure would encourage employers to refuse to give references for any of their former employees. This court holds that an employer owes to third parties the duty not to misrepresent the facts in describing the character and qualifications of a former employee in a recommendation letter where making such a misrepresentation runs the substantial and foreseeable risk that the third party would be physically injured. Where there is no risk of physical injury and no special relationship between the employer and the third party, there is no duty to disclose. The second inquiry in this case is whether the districts' (D) letters amounted to actionable misleading misrepresentation or mere nondisclosure. The districts' (D) letter in this case amount to "misleading half-truths." The districts (D) were under the obligation to provide all facts that would "materially qualify" the facts the districts (D) chose to disclose. The districts (D) argue that the letters were permissible half-truths because no reasonable person could believe that a recommendation letter contained the whole truth about a job applicant. However, in this case, the districts (D) made affirmative representations of Gadams' good character. These representations were made deceptively incomplete when the districts (D) failed to disclose the charges against Gadams. The letters implied that Gadams was fit to interact with female students, even though the districts (D) knew that he was not fit. For all the reasons outlined above and because Randi W. (P) has made sufficient allegations concerning the Livingston district's reliance on the letters, the court of appeals judgment is reversed in part, and affirmed in part.

Analysis:

Tarasoff dealt with a therapist's duty to warn a potential victim when his patient confides that he intends to commit a violent action. *Randi* deals with a different issue. The case is not about the duty to warn—the court makes it clear that the districts (D) were under no tort-law obligation to report Gadams's misconduct to the authorities and that the districts (D) could have written simple reports detailing Gadams's dates of employment, salary, etc., without including any mention of the complaints against him. The districts (D), unlike the therapist in *Tarasoff,* are not under the affirmative obligation to prevent Gadams from injuring a third party. They are instead under the negative obligation to refrain from making material misrepresentations in their letters of recommendations. If the districts (D) raise the issue of Gadams's general character and fitness to be around female students, they must provide all the material information they have, even the negative information.

■ CASE VOCABULARY

DEFAMATION: Harming the reputation of another person by making false or misleading statements to a third person or to the general public.

Tarasoff v. Regents of University of California

(Parents of Murdered Woman) v. *(Employer of Therapists)*

17 Cal.3d 425, 131 Cal.Rptr. 14, 551 P.2d 334 (1976)

A THERAPIST OWES A LEGAL DUTY NOT ONLY TO HIS PATIENT, BUT ALSO TO HIS PATIENT'S WOULD-BE VICTIM

■ **INSTANT FACTS** A murdered woman's parents sued the University (D) because therapists employed there failed to warn their daughter of death threats made towards her by a patient.

■ **BLACK LETTER RULE** Once a therapist does in fact determine, or under applicable professional standards reasonably should have determined, that a patient poses serious danger of violence to others, he bears a duty to exercise reasonable care to protect the foreseeable victim of that danger.

■ **PROCEDURAL BASIS**

Appeal from the superior court's ruling which sustained the defendant's demurrers to plaintiffs' second amended complaints without leave to amend.

■ **FACTS**

Prosenjit Poddar confided his intention to kill Tatiana Tarasoff to a psychologist, Dr. Moore, who was employed by the University of California at Berkley (D). On Moore's request, the campus police briefly detained Poddar, but released him when he appeared rational. Dr. Powelson, Moore's superior, directed that no further action be taken to detain Poddar. No one warned Tatiana of the threats made on her life, and two months later Poddar killed her. Tatiana's parents (P) brought suit against the therapists, the campus police, and the Regents of the University of California as their employer. The superior court concluded that the facts did not set forth causes of action against the defendants, and sustained the defendant's demurrers to the Tarasoffs' (P) second amended complaints without leave to amend. This appeal followed.

■ **ISSUE**

Does a therapist have a duty to protect a foreseeable victim from dangers posed by their patients?

■ **DECISION AND RATIONALE**

(Tobriner, J.) Yes. Although the Tarasoffs' (P) pleadings assert no special relation between Tatiana and the therapists (D), they establish as between Poddar and the therapists (D) the special relation that arises between a patient and his doctor or psychotherapist. Such a relationship may support affirmative duties for the benefit of third persons. Thus, for example, a hospital must exercise reasonable care to control the behavior of a patient which may endanger other persons. A doctor must also warn a patient if the patient's condition of medication renders certain conduct, such as driving a car, dangerous to others. The University (D) contends, however, that imposition of a duty to exercise reasonable care to protect third persons is unworkable because therapists cannot accurately predict whether or not a patient will resort to violence. In support of the argument, amicus representing the American Psychiatric Association and other professional societies cite numerous articles which indicate that therapists, in the present state of the art, are unable reliably to predict violent acts; their forecasts, amicus claims, tend consistently to overpredict violence, and indeed are often more wrong than right. We recognize the difficulty that a therapist encounters in attempting to forecast whether a patient presents a serious danger of violence. Obviously we do not require that the therapist in making that determination, render a perfect performance; the therapist need only exercise "that reasonable degree of skill, knowledge, and care ordinarily possessed and exercised by members of that professional specialty under similar circumstances." Within the broad range of reasonable practice and treatment in which professional opinion and judgment may differ, the therapist is free to exercise his or her own best judgment without liability; proof, aided by hindsight, that he or she judged wrongly is insufficient to establish negligence. Amicus contends, however, that even if a therapist does in fact predict that a patient poses a serious danger of violence to others, the therapist should be absolved of any responsibility for failing to act to protect the potential victim. In our view, however, once a therapist does in fact determine, or under applicable professional standards reasonably should have determined, that a patient poses serious danger of violence to others, he bears a duty to exercise reasonable care to protect the foreseeable victim of that danger. While the discharge of this duty of due care will necessarily vary with the facts of each case, in each instance the adequacy of the therapist's conduct must be measured against the traditional negligence standard of the rendition of reasonable care under the circumstances. The ultimate question of resolving the tension between the conflicting interest of patient and potential victim is one of social policy, not professional expertise. In sum, the therapist owes a legal duty not only to his patient, but also to his patient's would-be victim and is subject in both respects to scrutiny by judge and jury. For the foregoing reasons, we find that the Tarasoffs' (P) complaints can be amended to state a cause of action against the therapists and the University, as their employer, for breach of a duty to exercise reasonable care to protect Tatiana. We conclude, however, that the police defendants do not have any such special relationship to either Tatiana or to Poddar sufficient to impose upon them a duty to warn respecting Poddar's violent intentions.

■ CONCURRENCE

(Mosk, J.) I concur in the result because the Tarasoffs (P) assert that the therapists (D) predicted that Poddar would kill Tatiana and negligently breached their duty to warn Tatiana of the danger she was in. But the majority applies a rule that a therapist can be held liable for failure to predict his patient's violent behavior when other practitioners, acting according to professional standards, would have predicted violent behavior. The problem with this rule is that there are no professional standards regarding the prediction of violent behavior, and in fact, the argument that psychiatric predictions of violence are inherently unreliable is supported by an impressive body of literature on the subject, which is cited in a recent opinion by this court.

■ DISSENT

(Clark, J.) General principles of tort law favor nondisclosure in cases like this one. Confidentiality is important for three reasons: to prevent those in need of therapy from being deterred, to promote effective treatment by encouraging patients to confide in their doctors, and to allow patients to maintain trust in their therapists. The majority's decision in this case will either encourage doctors to give too many warnings, creating a possible "cry wolf" situation, or will encourage doctors to commit every patient that expresses a violent fantasy.

Analysis:

Whenever one person is by circumstances placed in such a position with regard to another that if he did not use ordinary care and skill in his own conduct he would cause danger of injury to the person or property of the other, a duty arises to use ordinary care and skill to avoid such danger. Departure from this fundamental principle only occurs upon the balancing of a number of considerations. The most important of these considerations in establishing duty is foreseeability. As a general principle, a defendant owes a duty of care to all persons who are foreseeably endangered by his conduct, with respect to all risks which make the conduct unreasonably dangerous. However, when the avoidance of foreseeable harm requires a defendant to control the conduct of another person, or to warn of such conduct, the common law has traditionally imposed liability only if the defendant bears some special relationship to the dangerous person or to the potential victim. The court here found that the risk that unnecessary warnings may be given is a reasonable price to pay for the lives that may be saved. Additionally, the revelation of a communication under these circumstances is not a breach of trust or a violation of professional ethics, as section 9 of the AMA's Principles of Medical Ethics provides that. "[a] physician may not reveal the confidence entrusted to him in the course of medical attendance . . . *unless he is required to do so by law or unless it becomes necessary in order to protect the welfare of the individual or of the community.*" (Emphasis added.) Thus, the public policy favoring protection of the confidential character of patient-psychotherapist communications must yield to the extent to which disclosure is essential to avert danger to others.

■ CASE VOCABULARY

AFFIRMATIVE ACTS: Positive, forthcoming actions taken.

AMICUS: A group with a strong interest in or views on the subject matter of an action, but which is not a party to the action.

DEMURRER: An allegation of a defendant, which, admitting the matters of fact alleged by the complaint to be true, shows that as they are therein set forth they are insufficient for the plaintiff to proceed upon.

DUE CARE: That degree of care which an ordinarily prudent person would have exercised under the same or similar circumstances.

Uhr v. East Greenbush Central School District

(Student's Family) v. *(School District)*

94 N.Y.2d 32, 720 N.E.2d 886, 698 N.Y.S.2d 609 (1999)

NEW YORK COURT IMPOSES STRICT REQUIREMENTS FOR DETERMINING WHETHER AN IMPLIED RIGHT OF ACTION EXISTS UNDER A STATUTE

■ **INSTANT FACTS** A family sues the school district when, in violation of state law, the school failed to test their daughter for scoliosis with the result that her illness progressed undetected.

■ **BLACK LETTER RULE** A court will not infer a private right of action under a statute unless the plaintiff is a member of the class the statute was intended to benefit; recognizing a private right of action would promote the legislative purpose; and recognizing a private right of action would be consistent with the legislative scheme.

■ **PROCEDURAL BASIS**

Appeal to the Court of Appeals of New York of the supreme court's granting the East Greenbush Central School District's motion for summary judgment in a negligence action for damages.

■ **FACTS**

New York Education Law § 905(1) requires that medical inspectors, principals, or teachers in all New York state schools examine all pupils between the ages of eight and sixteen for scoliosis at least once in every school year. § 905(2) provides that school authorities subject to the requirements of § 905(1) are immune from any civil liability resulting from making such an examination. The Uhrs (P) sued the East Greenbush Central School District (''District'') (D) after their daughter developed scoliosis. The District (D) had failed to test the Uhrs' (P) daughter during the 1993–1994 school year and as a result, her condition proceeded undetected for so long that she was eventually required to undergo surgery. The trial court determined that because § 905 does not create a private right of action and because the Uhrs (P) had failed to state a claim for common-law negligence, they could not maintain an action for damages against the District (D). The Appellate Division affirmed.

■ **ISSUE**

Can a court infer a private right of action from a statute where no special relationship or obligation to act exists that would have created a duty under the common law?

■ **DECISION AND RATIONALE**

(Rosenblatt, J.) No. Ordinarily, when the legislature wishes to create a private right of action under a statute it drafts an express right of action. When the statute is silent, as in this case, courts may determine whether a private right of action can be fairly inferred. To determine whether a private right of action is implied in a statute, courts will examine: 1) whether the plaintiff is a member of the class of persons the statute was intended to benefit; 2) whether recognizing a private right of action would promote the legislative purpose behind the statute; and 3) whether the creation of such a right would be consistent with the legislative scheme. In this case, the first prong is easily satisfied. The second prong is also satisfied. The purpose of the statute is to prevent the crippling effects scoliosis has on children by providing a means of early detection. By enacting § 905(1), the legislature sought to benefit the population as a whole by promoting public health and by saving the state money by preventing expensive hospitalizations. Recognizing a private right of action would promote the legislative purpose behind § 905(1) because the risk of liability for failure to examine pupils annually would encourage compliance with the law. However, the third prong is not satisfied—in this case, a private right of action would not be consistent with the legislative scheme. The "consistency" prong is distinguishable from the "promotion" prong, although the two may overlap. The Uhrs (P) argue that a private right of action is not only consistent with § 905(1), but necessary as the statute does not offer any other practical means of enforcement. However, the statute does have its own enforcement mechanism—it provides that the Commissioner of Education may withhold public funding from any school that does not comply with § 905(1). It is not clear that allowing a private right of action, in addition to the means of administrative enforcement provided by the statute, would be consistent with the statutory scheme. The history and language of § 905(2) are evidence of the Legislature's intention to immunize school districts from liability under § 905(1).

Analysis:

When the state legislature passes a new statute, it can provide that the statute be enforced by the executive branch, by citizens through civil suits, both. Providing for a private right of action under a statute may be seen as an efficient and inexpensive (for the government) means of enforcement. This may be one reason why courts tend to look for implied rights of action. The court in *Uhr* uses a three-prong test to determine whether a private right of action may be inferred from § 905(1). The last two prongs question whether an implied private right of action can promote the legislative purpose and be consistent with the legislative scheme. The first question requires an analysis of the legislative intent behind the statute and the effect a private right of action would have on compliance with the statute. The second question requires an analysis of the statute as a whole to determine whether an implied private right of action would be consistent with the enforcement mechanism the legislature expressly provided and with the legislative intent behind that mechanism. The *Uhr* court determined that the legislature intended to promote public health, but at the same time to insulate school districts from civil liability.

■ CASE VOCABULARY

MISFEASANCE: The wrongful performance of a lawful act.

NONFEASANCE: The failure to act where a duty exists.

SCOLIOSIS: A lateral curvature of the spine.

Strauss v. Belle Realty Co.

(*Tenant*) v. (*Landlord*)

65 N.Y.2d 399, 482 N.E.2d 34, 492 N.Y.S.2d 555 (1985)

PUBLIC UTILITIES OWE A DUTY ONLY TO CUSTOMERS

■ **INSTANT FACTS** A man sues his landlord and the electric company after he fell down a flight of stairs in his apartment building during a blackout.

■ **BLACK LETTER RULE** A public utility does not owe a duty of care to those who do not have a contractual relationship with it.

■ **PROCEDURAL BASIS**

Appeal to the New York Court of Appeals of the Appellate Division's dismissal of a plaintiff's negligence action for damages.

■ **FACTS**

On July 13, 1977, New York City suffered a blackout as a result of a failure of Consolidated Edison's ("Con Ed") (D1) power system. Julius Strauss (P) lived in an apartment building in Queens. Con Ed provided electricity to his apartment in accordance with a contract between Con Ed and Strauss, and provided electricity to the common areas of the building under a contract with the building's owner, Belle Realty Co. ("Belle") (D2). Because of the blackout, Strauss (P) had no running water in his apartment. On the second day of the blackout, Strauss (P) went to the basement to get water, but fell down the darkened and defective stairway. He sued Belle (D2) for failing maintain the stairs and warn of their condition, and sued Con Ed (D1) for its negligent breach of duty to supply electricity.

■ **ISSUE**

Does a public utility company owe a duty of care to an individual with whom it has no contractual relationship?

■ **DECISION AND RATIONALE**

(Kaye, J.) No. Con Ed (D1) is not liable to a tenant of an apartment building for injuries sustained in a common area as a result of Con Ed's (D1) negligent failure to provide electricity. Although a contractual relationship is not a prerequisite to finding that a duty of care exists, the courts have a duty to protect a defendant from "crushing liability." A utility's liability in a case where its gross negligence has caused it to fail to provide services would be enormous if not limited only to plaintiffs with a contractual relationship with the company. In *Moch Co. v. Rensselaer Water Co.,* the New York Court of Appeals determined that to allow a company whose warehouse burned down in a fire to sue a water company for failing to provide an adequate amount of water to city fire hydrants would unduly extend the water company's liability. The *Moch* court reserved the question of what remedy would apply in a case where the utility company was guilty of reckless and wanton indifference. Because Con Ed (D1) was guilty of gross negligence, which is a lower level of misconduct than that contemplated by the *Moch* court, *Moch* controls in this case. The arguments that the injuries were foreseeable and that Strauss (P) was part of a specific, limited, and circumscribed class with a close relationship to Con Ed (D1)—namely, people living in apartment buildings where Con Ed supplied all electricity—do not alter the outcome in this case. Strauss (P) may belong to a specific class, but because Con Ed (D1) provides electricity to millions of customers, that class is enormous and allowing a member of this class to sue Con Ed (D1) for injuries sustained in an area where Con Ed (D1) supplies electricity under a contract to which the victim is not a party does nothing to limit Con Ed's (D1) exposure to liability to reasonable levels. It is also worth noting that Strauss' (P) argument contains no limiting principle that would serve to prevent a landlord's invitees, or people making deliveries to sue Con Ed (D1) while allowing tenants to sue.

■ **DISSENT**

(Meyer, J.) The majority has based its decision on public policy but has failed to look at the public policy issue from all angles. A decision in Strauss' (P) favor may not lead to Con Ed's (D1) exposure to crushing liability. Con Ed (D1) may not be ruined because of lawsuits brought by millions of New Yorkers. It may be able to pass the burden of financing damage awards on to its stockholders and customers. In trying to limit the negligent party's exposure to liability, the majority has ignored the burdens placed on the injured parties, some of whom have lost their life savings, and seems to be making the perverse argument that the more people injured through a tortfeasor's gross negligence, the less liable that tortfeasor is.

Analysis:

The majority determined that the public interest in lower electricity rates would not be served if Con Ed (D1) were exposed to massive liability for injuries caused by its negligent failure to provide electricity. It also determined that it could protect Con Ed (D1) from such liability by requiring that in order to maintain a negligence suit against Con Ed (D1), a plaintiff must be in privity of contract with Con Ed (D1). The majority's holding may not be successful in this regard. It still leaves Con Ed (D1) open to lawsuits brought by people injured in areas where they are the ones paying for Con Ed's (D1) service and landlords. In a city as big as New York, this could still be an enormous number of people and a source of crushing liability.

■ **CASE VOCABULARY**

COLLATERAL ESTOPPEL: Another term for res judicata, this doctrine prevents a party from re-litigating a legal issue that a court has already decided.

PRIVITY: A similarity, or identity, of legal interests between parties.

SUI GENERIS: Literally, "Of its own kind"; a proceeding for a remedy that cannot be characterized as strictly legal or strictly equitable.

Reynolds v. Hicks

(Injured Driver) v. *(Bride and Groom)*
134 Wash.2d 491, 951 P.2d 761 (1998)

SOCIAL HOSTS THAT SERVE ALCOHOL TO MINORS DO NOT OWE A DUTY OF CARE TO THIRD PERSONS THAT MIGHT BE INJURED THROUGH THE DRUNK MINOR'S MISCONDUCT

■ **INSTANT FACTS** The under-age nephew of the groom was served alcohol at a wedding reception and when he caused a car accident on his way home, the injured driver sued the bride and groom.

■ **BLACK LETTER RULE** A social host that supplies a minor with alcohol does not owe a duty of care to third persons.

■ **PROCEDURAL BASIS**

Appeal to the Supreme Court of Washington of trial court decision dismissing a personal injury action for damages.

■ **FACTS**

On September 10, 1988, Jamie and Anna Hicks (D) were married. Three hundred people, including Jamie's under-age nephew, Steven, attended the wedding and the reception afterward. Steven Hicks consumed alcohol at the reception, and at midnight he left the reception in his sister's car. At around 1:00 a.m., Steven Hicks got into a car accident with Reynolds (P). Reynolds (P) sued Jamie and Anna Hicks (D), claiming that they were negligent in knowingly serving alcohol to an under-age driver. Jamie and Anna Hicks (D) moved for summary judgment on the grounds that Washington does not extend social host liability to situations where intoxicated under-age guests injure third parties. The trial court granted the Hicks (D) motion and the appellate court certified the case directly to the Washington Supreme Court.

■ **ISSUE**

Does a social host that serves alcohol to an under-age driver owe a duty of care to a third person injured by the intoxicated minor?

■ **DECISION AND RATIONALE**

(Madsen, J.) No. In *Hansen v. Friend,* the Washington Supreme Court held that a minor that is injured as a result of his intoxication has a cause of action against the social host that supplied him with alcohol. Reynolds (P) argues that the court should extend this holding to provide a cause of action for third persons. Such an expansion is not warranted by Washington law. This court has been reluctant to extend to social hosts the same kind of liability extended to commercial vendors of alcohol. There are several policy rationales behind this approach. Unlike commercial vendors, social hosts are capable of monitoring their paying customers' alcohol consumption and commercial vendors have pecuniary and proprietary interests in exercising supervision. Social host liability would have more far-reaching implications than commercial-vendor liability because while there are only a limited number of bars, liquor stores, etc., there is a much greater number of adult Washington residents that throw parties. Social host liability would affect almost every adult in the state. It is also worth noting that it is unrealistic to expect a couple like Jamie and Anna Hicks (D) to monitor the alcohol consumption of their

---

minor guests on their wedding day, or to create a legal regime that would require social hosts to hire bartenders and bouncers for any social gathering. Finally, the legislative intent behind the Washington statute that makes it unlawful for any person except a parent to supply liquor to a minor was not to protect third persons that might be injured by intoxicated minors, but rather, was enacted to protect intoxicated minors from their own injuries. The trial court decision is affirmed.

■ CONCURRENCE

(Durham, C.J.) The majority errs in suggesting that the exception for parents in the Washington statute that criminalizes the supplying of alcohol to minors indicates that third parties do not have a private right of action under the statute against social hosts that supply minors with alcohol. The result in this case would have been more firmly grounded in the view, expressed in the dissent to *Hansen,* that the judiciary is not equipped to impose social-host liability.

■ DISSENT

(Johnson, J.) The majority's analysis confuses the issues of duty and ultimate liability. The Washington Supreme Court has recognized that a minor has a private right of action under the statute for his own injuries against the social host that supplied him with alcohol. The court has also recognized that where the legislature has made it a criminal offense to sell alcohol to a minor, third persons injured as a result of an intoxicated minor's conducts have a private right of action against the vendor. The distinction the majority draws between commercial vendors and social hosts is insupportable because it ignores the fact that both a vendor and a social host are breaking the law when they provide a minor with alcohol. The majority holding that a social host commits a crime by serving alcohol to a minor guest but avoids all civil liability makes no sense because it focuses on the impracticality of requiring social hosts to take appropriate precautions instead of focusing on providing a remedy to injured parties.

Analysis:

The majority opinion focuses on the practical and policy implications of requiring social hosts to adhere to the same standard of care as the proprietors of bars. The majority is concerned with the implications its decision might have on society as a whole. Subjecting social hosts to the same standard of care as the proprietors of bars would certainly discourage social gatherings. It might raise homeowners' insurance rates, and make weddings and other family gatherings more expensive by requiring hosts to hire bartenders to monitor alcohol consumption. It would turn parties into fertile ground for frivolous lawsuits. The concurring justices are concerned with judicial encroachment into the legislature's territory. Finally, the dissenting justice is concerned with protecting potential plaintiffs. A person that is injured through the actions of an intoxicated minor may not have many deep pockets to recover from. The minor may not be insured, or his insurance may not cover the full extent of the plaintiff's injuries.

■ CASE VOCABULARY

SUMMARY JUDGMENT: A judgment granted on a motion that there is no factual issue to be determined and that the moving party is entitled to judgment in his favor as a matter of law.

Vince v. Wilson

(Injured Driver) v. *(Aunt of Incompetent Driver)*

151 Vt. 425, 561 A.2d 103 (1989)

NEGLIGENT ENTRUSTMENT RULE APPLIES TO CAR DEALERS, MONEY LENDERS, AS WELL AS THOSE WHO LEND CARS TO INCOMPETENT DRIVERS

■ **INSTANT FACTS** After getting into a car accident with a drunk, unlicensed driver, the injured passenger sues the dealership that sold the car to the drunk driver and the woman that paid for the car.

■ **BLACK LETTER RULE** The doctrine of negligent entrustment, under which liability arises out of the combined negligence of the incompetent driver and the person that sold him the car, is applied to anyone who sells, lends, leases, or gives a car to an incompetent driver, as well as anyone who finances a car for an incompetent driver.

■ **PROCEDURAL BASIS**

Appeals to the Supreme Court of Vermont of trial court's directed verdicts in favor of defendants Ace Auto Sales, Inc. and Gary Gardner and of judgment against defendant Wilson in a negligent entrustment action for damages.

■ **FACTS**

Wilson (D1) bought her grandnephew a car from Ace Auto Sales, Inc. ("Ace") (D2). Gary Gardner (D3) was the salesman. At the time she bought the car, Wilson (D1) not only knew that her grandnephew had no driver's license and had failed the test several times, but also informed Ace (D2) and Gardner (D3) of these facts. Wilson (D1) also knew that her grandnephew drank and used drugs. When the grandnephew got into a car accident that injured his passenger, Vince (P), Vince (P) sued Wilson (D1), Ace (D2), and Gardner (D3) for negligently entrusting an automobile to an incompetent driver. The trial court directed a verdict in favor of Ace (D2) and Gardner (D3), but the jury returned a verdict against Wilson (D1). Vince (P) appealed the directed verdict in Ace (D2) and Gardner's (D3) favor and Wilson (D1) appealed the jury verdict against her.

■ **ISSUE**

Does the doctrine of negligent entrustment apply to persons that knowingly provide funding to incompetent drivers and to persons that knowingly sell automobiles to incompetent drivers?

■ **DECISION AND RATIONALE**

(Mahady, J.) Yes. The general rule of negligent entrustment is that liability arises out of the combined negligence of the incompetent driver and of the car owner, who lends his automobile to the incompetent driver. Vince (P) argues that the rule should be applied to those who would provide funding to incompetent drivers that wish to buy cars and to those who would sell cars to incompetent drivers. Wilson (D1), Ace (D2), and Gardner (D3) argue that the rule should be limited to allow recovery only from car owners, or those who have "the right to control" the car. Courts in other states have interpreted the negligent entrustment doctrine more broadly than Wilson (D1), Ace (D2), and Gardner (D3) do here. These courts have held that the fact that an individual had ownership and control over the car at the time it was turned over to the incompetent driver is sufficient to give rise to liability. This interpretation is in line with the Restatement of Torts. Under the Restatement approach, one who supplies an automobile to an individual that the supplier knows or has reason to know is likely, because of youth or otherwise, to use the car in a way that would involve an unreasonable risk of physical harm is subject to liability. The Restatement rule covers sellers, lessors, and donors, as well as lenders. The cases that Wilson (D1), Ace (D2), and Gardner (D3) use to support their position have been severely criticized by legal commentators. Viewing the evidence in the light most favorable to Vince (P) because of the jury verdict in Vince's (P) favor, it is clear that the evidence makes out a sufficient prima facie case for negligent entrustment against Ace (D2) and Gardner (D3) as well as Wilson (D1). The trial court erred in directing a verdict in Ace (D2) and Gardner's (D3) favor. The cases against Wilson (D1), Ace (D2), and Gardner (D3) are remanded for proceedings consistent with the Supreme Court opinion.

Analysis:

The Vermont Supreme Court has taken an approach to negligent entrustment that is broader than the Restatement approach. The Vermont approach has the effect of increasing the number of available deep pockets for a plaintiff to sue. In the event of a drunk driving accident, for example, an injured person might be able to sue the driver, the dealer who sold the car, and the bank that lent the money. But the Vermont approach might also have the negative effect of discouraging dealers from selling cars to first-time buyers with no track record of responsible car ownership, young people, elderly people, people with a history of alcohol or drug abuse (even if they are not currently abusing any substances), and people with medical problems, such as epilepsy or diabetes, that might conceivably cause them to be dangerous behind the wheel.

■ CASE VOCABULARY

DIRECTED VERDICT: A trial judge will direct the jury to enter a particular verdict where the evidence presented at trial is so persuasive that no reasonable jury could make any other determination.

Carter v. Kinney

(*Bible Student*) v. (*Homeowner*)

896 S.W.2d 926 (Mo. 1995)

SOCIAL GUESTS ARE NOT INVITEES FOR THE PURPOSES OF DETERMINING A HOMEOWNER'S DUTY OF CARE

■ **INSTANT FACTS** A man sues the host of a weekly Bible study group after he slipped and fell in the host's icy driveway.

■ **BLACK LETTER RULE** A guest at a weekly social gathering in a private home is not an invitee, but rather a licensee; and the homeowner is not subject to the elevated duty of care owed to persons entering his property in order to do business with him.

■ **PROCEDURAL BASIS**

Appeal to the Supreme Court of Missouri of trial court's granting a motion for summary judgment in a negligence action for damages.

■ **FACTS**

Ronald and Mary Kinney (D) hosted a weekly Bible study class in their home for members of their church. The Kinneys (D) hosted the Bible study class as part of a series of classes sponsored by their church; and church members interested in taking their class added their names to a sign-up sheet. The Kinneys (D) did not receive any financial or other tangible benefit from hosting the class. Jonathan Carter (P) attended an early morning class on February 3, 1990. Carter (P) had no social relationship with the Kinneys (D) or with any other member of the class. Ronald Kinney (D) had shoveled his driveway the night before, but ice had formed on the driveway overnight without his knowledge. When Carter (P) arrived around 7:00 a.m., he slipped on the ice and broke his leg. Carter (P) sued the Kinneys (D), but his claim was dismissed when the Kinneys (D) moved for summary judgment.

■ **ISSUE**

Is a homeowner that hosts a weekly social gathering subject to the same duty of care as someone that opens his property to the public or derives some sort of material benefit from visitors to his property?

■ **DECISION AND RATIONALE**

(Robertson, J.) No. There are three types of plaintiffs in premises liability cases: trespassers, licensees, and invitees. Anyone that enters land without the permission of the owner is a trespasser. An individual that enters land with permission is a licensee, unless the landowner has an interest in the visit, in which case the visitor is classified as an invitee. Landowners do not owe trespassers a duty of care. A landowner owes a licensee the duty to make safe any dangers the landowner is aware of, and owes an invitee the duty to exercise reasonable care to protect the invitee from both known dangers and dangers the landowner would have found out about through inspection of his premises. Carter (P) argues that as the Kinneys' (D) social guest, he was an invitee. The Kinneys (D) argue that he was a licensee. Even though social guests are, in a sense, invited onto a landowner's property, Missouri law does not recognize social guests as a type of invitee because a social host does not, as a rule, obtain any material benefit from his guests, nor does he extend an invitation to the general public. Because

---

Carter (P) did not enter the Kinneys' (D) property as a "business visitor," he is a licensee, not an invitee, and the Kinneys (D) are subject to the lesser standard of care. Ronald Kinney (D) did not know that ice had formed on his driveway overnight, and cannot therefore be held liable for Carter's (P) injury.

Analysis:

This case presents the traditional approach to premises liability: dividing entrants to land into three categories, each owed a separate duty of care by the landowner. In general, a licensee is someone that is present on the landowner's property with the landowner's consent, but is there for his own purposes rather than to engage in any kind of business transaction with the landowner. Because the Kinneys (D) did not make a business of conducting Bible study classes in their home, anyone attending their class was a licensee, not an invitee. The duty a landowner owes to a licensee is almost the same as the duty owed to a trespasser. Granting permission to enter the property is not meant to be understood as a type of assurance that the property is safe to visit. The landowner is not under any obligation to inspect his property to make sure that it is safe, although he is under the obligation to at least warn his visitor of the existence of any dangerous condition that he knows about.

■ CASE VOCABULARY

INVITEE: One who enters property at the express or implied invitation of the owner, either because he intends to do business with the owner or because the owner has opened his property to the general public.

LICENSEE: One who has the owner's permission to enter the property, but may only do so for his own purposes and not to confer any material benefit on the owner.

TRESPASSER: One who enters property without permission.

Heins v. Webster County

(Hospital Visitor) v. *(Hospital)*

250 Neb. 750, 552 N.W.2d 51 (1996)

INVITEE-LICENSEE DISTINCTION ABOLISHED IN NEBRASKA

■ **INSTANT FACTS** A man sues a county hospital after he slipped and fell on hospital property while visiting his daughter, a nurse.

■ **BLACK LETTER RULE** Nebraska courts will no longer apply the common-law distinction between invitees and licensees; instead, landowners will owe a duty of reasonable care to all lawful visitors.

■ **PROCEDURAL BASIS**

Appeal to the Supreme Court of Nebraska of judgment for the defendant in a negligence action for damages.

■ **FACTS**

After a heavy snowfall, Roger Heins (P) and his wife visited Webster County Hospital (Hospital) (D). According to Heins (P), he and his wife visited the Hospital (D) to meet with his daughter, Julie, the director of nursing, to discuss plans for him to play Santa at the Hospital (D) during the Christmas season. According to the Hospital (D), Heins (P) and his wife were paying a social call. When he left the Hospital (D) through the main exit, Heins (P) slipped and fell, injuring his hip. After a bench trial, the trial court determined that Heins (P) was a licensee rather than a public invitee because he went to the Hospital (D) to pay a social visit to his daughter. The trial court decided that the Hospital (D) did not owe a duty to Heins (P) as a social guest and ruled in the Hospital's (D) favor.

■ **ISSUE**

Is the invitee-licensee distinction of continuing usefulness in negligence actions against landowners?

■ **DECISION AND RATIONALE**

(Connolly, J.) No. Nebraska courts will no longer apply an invitee-licensee distinction and will instead impose on landowners a duty to exercise reasonable care in maintaining their property for the protection of all lawful visitors. A number of jurisdictions have abandoned the invitee-licensee distinction. The United States Supreme Court has declined to apply the distinction in admiralty cases because centuries of judicial interpretations of the common-law rule has turned the distinction into a Semantic morass. The California and Massachusetts supreme courts have abandoned the invitee-licensee distinction for the policy reason that a visitor's status should not determine the duty that a landowner owes him. The present case exemplifies the kind of frustration the common-law distinction raises. Heins (P) was injured while exiting the Hospital (D) through a main exit over the lunch hour. If he had been visiting a patient he would have been able to recover under the common-law rule. But because he was visiting his daughter, a nurse, the common law offers him no protection. The Hospital (D), under the common-law rule, owes a duty to its public and business visitors to keep its main exits and entrances free of ice and snow. A business visitor using the same exit as Heins (P) would have been able to recover for his injury under the common law, but Heins (P) would not. The common-law distinction should not be able to protect a landowner from liability when he would otherwise be held to a standard of reasonable care. This court eliminated the invitee-licensee distinction. It will, however, keep the separate classification for trespassers. The court imposes on landowners the duty to exercise reasonable care in maintaining their property for the protection of lawful visitors. In determining whether a landowner has exercised reasonable care, a court may examine seven factors: 1) the foreseeability of harm, 2) the purpose of the entrant's visit, 3) the time, manner, and circumstances of the visit, 4) the use to which the property is or is expected to be put, 5) the reasonableness of the inspection, repair, or warning, 6) the opportunity and ease of inspection, repair, or warning, and 7) the burden on the landowner and/or community in providing protection. Judgment reversed and case remanded.

■ DISSENT

(Fahrnbruch, J.) Under the majority's new rule, a landowner owes a duty of care to an individual who, like Heins (P), may be engaging in activities on the property without the landowner's knowledge or express permission. In socializing the use of private property to the point where a landowner owes the same duty to all visitors except trespassers, the court is acting outside its usual function: It is not the court's role to create liability where the law does not.

Analysis:

If *Carter* represents the traditional approach to the duties of landowners, *Heins* represents the reformist approach, which is becoming more widely applied. Beginning with the California case of *Rowland v. Christian,* cited in *Heins,* American jurisdictions have started to abolish the common-law distinctions between types of visitors to property and instead impose a single duty of reasonable care on all landowners. Some of these jurisdictions, California among them, have even abolished the trespasser distinction. The reasonable care standard is not as harsh as it might at first seem. *Heins's* first factor takes into account the foreseeability of danger. This means not only that a landowner has the duty to repair or warn of dangers that might foreseeably cause injury, but also that a landowner owes a duty only to entrants whose visits are known or reasonably foreseeable. Even if the court had not preserved the trespasser distinction, a trespasser would still not be likely to recover under *Heins's* first factor. The most significant result of abolishing the common-law distinctions may be the transfer of a level of decision-making from judges to juries. In the common-law cases, judges determined whether a plaintiff fell under one of the three categories as a matter of law. In cases applying the *Heins* approach, juries will determine whether a landowner breached his duty toward all lawful visitors. This benefits plaintiffs by allowing them to survive motions for summary judgment brought early on in the proceedings and bring their cases before juries, which might be more sympathetic to their injuries than judges.

■ CASE VOCABULARY

BENCH TRIAL: A trial before a judge, with no jury.

Posecai v. Wal-Mart Stores, Inc.

(Mugging Victim) v. *(Warehouse Store)*

752 So.2d 762 (La. 1999)

BUSINESSES ARE UNDER THE DUTY TO PROTECT THEIR PATRONS FROM THE CRIMINAL ACTIVITY OF THIRD PERSONS

■ **INSTANT FACTS** A woman sues Sam's Club for negligence after she is mugged in the store's parking lot.

■ **BLACK LETTER RULE** Businesses have the duty to exercise reasonable care to protect their patrons from the reasonably foreseeable criminal actions of third persons.

■ **PROCEDURAL BASIS**

Appeal to the Supreme Court of Louisiana of a judgment for plaintiff in a negligence action for damages.

■ **FACTS**

Shirley Posecai (P) went shopping at Sam's Wholesale Club (Sam's Club) (D) in Kenner, Louisiana, on July 20, 1995. At around 7:20 p.m., she left the store and returned to her car in the Sam's Club (D) parking lot. As she was loading her shopping bags into the trunk, a man that had been hiding under her car grabbed her by the ankle and robbed her at gunpoint of about $19,000 in jewelry. After the robbery, Mrs. Posecai (P) ran back to the store for help. Although two officers from the Kenner Police Department investigated the incident, the robber was never found and Mrs. Posecai (P) was never able to recover her jewelry. During the robbery, a security guard was stationed inside the store to protect the cash office from 5:00 p.m. until 8:00 p.m. There were no security guards watching the parking lot. At trial, the security guard testified that he had been working at Sam's Club (D) for nine years, that he was not aware that any similar crime had been committed in the parking lot, and that he did not consider the parking lot to be a high-crime area. One of the police officers testified that he had been patrolling the area for two years and that although the police were rarely called to Sam's Club (D), the subdivision behind the store was a high-crime area. The other officer testified that the neighborhood was a high-crime one, but that Sam's Club (D) was not a high-crime location. A security expert testified that the robbery could have been prevented if Sam's Club (D) had stationed a security guard outside the store. He also testified that his research of the neighborhood showed that there had been three robberies or other predatory offenses in the Sam's Club (D) parking lot in the past six years. A delivery truck driver had been mugged at 12:45 a.m. in March of 1989, a person was mugged in the store parking lot in May of 1992, and a store employee had her purse snatched in February of 1994. Eighty-three predatory offenses had been committed in and around the thirteen other businesses located on the same block as Sam's Club (D) in the six and a half years before Mrs. Posecai's (P) mugging. Mrs. Posecai (P) argued that Sam's Club's (D) failure to provide security guards in its parking lot was negligent. After a bench trial, the trial court concluded that Sam's Club (D) had a duty to provide security in its parking lot because the danger to Mrs. Posecai (D) was foreseeable.

■ **ISSUE**

Does a landowner owe a duty to protect an invitee from the criminal acts of third persons?

■ DECISION AND RATIONALE

(Marcus, J.)   Yes, under certain circumstances.   Although there is no general duty to protect others from the criminal activity of third persons, business owners have a duty to take reasonable care to protect their customers from the criminal acts of third persons.   This duty only arises under limited circumstances when the criminal act was reasonably foreseeable to the owner.   Although this is a case of first impression in Louisiana, other jurisdictions have developed four different approaches to the foreseeability issue.   The first approach is the specific harm rule.   Under the specific harm rule, a landowner owes a duty to protect customers from the criminal acts of others only when he is aware of the specific, imminent harm about to occur.   The second approach is the similar incidents test.   Under the similar incidents test, a plaintiff established foreseeability by presenting evidence of similar crimes on or near the property.   The third, and most widely used, approach is the totality of the circumstances test.   The totality of the circumstances test takes factors besides similar incidents into account, including the nature, condition, and location of the land, the level of crime in the surrounding area, and any other relevant factual circumstances that might bear on foreseeability.   The fourth approach, adopted by California and Tennessee courts, is the balancing test.   Under the balancing test, courts weigh the foreseeability and gravity of harm against the burden imposed on business to protect its customers from that harm.   The balancing test will be adopted in Louisiana.   Under the new Louisiana test for foreseeability, the greater the foreseeability and gravity of harm, the higher the duty of care imposed on businesses.   The foreseeability and gravity of harm are to be determined by examining the circumstances of each case.   The most important factor will be the existence, frequency, and similarity of other crimes committed on the property.   In this case, there were only three predatory crimes in the six years preceding Mrs. Posecai's (P) mugging, only one of which can be said to be similar to the mugging.   The degree of foreseeability in this case is not sufficient to support a duty on Sam's Club's (D) part to provide security guards in the parking lot or to implement lesser security measures. Judgment affirmed.

■ CONCURRENCE

(Johnson, J.)   The majority adopted the balancing test when the totality of the circumstances test is more appropriate.   The totality of the circumstances test takes all relevant factors into consideration while requiring that a business undertake reasonable steps to prevent danger to their invitees.

Analysis:

The balancing test basically adds a second step to the totality of the circumstances test.   A court must first decide whether the criminal activity in question was reasonably foreseeable based on the circumstances of the case.   Then, it must take into account the gravity of the injury and weigh both against the cost to the business of providing protection.   In *Posecai,* the balancing test revealed that a duty to provide a security detail in the parking lot, or even to step up security inside the store, might prevent more muggings, but because a mugging or other predatory offense occurs at Sam's Club (D) on average only once every two years, the added cost of providing security outweighs the benefit of preventing more muggings.   The balancing test will lead to a different result than the totality of the circumstances test in cases such as *Posecai,* where the crime is rare and the cost of prevention high. It might also lead to a different result in cases where the criminal activity is more common, but causes less of an injury.

■ CASE VOCABULARY

PREDATORY OFFENSE: A "crime against the person."

Broadbent v. Broadbent

(*Child*) v. (*Mother*)

184 Ariz. 74, 907 P.2d 43 (1995)

DOCTRINE OF PARENTAL IMMUNITY ABANDONED IN ARIZONA

■ **INSTANT FACTS** A father, acting as his son's conservator, sues the child's mother for negligence after the son was severely injured due to the mother's negligent supervision while he was swimming in her backyard pool.

■ **BLACK LETTER RULE** A parent is no longer immune from tort liability toward his child solely by virtue of the parental relationship.

■ **FACTS**

Mrs. Broadbent (D) was watching her two-year-old son (P) playing in the family pool when the phone rang inside the house. After going inside to answer the phone, she looked out and did not see her son (P). She ran outside, and found him lying at the bottom of the pool. He suffered severe brain damage and loss of motor function as a result of lack of oxygen. In order to recover from Mrs. Broadbent's (D) liability insurer, Mr. Broadbent, as his son's (P) conservator, sued Mrs. Broadbent (D) for damages. The trial court dismissed the suit on the doctrine of parental immunity and the appeals court affirmed.

■ **ISSUE**

Does the doctrine of parental immunity bar a suit by an unemancipated minor against his mother for negligence?

■ **DECISION AND RATIONALE**

(Corcoran, J.) No. Under common law children have traditionally been seen as separate legal entities from their parents, and have been allowed to maintain contract and property causes of action against them. The doctrine of parental immunity is unknown in English common law, and is not applied in Scotland or Canada. In the United States, the doctrine has been applied since the nineteenth century and was designed to promote domestic peace. Over the years, American courts have fashioned several exceptions to the doctrine, and some states have eliminated the doctrine altogether. Arizona recognized the doctrine in 1967, but by 1970, in *Streenz v. Streenz,* had abrogated it in all but two circumstances. Parental immunity applies where the negligent act involves an exercise of parental authority and where the negligent act involves an exercise of ordinary parental discretion with respect to providing food, clothing, housing, medical care, and other care. The main justifications for the parental immunity doctrine are that suing one's parents would disrupt domestic tranquility, that suing one's parents raises the risk of fraud and collusion, that awarding damages to a child would deplete family resources, that awarding damages would benefit the negligent parent in the event the child predeceases him, and that suing one's parents would interfere with parental discipline and control. These justifications are weak. An injury to a child disrupts a family more than a lawsuit. Issues of fraud and collusion may be discovered and resolved case by case. Awarding damages would not deplete family resources as cases are brought against parents mainly to recover from the parents' liability insurers. The chances of a child predeceasing his parents are relatively slim and any issues raised by this situation could be addressed by the law of intestate succession. Finally, although there is a public policy interest in allowing parents the freedom to raise their children according to their own methods, a parent's discretion in this area is not unfettered. Child abuse statutes already infringe on a parent's discretion in the area of discipline and control. It is clear that a parent owes a duty of care toward his child. This court hereby adopts a "reasonable parent" test, under which a parent's conduct in a given case is compared with that of a reasonable and prudent parent in a similar situation. This standard will be applied in all circumstances, and the *Streenz* extension of parental immunity to cover acts involving the exercise of parental authority and ordinary discretion is hereby revoked. A parent is no longer immune from tort liability toward his child solely on the basis of the parental relationship. The judgment is reversed and the case remanded.

■ CONCURRENCE

(Feldman, C.J.) In areas where parents have traditionally held broad discretion, the rule ought to be that a parent's conduct has to be palpably unreasonable before liability will be imposed.

Analysis:

Although universally applied throughout the twentieth century, the parental immunity doctrine has now been almost universally abrogated. The majority in this case imposes a duty of reasonably prudent conduct and allows a child to recover damages when that duty is breached. The Chief Justice, concurring in the result in this case, would have maintained the *Streenz* distinction between types of parental conduct. Under the Chief Justice's approach, if a parent injures his child while engaging in activity involving the exercise of ordinary parental discretion, his conduct ought to be held to a lower standard than the one the majority would impose. The "palpably unreasonable" standard the Chief Justice supports is lower than the "reasonably prudent parent" standard because it is more objective. It does not require a jury to make comparisons between the parent's conduct in this case and that of the hypothetical reasonable parent. The Chief Justice would protect a parent's traditional right to exercise his parental discretion free from governmentally imposed restrictions, except in extraordinary cases.

■ CASE VOCABULARY

CONSERVATOR: An individual appointed by the court to serve as the temporary guardian and custodian of the property of a missing, incompetent, or insane person, or as in this case, of a child.

INTESTATE SUCCESSION: Succession or inheritance from someone who has not left a valid will.

Riss v. City of New York

(Victim of Attack) v. *(City)*

22 N.Y.2d 579, 240 N.E.2d 860, 293 N.Y.S.2d 897 (1968)

CITY IS IMMUNE FROM LIABILITY WHERE POLICE OFFICERS FAILED TO PROVIDE PROTECTION

■ **INSTANT FACTS** Riss (P) sued City (D) for negligence due to the police failing to provide protection from attacker who had previously threatened her on numerous occasions.

■ **BLACK LETTER RULE** A municipality is not liable for failure to provide special police protection to a member of the public who was repeatedly threatened with personal harm and eventually suffered injuries for lack of protection.

■ **PROCEDURAL BASIS**

Appeal following dismissal of action after presentation of the evidence in negligence action seeking damages for personal injuries.

■ **FACTS**

Riss (P) sued the City of New York (D) for negligence alleging that the city police failed to provide police protection. Riss (P) had been terrorized for months by a rejected suitor who threatened to kill or maim her. She repeatedly sought protection from the police. Thereafter, she received a phone call warning that it was her "last chance." She again called the police but nothing was done. The next day, the rejected suitor hired someone to throw lye into Riss' (P) face, causing blindness in one eye, loss of a portion of vision in the other eye, and permanent facial scarring. The trial court [recognizing that the law is not always fair] dismissed Riss' (P) complaint at the end of all the evidence and the appellate division affirmed. Riss (P) appealed.

■ **ISSUE**

Is a municipality liable for failure to provide special police protection to a member of the public who was repeatedly threatened with personal harm and eventually suffered injuries for lack of protection?

■ **DECISION AND RATIONALE**

(Breitel, J.) No. The municipality is not liable for failing to provide police protection to a member of the general public. We first must distinguish certain types of governmental activities where liability may be found. Activities that displace or supplement traditionally private enterprises may lead to liability, such as rapid transit systems, hospitals and places of public assembly. Activities that provide services and facilities for the use of the public may also lead to liability, such as highways, public buildings and the like. The basis for liability is that the services or facilities are for the direct use of members of the public. This case involves governmental protection services from external hazards, such as controlling the activities of criminal wrongdoers. [This is certainly an impossible task.] If we were to permit tort liability for those who seek police protection based on specific hazards, it would cause a determination as to how the limited resources of the community should be allocated and without predictable limits. We should not so dictate the allocation of the resources and it should be left to the legislature to make the determination concerning the scope of public responsibility. Imposing liability in such situations will not cure the problem of crime in cities [and would bankrupt the city]. It is not for the courts, in the absence of legislation, to carve out an area of tort liability for police protection to members of the public. This case is distinguishable from the situation where the police authorities undertake responsibilities to particular members of the public and expose them, without adequate protection, to the risks that then materialize into actual losses. Judgment is affirmed.

■ DISSENT

(Keating, J.) The city's (D) argument can be summarized as follows: "Because we owe a duty to everybody, we owe it to nobody." This would be a preposterous argument if it were not for the fact that it has long been respected by the courts. When the city chooses to provide police and fire protection, it should not escape liability for its failure to do an adequate job. The city's (D) crushing liability argument has several flaws. First, the idea that extending liability to the city would cause financial disaster is a myth. No municipality has ever gone bankrupt because of damages awarded when a city or state employee engages in tortious conduct. Second, the majority's determination that there are no limits to the potential liability for the city's failure to provide adequate police protection is untenable because governmental immunity has been removed from other areas of governmental activity without leading to disaster. Third, the argument that extending liability in this case would create a situation where a lawsuit is brought against the city every time a crime is committed is also untenable because tort law contains many limiting principles, such as fault, proximate cause, and foreseeability, that limit liability to reasonable bounds. The judicial interference argument is also flawed because it ignores the fact that courts indirectly review the administrative activity of states and municipalities in every tort case brought against the government. When courts review administrative activity in tort cases, they do not make public policy decisions for the government. In municipal negligence cases, courts are accomplishing two things. First, they are applying the principle of vicarious liability to government activity. Second, they are presenting government officials with two alternatives in cases where the insufficient allocation of public funds has resulted in injury: the officials can either improve public administration or accept the cost of paying damages to injured persons.

Analysis:

States have adopted various types of statutes that abolished sovereign immunity. Accordingly, there are many situations whereby a municipality may be liable under principles of ordinary tort law. However, as with the Federal Tort Claims Act, there are exceptions in certain circumstances that allow the immunity to remain. This case demonstrates that the police are not liable for failing to provide protection to the public, even if they negligently fail to do so. The court's reasoning is that there is no statutory basis that would provide for such liability, and it was unwilling to judicially create such liability. If it were to do so, the court would be directing the municipality where to put its resources. Note that the court's decision also distinguished the situation of the police undertaking a duty to particular members of the public, which therefore could lead to liability for negligently failing to act. The difference is that a special relationship has developed with a certain member of the public, as distinguished from the public at large.

Lauer v. City of New York

(Parents) v. *(Medical Examiner)*

95 N.Y.2d 95, 733 N.E.2d 184, 711 N.Y.S.2d 112 (2000)

CRIMINAL SUSPECT CANNOT SUE MEDICAL EXAMINER FOR NEGLIGENCE BECAUSE MEDICAL EXAMINER DOES NOT OWE A DUTY TO CRIMINAL SUSPECTS

■ **INSTANT FACTS** A man sues the city medical examiner when he was investigated for the murder of his son after the medical examiner mistakenly reported the death as a homicide and then failed to correct his error as soon as he found out about it.

■ **BLACK LETTER RULE** A member of the public can recover from a municipality when the ministerial negligence of one of its employees causes injury in breach of a duty the employee owes to the injured party.

■ **PROCEDURAL BASIS**

Appeal to the Court of Appeals of New York of an emotional distress action for damages.

■ **FACTS**

Andrew Lauer, a three-year-old, died on August 7, 1993. Dr. Eddy Lilavois performed an autopsy that same day and determined that Andrew's death was a homicide caused by blunt injuries to the head and neck. Dr. Lilavois preserved the brain for further investigation, but issued a death certificate stating that the cause of death was homicide. The police began an investigation that focused on Andrew's father (P). A few weeks later, Dr. Lilavois and a neuropathologist conducted a thorough study of Andrew's brain and determined that his death was not a homicide, but was instead caused by a brain aneurysm. Dr. Lilavois failed to correct his report or the death certificate, and the investigation of Andrew's father (P) continued. Over a year later, after a newspaper expose of the incident, the police investigation stopped, the Medical Examiner's Office revised the autopsy report and the death certificate, and Dr. Lilavois resigned. Andrew's father (P) brought a number of claims against the city of New York (D). The trial court dismissed all claims; the appellate court reinstated one, the emotional distress claim.

■ **ISSUE**

Can a member of the public recover from a municipality for the ministerial negligence of one of its employees?

■ **DECISION AND RATIONALE**

(Kaye, C.J.) Not necessarily. A ministerial breach by a public employee does not necessarily give rise to liability. Municipalities no longer have tort immunity and can be sued for the negligence of their employees. However, there is a distinction between the ministerial acts of a government employee and the discretionary acts. A discretionary act is one that involves the employee's use of reasonable judgment—a municipality cannot be held liable for any injury that arises from such an act. A municipality can, however, be held liable for an injury arising from an employee's ministerial conduct, or conduct requiring compliance with a governing rule requiring a compulsory result. Mr. Lauer (P) argues that the city of New York (D) is liable for the ministerial negligence of its employee, Dr. Lilavois.

However, an act of ministerial negligence does not necessarily give rise to liability. There still needs to be a breach of duty. Without a duty running from the negligent party directly to the injured person, there can be no liability. A plaintiff must show that a duty exists toward him in particular, not just to society in general. Mr. Lauer's (P) claim fails because he cannot show that the Medical Examiner owes a duty to him in particular. Mr. Lauer (P) argues that under § 557 of the New York Charter the Chief Medical Examiner owed him a duty to communicate accurate information to the police. The violation of a statute can give rise to a tort action only when the purpose of the statute is to protect the property or personal interest of an individual. The court will not impose crushing liability on a municipality without clear guidance from the Legislature. Charter enactments like § 557 do not reveal a legislative intent to protect any interests of an individual that are not shared by the general public. The statute was not enacted for the special benefit of Mr. Lauer (P) or any other individual that might become a criminal suspect upon the death of another. Additionally, no special relationship existed between Mr. Lauer (P) and the Medical Examiner's Office that might give rise to a duty of care. Dr. Lilavois never undertook to take action on Mr. Lauer's (P) behalf. He made no promises that Mr. Lauer (P) might have justifiably relied on. Mr. Lauer (P) had no direct contact with Dr. Lilavois and there is no evidence that Dr. Lilavois knew that Mr. Lauer (P) was a suspect. Medical Examiners in general do not owe a special duty to criminal suspects. The order of the appellate court if reversed and the complaint dismissed.

■ **DISSENT**

(Smith, J.) Mr. Lauer (P) has a prima facie case for emotional distress.

■ **DISSENT**

(Bellacosa, J.) Mr. Lauer (P) has a prima facie case for emotional distress and the appellate court order should be affirmed. This ruling is justified in a case such as this one, where the public employee that precipitated the investigation that injured the plaintiff fails to take action to remove or mitigate the risk of harm. Dr. Lilavois had the exclusive knowledge and power to correct the wrong before it caused further injury. He should be liable for his failure to act reasonably at the time when he found out about Mr. Lauer's (P) innocence. Immunizing misconduct like Dr. Lilavois' will only encourage the government to cover up its wrongdoing in the future.

Analysis:

The majority in this case is trying to limit the city's (D) liability while preserving the rule that the city is not completely immune from tort liability. The court applies a distinction between a government employee's discretionary activity and his ministerial activity. Ministerial activity is that mandated by a government rule, regulation, or policy. In this case, Dr. Lilavois acted ministerially when he filed an autopsy report and issued a death certificate. The city (D) cannot be sued for the unilateral, discretionary activities of its employees, but it can be sued for the actions that the city itself mandates. Dr. Lilavois' actions exposed the city (D) to the possibility of liability, but Lauer (P) still had to show that the city owed him a duty of care. The court's analysis narrows the range of activity that gives rise to liability by requiring first that it be ministerial, and then that it give rise to a duty of care. The majority limits the city's (D) liability out of concern for the expense that "crushing liability" might impose on the city (D) and, by extension, the taxpayer.

■ **CASE VOCABULARY**

A FORTIORI: "By an even stronger force of logic." The phrase can also be used as an adjective, to mean "even stronger."

Friedman v. State of New York

(*Driver*) v. (*Department of Transportation*)

67 N.Y.2d 271, 493 N.E.2d 893, 502 N.Y.S.2d 669 (1986)

WHEN THE GOVERNMENT DECIDES TO TAKE ACTION, IT MUST TAKE ACTION WITHIN A REASONABLE TIME

■ **INSTANT FACTS** A woman sues the New York Department of Transportation after she got into a head-on collision on a state highway with no protective median barrier separating lanes of traffic.

■ **BLACK LETTER RULE** When the government decides to take action to remedy a dangerous condition, it may be held liable when it fails to do so in a reasonable time.

■ **PROCEDURAL BASIS**

Appeal to the Court of Appeals of New York of three consolidated personal injury actions for damages.

■ **FACTS**

Three personal injury actions against the state, all involving crossover collisions, have been consolidated for this appeal. In *Friedman v. New York,* Ms. Friedman (P1) sued the state of New York (D1) after her car was sideswiped on a viaduct, which caused her to swerve into oncoming traffic where she was hit head-on. The Department of Transportation (DOT) had studied the issue of whether to construct a median barrier on that stretch of road five years before her accident and had decided to build a median. At the time of her accident, the state (D1) had not yet built the barrier. The trial court ruled in Ms. Friedman's (P1) favor and the appellate court affirmed. *Cataldo v. New York State Thruway Authority* and *Muller v. New York,* both involved crossover collisions on the Tappan Zee bridge. Government studies conducted in 1962 and 1972 concluded that the risks of stranded cars and "bounce-back" collisions outweighed the benefits of constructing a median along the bridge. Ms. Cataldo's (P2) accident happened shortly after the 1972 study, and the appellate court rejected her claim that the study reached the wrong conclusion. Muller's (P3) accident occurred after the Thruway Authority (D2) had changed its mind about the median and decided to build one. Three years had passed without the state's (D1) taking any action to build the barrier. The appellate court held that the three-year delay was not unreasonable and dismissed Muller's (P3) claim.

■ **ISSUE**

When the government has decided to take action to remedy a dangerous condition, can it be held liable when its failure to take action within a reasonable time causes injury?

■ **DECISION AND RATIONALE**

(Alexander, J.) Yes. It is a longstanding rule that a municipality owes to the public the duty to keep its street in a safe condition. This duty is nondelegable, but the courts are concerned about limiting their intrusion into the government's planning and decision-making roles. As a result, the government is granted qualified immunity from liability arising from highway planning decisions. The government may only be held liable where its study of a traffic condition is plainly inadequate or unreasonable. When the government is informed of a dangerous condition it is required to undertake a reasonable study and once the government decides to implement a traffic plan it is under the duty to review the plan in light of its actual operation. In *Cataldo* and *Muller,* no liability flows from the Thruway Authority's (D2) decision in 1962 not to construct a median. Cataldo (P2) and Muller (P3) argue that when the Thruway Authority (D) failed to review that decision between 1962 and 1972 it breached its duty to review its plan in the light of its actual operation. This argument fails because both accidents took place after 1972, when the Thruway Authority (D) had undertaken a second study. Cataldo (P2) and Muller (P3) argue that this study was inadequate, but this argument fails because the court is reluctant to examine the factors the government's engineers used in the study and rule them inadequate with the benefit of hindsight. The appellate court properly dismissed Cataldo's (P2) claim because her accident took place shortly after the government's reasonable decision not to construct a barrier on the Tappan Zee bridge. Friedman (P1) and Muller (P3) advance a further basis on which the state (D1) might be held liable. They argue that once the state (D1) has made the decision to take action to correct a dangerous condition it may be held liable where the failure to take action within a reasonable time causes injury. This argument is in accordance with several appellate court decisions. When the analysis of a dangerous condition causes the government to make a remedial plan, an unjustifiable delay in executing the plan constitutes a breach of the government's duty. In both *Friedman* and *Muller* there is sufficient evidence to support a finding that the state's (D1) delay in taking action to remedy a dangerous traffic condition was unreasonable. The appellate court's rulings in *Friedman* and *Cataldo* are affirmed, and its ruling in *Muller* is reversed.

Analysis:

The court in *Friedman* holds that once the state has decided to take action to remedy a dangerous condition, it has a duty to do so in a reasonable amount of time. The state cannot be held liable for its decision to take no action, as long as that decision was based on a reasonable study of the dangerous condition. The state has qualified immunity from liability for its traffic safety decisions in the sense that it only assumes liability when it decides to take action to fix a problem. This result is in accordance with the court's concern that the government's liability be as limited as possible without conflicting with the abrogation of sovereign immunity.

■ CASE VOCABULARY

IMMUNITY FROM LIABILITY: An exemption from tort liability based on the nature of the particular defendant.

Cope v. Scott

(Injured Driver) v. *(Negligent Driver and the National Parks Service)*

45 F.3d 445 (D.C. Cir. 1995)

GOVERNMENT DECISIONS ON ROAD MAINTENANCE ARE IMMUNE FROM SUIT, BUT DECISIONS ON POSTING SIGNS ARE NOT IMMUNE

■ **INSTANT FACTS** A man sues the National Parks Service after getting into a car accident on a poorly maintained roadway with no warning signs.

■ **BLACK LETTER RULE** A federal agency's decision not to maintain a roadway is discretionary and immune from suit under the Federal Tort Claims Act; however, its decision not to post warning signs, although discretionary, is not immune from suit because it is not a decision that is fraught with public policy considerations.

■ **PROCEDURAL BASIS**

Appeal to the United States Court of Appeals for the District of Columbia Circuit of a negligence action for damages.

■ **FACTS**

Beach Drive is the main route through Rock Creek Park, an urban park in Washington, D.C. maintained by the National Park Service (Service) (D1). Although the road was originally designed for recreational driving and has many sharp curves, in recent years the Service (D1) has allowed the road to be used as a major commuter route through the city, with the result that the road now carries heavy traffic throughout the day. John R. Cope (P) was driving on Beach Drive on a rainy evening in 1987 when a southbound vehicle driven by Roland Scott (D2) slid into Cope's (P) lane and collided with his (P) car while rounding a curve. Cope (P) suffered neck and back injuries. The Service officer called to the scene of the accident characterized the pavement in his report as a "worn polished surface" that was "slick when wet." Cope (P) sued both Scott (D2) and the Service (D1) alleging that the Service (D1) was negligent in failing to maintain the road and failing to place adequate warning signs. During discovery, Cope (P) obtained an engineering study of the roads in Rock Creek Park that had been conducted between 1986 and 1988. The study concluded that the section of Beach Drive where Cope's (P) accident took place was a "high accident" area, that the road fell below "acceptable skid resistance levels," and recommended that any future repaving use "polish-resistant coarse aggregate" as an overlay in dangerous curves. The study also noted that the curves should be adequately signed. Finally, the study listed the section of Beach Drive where Cope's (P) accident occurred as 33rd on a maintenance priority list of 80 sections of road. On the date of the accident, at least two "slippery when wet" signs were located on the stretch of Beach Drive where the accident took place, but the record does not show how close either sign was to the curve where Scott's (D2) car skidded. In the District Court, the Service (D1) moved for summary judgment arguing that its inaction was discretionary and therefore exempt from suit under the Federal Tort Claims Act (FTCA). The District Court granted the motion, ruling that it had no jurisdiction to hear the case.

■ ISSUE

Does the government's failure to maintain a roadway constitute discretionary activity that is immune from suit under the Federal Tort Claims Act? Does its failure to post signs warning of dangerous conditions constitute discretionary activity under the FTCA?

■ DECISION AND RATIONALE

(Tatel, J.) No and yes. The government's inaction with respect to maintaining the roadway was discretionary and therefore exempt from suit under the FTCA. However, its failure to post warning signs was not discretionary. The exception to the FTCA created for discretionary government acts was intended to prevent the courts from second-guessing the economic, social, and political decisions made by federal agencies. Determinations on discretionary function are jurisdictional determinations, which means that even if Cope (P) can show that the federal courts have jurisdiction over his claim, he must still show negligence. The Supreme Court in *United States v. Gaubert* established a two-part test to determine whether a government action is exempt from suit under the discretionary function exemption to the FTCA. First, the court will ask whether any federal statute, regulation, or policy specifically prescribes a course of action that the government employee must follow, and therefore precludes choice on the employee's part. Second, if the activity does involve choice, the court asks whether the employee's discretionary action was of the nature and quality that Congress intended to exempt from tort liability. Actions requiring choice will only be exempt from the FTCA if they are susceptible to policy judgment and involve an exercise of political, social, or economic judgment. Because practically every government decision is subject to some sort of policy analysis, a court's determination that a decision is essentially political, social, or economic is a difficult one to make. The Service's (D1) argument that any decision involving choice and a hint of policy concern is discretionary and exempt from the FTCA reads the exception too broadly. Exempt discretionary decisions are those fraught with policy considerations. The court will not accept Cope's (P) proposed limitation of the exception, either. Cope (P) argues that the Service (D1) cannot claim the discretionary function exception unless it can show that its decision involved balancing competing policy considerations. However, under the second prong of the *Gaubert* test, what matters is whether the decision was grounded in policy concerns, not what the decisionmaker was thinking. The court will also reject Cope's (P) argument that because the Service (D1) implements federal policy its actions are not discretionary because the Supreme Court has already determined that analytical frameworks such as the one Cope (P) has proposed are not an appropriate way to address the discretionary function exemption to the FTCA. Cope (P) has made two allegations against the Service (D1): 1) That the Service (D1) was negligent in failing adequately to maintain Beach Drive and 2) that the Service (D1) was negligent in failing to place adequate warning signs along the roadway. The first allegation fails both the first and second prongs of the *Gaubert* test. Cope (P) argues that a manual titled "Park Road Standards" provides specific prescriptions regarding skid resistance and road surfacing, but the manual does not rise to the level of a specific prescription. Cope (P) fails the second *Gaubert* prong because the Service's (D1) discretion over the maintenance of the roadway is subject to policy analysis. Regular maintenance would not have prevented the deterioration of Beach Drive. Instead, to determine the proper course of action in addressing the dangerous conditions of Beach Drive, the Service (D1) would have to balance factors such as the overall purpose of the road, the allocation of funds between various of the Service's (D1) other projects, the safety of drivers, and the inconvenience construction might cause to commuters. The Service's (D1) management of Beach Drive is fraught with policy considerations and therefore discretionary and exempt from the FTCA. Cope's (P) second allegation is that the Service (D1) is under the duty to provide an adequate "slippery when wet" road signs on Beach Drive because of the specific slippery road problem. As to the First prong of the *Gaubert* test, the Service (D1) argues that there are no specific prescriptions regarding the posting of road signs. Although the Service (D1) uses a "Manual on Uniform Traffic Control Devices" when posting signs, this manual is not a specific prescription, but rather a set of guidelines governing the installation of road signs. The Service's (D1) posting of road signs does involve discretion. However, as to the second prong of the *Gaubert* test, the discretion involved in posting road signs is not the type of discretion protected by the discretionary function exemption to the FTCA. The decision on whether to post a road sign is not fraught with policy considerations; instead, it relies on engineering judgments. The District Court's dismissal of Cope's (P) claim that the Service (D1) negligently maintained the road is affirmed, but its dismissal of Cope's (P) second claim is vacated and the case is remanded.

Analysis:

Congress has delegated to the National Parks Service (D1) the responsibility to regulate and administer the National Parks system. Administering the parks involves studying the economic, social, and political issues raised by the parks system. The D.C. Circuit recognizes that an individual government agency is an expert in its field and that overseeing its functions and second-guessing its decisions would place a heavy burden on the court, which has not made a study of all the policy considerations surrounding park management. Overseeing a government agency would also contravene Congress's intent, which was to delegate the administration of the national parks to the executive branch, not to the federal judicial system. The court in *Cope* applies the rule that agency decisions that involve social, political, or economic considerations, areas in which the agency is an expert, are covered by the discretionary functions exemption to the FTCA while decisions involving garden-variety discretion, such as a government employee's decision to drive in a negligent manner, are not protected by the exemption.

■ **CASE VOCABULARY**

DE NOVO: Literally, "anew" or "over again." In a trial de novo, the court hears all evidence and arguments anew, without using any of the lower court's findings.

CHAPTER FOUR

The Duty Requirement: Nonphysical Harm

Falzone v. Busch

Instant Facts: A woman was seated in her car on the side of the road when she was nearly hit by a vehicle that had veered across the highway.

Black Letter Rule: A plaintiff may recover damages for bodily injury or sickness that are the result of a reasonable fear of immediate personal injury instilled by the defendant's negligent act.

Metro–North Commuter Railroad Company v. Buckley

Instant Facts: A railroad employee filed suit under the Federal Employer's Liability Act, claiming that he suffered emotional distress as a result of the fear of contracting cancer or asbestosis.

Black Letter Rule: A plaintiff suing under the Federal Employer's Liability Act may not recover for emotional distress where he has been exposed to the risk of contracting a disease but has not yet suffered any symptoms of the disease.

Gammon v. Osteopathic Hospital of Maine, Inc.

Instant Facts: After the decedent died in a hospital, the decedent's son was given a bag which contained the severed leg of a pathology specimen; as a result, the son suffered severe emotional distress.

Black Letter Rule: A defendant may be liable for any foreseeable emotional or psychic harms he negligently causes.

Portee v. Jaffee

Instant Facts: After her son was trapped in an elevator shaft and died as a result, a woman sued for the mental and emotional distress caused by witnessing her son's predicament and resulting death.

Black Letter Rule: A cause of action for the negligent infliction of emotional distress may be maintained were the plaintiff witnesses the death or severe injury of a close relative at the scene of the accident caused by the defendant's negligence.

Johnson v. Jamaica Hospital

Instant Facts: The parents of a baby abducted from a hospital sought to recover from the hospital damages for emotional distress caused by the abduction of their child.

Black Letter Rule: A parent may not recover damages attributable to emotional distress she suffered as a result of the direct injury inflicted on her child by the defendant's negligence, unless the parent was in the zone of danger and witnessed the infliction of the injury.

Nycal Corporation v. KPMG Peat Marwick LLP

Instant Facts: A company that entered into a stock purchase agreement with the controlling shareholders of a target corporation filed suit against the accounting firm that performed an audit of the target.

Black Letter Rule: An accountant who performs his duties negligently may be liable to third parties with whom he is not in a contractual relationship, if the accountant had actual knowledge of the limited groups of potential parties who would rely on his work and actual knowledge of the particular transaction his work was designed to influence.

532 Madison Avenue Gourmet Foods, Inc. v. Finlandia Center, Inc.

Instant Facts: 532 Madison Avenue Gourmet Foods, Inc. (P) brought suit against Finlandia Center, Inc. (D) and others for economic losses it suffered as a result of a partial collapse of a building in New York City and the subsequent closure of streets in the area, which cut off the public's access to the plaintiff's twenty-four-hour delicatessen.

Black Letter Rule: A landowner may not recover for economic losses caused by an adjoining landowner's construction defects absent personal injury or property damage.

Emerson v. Magendantz

Instant Facts: After a married couple gave birth to a child despite the wife having undergone a tubal-ligation, the couple filed suit against the doctor for negligently performing the sterilization procedure.

Black Letter Rule: A plaintiff who gives birth after having undergone a negligently performed sterilization procedure has a cause of action against the negligent doctor for certain damages, which do not include the costs of child rearing or the emotional distress associated with childbirth, unless the child is born with congenital defects.

Falzone v. Busch

(Emotionally Traumatized Witness) v. *(Negligent Driver)*
45 N.J. 559, 214 A.2d 12 (1965)

A PLAINTIFF NEED NOT HAVE SUFFERED A PHYSICAL INJURY TO RECOVER DAMAGES FOR EMOTIONAL DISTRESS CAUSED BY THE DEFENDANT'S NEGLIGENCE

■ **INSTANT FACTS** A woman was seated in her car on the side of the road when she was nearly hit by a vehicle that had veered across the highway.

■ **BLACK LETTER RULE** A plaintiff may recover damages for bodily injury or sickness that are the result of a reasonable fear of immediate personal injury instilled by the defendant's negligent act.

■ **PROCEDURAL BASIS**

Certification to the Supreme Court of New Jersey to review the trial court's decision to grant summary judgment for the defendant.

■ **FACTS**

Mabel Falzone (P) was seated in a parked car when Busch's (D) automobile veered across the highway and stuck Mabel's (P) husband, Charles Falzone (P). Mrs. Falzone (P) claimed that Busch's (D) vehicle came so close to her as to put her in fear for her safety. As a result, she became ill and required medical attention. Both Mr. & Mrs. Falzone (P) filed suit, but the trial court granted summary judgment against Mrs. Falzone's (P) claim on the ground that New Jersey required some physical impact before a plaintiff could recover for negligently induced fright. The Supreme Court of New Jersey certified the appeal before it was heard by the Court of Appeals.

■ **ISSUE**

May a plaintiff recover for bodily injury or sickness resulting from fear for her safety caused by the defendant's negligence, although the plaintiff was not physically struck?

■ **DECISION AND RATIONALE**

(Proctor, J.) Yes. A plaintiff may recover damages for bodily injury or sickness that are the result of a reasonable fear of immediate personal injury instilled by the defendant's negligent act. This court has justified denying recovery for physical injury's not the result of a physical impact on three grounds, all of which we no longer find tenable. First, it was thought that emotional injury was not the "natural and proximate" result of the negligent act. However, we believe that this court decided as a matter of law an issue that is better left to medical evidence. Moreover, medical knowledge on the relationship between emotional disturbance and physical injury no longer seems open to serious challenge. As a matter of fact, this court has permitted recovery for physical ailments resulting from emotional disturbance in other contexts, namely where there was some slight physical contact and where the emotional harm was willfully inflicted. Second, this court concluded that the consensus of the bar was that no liability exists in the absence of an impact. We cannot agree that consensus of lawyers as to the state of the law should stagnate its development. Finally, this court has refused recovery in cases like this due to a fear that allowing such a cause of action would result in a flood of litigation in cases where the injury complained of may be feigned without detection and rest the issue of damages on speculation and conjecture. We find this concern unpersuasive. There may be difficulties in tracing the causal connection between fright and physical injury, but causation is a difficult issue in many cases. We must confide in our courts and juries to weed out the fraudulent claims. A court should not deny recover to one who is injured simply because there are others who may institute fraudulent claims. Finally, we find absolutely no evidence establishing that there is an excessive number of actions of this type in those states permitting a cause of action as alleged here. Even if there were an increase in litigation, the proper remedy is expansion of the judicial machinery, not to deny justice to those who are wronged. Accordingly, the rule requiring a physical impact should no longer be followed in this jurisdiction. The interest served by the rule of *stare decisis,* predictability is not as strong in the law of torts as it would be in property law, contract law or some other field. Reversed.

Analysis:

In rejecting the requirement that the plaintiff be subjected to some physical impact before recovery for emotional disturbance, the court here joined what is now the rule in almost every state. Indeed, the requirement of a physical impact seems silly. After all, if the injury being remedied is purely emotional, why should it matter that the plaintiff was physically impacted? The line drawn at physical contact was an arbitrary means of limiting the number of emotional distress claims so that courts would not have to deal with the inherent difficulties—the threat of fraud and speculative or unlimited liability—that come with adjudicating such cases. However, as the court points out here, the reason we have courts, trials, and juries is to separate honest claims from fraudulent ones. Courts now allow recovery for emotional distress where there is no physical impact in only limited categories of cases. This case would fit into the category of cases where the emotional distress results in a manifestation of physical harm. Although the court never expressly requires such manifestation, its requirement of "bodily injury" or "sickness" implicitly limits recovery to situations where the emotional distress is objectively discernible.

■ CASE VOCABULARY

PROXIMATE CAUSE: The event, act or occurrence which, in the natural sequence of events, usually produces the injury complained of.

Metro-North Commuter Railroad Company v. Buckley

(*Federal Employer*) v. (*Employee Exposed to Asbestos*)

521 U.S. 424, 117 S.Ct. 2113, 138 L.Ed.2d 560 (1997)

A PLAINTIFF SUING UNDER THE FEDERAL EMPLOYER'S LIABILITY ACT MAY RECOVER FOR EMOTIONAL DISTRESS ONLY WHERE THE PLAINTIFF HAS SUFFERED A PHYSICAL IMPACT OR WAS PLACED IN A RISK OF IMMEDIATE IMPACT

■ **INSTANT FACTS** A railroad employee filed suit under the Federal Employer's Liability Act, claiming that he suffered emotional distress as a result of the fear of contracting cancer or asbestosis.

■ **BLACK LETTER RULE** A plaintiff suing under the Federal Employer's Liability Act may not recover for emotional distress where he has been exposed to the risk of contracting a disease but has not yet suffered any symptoms of the disease.

■ **PROCEDURAL BASIS**

Certiorari granted by the United States Supreme Court to review the holding of the Second Circuit Court of Appeals, which reversed the district court's ruling dismissing the plaintiff's cause of action.

■ **FACTS**

While working as a pipefitter for Metro-North Commuter Railroad Company (Metro) (D), Michael Buckley (P) was exposed to asbestos for an average of one hour per day. When Buckley (P) was made aware of the danger posed by asbestos he began to fear he would develop cancer. Medical experts established that Buckley's (P) fear was not unfounded, as he had up to a five percent greater chance of death due to cancer. Despite periodic checkups, Buckley (P) never exhibited any signs of cancer or any other asbestos-related malady. Nevertheless, Buckley (P) filed suit under the Federal Employer's Liability Act (FELA), seeking damages for his emotional distress and the cost of checkups. Admitting its negligence, Metro (D) denied its liability on the ground that Buckley (P) could not recover for emotional distress because he suffered no physical injury. The trial court agreed and dismissed Buckley's (P) cause of action, stating that FELA did not permit recovery for emotional injury in cases where there was no "physical impact."

■ **ISSUE**

May a plaintiff who has been exposed to an increased risk of disease or death recover under FELA damages for emotional distress, even if the plaintiff has suffered no physical injury or exhibited symptoms of disease?

■ **DECISION AND RATIONALE**

(Breyer, J.) No. A plaintiff suing under the Federal Employer's Liability Act may not recover for emotional distress where he has been exposed to the risk of contracting a disease but has not yet suffered any symptoms of the disease. This Court has previously held that FELA permits recovery for emotional injury only where there has been some "physical impact." The common law permits recovery for emotional distress in limited categories of cases. For example, the law permits recovery where: (1) the emotional distress accompanies a physical injury; (2) the emotional distress is the result of witnessing the physical injury of a close relative; (3) the emotional distress is inflicted intentionally; and (4) the plaintiff sustained a physical impact or was placed in immediate risk of physical harm—i.e., in the "zone of danger" created by the defendant's negligence. The critical question here is whether Buckley's (P) contact with asbestos is the "physical impact" contemplated by the common law. In our view, physical contact with a substance that might cause physical harm in the future is not the type of physical impact that would support a claim for emotional distress. First, Buckley (P) suffered no threat of immediate physical trauma. Second, the "zone of danger" test allows recovery in certain cases because there is a recognition that a near miss may be as frightening as a direct hit. Third, the common law has traditionally not permitted recovery where the plaintiff is disease and symptom free. Fourth, general policy reasons, such as the difficulty in weeding out fraudulent claims, the threat of unlimited liability and the potential for a flood of unimportant claims all mitigate against permitting recovery where there is no physical contact. For example, apart from Buckley's (P) own testimony there was no evidence of emotional distress. How then is a court to evaluate the validity of his claim? One answer might be that Buckley (D) was actually exposed to asbestos. But this answer is of no help because it raises a troublesome question: How can one determine from the external circumstance of exposure whether, or when, a claimed emotional reaction to an increase in the risk of death is reasonable and genuine, rather than overstated? As to the fear of unlimited and uncertain liability, we wonder whether permitting recovery would unreasonably require the public to pay higher prices. Also, permitting recover in a large number of emotional distress cases creates a risk that resources will be unavailable to compensate those who later contract the disease. Buckley (D) argues that these concerns are not genuine because recovery for emotional distress is permitted in other cases where these same concerns are raised. But the common law permits recovery in these cases, not because the concerns are not present, but as a method of limiting cases where those concerns are present.

■ CONCURRENCE AND DISSENT

(Ginsburg, J.) In my view, Buckley's contact with asbestos does constitute a "physical impact." However, his claim must fail because there is no objective evidence of emotional distress.

Analysis:

The Court here points to the lack of any objective evidence of Buckley's (P) distress as a reason for concern. Although the Court's concern may be valid, perhaps it should only lead to a requirement of objective evidence or, at most, a presumption against damages, not a complete denial of recovery. This is the precise point brought up by Justice Ginsburg's dissent. The Court also denies recovery because it believed that there is no way to determine the point at which a plaintiff's emotional distress is genuine or reasonable, but courts and juries exist for that very purpose. The Court also speaks of a concern that unpredictable liability will mean that resources will not be available to those who actually deserve them. The Court demonstrates that the traditional limits placed on recovery for emotional distress are arbitrary means for limiting those cases where the threat of fraud is high.

■ CASE VOCABULARY

ZONE OF DANGER: That area where the defendant's negligence has created a risk of harm; some courts restrict recovery for emotional distress that results from a fear of being injured by the defendant's negligence to those plaintiffs that were truly at risk of physical injury due to their spatial proximity to the defendant.

Gammon v. Osteopathic Hospital of Maine, Inc.

(Son of Deceased Patient) v. *(Hospital)*
534 A.2d 1282 (Me. 1987)

A DEFENDANT'S LIABILITY FOR EMOTIONAL OR PSYCHIC HARMS HE INFLICTS UPON THE PLAINTIFF SHOULD BE LIMITED BY THE FORESEEABILITY OF THE HARM

■ **INSTANT FACTS** After the decedent died in a hospital, the decedent's son was given a bag which contained the severed leg of a pathology specimen; as a result, the son suffered severe emotional distress.

■ **BLACK LETTER RULE** A defendant may be liable for any foreseeable emotional or psychic harms he negligently causes.

■ **PROCEDURAL BASIS**

Appeal to the Supreme Judicial Court of Maine challenging the trial court's grant of a directed verdict on the plaintiff negligence claim for severe emotional distress.

■ **FACTS**

When his father died at the Osteopathic Hospital of Maine (D), Gammon (P) hired a funeral home to make the necessary arrangements. When Gammon (P) opened a bag supposedly filled with his father's personal effects, he discovered a bloodied, severed leg, bluish in color. Gammon (P) suffered an immediate traumatic emotional reaction. Thereafter, Gammon (P) began to suffer nightmares and his personality and relationship with his family both took a turn for the worse. After several months Gammon's (P) emotional state eventually improved, but he still suffered from nightmares. Gammon (P) never sought treatment, nor did he present medical evidence at trial.

■ **ISSUE**

May a plaintiff recover for emotional or psychic injuries negligently inflicted by the defendant without any evidence of physical injury?

■ **DECISION AND RATIONALE**

(Roberts, J.) Yes. A defendant may be liable for any foreseeable emotional or psychic harms he negligently causes. A person's psychic well-being is as much entitled to legal protection as his physical well-being. In the past courts have limited recover for emotional harms to certain categories of cases, usually involving physical harm. In those cases where there is no physical injury, we have required a showing of physical impact, objective manifestation, underlying or accompanying tort, or special circumstances. We find, however, that these limitations are arbitrary and should not bar Gammon's recovery. They are simply artificial devices employed by courts to protect against fraudulent claims and undue burden on the defendant. We believe the trial process is well-suited to protect against fraudulent claims. Furthermore, the concept of foreseeability imposes an adequate limit on the defendant's liability. A defendant is bound to foresee psychic harm only when such harm reasonably could be expected to befall the ordinary sensitive person. The high probability that a person will suffer emotional harm from the mishandling of a family member's corpse should allay any fears of fraudulent claims. Reversed and remanded.

Analysis:

Traditionally, courts have justified limiting recovery for emotional distress on grounds that they are protecting against fraud and reasonably limiting the defendant's liability. However, the real and often silent issue in these cases is whether the court believes that emotional harm is likely under the facts of the case. In other words, if the court believes that emotional harm is more likely than not under a general set of facts, it will permit recovery in those cases that come within the particular category. Thus, courts have evinced an unwillingness to permit juries to make the likelihood determination. In contrast, the court here demonstrates a willingness to permit juries to make that same inference. As to limiting a defendant's liability, the court simply employs the rule of foreseeability, which courts have employed to limit defendants' liability in all cases of negligence. The court simply rejects the notion that emotional harm is more difficult to evaluate than other intangible injuries.

Portee v. Jaffee

(Mother of Deceased Child) v. *(Landlord)*

84 N.J. 88, 417 A.2d 521 (1980)

A DEFENDANT WHO NEGLIGENTLY CAUSES THE DEATH OR SEVERE INJURY OF HIS VICTIM WILL BE HELD LIABLE TO ANY CLOSE RELTIVES OF THE VICTIM WHO WITNESSED THE ACCIDENT FIRST-HAND

■ **INSTANT FACTS** After her son was trapped in an elevator shaft and died as a result, a woman sued for the mental and emotional distress caused by witnessing her son's predicament and resulting death.

■ **BLACK LETTER RULE** A cause of action for the negligent infliction of emotional distress may be maintained were the plaintiff witnesses the death or severe injury of a close relative at the scene of the accident caused by the defendant's negligence.

■ **PROCEDURAL BASIS**

Appeal to the New Jersey Supreme Court for a direct review of the decision of the trial court granting the defendants' motions for summary judgment on a claim of mental and emotional distress.

■ **FACTS**

A seven-year-old boy was trapped in an elevator shaft located in the building where the boy and his mother, Ms. Portee (P), lived and which was owned by Jaffee (D). Mrs. Portee (P) witnessed the rescue attempt, as her son moaned cried and flailed his arms. The rescue proved unsuccessful and Portee's (P) son died while trapped. After the accident, Portee (P) became severely depressed and attempted suicide, which required extensive physical and psychotherapy.

■ **ISSUE**

May a plaintiff maintain a cause of action for the negligent infliction of emotional distress caused by witnessing the death of a close relative?

■ **DECISION AND RATIONALE**

(Pashman, J.) Yes. A cause of action for the negligent infliction of emotional distress may be maintained were the plaintiff witnesses the death or severe injury of a close relative at the scene of the accident caused by the defendant's negligence. This case requires us to remedy a violation of the duty of care while avoiding speculative results or punitive liability. Our focus then is on the injured personal interest, here the emotional tranquillity that comes with the knowledge that one's child is safe. In circumstances similar to those before us, the California Supreme Court identified several factors which would determine whether an emotional injury would be compensable because "foreseeable:" (1) Whether the plaintiff was located near the scene of the accident; (2) whether the shock resulted from the direct and contemporaneous sensory observation of the accident, as opposed to learning of it from third parties; and (3) whether the plaintiff and the victim were closely related. We agree that all three of these factors support a cause of action. First, we believe it essential that the plaintiff be closely related to the victim because the genuine suffering which flows from harm to close relatives starkly contrasts with everyday emotional setbacks. Second, we also find it necessary for the plaintiff to have witnessed the accident personally in order to reasonably limit a defendant's liability for emotional harm inflicted upon his victim's close relatives. When the plaintiff witnesses the accident at the scene, it is likely that he has suffered a traumatic sense of loss that will cause severe emotional distress. Finally, that the plaintiff be near the scene of the accident seems to us a necessary corollary to and involves the same policies as the observation requirement. An additional factor is the severity of the injury. The harm witnessed must be that of death or severe bodily injury. The risk of an extraordinary reaction to a slight injury does not justify the imposition of liability. Reversed.

Analysis:
Many courts faced with the issue of plaintiffs who witness physical trauma to close relatives have held that such circumstances justify the imposition of liability. Other courts have limited recovery to only those relatives in the "zone of danger." The problem with the "zone of danger" limitation is that the risk of physical harm has little to do with the interest sought to be protected. The zone of danger rule is intended to limit recovery for emotional distress that results from the fear of physical impact generally caused by the defendant's conduct. This case has nothing to due with the fear of physical injury; it has to due with the psychological impact of having to witness injury to a relative.

Johnson v. Jamaica Hospital

(Parents of Abducted Baby) v. *(Negligent Hospital)*

62 N.Y.2d 523, 467 N.E.2d 502, 478 N.Y.S.2d 838 (1984)

A CAUSE OF ACTION CANNOT BE MAINTAINED WHERE THE PLAINTIFF SUFFERS EMOTIONAL HARM AS THE RESULT OF AN UNWITNESSED INJURY TO A RELATIVE

■ **INSTANT FACTS** The parents of a baby abducted from a hospital sought to recover from the hospital damages for emotional distress caused by the abduction of their child.

■ **BLACK LETTER RULE** A parent may not recover damages attributable to emotional distress she suffered as a result of the direct injury inflicted on her child by the defendant's negligence, unless the parent was in the zone of danger and witnessed the infliction of the injury.

■ **PROCEDURAL BASIS**

Certification to the Court of Appeals of New York by the Appellate Division, which affirmed by the divided vote the trial court's decision to deny a motion to dismiss for failure to state a cause of action.

■ **FACTS**

Kawana Johnson, the daughter of Mr. & Mrs. Johnson (P), was born in and abducted from Jamaica Hospital (Hospital) (D), the abduction occurring on a day the hospital received two bomb threats. While Kawana was still missing, Mr. and Mrs. Johnson (P) instituted a suit for the emotional distress caused by the Hospital's (D) negligence. The trial court denied the Hospital's (D) motion to dismiss for failure to state a cause of action and the Appellate Division affirmed.

■ **ISSUE**

May parents recover damages attributable to their emotional distress suffered as a result of a direct injury inflicted upon their child?

■ **DECISION AND RATIONALE**

(Kaye, J.) No. A parent may not recover damages attributable to emotional distress she suffered as a result of the direct injury inflicted on her child by the defendant's negligence, unless the parent was in the zone of danger and witnessed the infliction of the injury. We have allowed parents to recover for emotional distress caused by the infliction of an injury to their child only where the parents were both in the zone of danger and their distress resulted from first-hand observation of the injury. This court has refused to recognize a duty owed by the hospital to the parents of hospitalized children. The direct injury caused by the Hospital's (D) negligence—abduction—was suffered by Kawana, and the Johnson's (P) grief is not actionable. The foreseeability of such psychic trauma does not establish a duty owing to the parents. To hold otherwise would invite open-ended liability for indirect emotional injury suffered by families in every instance where the young, elderly or incapacitated experience negligent care. In summary, the Hospital (D), even if negligent in caring for Kawana, is not liable for the emotional distress suffered by the Johnsons (P) as a result of the abduction. The holding of the Appellate Division is reversed and the compliant is dismissed.

■ DISSENT

(Meyer, J.) I thought that this court rejected the fear of "open ended liability" as a justification for denying recovery for emotional harms when it permitted recovery of damages flowing from emotional harm caused to one who witnessed the death of a close relative. The flood of litigation is unlikely here because this is not a common occurrence. The burden on defendants is not so great as to foreclose liability altogether.

Analysis:

The court rests its decision here on its conclusion that the Hospital (D) owed no duty to the Johnsons (P). In doing so the court draws a line between harms that are "direct" and "indirect." First, the court holds that the direct injury caused by the hospital's negligence was suffered by Kawana. The court then turns to the notorious "open-ended liability" concern. However, the court could simply limit recovery to the parents in this situation. The court's conclusion that no duty was owed to the Johnsons (D) neglects the important deterrent effect tort law is designed to have. One answer is to give Kawana a cause of action, as the court recognized that she had. However, once Kawana was returned to her parents it would be difficult to argue that she suffered any damage for which the Hospital could be held liable. What incentive is a hospital given to ensure the safety of infants if they face no liability for their negligence?

Nycal Corporation v. KPMG Peat Marwick LLP

(*Investor in Bankrupt Corporation*) v. (*Accounting Firm of Bankrupt Corporation*)
426 Mass. 491, 688 N.E.2d 1368 (1998)

A PROFESSIONAL MAY INCUR LIABILITY FOR THE NEGLIGENT PERFORMANCE OF HIS DUTIES WHICH CAUSE ECONOMIC HARM TO INDIVIDUALS WITH WHOM THE PROFESSIONAL IS NOT IN PRIVITY

■ **INSTANT FACTS** A company that entered into a stock purchase agreement with the controlling shareholders of a target corporation filed suit against the accounting firm that performed an audit of the target.

■ **BLACK LETTER RULE** An accountant who performs his duties negligently may be liable to third parties with whom he is not in a contractual relationship, if the accountant had actual knowledge of the limited groups of potential parties who would rely on his work and actual knowledge of the particular transaction his work was designed to influence.

■ **PROCEDURAL BASIS**

The Supreme Judicial Court of Massachusetts granted an application for the direct review of the decision of the trial court, which granted summary judgment to the defendant.

■ **FACTS**

Relying in part on an auditor's report of the financial condition of Gulf Resources & Chemical Corporation (Gulf) prepared by KPMG Peat Marwick LLP (KPMG) (D) in connection with Gulf's annual report, the Nycal Corporation (Nycal) (P) entered into a stock purchase agreement with the controlling shareholders in Gulf. Two years after the purchase agreement was signed, Gulf filed for bankruptcy. Nycal's (P) investment was rendered worthless. Nycal (P) then filed suit, claiming that KPMG (D) materially misrepresented the financial condition of Gulf. KPMG's (D) motion for summary judgment was granted, and Nycal (P) applied for direct review by the Supreme Judicial Court.

■ **ISSUE**

May an accountant be liable for negligently performed work relied on by a party who the accountant was unaware of and for a transaction the accountant had no knowledge of?

■ **DECISION AND RATIONALE**

(Greaney, J.) No. An accountant who performs his duties negligently may be liable to third parties with whom he is not in a contractual relationship only if the accountant had actual knowledge of the limited groups of potential parties who would rely on his work and actual knowledge of the particular transaction his work was designed to influence. Courts have employed three different test to identify those nonclients to whom an accountant owes a duty of care. One of these tests is the foreseeability test, which holds an accountant liable to any person whom the accountant could have foreseen would obtain and rely on the accountant's opinion. The foreseeability standard usually determines the duty of care owed in most tort cases. Nevertheless, we find that standard inadequate under these circumstances because once the report is handed to the client, the accountant loses complete control over its dissemination, which could expose the accountant to a liability for an indeterminate amount and time

---

and to an indeterminate class. The "near-privity" test, on the other hand, limits an accountant's liability to those with whom he is in privity or a similar relationship, if the accountant knew both the party and the transaction his work was intended to influence and somehow created a link to the injured party. We also reject this test because we find nothing in our case law requiring an accountant to actively create a link with the nonclient. Instead, we believe that § 552 of the Restatement (Second) of Torts comports with the standard applied in cases of other professionals. Under § 552 an accountant's liability is limited (1) to those parties for whose benefit he intends to supply information or knows that the recipient intends to supply it; and (2) for those transactions he intends to influence or know the recipient will use to influence. We believe that this standard guards against the threat of unlimited liability posed by the foreseeability test, while still holding an accountant liable for work he intends will influence other parties and transactions. Contrary to the fears expressed by Nycal (P) we believe that this standard will not exonerate an accountant who remains willfully ignorant of the persons and transactions his report will influence. Accordingly, we believe that summary judgment was correctly granted. There is no evidence showing that KPMG (D) knew of or intended to influence any proposed stock purchase by Nycal (P). In fact, the evidence establishes that KPMG (D) prepared its report solely for its inclusion in Gulf's annual report.

Analysis:

As have almost half the states have done, the Massachusetts Court adopts the Restatement approach to determining the liability of an accountant for negligently performed work. In doing so, the court rejects foreseeability as the measuring stick for the duty of care. The reason is pure economics. It is often the case that countless people may or will rely on an accountant's work. It is also the case that accountants charge fees that, however high they may be, pale in comparison to the value of many of the transactions their work helps foster. For example, KPMG (D) prepared an audit for Gulf's annual report. In one sense, this report is relied on by all of Gulf's shareholders and the investing community (both here and abroad) at large. KPMG (D) was certainly aware that its audit would be included in a report essential to the investing community, making it foreseeable that a person would look to Gulf's annual report to decide whether to buy stock. However, it is unlikely that KPMG (D) charged a fee large enough to insure against the possibility of suit by anyone who bought or sold Gulf's stock in reliance on their report. If accountants who performed corporate audits were liable to anyone they could foresee relying on their report, the price of their services would be cost prohibitive.

■ CASE VOCABULARY

ANNUAL REPORT: A report, issued by a corporation to the stockholders, which includes financial statements and comments by management as to the meaning of the statements; all publicly held companies are required by federal law to issue annual reports to their shareholders.

PRIVITY: The relationship between two parties to a contract; an accountant and his client are in *privity of contract* because the two have an agreement that the former will perform services for the latter.

532 Madison Avenue Gourmet Foods, Inc. v. Finlandia Center, Inc.

(Operating Business) v. *(Building Owner)*

96 N.Y.2d 280, 750 N.E.2d 1097, 727 N.Y.S.2d 49 (2001)

ADJOINING LANDOWNERS MAY NOT RECOVER PURELY ECONOMIC LOSSES RESULTING FROM CLOSURE OF PUBLIC STREETS

I suffered a huge economic loss from having to close my deli while the city repaired the street damaged by my neighbor. What can I do?

Nothing. Purely economic loss is the one thing in America you can't sue for.

stus.com

■ **INSTANT FACTS** 532 Madison Avenue Gourmet Foods, Inc. (P) brought suit against Finlandia Center, Inc. (D) and others for economic losses it suffered as a result of a partial collapse of a building in New York City and the subsequent closure of streets in the area, which cut off the public's access to the plaintiff's twenty-four-hour delicatessen.

■ **BLACK LETTER RULE** A landowner may not recover for economic losses caused by an adjoining landowner's construction defects absent personal injury or property damage.

■ **PROCEDURAL BASIS**

Consolidated appeal of intermediate court's affirmance of dismissal of a claim for public nuisance in one case, and its reinstatement of dismissed claims in two cases.

■ **FACTS**

This case consolidated three different cases stemming from the closure of public streets in New York City. Two of the cases involved a partial collapse of a section of a building located at 540 Madison Avenue, which resulted from the aggravation of structural defects by construction activities at a nearby construction site. New York City officials closed a fifteen-block area for two weeks, but some businesses were forced to remain closed for longer. The twenty-four-hour delicatessen operated by 532 Madison Avenue Gourmet Foods, Inc. (P) remained closed for five weeks. The trial court dismissed the plaintiffs' claims, finding that the defendants owed them no legal duty. The other case involved the collapse of a forty-eight-story construction elevator on West 43rd Street, in the heart of Times Square. The city prohibited traffic flow in a wide area and evacuated nearby buildings. The plaintiffs, a law firm, public relations firm, and clothing manufacturer, alleged economic losses resulting from the closure of public streets. The trial court dismissed the complaints, finding no legal duty.

■ **ISSUE**

Is a business that suffers economic loss as a result of closed city streets entitled to recover for purely economic losses?

■ **DECISION AND RATIONALE**

(Kaye, C.J.) No. While a landowner owes a duty to adjoining landowners to take reasonable precautions to avoid injuring their property interests, this duty does not extend to protecting an entire neighborhood against purely economic losses. The law of torts involves drawing lines between those parties foreseeably injured by another's actions and those that are not in order to equitably apportion liability and hold tortfeasors accountable for their actions. Those parties suffering purely economic damages,

---

however, constitute a large, indeterminate group conceivably extending to endless limits. Accordingly, on the facts of this case, the scope of the defendant's duty does not extend beyond those who suffer actual physical injury or property damage. Affirmed in part and reversed in part.

Analysis:

The court considers the economic loss rule in the construction defect context, limiting its holding to those factual scenarios, but the rule extends across tort law to bar claims for purely economic injuries. Some critics of the economic loss rule claim that general principles of causation and foreseeability sufficiently protect tortfeasors from far-reaching liability, calling for an end to the rule. For instance, while an adjoining business could foreseeably be economically injured by a construction defect, a business four blocks away may not. Under such circumstances, the economic loss rule bars both claims, but general tort principles would arguably permit the former.

■ CASE VOCABULARY:

ECONOMIC LOSS RULE: The principle that a plaintiff cannot sue in tort to recover for purely monetary loss—as opposed to physical injury or property damage—caused by the defendant. Many states recognize an exception to this rule when the defendant commits fraud or negligent misrepresentation, or when a special relationship exists between the parties (such as an attorney-client relationship).

Emerson v. Magendantz

(*Husband and Wife who Gave Birth Despite Sterilization*) v. (*Doctor Who Performed Tubal-Ligation*)
689 A.2d 409 (R.I. 1997)

A PHYSICIAN MAY BE HELD LIABLE FOR NEGLIGENCE THAT LEADS TO AN UNWANTED PREGNAN-CY OR BIRTH

■ **INSTANT FACTS** After a married couple gave birth to a child despite the wife having undergone a tubal-ligation, the couple filed suit against the doctor for negligently performing the sterilization procedure.

■ **BLACK LETTER RULE** A plaintiff who gives birth after having undergone a negligently performed sterilization procedure has a cause of action against the negligent doctor for certain damages, which do not include the costs of child rearing or the emotional distress associated with childbirth, unless the child is born with congenital defects.

■ **PROCEDURAL BASIS**

Certification by the trial judge to the Supreme Court of Rhode Island.

■ **FACTS**

After giving birth to their first child, the Emersons (P) decided that Diane Emerson (P) would undergo a sterilization procedure to limit the size of their family. To that end, Dr. Magendantz (D) performed a tubal-ligation of Mrs. Emerson (P). However, four-and-a-half months later, Mrs. Emerson (P) saw an obstetrician who informed her she was pregnant. After the birth of her second child, Kirsten Emerson, allegedly born with congenital problems, Mrs. Emerson (P) underwent another sterilization procedure. The Emersons (P) then filed suit, seeking to recover from Dr. Magendantz (D) damages suffered as the result of the physical pain involved in undergoing another procedure, the mental anguish and distress and loss of wages and earning capacity associated with the unwanted pregnancy and the cost of caring for and rearing Kirsten.

■ **ISSUE**

Is there a cause of action when a negligently performed sterilization procedure leads to an unwanted pregnancy and the birth of a child; and if so, what are the damages?

■ **DECISION AND RATIONALE**

(Weisberger, C.J.) Yes. A plaintiff who gives birth after having undergone a negligently performed sterilization procedure has a cause of action against the negligent doctor for certain damages, which do not include the costs of child rearing or the emotional distress associated with childbirth, unless the child is born with congenital defects. Those courts recognizing a cause of action for negligence in the performance of a sterilization procedure have adopted three different approaches to the issue of damages in such a case. The majority of courts have allowed a limited recovery which includes the damages flowing from the cost of the ineffective procedure, the medical costs associated with pregnancy, the expense of subsequent sterilization, the loss of wages, the loss of consortium arising out of the unwanted pregnancy and the medical expenses for prenatal care, delivery and postnatal care. Other courts permit the parents to recover the cost of child rearing but balance that cost against the benefits associated with parenthood. Two jurisdictions permit the recovery of rearing costs without offsetting any benefit, emotional or pecuniary, to the parents. We believe that the limited recovery rule is best. First, attempting to offset the benefits of parenthood against the costs of child rearing is an exercise in prophecy. The fact is that no one can reasonably determine what those benefits will be until all is said and done. The child could turn out to be President of the United States or most horrific criminal known to mankind. Second, public policy precludes the recover of rearing costs when the parents have decided to forgo adoption and retain the child. The fact that the Emersons (P) chose to keep Kirsten should serve as evidence that the benefits outweigh the costs. If, however, the child turns out to have congenital defects, as is alleged, the parents may recover the special costs associated with bringing up a handicapped child and any emotional distress flowing from rearing such a child. We believe that the financial and emotional drain associated with raising such a child is often overwhelming to the parents. We do, however, require that the parents place the physician on notice that they have the expectation of giving birth to a handicapped child, before recover of special damages will be allowed. Remanded.

■ CONCURRENCE AND DISSENT

(Bourcier, J.) I agree that this state should recognize the cause of action before this Court. However, I disagree as to the majority's opinion regarding the measure of available damages. This is simply a cause of action for medical malpractice. Accordingly, the parents should be allowed to recover all damages proximately caused by the physician's negligence, while permitting the jury to mitigate or reduce recovery by what may be proven to be the value of parenthood. There is no justification for the court to force upon parents the difficult choices involved in deciding to undergo an abortion, give the child up for adoption or to accept parenthood and all the costs associated therewith. The unwanted pregnancy is not the type of "joy" or "blessing" that can absolve a negligent doctor of the damage he has done by imposing extraordinary costs on his patients. Furthermore, the fact that the Emersons (P) decided to undergo, not one, but *two* sterilization procedures is evidence that they are not convinced that the benefits of parenthood outweigh the costs. There are opportunity costs associated with pregnancy and child rearing. A "blessing" versus economic costs approach is too simplistic.

Analysis:

The main issue in this case is the measure of damages when a failed sterilization procedure leads to an unwanted pregnancy and the resulting birth of a child. Although most courts recognize the a cause of action in such circumstances, they limit recovery with unusual damages rules. The rule that allows recovery of all damages proximately caused by the defendant's negligence is rarely applicable in this type of case. As have many other courts, the Rhode Island court denies both kinds of damages on the grounds that the costs of child-rearing should be borne by the parents because it is they who receive the benefit of parenthood. The court refuses to permit an offset because it believes the benefits of parenthood are incalculable. Nevertheless, the court seems to make its own general calculation when it holds that the benefits of parenthood outweigh the costs. The same rationale for denying the costs of child rearing has led this and other courts to deny damages for the emotional distress associated with having a child. However, this court draws an odd line at the birth of children with genetic defects. Apparently, in its view, the emotional and economic costs involved in raising such a child are not outweighed by the benefits of parenthood.

■ CASE VOCABULARY

CONGENITAL DEFECT: A birth defect.

CHAPTER FIVE

Causation

Stubbs v. City of Rochester

Instant Facts: A man who lived and worked in Rochester filed suit against the city, claiming that the water supply was negligently maintained so that the potable water became contaminated with sewage and that such contamination was the cause of his typhoid fever.

Black Letter Rule: Where there are two or more possible causes of the plaintiff's injury, one of which is the defendant's negligent conduct, a plaintiff is required to establish facts allowing for a reasonable inference that the defendant's conduct was more than likely the cause of his injury.

Zuchowicz v. United States

Instant Facts: Although the precise cause of her disease was unascertainable, a woman filed suit, claiming that a hospital's negligence in prescribing her double the maximum authorized dosage of a particular drug caused her to suffer from the rare disease.

Black Letter Rule: A reasonable inference of causation can be made where the defendant's conduct is deemed negligent because it creates the particular risk of harm suffered by the plaintiff.

Alberts v. Schultz

Instant Facts: After losing his leg on account of gangrene, an amputee filed suit against his physician on the ground that the doctor's negligence in failing to order the proper exams and promptly refer the case to a specialist caused the patient to lose a significant chance at saving his leg.

Black Letter Rule: A plaintiff in a lost chance cause of action must show, to a reasonable degree of medical probability that, the doctor's negligence caused a diminution in the chance of recovery.

Summers v. Tice

Instant Facts: Two hunters negligently fired in the direction of a third man who was struck in the eye and lip.

Black Letter Rule: Where two defendants have acted negligently, a third person is injured as a result and it cannot be determined which defendant caused the plaintiff's injury, even though the negligence of only one could have been the cause, the burden of disproving causation is placed on the negligent defendants.

Hymowitz v. Eli Lilly & Co.

Instant Facts: Several plaintiffs brought separate suits against the several manufacturers of a drug used to prevent miscarriages which injured the plaintiffs prenatally. Due to the fungible nature of the drug, however, none of the plaintiffs could establish which company manufactured the precise drug taken by their mother.

Black Letter Rule: If the plaintiff cannot prove which of multiple persons caused his injury, but can show that all produced a defective product, all of the defendant manufacturers will be held liable for the plaintiff's injuries in proportion to each manufacturer's market share of that product at the time of injury.

Benn v. Thomas

Instant Facts: The estate of a man who died from a heart attack occasioned by a rear-end auto accident filed a suit against the driver who caused the accident for damages flowing from the death.

Black Letter Rule: A tortfeasor whose act, superimposed upon a prior condition of the defendant, results in a greater than expected injury is, nevertheless, liable for the full extent of the harm.

Overseas Tankship (U.K.) Ltd. v. Morts Dock & Engineering Co., Ltd. (The Wagon Mound)

Instant Facts: After being sued for causing an oil spill that later ignited, setting a nearby wharf ablaze, a shipping company sought to avoid liability on the ground that they could not be held liable because the fire was an unforeseeable consequence of the oil spill.

Black Letter Rule: A defendant is liable for only those consequences of his conduct that are reasonably foreseeable at the time he acts.

Doe v. Manheimer

Instant Facts: Doe (P) was assaulted by a man on Manheimer's (D) property, and Doe (P) claimed that Manheimer's (D) failure to remove the brush on the property caused the attack.

Black Letter Rule: A negligent act is the legal cause of a plaintiff's injury only if the injury would not have occurred without the act, and if the negligent act was a substantial factor in producing the plaintiff's injury.

Palsgraf v. Long Island R.R. Co.

Instant Facts: Palsgraf (P) sued Long Island R.R. Co. (D) ("the railroad") for the injuries sustained when a package fell out of the hand of one of the train passengers and exploded.

Black Letter Rule: A defendant owes a duty of care only to those plaintiffs who are in the reasonably foreseeable zone of danger.

Stubbs v. City of Rochester

(Typhoid-Stricken Plaintiff) v. *(City that Negligently Maintained Water Supply)*

226 N.Y. 516, 124 N.E. 137 (1919)

A PLAINTIFF HAS THE BURDEN OF PROVING THAT THE DEFENDANT'S NEGLIGENCE WAS MORE LIKELY THAN NOT THE CAUSE OF HIS INJURY

■ **INSTANT FACTS** A man who lived and worked in Rochester filed suit against the city, claiming that the water supply was negligently maintained so that the potable water became contaminated with sewage and that such contamination was the cause of his typhoid fever.

■ **BLACK LETTER RULE** Where there are two or more possible causes of the plaintiff's injury, one of which is the defendant's negligent conduct, a plaintiff is required to establish facts allowing for a reasonable inference that the defendant's conduct was more than likely the cause of his injury.

■ **PROCEDURAL BASIS**

Appeal to the New York Court of Appeals challenging the holding of the Appellate Division, which affirmed a nonsuit granted by the trial judge after the plaintiff's case.

■ **FACTS**

Stubbs (P), a resident and employee in the City of Rochester (D), filed suit against the City (D) after he contracted typhoid, claiming that the City (D) negligently maintained its water system so that it became contaminated with sewage, which caused his disease. At trial, expert witnesses stated their opinion that Stubbs' (P) case of typhoid was likely caused by contaminated water. Stubbs' (P) evidence also showed that he drank water from no other supply. Statistical evidence established that in the year Stubbs (P) became ill there were at least 50 more cases of typhoid than in any of the ten preceding years, with 58 of 180 cases coming from the district affected by the contamination. The City (D) claimed that this evidence did not establish that Stubbs (P) contracted typhoid from the contaminated water because it failed to eliminate the possibility that the disease was contracted as a result of any of the other causes which were a possibility in this case. Agreeing with the City (D), the trial court granted a nonsuit against Stubbs (P).

■ **ISSUE**

Must a plaintiff exclude the possibility that his injury was the result of some cause other than the defendant's conduct where there exists a possibility of more than one cause?

■ **DECISION AND RATIONALE**

(Hogan, J.) No. Where there are two or more possible causes of the plaintiff's injury, one of which is the defendant's negligent conduct, a plaintiff is required to establish facts allowing for a reasonable inference that the defendant's conduct was more than likely the cause of his injury. The law requires the plaintiff to prove his injury was caused wholly or in part by the defendant's conduct when there are several possible causes. However, we do not agree with the City's (D) argument that this standard required Stubbs (P) to eliminate all other causes of typhoid. Holding otherwise would mean that a plaintiff could never recover under facts such as these. For example, one of the possible causes of

---

typhoid is personal contact with a carrier of the disease. In order to exclude this possibility, Stubbs (P) would have to prove that no person he came in contact with, even momentarily, during the relevant period was free of the disease. Such a burden would be impossible to meet. That is not even to mention those causes of typhoid unknown to science. Viewed in the light most favorable to Stubbs (P), the evidence justifies a submission of the facts to the jury as to whether they raise a reasonable inference of causation. A verdict rendered for Stubbs (P) would not be based in conjecture but upon reasonable possibilities. Reversed and remanded for a new trial.

Analysis:

This case illustrates two principles with regard to proving causation. The first is that the plaintiff carries the burden of proving that the defendant's negligent conduct was the cause of the injury complained of. Indeed, causation is an element of every negligence suit. However, as with any other element in virtually any civil suit, the plaintiff need only meet his burden with respect to causation by a preponderance of the evidence. Here, the City (D) was seeking to impose a higher burden upon Stubbs (P), by arguing he was required to eliminate all other possibilities. Under established principles, if Stubbs's (P) evidence raises the reasonable inference that his disease was caused by polluted water, it becomes incumbent upon the City (D) to rebut that inference by establishing that Stubbs's (P) disease just as likely resulted from some other cause. It is important to remember that the law of torts (and most law) does not deal in certainties, but rather reasonable possibilities.

Zuchowicz v. United States

(Patient) v. *(Government Naval Hospital)*

140 F.3d 381 (2d Cir. 1998)

CAUSE IN FACT MAY BE INFERRED WHERE THE PLAINTIFF'S HARM IS ONE OF THE CORE RISKS CREATED BY THE DEFENDANT'S NEGLIGENCE

■ **INSTANT FACTS** Although the precise cause of her disease was unascertainable, a woman filed suit, claiming that a hospital's negligence in prescribing her double the maximum authorized dosage of a particular drug caused her to suffer from the rare disease.

■ **BLACK LETTER RULE** A reasonable inference of causation can be made where the defendant's conduct is deemed negligent because it creates the particular risk of harm suffered by the plaintiff.

■ **PROCEDURAL BASIS**

Appeal to the Second Circuit challenging the trial court's conclusions of fact and law as to causation in a suit brought under the Federal Tort Claims Act.

■ **FACTS**

Mrs. Zuchowicz's (P) estate brought a claim under the Federal Tort Claims Act, alleging that the naval hospital's (Hospital) (D) admitted negligence in directing her to take double the maximum authorized dosage of the drug Danocrine caused her to develop primary pulmonary hypertension (PPH), a rare and fatal disease that led to Mrs. Zuchowicz's (P) death. The evidence at trial could not establish a link between excessive doses of Danocrine and the onset of PPH due to the fact that no studies had been done where women were given such high doses. Based on Mrs. Zuchowicz's (P) history, the temporal relationship between the overdose and the onset of PPH and his ability to eliminate many (though not all) other possible causes, one expert testified that Danocrine caused Mrs. Zuchowicz's (P) PPH and that he believed the overdose was responsible for the disease. Another expert testified that hormonal factors caused by the overdose of Danocrine likely caused Mrs. Zuchowicz's (P) PPH.

■ **ISSUE**

Must the plaintiff produce direct evidence that her harm was caused by the defendant's negligence?

■ **DECISION AND RATIONALE**

(Calabresi, C.J.) No. A reasonable inference of causation can be made where the defendant's conduct is deemed negligent because it creates the particular risk of harm suffered by the plaintiff. The law of causation in Connecticut requires that the defendant's conduct have been a substantial factor in bringing about the plaintiff's injury. To meet the substantial factor requirement the plaintiff must prove that: (1) the defendant's negligence was the *but for* cause of the injury; (2) the negligence was causally linked to the injury; and (3) the defendant's negligence was proximate to the injury. The issue here is whether Mrs. Zuchowicz (P) estate has shown that the overdose was the *but for* cause of her PPH. To have met its burden Mrs. Zuchowicz's (P) estate must have shown that both Danocrine and the overdose thereof were but for causes of her PPH. We believe the expert testimony established that it was more likely than not that the Danocrine was a *but for* cause of the PPH. The Hospital (D) challenges the trial court's admission into evidence of the experts' testimony. However, we find that the trial fulfilled its gatekeeping function in accordance with the standard set by the Supreme Court. The court's statement that it was admitting the testimony because the experts were basing their opinions on methods reasonably relied on by experts in their particular fields serves to show that the proper standard was applied. This notwithstanding, the issue remains as to whether the overdose was more likely than not a *but for* cause. The law no longer demands that causation be proved by direct evidence. Particularly, but for causation may be inferred where the plaintiff's harm is one of the core risks created by the defendant's negligence. The reason the FDA does not approve the prescription of new drugs at dosages higher than those that have been subject to extensive study is because all drugs involve a risk of unknown side effects, often exacerbated when the drug is taken excessively. Thus, it follows that when a negative side effect is demonstrated to be the result of a drug, and the drug was wrongly prescribed in an unapproved and excessive dosage, the plaintiff has shown enough to permit the jury to conclude that the excessive dosage was a substantial factor in producing the harm. Based on this allowable inference and some expert testimony linking the overdose with the PPH the court did not err in finding that causation was proved. Affirmed.

Analysis:

The court's holding in this case makes sense in the view of several factors. First, there was no other reasonable explanation for Mrs. Zuchowicz's (P) PPH. Second, one of the experts testified that he believed the overdose, not just the Danocrine, was responsible for the PPH. Finally, it would be unfair for the Hospital (D) to escape liability where the extent of its own negligence made causation impossible to establish by direct evidence. However, the inference does not mean the plaintiff is relieved of proving causation by a preponderance of the evidence. There could be situations where the inference of causation is just as reasonable as another theory. In such a case, the plaintiff must prove that the defendant's conduct is the most reasonable explanation for his injury.

■ CASE VOCABULARY

BUT-FOR CAUSE: To prove cause in fact courts employ a but-for test, which asks whether the plaintiff would not have suffered his injury *but-for* the defendant's negligence.

Alberts v. Schultz

(*Amputee*) v. (*Diagnosing Doctor*)
126 N.M. 807, 975 P.2d 1279 (1999)

A DEFENDANT CAREGIVER MAY BE LIABLE TO A PATIENT WHO THE CAREGIVER HAS NEGLIGENTLY CAUSED TO LOSE SOME CHANCE AT SURVIVAL OR RECOVERY

■ **INSTANT FACTS** After losing his leg on account of gangrene, an amputee filed suit against his physician on the ground that the doctor's negligence in failing to order the proper exams and promptly refer the case to a specialist caused the patient to lose a significant chance at saving his leg.

■ **BLACK LETTER RULE** A plaintiff in a lost chance cause of action must show, to a reasonable degree of medical probability that, the doctor's negligence caused a diminution in the chance of recovery.

■ **PROCEDURAL BASIS**

Interlocutory appeal certified to the Supreme Court of New Mexico.

■ **FACTS**

Dee Alberts (P) went to Dr. Schultz (D) complaining of pain in his leg in the absence of any exercise or activity. Although these were signs of impending gangrene that could lead to amputation, Dr. Schultz (D) did not order an arteriogram or conduct any other tests, nor did he promptly refer Mr. Alberts (D) to a specialist. Two weeks later, Dr. Schultz (D) referred Mr. Alberts to a Dr. Reddy (D), who, one day later, attempted a by-pass surgical procedure with little success. Mr. Alberts' (P) leg was amputated shortly thereafter. Expert testimony established that Dr. Schultz (D) should have performed certain diagnostic tests, ordered an arteriogram and promptly referred Mr. Alberts (P) to a specialist. The same expert testified that Dr. Reddy (D) was negligent in waiting one day to perform the by-pass. In the view of the expert, the passage of even the smallest amount of time could make the difference between success and failure in cases like Mr. Alberts' (P). Such success, however, could only be achieved if Mr. Alberts (P) had arteries which were suitable for by-pass, a fact not in the medical record and which the expert presumed was true. Finally, the expert also testified that, in his opinion, the negligence of Drs. Schultz (D) and Reddy (D) significantly decreased Mr. Alberts' (P) chances of saving his leg; but he could not conclude to a reasonable degree of medical certainty that, in the absence of negligence, Mr. Alberts' leg could have been saved.

■ **ISSUE**

Where the defendant's negligence reduces the plaintiff's chances at recovery, must the plaintiff prove that recovery would have occurred in the absence of the physician's negligence?

■ **DECISION AND RATIONALE**

(Franchini, C.J.) No. A plaintiff in a lost chance cause of action must show, to a reasonable degree medical probability that, the doctor's negligence caused a diminution in the chance of recovery. A claim for loss of chance is predicated upon the negligent denial by a healthcare provider of the most effective therapy for a "presenting problem," the particular medical complaint for which the patient sought medical advice. The negligent conduct can be an incorrect diagnosis, the application of inappropriate treatments, or the failure to timely provide effective treatment. Thus, under loss of chance theory of liability, the claim is not that the physician caused or exacerbated the plaintiff's injury, rather that the doctor has obliterated or reduced whatever chance the patient had at recovery prior to the negligence. The injury is the lost opportunity at a better result, not the injury caused by the presenting problem. The causal connection between the negligence and the lost opportunity must be medically probable. As in any medical malpractice case, this causal link must be proved by a preponderance of the evidence or established to a "reasonable degree of medical certainty." Absolute certainty is not required because the physician's negligence has made it impossible to determine how the patient would have fared in the absence of any negligence. As to the calculation of damages in a loss of chance cause of action, we believe that they could be awarded on a proportional basis determined by the percentage value of the patient's chance for recover prior to the negligent act. In other words, if the patient had a chance of recovery of 50 percent prior to the negligent act and a 20 percent chance after the same, the doctor will be liable for 30 percent of the patient's total loss. Applying these principles to the facts of this case, we find that Mr. Alberts (P) has not established the causation element. The negligence of Drs. Schultz (D) and Reddy (D) could have reduced Mr. Alberts (P) chances at recover only if Mr. Alberts (D) actually had any chance at recovery. However, Mr. Alberts (P) cannot demonstrate that recovery was possible prior to the negligent conduct. Mr. Alberts (P) did not establish that a successful by-pass would have precluded amputation, that he had arteries suitable for a by-pass at the time he went to see Dr. Schultz (D) or that he had suitable arteries at the time he went to see Dr. Reddy (D) but not the day after, the day of his surgery. The expert's testimony as to the reduction of chance was predicated on an assumption that Mr. Alberts (P) was, at the time he visited either Dr. Schultz (D) or Dr. Reddy (D), a suitable candidate for by-pass. This assumption was never proved at trial.

Analysis:

As have most jurisdictions, New Mexico here adopts the loss of chance theory of liability in medical malpractice cases. The loss of chance is subject to criticism. Some argue that there must me some certainty that the defendant's conduct caused the plaintiff's injury. In the view of these critics, the New Mexico court's statement that, "absolute certainty is not required because the physician's negligence has made it impossible to determine how the patient would have fared in the absence of any negligence," is an inappropriate departure from traditional tort principles. In other words, affording less than full recovery for a less than certain chance that the defendant was at fault eliminates the tort system's truth-seeking function, turning that system into a lottery. Related to this argument is the fact that the loss of chance theory, in principle, would hold the physician liable even if the patient beat the odds and made a full recovery. Supporting the loss of chance theory, as the court notes here, is the fact that the defendant should not escape liability simply because his own negligence is precisely what makes causation difficult to prove.

■ CASE VOCABULARY

ARTERIOGRAM: An X-ray of an artery.

PRESENTING PROBLEM: The court uses the term presenting problem to distinguish the malady which caused the plaintiff's injury and was mistreated from the injury caused by the doctors—the loss of chance.

Summers v. Tice

(*Injured Hunter*) v. (*Negligent Hunters*)
33 Cal.2d 80, 199 P.2d 1 (1948)

THE PLAINTIFF IS RELIEVED OF THE BURDEN OF PROVING CAUSATION WHEN THERE ARE TWO NEGLIGENT DEFENDANTS, ONLY ONE OF WHICH CAUSED THE PLAINTIFF'S HARM, BUT IT IS IMPOSSIBLE TO PROVE WHICH DEFENDANT WAS THE CAUSE IN FACT

■ **INSTANT FACTS** Two hunters negligently fired in the direction of a third man who was struck in the eye and lip.

■ **BLACK LETTER RULE** Where two defendants have acted negligently, a third person is injured as a result and it cannot be determined which defendant caused the plaintiff's injury, even though the negligence of only one could have been the cause, the burden of disproving causation is placed on the negligent defendants.

■ **PROCEDURAL BASIS**

Appeal to the Supreme Court of California.

■ **FACTS**

While quail hunting with Tice (D) and Simonson (D). Summers (P) was struck in the eye and lip when the other two men negligently fired in his direction. Because both men used the same gauge shotgun and the same size shot, it could not be proved which man caused Summers' (P) injury. Nevertheless, the judge awarded judgment to Summers (P). Tice (D) and Simonson (D) appealed.

■ **ISSUE**

Where one of two negligent defendants causes the plaintiff's injury, does the plaintiff's case fail if it is impossible to prove which of the two negligent men was the cause?

■ **DECISION AND RATIONALE**

(Carter, J.) No. Where two defendants have acted negligently and a third person is injured as a result and it cannot be determined which negligent acotr caused the plaintiff's injury, the burden of identifying who caused the injury is placed on the negligent defendants. We believe that the facts make manifest the need to shift the burden of persuasion to Tice (D) and Simonson (D). After all, the defendants are wrongdoers; it was there acts that placed Summers (P) in the unenviable position of having to prove causation where causation cannot be proved. Furthermore, defendants are ordinarily in a better position to determine which one caused the injury. There is no reason to leave Summers (P) without remedy. We also hold that both Tice (D) and Simonson (D) are jointly and severally liable for the whole of the loss. To hold otherwise, would exonerate Tice (D) and Simonson (D), although each was negligent, and the injury resulted from such negligence.

Analysis:

''Alternative liability'' shifts to the defendants the burden of proving who caused the plaintiff's injury when multiple defendants are negligent and any one of them could have caused the plaintiff's injury, but the identity of the exact defendant who caused the injury is unascertainable. The court suggests that the shift in burden is proper because defendants are ordinarily "in a far better position to offer evidence to determine which caused the injury." However, it is clear that Tice (D) and Simonson (D) are in no better position to offer evidence as to cause. The court's holding rests more on considerations of fairness, mainly the idea that an innocent plaintiff should not bear the loss occasioned by two wrongdoers. The rule of alternative causation, as it has become known, has been limited by courts to those cases where there are only a few negligent defendants. The rationale for such a limitation is that as the number of defendants increases, the probability that any of them was the cause diminishes, making the shift in burden less fair. The case is also important for the court's application of the principle of joint and several liability. In other words, both Tice (D) and Simonson (D) are held responsible for the whole of Summers' (P) injury. Summers could go after either one to satisfy the judgment.

■ CASE VOCABULARY

JOINT AND SEVERAL LIABILITY: The law has traditionally held that joint tortfeasors are each wholly responsible for the plaintiff's injury. Although joint tortfeasors are entitled to contributions from each other, the plaintiff may go after only one of them in order to satisfy his judgment.

Hymowitz v. Eli Lilly & Co.

(Plaintiffs Injured Prenatally by Drug) v. *(Drug Manufacturers)*

73 N.Y.2d 487, 539 N.E.2d 1069, 541 N.Y.S.2d 941 (1989), cert. denied, 493 U.S. 944, 110 S.Ct. 350 (1989)

A DEFENDANT MANUFACTURER'S MARKET SHARE MAY BE USED AS A SUBSTITUTE FOR CAUSATION WHERE THE PLAINTIFF WAS INJURED BY A FUNGIBLE PRODUCT, THE PRECISE MANUFACTURER OF WHICH IS UNASCERTAINABLE

■ **INSTANT FACTS** Several plaintiffs brought separate suits against the several manufacturers of a drug used to prevent miscarriages which injured the plaintiffs prenatally. Due to the fungible nature of the drug, however, none of the plaintiffs could establish which company manufactured the precise drug taken by their mother.

■ **BLACK LETTER RULE** If the plaintiff cannot prove which of multiple persons caused his injury, but can show that all produced a defective product, all of the defendant manufacturers will be held liable for the plaintiff's injuries in proportion to each manufacturer's market share of that product at the time of injury.

■ **PROCEDURAL BASIS**

Certification to the New York Court of Appeals by the Appellate Division to answer the question of whether trial court correctly denied the defendants' motions for summary judgment on the ground that the plaintiffs were not required to prove which company manufactured the precise pill that caused their injury.

■ **FACTS**

From 1947 to 1971, approximately 300 manufacturers produced and marketed the drug DES for the purpose of preventing human miscarriages. In 1971, the Food & Drug Administration banned the use of DES for miscarriage purposes because studies had shown the drug to cause harmful latent effects on the offspring of mothers who took the drug. Eli Lilly & Co. (D) and several other DES manufacturers were sued in several causes of action by hundreds of plaintiffs claiming they were injured by DES ingested while their mothers were pregnant. However, no plaintiff in any case was able to identify the exact manufacturer of the DES pill taken by his or her mother. The reason for the identification problem stemmed from several causes: All DES was of the same chemical composition; druggists filled prescriptions from whatever was on hand; drug companies continuously entered and left the DES market; and the women who ingested the pills had no reason to remember who manufactured their pill because the effects of DES were latent for several years.

■ **ISSUE**

May a plaintiff recover against several drug manufacturers when identification of the producer of the specific drug that caused the injury is impossible?

■ **DECISION AND RATIONALE**

(Wachtler, C.J.) Yes. If the plaintiff cannot prove which of multiple persons caused his injury, but can show that all produced a defective product, all of the defendant manufacturers will be held liable for the plaintiff's injuries in proportion to each manufacturer's market share of that product at the time of injury. The doctrine of alternative liability, as announced in *Summers v. Tice* [California Supreme Court holds two hunters jointly liable for negligently firing in the direction of the plaintiff, even though only one could have caused the plaintiff's injury] would be improperly applied to these facts for several reasons. Shifting the burden of causation onto the defendants in Summers was fair because there was a 50 percent likelihood that one of them caused the injury. However, here the defendants are numerous and the likelihood that any one caused the plaintiffs' injury is significantly diminished. Application of alternative liability would also be improper because the doctrine rests on the assumption that the defendants have better access to information as to who caused the plaintiffs' injury. The drug companies are as unaware of which pill caused which injury as are the plaintiffs. The theory of concerted action, mostly used in drag race cases, provides for joint and several liability when the defendants have a tacit or express understanding to commit a tortious act. Since there is no evidence establishing that the manufacturers of DES agreed to tortiously market the drug, the doctrine of concerted action is also inapplicable. Notwithstanding the fact that some courts have refused to recognize a cause of action in DES cases, we believe that the circumstances call for recognition of a realistic avenue of relief for those injured by DES. Both justice and fairness demand that a culpable party should not escape liability because the devastating effects of its tortious act remain latent for years, or because so many other culpable parties contributed to the harm. It is only proper that those who produced and profited from sales of the drug should bear the loss suffered by innocent plaintiffs. Accordingly, we adopt a version of the market share liability concept first announced by the California Supreme Court. This doctrine limits any one manufacturer's liability to its market share of sales of the drug. The justification for such an approach is that, over the run of hundreds or thousands of cases, a manufacturer's liability will approximate the number of injuries it actually caused. However, fairness dictates that the manufacturers' liability be several so that no one company is forced to pay more than its share in any case. We must now turn to the question of what standard will be used to measure market share. To that end, we believe that a market share theory using a national market is best. Although this standard will result in disproportionate liability of the individual manufacturers and the actual injuries each manufacturer caused in this State, it corresponds best with the overall culpability of each defendant, measured by the risk of injury each defendant created to the public-at-large. The national market share is fair to the defendants if one considers that each will be involved in similar cases in virtually every state. A particular manufacturer may exculpate himself if he is able to prove that it did not market DES for pregnancy use. However, exculpation is not allowed when a plaintiff can show that his drug did not cause the plaintiffs' injury. Such exculpation is inappropriate where liability is based on market-share and risk produced rather than actual causation. Affirmed.

■ CONCURRENCE AND DISSENT

(Mollen, J.) I agree with the court's adoption of the market share theory of liability, based on a national market. Thus, the cause of action would require the plaintiffs to prove that their mothers ingested DES, that DES caused their injuries and that the defendant(s) produced and marketed DES for pregnancy use. However, I believe that the theory should be used to shift the burden of causation onto the manufacturer, who may exculpate themselves by proving that their pill could not have caused the plaintiffs' injuries. Those defendants unable to exculpate themselves would be held liable according to their market share. I also believe that liability in any case should be joint and several, thereby ensuring that the plaintiffs will receive full recovery for their damages. Unlike that taken by the majority, this approach does not radically depart from basic tort principles.

Analysis:

Similar to the alternative causation doctrine, as announced in *Summers v. Tice,* the market share theory imposes liability on a defendant who has not been shown to cause the plaintiff's harm. Both alternative causation and market share are grounded in the same basic principle: that a wrongdoer should not escape liability simply because the circumstances make it impossible to prove that it caused the harm. For a plaintiff to avail himself of the market share theory, courts require that the defendants' products be completely fungible and pose the same risk of harm. Thus, if it were possible for some of the women to have taken a special form of DES that posed a reduced risk of prenatal harm, the theory would be wholly inapplicable. The fungibility and equivalent risk requirements have, with only one exception, limited the theory's application to DES cases. A few courts reject the theory completely on the ground that, contrary to established principles of tort law, it bases liability on statistical and not actual causation.

■ CASE VOCABULARY

FUNGIBILE: Goods that have the same nature are said to be fungible. For example, sugar is a fungible good because it is the same regardless of who markets it.

Benn v. Thomas

(Decedent's Estate) v. *(Negligent Driver)*

512 N.W.2d 537 (Iowa 1994)

THE EXTENT OF THE PLAINTIFF'S DAMAGE NEED NOT HAVE BEEN FORESEEABLE IN ORDER FOR THE DEFENDANT TO BE MADE LIABLE FOR THE TOTAL AMOUNT

■ **INSTANT FACTS** The estate of a man who died from a heart attack occasioned by a rear-end auto accident filed a suit against the driver who caused the accident for damages flowing from the death.

■ **BLACK LETTER RULE** A tortfeasor whose act, superimposed upon a prior condition of the defendant, results in a greater than expected injury is, nevertheless, liable for the full extent of the harm.

■ **PROCEDURAL BASIS**

Appeal to the Supreme Court of Iowa challenging the court of appeals' decision to reverse the judgment of the trial court on the ground that the trial judge failed to properly charge the jury.

■ **FACTS**

As soon as the van in which he was riding was rear-ended, Loras Benn (P) suffered from a heart attack and died. Due to a history of medical problems, including coronary disease, Benn (P) was at risk of having a heart attack. Expert testimony established that the car accident was "the straw that broke the camel's back," and caused Benn (P) to have a fatal heart attack. The accident itself, however, did not cause Benn's (P) death. Benn's (P) estate filed suit against the driver who caused the accident, seeking damages for Benn's (P) injuries and death. The trial judge denied a request to charge the jury to the effect that a defendant was liable for all injuries he proximately caused, even though they were greater than those that might have been experienced by a person of normal sensitivity. Instead, the judge gave an instruction that stated that negligent conduct is the proximate cause of the damage if it is a substantial factor in producing the damage. The judge defined "substantial" as, "[having] an effect in producing damage as to lead a reasonable person to regard it as a cause."

■ **ISSUE**

Is a defendant liable for the full extent of the injuries he causes, even if the injuries are attributable to the plaintiff's particular sensitivity?

■ **DECISION AND RATIONALE**

(McGiverin, C.J.) Yes. A tortfeasor whose act, superimposed upon a prior condition of the defendant, results in a greater than expected injury is, nevertheless, liable for the full extent of the harm. This concept, known as the "eggshell plaintiff" or "thin-skull" rule, deems the negligent act, not the preexisting condition, as the proximate cause of the plaintiff's injury. Fundamentally, what the rule does is reject the limit of foreseeability when the extraordinary consequence results from the plaintiff's particular sensitivity. Although the instruction given was a correct summary of the law, it failed to convey the thin-skull rule, which could have applied under the facts. Reversed.

Analysis:

Another example helps illustrate the difference between two applications of the "thin-skull rule." Suppose that the defendant negligently causes something to fall on the plaintiff's leg, and as a result the plaintiff must undergo an amputation, even though in ninety-nine percent of the people the accident would lead to only a fracture or bruise. In such a case it was foreseeable that the leg would be injured somehow, but the extent of the harm could not be predicted. Suppose, however, that instead of an amputation, the plaintiff suffers a heart attack when his leg is injured. Here, it is not the extent of the harm that is unforeseeable, but the nature of the injury. People usually do not suffer heart attacks when something falls on their leg. Regardless, the end result is the same in both cases—the defendant is liable.

Overseas Tankship (U.K.) Ltd. v. Morts Dock & Engineering Co., Ltd. (The Wagon Mound)

(Freighter Owners) v. *(Wharf Operators)*
[1961] A.C. 388 (Privy Council, 1961)

A DEFENDANT IS LIABLE ONLY FOR THE FORESEEABLE CONSEQUENCES OF HIS NEGLIGENT CONDUCT

■ **INSTANT FACTS** After being sued for causing an oil spill that later ignited, setting a nearby wharf ablaze, a shipping company sought to avoid liability on the ground that they could not be held liable because the fire was an unforeseeable consequence of the oil spill.

■ **BLACK LETTER RULE** A defendant is liable for only those consequences of his conduct that are reasonably foreseeable at the time he acts.

■ **PROCEDURAL BASIS**

Appeal to the Privy Council challenging the decision of the Full Court of the Supreme Court of New South Wales, which dismissed the defendant's appeal.

■ **FACTS**

While Morts Dock & Engineering Co., Ltd. (Morts) (P), a ship-repairing firm, was refitting a ship at a wharf it owned, the ship Wagon Mound, owned by Overseas Tankship (U.K.) Ltd. (D), was taking on oil at a nearby wharf. Some of that oil wound up spilling and concentrating at the wharf owned by Morts (P). When the manager at Morts (P) became aware of the spill he stopped all welding activities until he assessed the danger. Based on discussions with others and his own understanding about furnace oil in open waters, the manager felt he could resume operations with necessary precautions. Two days later, the oil ignited and a fire spread, causing damage to Morts' (P) wharf and other equipment. The trial judge found that the parties could not have reasonably known that the oil was capable of igniting when spread on water. However, the evidence established that atop the spilled oil lay a piece of cotton which was supported by some debris laying underneath the wharf, and that molten metal from the wharf ignited the cotton, leading to the blaze.

■ **ISSUE**

Is a negligent defendant responsible for all the consequences of his conduct whether reasonably foreseeable or not?

■ **DECISION AND RATIONALE**

(Viscount Simonds, J.) No. A defendant is liable for only those consequences of his conduct that are reasonably foreseeable at the time he acts. The rule announced in the case of *In re Polemis* (English case rejecting foreseeability as the standard by which to measure proximate cause), which held a defendant liable for even the unforeseeable consequences of his negligence, is no longer good law. It is a principle of civil liability that the defendant's liability should be limited to those acts that are the natural and probable consequences of his act. The question then arises: What are the natural and probable consequences of a defendant's act? We believe that the answer is those consequences which are foreseeable. A defendant is held liable for the natural and probable consequences of his negligence precisely because those are the foreseeable consequences. To follow *Polemis* and make the test hinge on a determination of what causes are ''direct'' would be to invite never-ending problems of causation. Instead, the essential inquiry should be whether the damage caused was of such a kind as the reasonable man should have foreseen. Accordingly, the owners of the Wagon Mound cannot be liable for the damage occasioned by the fire. Dismissed.

Analysis:

The Wagon Mound is the paradigm case for the rule that a defendant is liable only for those types of harms he could have reasonably foreseen. In other words, if the defendant is negligent because he created a risk that ''X'' will happen, but for some reason ''Y'' occurs instead, the defendant will not be held liable. The rule is based on fairness—that a defendant's liability must be reasonably limited. However, there is a question as to whether the rule of foreseeability was even applicable in this case. Although the appellate court has to give deference to the trial judge's finding that the accident was not foreseeable, the conclusion seems erroneous in this case. The fact that the manager of the dock suspended operations on account of the spill would serve as evidence that a fire was foreseeable. Indeed, in *Wagon Mound II* it was held that the defendant was liable because the risk of fire was foreseeable.

■ CASE VOCABULARY

PRIVY COUNCIL: Court of last resort for those cases originating the in the British Commonwealth states.

Doe v. Manheimer

(Rape Victim) v. *(Property Owner)*

212 Conn. 748, 563 A.2d 699 (1989)

THERE IS NO LIABILITY UNLESS NEGLIGENCE IS A SUBSTANTIAL FACTOR IN CAUSING THE INJURY

The defendant landowner caused the rape of my client by failing to trim the grass and brush on his property, thereby providing the assailant with a hiding place.

"Tortious failure to garden?" I think not.

stus.com

■ **INSTANT FACTS** Doe (P) was assaulted by a man on Manheimer's (D) property, and Doe (P) claimed that Manheimer's (D) failure to remove the brush on the property caused the attack.

■ **BLACK LETTER RULE** A negligent act is the legal cause of a plaintiff's injury only if the injury would not have occurred without the act, and if the negligent act was a substantial factor in producing the plaintiff's injury.

■ **PROCEDURAL BASIS**

Appeal from an order setting aside a jury verdict.

■ **FACTS**

Doe (P) was attacked and raped on property owned by Manheimer (D). Although the attack occurred in the morning, the area was shielded from view by overgrown bushes and grass. There was evidence that the attack and rape were premeditated. The property on which Doe (P) was attacked was located in a high crime area. A rape had taken place in a nearby building a few months earlier. Manheimer's (D) mother had been assaulted and robbed in a liquor store located on the property fourteen months earlier.

Doe (P) brought suit against Manheimer (D) for her injuries. She claimed that Manheimer (D) failed to remove the overgrown vegetation on the property even though he knew, or should have known, that third persons might use the overgrowth to conceal crimes against pedestrians. Doe (P) claimed that the overgrowth caused and contributed to the assault and the duration of the assault. At trial, an expert testified on behalf of Doe (P) that the condition of the property served as an inducement for crime.

The jury returned a verdict for Doe (P). The trial judge set aside the verdict. The judge noted that the rape most probably would not have taken place on the property without the shielding provided by the overgrowth, and implicitly found that Manheimer (D) owed Doe (P) a duty of reasonable care, in that it could be found that violence was reasonably foreseeable in such a sheltered location. The position of the overgrown bush was the breach of that duty. The court went on to find, however, that the shielded bushing did not cause the injury. The rape and assault caused the injury and the damages. The shielding could have been provided by some other object if the overgrowth were not there.

■ **ISSUE**

Was the overgrowth on Manheimer's (D) property the cause of Doe's (D) injuries from being raped?

■ **DECISION AND RATIONALE**

(Glass, J.) No. A negligent act is the legal cause of a plaintiff's injury only if the injury would not have occurred without the act, and if the negligent act was a substantial factor in producing the plaintiff's injury. The question of whether something was a substantial factor or the proximate cause of the injury looks to whether the plaintiff's injury was of the same general nature as the foreseeable risk created by the defendant's negligence. If a defendant's negligence creates or increases the risk of a particular harm, the defendant is not relieved from liability by the intervention of a third party, unless the third party intentionally caused the harm and the harm was not within the scope of risk created by the defendant. The tortious or criminal act of another could be foreseeable, and thus within the scope of the created risk.

There is no reason to question the trial court's finding that the assault would not have taken place without the overgrowth on the property. Manheimer (D) has not disputed that finding. There is no evidence, however, to support Doe's (P) contention that the overgrowth was the proximate cause of her injuries. The harm she suffered cannot reasonably be understood to be within the scope of risk created by Manheimer's (D) conduct.

Doe's (P) argument that it was within the scope of risk that the condition of the property might be the catalyst for an assault is rejected. This argument would make the conduct of Doe's (P) assailant a predictable response or reaction to the stimulus created by Manheimer (D). Liability is imposed, however, only for reasonably foreseeable misconduct by others, rather than all misconduct that proceeds from a situation caused by a defendant. It was not foreseeable that the overgrown vegetation on Manheimer's (D) property would provide an incentive or inducement for an assault on a stranger. There was nothing that took place in the past to lead Manheimer (D) to make the association between the overgrowth and violent crime. The prior crime in the area was either nonviolent or took place inside a nearby building. The other crimes were not of a type that would lead a reasonable person to suppose that a violent sexual crime would take place in a vacant lot.

Furthermore, the idea of a catalyst for crime creating liability would do violence to the idea of proximate causation. In order to be within the scope of risk, an injury must be of the same general type as to make conduct negligent in the first place. Affirmed.

Analysis:

After the attack on Doe (P), is it now "reasonably foreseeable" that the overgrowth could give rise to a violent crime? The court's "scope of the risk" analysis seems to preclude any liability, even though one attack has taken place. The court notes that the type of injury normally associated with overgrowth or unkempt shrubbery would be tripping and falling, rather than an assailant concealing himself. In addition, as the court notes, the assailant could have found some other way of concealing his crime if the bushes had not been there.

■ CASE VOCABULARY

PROXIMATE CAUSE: A cause that is legally sufficient to result in liability; a cause that directly produces an event and without which the event would not have occurred.

Palsgraf v. Long Island R.R. Co.

(Passenger) v. *(Railroad)*

248 N.Y. 339, 162 N.E. 99 (1928)

A DEFENDANT IS ONLY LIABLE FOR DAMAGES TO A PLAINTIFF TO WHOM THE DEFENDANT FORESEEABLY OWES THE DUTY OF CARE

■ **INSTANT FACTS** Palsgraf (P) sued Long Island R.R. Co. (D) for the injuries sustained when a package fell out of the hand of one of the train passengers and exploded.

■ **BLACK LETTER RULE** A defendant owes a duty of care only to those plaintiffs who are in the reasonably foreseeable zone of danger.

■ **PROCEDURAL BASIS**

Appeal in action in negligence for recovery of damages.

■ **FACTS**

Palsgraf (P) was standing on the platform of the train station when a man jumped on a already-moving train. The man was being pulled in by an employee of the railroad (D), when an unmarked package containing firecrackers fell out of his hand. When the package fell, the firecrackers within it exploded, and the shock of the explosion threw down scales many feet away from the explosion. The scales fell on Palsgraf (P) injuring her. Palsgraf (P) sued the railroad (D) for her injuries. The trial court and the Appellate Division ruled in favor of Palsgraf (P). The railroad (D) appeals.

■ **ISSUE**

Does a defendant owe a duty of care only to those plaintiffs who are in the reasonably foreseeable zone of danger?

■ **DECISION AND RATIONALE**

(Cardozo, C.J.) Yes. A defendant owes a duty of care only to those plaintiffs who are in the reasonably foreseeable zone of danger. In this case, the conduct of the railroad employee (D) was not negligent at all with respect to Palsgraf (P). No one was on notice that the package contained explosives which could harm a person so far removed. In every negligence case, before negligence of the defendant can be determined, it must be found that the defendant owed a duty to the plaintiff, and that the defendant could have avoided the injury to the plaintiff, had he observed this duty. The plaintiff in a negligence case may sue in her own right only for a wrong personal to her. The orbit of the danger or risk as disclosed to a reasonable person would be the orbit of the duty. Thus, a plaintiff must show a wrong to herself, or a violation of her own rights, but not a "wrong" to anyone. In this case, there is no indication in the facts to suggest to the most cautious mind that the wrapped package would explode in the train station. Even if the guard had thrown the package intentionally, he would not have threatened Palsgraf's (P) safety, so far as appearances could warn him. Thus, liability cannot be greater where the act of the guard was unintentional or inadvertent. (Reversed.)

■ **DISSENT**

(Andrews, J.) Where an act threatens the safety of others, the doer is liable for all its proximate consequences, even when the injury is to one who would generally be thought to be outside of the radius of danger. It is important to inquire only as to the relation between cause and effect. Due care is a duty imposed on each member of the society to protect others in the society from unnecessary danger, and not just to protect A, B, or C. Negligence involves a relationship between a man and his fellows, but not merely a relationship between man and those whom he might reasonably expect his act would injure. Everyone owes to the world at large the duty of refraining from those acts which may unreasonably threaten the safety of others. If such an act occurs, not only has he wronged those to whom harm might reasonably be expected to result, but also those whom he has in fact injured, even if they may be thought of as outside the zone of danger.

Analysis:

This case deals with the question of causation in terms of the plaintiff. In other words, to whom does a defendant owe a duty of care? According to the majority opinion written by Chief Justice Cardozo, the defendant only owes a duty of care to those individuals who are within the foreseeable zone of danger. Thus, according to the majority opinion in this case the plaintiff, who was standing far away from the explosion, is not entitled to damages even though she was injured. According to the dissent, however (the famous Andrews dissent), every plaintiff is a foreseeable plaintiff. Thus, regardless of how far or how near or how unforeseeable, any individual is entitled to recover for damages that resulted from the defendant's negligent conduct. The Cardozo opinion is adhered to by a majority of courts. The Andrews opinion is a minority view followed in a few jurisdictions.

■ CASE VOCABULARY

ATTENUATE: To lessen or weaken.

CONFLAGRATION: A great destructive burning or fire.

FORESEEABILITY: The foreseeability of the consequences of a defendant's actions depend on the balancing between the likelihood of risk and the magnitude of damages flowing therefrom.

INVASION: An encroachment upon the rights of another.

PROXIMATE CAUSE: The type of cause which in the natural and continuous sequence unbroken by any new independent cause produces an event, and without which the injury would not have occurred.

CHAPTER SIX

Defenses

Fritts v. McKinne

Instant Facts: Dr. McKinne (D) was sued for medical negligence after decedent died following surgery, and he asserted evidence of decedent's substance abuse as a comparative negligence defense.

Black Letter Rule: Except in limited situations, the comparative negligence of a party, which necessitates medical treatment, is irrelevant to the issue of possible subsequent medical negligence.

Dalury v. S–K–I, Ltd.

Instant Facts: Injured skier, Dalury (P), sought to invalidate exculpatory agreement based upon violation of public policy.

Black Letter Rule: A skier's assumption of the inherent risks of skiing does not abrogate the ski area's duty to warn of or correct dangers which, in the exercise of reasonable prudence under the circumstances, could have been foreseen and corrected.

Murphy v. Steeplechase Amusement Co.

Instant Facts: Murphy (P) sued Amusement park (D) for injuries but the court held that he assumed the risk of sustained injuries by electing to go on the ride.

Black Letter Rule: One who takes part in a sport accepts the dangers that inhere in it so far as they are obvious and necessary.

Davenport v. Cotton Hope Plantation Horizontal Property Regime

Instant Facts: Davenport (P) was injured during a fall down a stairway when he knew that the floodlight was broken, yet he continued to use the stairway.

Black Letter Rule: Assumption of risk is not a complete bar to recovery where a state has adopted a modified comparative negligence system, unless the degree of fault arising therefrom is greater than the negligence of the defendant.

Levandoski v. Cone

Instant Facts: Officer Levandoski (P) fell while chasing Cone (D) and sued Cone (D) for his injuries.

Black Letter Rule: The firefighter's rule does not bar recovery from a tortfeasor who is neither a landowner nor a person in control of the premises.

Geier v. American Honda Motor Company, Inc., et al.

Instant Facts: Geier (P) sued Honda (D) claiming that it should have equipped their car with airbags and Honda (D) asserted compliance with Federal standard and pre-emption.

Black Letter Rule: A common law tort action can be pre-empted by a Federal legislative standard intended to preempt tort claims.

Fritts v. McKinne

(Wife of Decedent) v. *(Doctor)*
934 P.2d 371 (Okla. Civ. App. 1996)

EVIDENCE OF COMPARATIVE NEGLIGENCE, UNRELATED TO MEDICAL TREATMENT, IS NOT ADMISSIBLE AS A DEFENSE IN MEDICAL NEGLIGENCE SUIT

■ **INSTANT FACTS** Dr. McKinne (D) was sued for medical negligence after decedent died following surgery, and he asserted evidence of decedent's substance abuse as a comparative negligence defense.

■ **BLACK LETTER RULE** Except in limited situations, the comparative negligence of a party, which necessitates medical treatment, is irrelevant to the issue of possible subsequent medical negligence.

■ **PROCEDURAL BASIS**

Appeal from judgment following jury verdict in action for wrongful death damages due to medical negligence.

■ **FACTS**

Mr. Fritts was seriously injured in an accident, which involved his pickup truck hitting a tree at approximately 70 miles per hour. He and his friend had been drinking prior to the accident, and there was a dispute about which one of them was driving at the time of the accident. Mr. Fritts required surgery five days after the accident to repair facial fractures. [The tree did not go to the hospital.] During surgery, Dr. McKinne (D) performed a tracheostomy to allow Mr. Fritts to breathe during surgery. Unfortunately, Mr. Fritts lost a major amount of blood and died three days later. Mrs. Fritts (P) sued Dr. McKinne (D) claiming that he negligently failed to identify and isolate the proper artery. In addition to defending on the ground that the artery was not normally where it should have been, Dr. McKinne (D) asserted a comparative negligence defense that Mr. Fritts was injured either while driving drunk or was drunk while riding in the truck with his friend who was also drunk. Dr. McKinne (D) also argued that the evidence of Mr. Fritts' drug and alcohol use was relevant to the issue of damages in that he had a substantially diminished life expectancy as a result thereof. The trial court denied Mrs. Fritts' (P) motion to exclude this evidence, and much of the trial was devoted to Mr. Fritts' drunkenness at the time of the accident as well as his past drug and alcohol abuse. The trial judge also instructed the jury on comparative negligence, stating that it is the duty of the driver of a motor vehicle to use ordinary care to prevent injury to himself or to other persons. The jury returned a verdict in favor of Dr. McKinne (D). Mrs. Fritts (P) appealed.

■ **ISSUE**

Is evidence of comparative negligence of a party, which necessitates medical treatment, admissible in defense of a subsequent medical negligence suit?

■ **DECISION AND RATIONALE**

(Stubblefield, J.) No. Generally, the comparative negligence of a party, which necessitates medical treatment, is irrelevant to the issue of possible subsequent medical negligence. There are limited situations where such evidence is permitted—the patient's failure to reveal important medical history, the patient's furnishing of false information about his condition, the patient's failure to follow the doctor's advise or the patient's failure or delay to seek further recommended medical attention. In these situations, such contributory negligence is admissible as a defense. A physician may not, however, simply avoid liability for negligent medical treatment by asserting that the patient's injuries were originally caused by the patient's own negligence. [There sure would be a lot less lawsuits!] Those patients are entitled to subsequent non-negligent medical treatment and to an undiminished recovery if such subsequent non-negligent treatment is not afforded. We thus conclude that the submission of the issue of comparative negligence—decedent's conduct unrelated to his medical treatment—was error. Although Mr. Fritt's history of substance abuse is relevant to the issue of probable life expectancy in connection with the damages claimed for loss of future earnings, the jury should have been advised that it was admissible on this point only. Bifurcation of the liability and damage phases of trial would have avoided the possibility of prejudice from this evidence. Judgment reversed and remanded for a new trial.

Analysis:

This case demonstrates that there are limitations on use of comparative negligence, as a defense. Generally, if the pre-treatment conduct does not relate to the alleged medical negligence it is not admissible. As the court notes, negligence of a party that necessitates the medical treatment is simply irrelevant. If this were not the general rule, then a doctor would never be held liable for negligent treatment where a patient was hospitalized due to his own fault. Of course, there are a limited number of circumstances where such evidence is admissible, but they pertain to conduct that relates in some fashion to the ultimate medical treatment. The court did say that the evidence of substance abuse was relevant to the issue of damages, but because the jury was not told to consider the evidence for only that limited purpose, there was the possibility of prejudice.

■ CASE VOCABULARY

BIFURCATION OF TRIAL: Where the liability phase is tried first, and then the damage phase.

LIMITING INSTRUCTIONS: Instructions given to the jury to consider certain evidence only for a limited purpose.

REVERSIBLE ERROR: An error that is significant enough to possibly cause prejudice to a party so as to require the reversal of a judgment.

Dalury v. S-K-I, Ltd.

(Skiing Accident Victim) v. *(Ski Resort Owner)*

164 Vt. 329, 670 A.2d 795 (1995)

EXPRESS ASSUMPTION OF THE RISK DOES NOT ABROGATE BUSINESS OWNER'S DUTY TO BUSINESS INVITEES TO CORRECT DANGERS THAT COULD HAVE BEEN FORESEEN AND CORRECTED

■ **INSTANT FACTS** Injured skier, Dalury (P), sought to invalidate exculpatory agreement based upon violation of public policy.

■ **BLACK LETTER RULE** A skier's assumption of the inherent risks of skiing does not abrogate the ski area's duty to warn of or correct dangers which, in the exercise of reasonable prudence under the circumstances, could have been foreseen and corrected.

■ **PROCEDURAL BASIS**

Appeal from entry of summary judgment in action for personal injuries.

■ **FACTS**

Dalury (P) was seriously injured while skiing at S-K-I, Ltd.'s (D) resort. He collided with a metal pole that formed part of the control maze for a ski lift line. [He hadn't yet perfected his stopping technique.] Previously, Dalury (P) had purchased a season ski pass and signed a release form that expressly stated that he voluntarily assumed the risks of injury and damage, and released the resort from all liability for personal injuries or property damage. The photo identification, signed by Dalury (P), contained the same information. The trial court granted summary judgment for S-K-I (D). Dalury appealed.

■ **ISSUE**

Does a skier's assumption of the inherent risks of skiing abrogate the ski area's duty to warn of or correct dangers which, in the exercise of reasonable prudence under the circumstances, could have been foreseen and corrected?

■ **DECISION AND RATIONALE**

(Johnson, J.) No. We hold that a skier's assumption of the inherent risks of skiing does not abrogate the ski area's duty to warn of or correct dangers which, in the exercise of reasonable prudence under the circumstances, could have been foreseen and corrected. We first conclude that the release was not ambiguous as to whose liability was waived. However, even a well-drafted exculpatory agreement may be void if it violates public policy. The Restatement provides that an exculpatory agreement should be upheld if it is (1) freely and fairly made, (2) between parties who are in an equal bargaining position, and (3) there is no social interest with which it interferes. The critical issue in this case concerns the social interests that are affected. In a leading California case, the court examined various characteristics to determine whether an exculpatory agreement violates public policy. It held that an agreement is invalid if it exhibits some or all of the following characteristics: (1) it concerns a business suitable for public regulation; (2) The service engaged in is of great importance to the public; (3) The party holds itself out as willing to perform the service for the public; (4) The party invoking the agreement has a decisive advantage of bargaining strength; (5) The party gives the public a standardized adhesion contract, with no option to obtain additional protection against negligence; and, (6) The purchaser is placed under the control of the seller, subject to the risk of carelessness by the seller or its agents. The Supreme Court of California, applying these factors, concluded that a release from liability for future negligence imposed as a condition for admission to a charitable research hospital was invalid. The Colorado Supreme Court has used these same factors in holding that there was no duty to the public in air service for a parachute jump, because that sort of service does not affect the public interest. Similarly, the Wyoming Supreme Court concluded that a ski resort's sponsorship of an Ironman Decathlon competition did not invoke the public interest. On the other hand, the Virginia Supreme Court held that a pre-injury release from liability for negligence in a triathlon competition was void as against public policy because it was simply wrong to put one party to a contract at the mercy of the other's negligence. S-K-I (D) urges us to uphold the exculpatory agreement on the ground that ski resorts do not provide an essential public service, and it is not a necessity of life. [Some obsessed skiers might disagree!] We do not agree that the sale of lift tickets does not implicate any public interest. When a substantial number of such sales take place as a result of the seller's invitation to the public to utilize the facilities and services, a legitimate public interest arises. The major public policy implications are those underlying the law of premises liability. In this State, a business owner has a duty of active care to make sure that its premises are in safe and suitable condition for its customers. This duty of care increases proportionately with the foreseeable risks of the operations involved. Thus, a business invitee has a right to assume that the premises are reasonably safe for the purpose for which he is upon them, and that proper precaution has been taken to make them so. It is illogical to undermine the public policy underlying business invitee law and allow skiers to bear risks they have no ability or right to control.

Analysis:

Dalury (P) signed an exculpatory agreement that expressly stated that he assumed the risks of injury and released the ski resort of liability, but this case illustrates that liability may be imposed in spite of express assumption of the risk. The court based its holding on the law of premises liability, under which a duty is imposed upon business owners to provide their business invitees with a safe and suitable condition of the premises. It is this fundamental public policy that allowed the court to hold that the exculpatory agreement was unenforceable. Note the decisions from other states cited in the court's opinion. Although some held that certain sporting events did not affect the public interest, it is unclear whether those courts relied upon premises liability law in reaching their decisions. Finally, most courts generally agree that no matter what the situation, gross negligence or recklessness may not be disclaimed by agreement.

■ CASE VOCABULARY

EXCULPATORY AGREEMENT: An agreement whereby one party in advance holds the other party harmless for any injury suffered or damage sustained.

SUMMARY JUDGMENT: Judgment entered after granting a legal motion for summary judgment in which party requests that the judge enter judgment, before trial, on the grounds that the action has no merit or there is no defense to the action.

Murphy v. Steeplechase Amusement Co.

(Rider of "The Flopper") v. *(Amusement Park)*
250 N.Y. 479, 166 N.E. 173 (1929)

IMPLIED ASSUMPTION OF THE RISK EXISTS FOR NORMAL USE OF AMUSEMENT PARK RIDES

■ **INSTANT FACTS** Murphy (P) sued Amusement park (D) for injuries but the court held that he assumed the risk of sustained injuries by electing to go on the ride.

■ **BLACK LETTER RULE** One who takes part in a sport accepts the dangers that inhere in it so far as they are obvious and necessary.

■ **PROCEDURAL BASIS**

Appeal from judgment entered following a jury verdict in action for negligence seeking damages for personal injuries.

■ **FACTS**

Murphy (P) was injured on an amusement ride known as "The Flopper" while attending Steeplechase Amusement park (D) at Coney Island, New York. The ride is a moving belt, running upward on an inclined plane, on which passengers sit or stand. Many of them are unable to keep on their feet because of the movement of the belt, and are thrown backward or aside. Murphy (P) watched as a friend step onto the moving belt and he too stepped on behind the friend. As he did so, he felt a sudden jerk, was thrown to the floor, and suffered a fractured kneecap. Murphy (P) sued Steeplechase Amusement Co. (D) alleging that the belt was dangerous in that it stopped and started violently and suddenly, was not properly equipped to prevent injuries, was operated at a fast and dangerous rate of speed and was not supplied with a proper railing, guard or other device to prevent a fall. [That's a lot of negligence.]

■ **ISSUE**

Does one who takes part in a sport accept the dangers that inhere in it so far as they are obvious and necessary?

■ **DECISION AND RATIONALE**

(Cardozo, J.) Yes. We hold that one who takes part in a sport accepts the dangers that inhere in it so far as they are obvious and necessary. A fall was foreseen as one of the risks of the adventure. Not only was the name of the ride a warning to the timid, but also Murphy's (P) friend witnessed other patrons' tumbling bodies and screams and she elected to take a chance. Visitors were also tumbling about the belt to the merriment of onlookers when Murphy (P) made his choice to join them. By so doing, he took the chance of a like fate. [Except not to his merriment.] It would be a different case if the dangers inherent in the sport were obscure or unobserved, or so serious as to justify the belief that precautions of some kind must have been taken to avert them. Nothing happened to Murphy (P) except what common experience tells us may happen at any time as the consequence of a sudden fall. Judgment reversed.

Analysis:

This opinion, written by the famous Justice Cardozo, is an example of implied assumption of the risk. The facts do not reveal any express agreement entered into between Murphy (P) and the amusement park (D), nor is there evidence of any posted warning signs or release of liability language on the ticket stubs. Nevertheless, the court concludes that Murphy (P) "took the chance" of tumbling about the belt as those patrons before him had done. The fact that Murphy (P) fell is something that common experience tells one may happen. The court equates the situation to that of a skater or a horseman who might experience a similar fall during his sport.

■ **CASE VOCABULARY**

VOLENTI NON FIT INJURIA: He who consents cannot receive an injury.

Davenport v. Cotton Hope Plantation Horizontal Property Regime

(Injured Party) v. *(Property Owner)*

333 S.C. 71, 508 S.E.2d 565 (1998)

DEFENSE OF ASSUMPTION OF THE RISK IS NOT A COMPLETE BAR TO RECOVERY IN COMPARATIVE NEGLIGENCE STATE

■ **INSTANT FACTS** Davenport (P) was injured during a fall down a stairway when he knew that the floodlight was broken, yet he continued to use the stairway.

■ **BLACK LETTER RULE** Assumption of risk is not a complete bar to recovery where a state has adopted a modified comparative negligence system, unless the degree of fault arising therefrom is greater than the negligence of the defendant.

■ **PROCEDURAL BASIS**

Certiorari granted by State Supreme Court to review court of appeal's reversal of trial court's directed verdict in negligence action for personal injuries.

■ **FACTS**

Davenport (P) was injured while descending a stairway near his apartment. He rented his third floor apartment from the condominium's owner, within Cotton Hope Plantation Horizontal Property Regime's (Cotton) (D) premises. There were three stairways that offered access, but Davenport (P) used the middle stairway because it was closest to his apartment. For two months before his fall, Davenport (P) had been reporting to management that the middle stairway's floodlights were not working, but he continued to use the stairway. [Sounds like the defense of assumption of risk may be asserted.] The night he fell, Davenport (P) believed that he was stepping on a step, but it was actually a shadow caused by the broken floodlights. The trial court directed a verdict against Davenport (P) based on assumed risk, and also held that even if comparative negligence applied, he was more negligent than Cotton (D). The court of appeals reversed on both points and Cotton (D) petitioned the State's Supreme Court for review.

■ **ISSUE**

Does assumption of risk act as a complete bar to recovery where a state has adopted a modified comparative negligence system?

■ **DECISION AND RATIONALE**

(Toal, J.) No. We hold that assumption of risk is not a complete bar to recovery where a state has adopted a modified comparative negligence system, unless the degree of fault arising therefrom is greater than the negligence of the defendant. There are four requirements to establishing the defense of assumption of the risk: (1) the plaintiff must have knowledge of the facts constituting a dangerous condition; (2) the plaintiff must know the condition is dangerous; (3) the plaintiff must appreciate the nature and extent of the danger; and (4) the plaintiff must voluntarily expose himself to the danger. Some comparative fault jurisdictions have abolished assumption of risk as an absolute bar to recovery. However, even in these jurisdictions, *express* assumption of risk continues as an absolute defense in an action for negligence. The reason is that express assumption of risk sounds in contract, not in tort. When *implied* assumption of risk occurs—where the plaintiff implicitly, rather than expressly, assumes known risks—we must consider the type of implied assumption of risk involved before determining whether there is a complete bar to recovery. *Primary* implied assumption of risk arises when the plaintiff impliedly assumes those risks that are inherent in a particular activity, and the determination is whether the defendant's legal duty encompasses the risk encountered by the plaintiff. If not, plaintiff has failed to establish a prima facie case of negligence by failing to establish the existence of a duty. *Secondary* implied assumption of risk arises when the plaintiff knowingly encounters a risk created by the defendant's negligence. Since express and primary implied assumption of risk are compatible with comparative negligence, we will refer to secondary implied assumption of risk simply as "assumption of risk." A few comparative fault jurisdictions have retained assumption of risk as an absolute defense. Other comparative fault jurisdictions have rejected assumption of risk as a total bar to recovery and only allow a jury to consider the plaintiff's negligence in assuming the risk. In these states, if the plaintiff's total negligence exceeds or equals that of the defendant, only then is the plaintiff completely barred from recovery. We choose to adopt the latter view rather than the former. Thus, even if Davenport (P) assumed the risk of injury, he will not be barred from recovery unless his negligence exceeds Cotton's (D) negligence. [How negligent could going down the stairs be, even if it was in the dark?] This question is properly submitted for jury determination. Remanded for new trial.

Analysis:

The elements of implied assumption of risk are set forth in this case, as well as an explanation of the difference between *primary* and *secondary* implied assumption of risk. The court's holding permits the use of secondary implied assumption of risk as a defense, but not as a total bar to recovery, unless of course the degree of fault of the plaintiff is greater than the negligence of the defendant. This represents the majority view. The court noted that a few states have retained assumption of risk as an absolute defense. In its discussion concerning primary and secondary implied assumption of risk, the court expressed its view that primary assumption is not really a defense, but a failure to meet the prima facie elements of a negligence claim. On the other hand, secondary assumption of risk is a true defense that is used after the plaintiff establishes the prima facie case of negligence.

■ CASE VOCABULARY

DIRECTED VERDICT: Judge entering judgment for one party before return of jury verdict.

Levandoski v. Cone

(Police Officer) v. *(Fleeing Suspect)*
267 Conn. 651, 841 A.2d 208 (2004)

THE FIREFIGHTER'S RULE APPLIES ONLY TO PROPERTY OWNERS

Freeze or I'll trip and injure myself and sue you.

stus.com

■ **INSTANT FACTS:** Officer Levandoski (P) fell while chasing Cone (D) and sued Cone (D) for his injuries.

■ **BLACK LETTER RULE:** The firefighter's rule does not bar recovery from a tortfeasor who is neither a landowner nor a person in control of the premises.

■ **PROCEDURAL BASIS**

Appeal from a jury verdict in favor of Levandoski (P).

■ **FACTS**

Levandoski (P), a police officer, responded to a complaint about a noisy party at the home of Baskin. Levandoski (P) and his partner observed the house from a distance before approaching. Levandoski (P) watched Cone (D) take some items from a bag in the garage, walk down the driveway while looking over his shoulder, and then put some small plastic bags in his pants. Levandoski (P) thought the bags contained marijuana, turned his flashlight on Cone (D), and asked him to remove the bags from his pants. Cone (D) began to run toward a wooded area. Levandoski (P) followed him and, just as he was about to apprehend Cone (D), fell off of a ledge onto some rocks. Levandoski (P) brought suit against Cone (D), and Cone (D) claimed that he should not be liable because of the firefighter's rule.

■ **ISSUE**

Does the firefighter's rule bar Officer Levandoski's (P) suit against a fleeing suspect for injuries sustained on the property of another?

■ **DECISION AND RATIONALE**

(Borden, J.) No. The firefighter's rule does not bar recovery from a tortfeasor who is neither a landowner nor a person in control of the premises. The rule has its origins in the law of premises liability. As the rule was originally formulated, firefighters (and later police officers) who entered premises in the performance of an official duty had the status of a licensee. Firefighters and police officers enter property regardless of the owner's consent, so courts have regarded it as unreasonable to require landowners to exercise the same standard of care for public officers. In addition, firefighters and police officers are in a line of work that is inherently dangerous, and they voluntarily assumed the risk of that danger by entering their professions. Finally, allowing firefighters and police officers to recover in tort against property owners would lead to double taxation. Property owners pay taxes to compensate police and firefighters for the risks they face, and exposing negligent property owners to liability would be imposing multiple burdens for police and fire protection. Workers' compensation benefits are available for injuries suffered.

The history and rationales for the firefighter's rule leads to a conclusion that the rule should remain a rule of premises liability, because of the reasonable expectations of property owners and because of the hardship on property owners in the absence of the rule. In addition, to the extent the rule relates to assumption of the risk, it would be inconsistent with the policy of the general tort law to extend the rule. Assumption of the risk has been abolished in negligence actions in Connecticut. Finally, the rationale of protecting property owners from double taxation does not apply in this case. Cone (D) is not a taxpayer. A taxpaying property owner pays the salary of the police officer, and so has the benefit of a lesser duty towards police officers. Likewise, the availability of workers' compensation does not matter, as the court has never used that availability to alter the burden in other tort cases.

Cone (D) also claims that it was not foreseeable that Levandoski (P) would be injured by Cone's (D) negligence. There was, however, ample evidence for the jury to conclude that Levandoski (P) could be injured chasing a fleeing suspect. Cone (D) does not argue that he had the right to flee Levandoski (P), and common sense suggests that one who flees a police officer ought to know that the pursuing officer could be injured scrambling through obstacles and over unlit terrain. Affirmed.

Analysis:

The firefighter's rule has been adopted by most state courts; however, the rule has been limited or abolished by legislation in several states. The narrow application of the rule set out by the court here—limiting the rule to premises liability cases—appears to represent the minority view. Most courts have held that the doctrine is based on assumption of risk, rather than the duty of property owners towards persons on the property.

■ CASE VOCABULARY:

FIREFIGHTER'S RULE: A doctrine holding that a firefighter, police officer, or other emergency professional may not hold a person, usually a property owner, liable for unintentional injuries suffered by the professional in responding to the situation created or caused by the person.

INVITEE: A person who has an express or implied invitation to enter or use another's premises, such as a business visitor or a member of the public to whom the premises are held open. The occupier has a duty to inspect the premises and to warn the invitee of dangerous conditions.

LICENSEE: One who has permission to enter or use another's premises, but only for one's own purposes and not for the occupier's benefit.

Geier v. American Honda Motor Company, Inc., et al.

(Auto Accident Victim) v. *(Car Manufacturer)*

529 U.S. 861, 120 S.Ct. 1913, 146 L.Ed.2d 914 (2000)

WHEN STATE-LAW TORT CLAIMS CONFLICT WITH A FEDERAL ACT THE CLAIMS ARE PRE-EMPTED

■ **INSTANT FACTS** Geier (P) sued Honda (D) claiming that it should have equipped their car with airbags and Honda (D) asserted compliance with Federal standard and preemption.

■ **BLACK LETTER RULE** A common law tort action can be pre-empted by a Federal legislative standard intended to preempt tort claims.

■ **PROCEDURAL BASIS**

Certiorari granted by United States Supreme Court following court of appeals affirming trial court's dismissal of product liability lawsuit seeking personal injury damages.

■ **FACTS**

Geier (P), while driving a 1987 Honda Accord, collided with a tree and was seriously injured. The car had shoulder and lap belts, which Geier (P) had buckled up at the time, but it was not equipped with airbags or other passive restraint devices. [But would the tree still win over the airbags?] Geier (P) and her parents sued American Honda Motor Company, Inc. (Honda) for negligently and defectively designing its car without a driver's side airbag. The Federal Motor Vehicle Safety Standard required auto manufacturers to equip some, but not all, of their 1987 vehicles with passive restraints. It gave car manufacturers a choice as to whether to install airbags. The trial judge dismissed Geier's (P) lawsuit because it concluded that the lawsuit, which sought to establish a different safety standard—i.e., an airbag requirement—was expressly pre-empted by a provision of the Act which pre-empts "any safety standard" that is not identical to a federal safety standard applicable to the same aspect of performance. The court of appeals affirmed but on the ground that the state-law tort claims conflicted with the federal act, and thus, under ordinary pre-emption principles, the Act pre-empted the lawsuit.

■ **ISSUE**

Can a common-law tort action be pre-empted by a Federal legislative standard intended to preempt tort claims?

■ **DECISION AND RATIONALE**

(Breyer, J.) Yes. We first conclude that the Act's express pre-emption provision does not pre-empt this lawsuit. With respect to the Act's pre-emption provision, it provides that whenever a Federal motor vehicle safety standard is in effect, no State shall have the authority to establish or continue any safety standard that is not identical to the Federal standard. However, the Act contains another provision—a "saving" clause—that says that compliance with a federal safety standard does not exempt anyone from liability under common law. This saving clause causes us to conclude that the pre-emption clause does not include common law actions. [Don't think the Geier's have won. Read on.] Second, we conclude that ordinary pre-emption principles apply, which require pre-emption of state laws and common-law rules that actually conflict with the statute or federal standards thereunder. In reaching this conclusion, we must decide whether the saving clause limits these ordinary pre-emption principles.

After a careful review of the saving clause, as well as the pre-emption clause, we can find nothing that would favor one set of policies over the other where a jury-imposed safety standard actually conflicts with a federal safety standard. Finally, we conclude that this "no airbag" lawsuit conflicts with the Federal standard, and hence the Act itself. The manufacturer was given a range of choices among different passive restraint devices, which would bring about a mix of different devices introduced gradually over time. The federal standard does not set a minimum airbag standard. A review of the history of the safety regulations and the government's explanation for them causes us to conclude that the government had concluded that it would be better to phase in airbag regulation, rather than to make them mandatory at that time.

DISSENT

(Stevens, J.) To be safe, a car must have an airbag. This technology has been available to the automobile manufacturers for over 30 years. The issue raised by Geier's (P) action is whether that proposition was sufficiently obvious when Honda (D) manufactured the car to make the failure to install airbags negligent or a design defect. I dissent from the majority's holding that an interim regulation, motivated by the government's desire for gradual development of passive restraint devices, deprives state courts of jurisdiction from this question. I also dissent from the majority's unprecedented extension of the doctrine of preemption. State laws are not to be pre-empted by a federal statute unless it is the clear and manifest purpose of Congress to do so. Because neither the text of the statute nor the text of the regulation contains any indication of an intent to pre-empt the cause of action, and because I cannot agree with the majority's unprecedented use of inferences from regulatory history and commentary as a basis for implied preemption, I am convinced that Honda (D) has not overcome the presumption against pre-emption.

Analysis:

The Supreme Court upheld the dismissal of this case based upon the doctrine of pre-emption. Under this doctrine, if the state law or common law cause of action conflicts with a federal statute, the state law or action is displaced and is pre-empted by the federal law. The court found that a conflict existed by analyzing the history and the government's explanations for the regulations. The dissent argued that the unprecedented use of inferences from this history and commentary to find implied pre-emption was wrong. It noted that neither the statute nor the regulation in question contained text that gave any indication of intent to pre-empt the claim. It appears that the dissent is requiring express pre-emption, and the majority is satisfied with implied pre-emption. Finally, remember that Honda (D) was asserting that it complied with federal regulations by having shoulder and lap belts, and thus it could not be sued for failure to include airbags in the car.

■ CASE VOCABULARY

PRE-EMPTED: Referring to the doctrine of preemption whereby certain claims are governed by federal law, and it takes precedence over state laws.

SAVING CLAUSE: A provision in a statute that exempts something from coverage under the statute that would otherwise be included.

CHAPTER SEVEN

Strict Liability

Fletcher v. Rylands

Instant Facts: A cotton mill operator built a reservoir on land adjacent to an underground mining operation. When the reservoir was filled, the water escaped through some old mine shafts and into the operational mines.

Black Letter Rule: The person who for his own purposes brings on his lands and collects and keeps there anything likely to do mischief if it escapes, must keep it in at his peril and be answerable for all the damage that is the natural consequence of its escape.

Rylands v. Fletcher

Instant Facts: A cotton mill operator built a reservoir on land adjacent to an underground mining operation. When the reservoir was filled, the water escaped through some old mine shafts and into the operational mines.

Black Letter Rule: A landowner is not responsible for damage to neighboring land caused by the natural use of his land, but is strictly liable for damage caused by the non-natural use of his land.

Sullivan v. Dunham

Instant Facts: A woman was walking on a public road when she was struck and killed by a piece of wood that was thrown by a landowner who was blasting a tree that was on his land.

Black Letter Rule: If a landowner cannot use his land in a particular way without causing damage, he must either use his land in some other way or be held responsible for the damage.

Indiana Harbor Belt R.R. Co. v. American Cyanamid Co.

Instant Facts: American Cyanamid (D) loaded a railway car with toxic chemicals. At Indiana Harbor's (P) railroad yard, these chemicals leaked, causing Indiana Harbor (P) to incur cleanup charges.

Black Letter Rule: The manufacture and shipping (as opposed to carrying) of toxic chemicals is not abnormally dangerous.

Fletcher v. Rylands

(Mine Operator) v. *(Mill Owner)*

L.R. 1 Ex. 265 (1866)

IF YOU KEEP SOMETHING ON YOUR LAND THAT ESCAPES AND CAUSES DAMAGE, YOU ARE RESPONSIBLE FOR THE DAMAGE

■ **INSTANT FACTS** A cotton mill operator built a reservoir on land adjacent to an underground mining operation. When the reservoir was filled, the water escaped through some old mine shafts and into the operational mines.

■ **BLACK LETTER RULE** The person who for his own purposes brings on his lands and collects and keeps there anything likely to do mischief if it escapes, must keep it in at his peril and be answerable for all the damage that is the natural consequence of its escape.

■ **PROCEDURAL BASIS**

Appeal from decision requiring proof of fault as a condition of recovery.

■ **FACTS**

Fletcher (P) operated a mine underneath land rented from a landowner. Rylands (D) operated a cotton mill on rented land nearby. Rylands (D) hired some independent contractors to build a reservoir on the land. The land rented by Rylands (D) had at some previous time been mined for coal, the old mine abandoned, and the old mineshafts filled with soil. Although the builders of the reservoir knew of the old mineshafts, they did not know or suspect that the old shafts were connected to the shafts being worked by Fletcher (P). When the reservoir was filled, the water leaked through the old shafts and into the working shafts. The judges below, in a 2–1 decision, held that there could be no recovery without evidence of negligence on Rylands' (D) part.

■ **ISSUE**

Is one who brings something onto his land [water] liable for the damage caused if that thing escapes, even though the escape was not due to his fault or the fault of any of his employees?

■ **DECISION AND RATIONALE**

(Blackburn, J.) Yes. Fletcher (P), though free from all blame, will have to bear the loss unless he can establish some theory under which to hold Rylands (D), who is also free from blame, liable. The question is what obligation the law casts on a person who lawfully brings something on his land that, thought harmless if it remains there, will naturally do mischief it if escapes from the land. It is undisputed that he must take care to keep what was brought onto his land from escaping and damaging his neighbors. The debate is whether he has an absolute duty to keep it in at his peril or whether, as the majority below has decided, he has merely a duty to take all reasonable and prudent precautions to keep it in. We think that the true rule of law is that the person who for his own purposes brings on his lands and collects and keeps there anything likely to do mischief if it escapes must keep it at his peril. If he does not do so, he is prima facie answerable for all the damage that is the natural consequence of its escape. He can excuse himself by showing that the escape was caused by some fault of the complaining neighbor or that it was caused by an act of God, though neither appears to be the case here. This principle of law seems just. Plaintiffs such as Fletcher (P) have been damaged through no fault of their own by the act of defendants such as Rylands (D) bringing onto their property things that were not naturally present. Such defendants should have the burden of making good for the ensuing damage if they cannot manage to confine the thing to their own property. It is true that there are many cases where an innocent party who has been injured by another cannot recover without proof of negligence; for example, where an unruly horse gets on the footpath of a public street and kills a pedestrian, or where a person walking past a warehouse is killed by a falling bale of cotton. However, these cases are distinguishable. Those who travel upon a highway and those who pass near to warehouses where goods are being raised and lowered take upon themselves some known risk of injury. But here, there can be no ground for saying that Fletcher (P) took upon himself any risk of injury. He did not know of Rylands' (D) plan to build the reservoir, nor could Fletcher (P) have stopped Rylands (D) from building the reservoir even if he had known. Reversed.

Analysis:

This case is the origin of the doctrine that is known as strict liability, though the doctrine has evolved into something different than what is seen here. Prior to this case, which imposes absolute liability absent proof of negligence, the plaintiff would have had to pursue his claims under some sort of trespass or negligence theory. However, both trespass and nuisance are intentional torts—they require that the defendant intended to do the thing that caused the problem. In this case, the problem was caused by the water running out of Rylands' (D) artificial pond, which was not something that he intended. Notice also that, even at this early stage, strict liability was not unlimited liability. Thus, if Fletcher (P) had wandered over to the artificial pond and fallen in and drowned, Rylands (D) would not have been strictly liable for the drowning.

■ CASE VOCABULARY

STRICT LIABILITY: Liability without fault; when a party is pursuing activities that are abnormally dangerous or likely to cause injury, that party is liable for the damages even if it took reasonable efforts to prevent the damage.

Rylands v. Fletcher

(Mill Owner) v. *(Mine Operator)*

L.R. 3 H.L. 330 (1868)

ONE WHO PUTS HIS LAND TO ARTIFICIAL USE IS STRICTLY LIABLE FOR THE DAMAGE CAUSED BY THAT USE

■ **INSTANT FACTS** A cotton mill operator built a reservoir on land adjacent to an underground mining operation. When the reservoir was filled, the water escaped through some old mine shafts and into the operational mines.

■ **BLACK LETTER RULE** A landowner is (not) responsible for damage to neighboring land caused by the natural use of his land, but is strictly liable for damage caused by the non-natural use of his land.

■ **PROCEDURAL BASIS**

Appeal from decision imposing strict liability.

■ **FACTS**

[This will sound familiar.] Fletcher (P) operated a mine underneath land rented from a landowner. Rylands (D) operated a cotton mill on rented land nearby. Rylands (D) hired some independent contractors to build a reservoir on the land. The land rented by Rylands (D) had at some previous time been mined for coal, the old mine abandoned, and the old mineshafts filled with soil. Although the builders of the reservoir knew of the old mineshafts, they did not know or suspect that the old shafts were connected to the shafts being worked by Fletcher (P). When the reservoir was filled, the water leaked through the old shafts and into the working shafts. The initial decision was that there could be no recovery without evidence of negligence on Rylands' (D) part. The reviewing court reversed this determination and imposed strict liability upon Rylands (D), holding that anyone who brings something not naturally there onto his land has an absolute duty to keep it in.

■ **ISSUE**

Is a person who puts his land to a non-natural use liable for damage to a neighbor's land that is caused by that use?

■ **DECISION AND RATIONALE**

(Cairns, J.) Yes. One may use his land in the ordinary course of enjoyment for any lawful purpose. If, in the course of the natural use of the land, water accumulates on the land and then, through the laws of nature, passes onto the land of a neighbor, then the neighbor cannot complain of the water. It is the neighbor's burden to guard against the natural flow of water onto his property. However, there is a different result if the owner or occupier of the land puts the land to a non-natural use. If he should introduce onto the land water that would not naturally accumulate there, then he does so at his own peril. If the water escapes onto a neighbor's land and causes injury, then the landowner should be liable. Based on these principles, I would arrive at the same result reached by Mr. Justice Blackburn below, that Rylands (D) is liable. Affirmed.

■ CONCURRENCE

(Cranworth, J.) The rule of law was correctly stated by Mr. Justice Blackburn in the court below. If a person brings or accumulates on his land anything which, if it should escape, may cause damage to his neighbor, he does so at his peril. If it does escape and cause damage, he is responsible no matter what precautions he may have taken to prevent the damage.

Analysis:

Notice the difference between the opinion of Cairns and that of Cranworth (adopting Blackburn's decision below in the case of *Fletcher v. Rylands*). The Cairns opinion speaks of natural and non-natural use, whereas Cranworth spoke of bringing and keeping something not naturally there onto the land. The differences seem subtle, but note that a non-natural *use* reflects the use to which the neighbors put the surrounding land. Thus, strict liability will also depend, in Cairns's opinion, on the community's usage and custom. In the present case, the area where this occurred had traditionally been a place with rich mineral deposits and a lot of mining activity. The Cairns opinion considered the question from something akin to a nuisance point of view—whether the invasion is unreasonable for the circumstances, while the Cranworth opinion is based on more of a trespass theory—whether there is a physical invasion.

Sullivan v. Dunham

(*Decedent's Representative*) v. (*Landowner*)

161 N.Y. 290, 55 N.E. 923 (1900)

THOSE WHO USE DYNAMITE ARE STRICTLY LIABLE FOR DAMAGE CAUSED BY THE BLASTING

■ **INSTANT FACTS** A woman was walking on a public road when she was struck and killed by a piece of wood that was thrown by a landowner who was blasting a tree that was on his land.

■ **BLACK LETTER RULE** If a landowner cannot use his land in a particular way without causing damage, he must either use his land in some other way or be held responsible for the damage.

■ **PROCEDURAL BASIS**

Appeal from a determination that strict liability applies.

■ **FACTS**

Dunham (D) is a landowner who employed two men (D) to dynamite a 60-foot tree that was on his land. Decedent was walking down a nearby road. The blast hurled a fragment of wood 412 feet onto the road, where it stuck and killed decedent. Sullivan (P), as decedent's representative, sued Dunham (D) and the two employees (D) for her wrongful death. The trial court below charged that negligence need not be proven in order to find the men liable for the death and entered a judgment on a verdict for Sullivan (P). The appellate court affirmed.

■ **ISSUE**

Is blasting with dynamite an activity that will expose those doing it to strict liability for any damage caused?

■ **DECISION AND RATIONALE**

(Vann, J.) Yes. The question presented on this appeal is whether one who, for a lawful purpose and without negligence or want of skill, explodes a blast upon his own land and thereby causes a piece of wood to fall upon a person lawfully traveling in a public highway is liable for the injury thus inflicted. There are many cases establishing strict liability for blasting. The leading case involves a defendant who used blasting to dig a canal on his own land, and in so doing the blasts threw fragments of rock against the plaintiff's house, which stood upon neighboring land. [*Hay v. Cohoes Co.*] Although there was no proof of negligence, the defendant was held liable for the injury sustained by his blasting. The court in *Hay* reasoned that the lawful use of one's land is not an absolute right, but is qualified and limited by the higher right of others to the lawful possession of their property. If a landowner cannot use his land in a particular way without damaging his neighbor's land, he must either use his land in some other way or be held responsible for the damages that he causes. While *Hay* addressed the case of trespass to land, the present case is one of trespass to a person. As the safety of a person is more sacred than the safety of property, the principle in *Hay* should govern our decision here unless it is no longer good law. In opposition to *Hay* is the case of [*Losee v. Buchanan*,] where it was held that one who, without negligence, operates a steam boiler upon his own premises is not liable to his neighbor for the damages caused by the accidental explosion thereof. The *Losee* court, however, distinguished

Hay because the boiler explosion was accidental, whereas blasting is the voluntary setting free of a tremendous force, which by its very nature casts rocks about. We believe that *Hay* is sound and valuable authority. It rests upon the principle that the safety of property generally is superior in right to a particular use of a single piece of property by its owner. It renders all property more secure by preventing one landowner from doing injury to his neighbors. It makes human life safer by tending to prevent a landowner from casting part of his land upon another person who is where he has a right to be. It lessens hardship by placing absolute liability upon the one who causes the injury. The accident in this case was a misfortune to Dunham (D) and his employees (D), but it was an even greater misfortune to the young woman who was killed. The safety of travelers upon the public highway is more important to the state than the improvement of one piece of property, by special method, is to its owner.

Analysis:

Ultrahazardous activities are those that are especially dangerous and cannot be made safe even with the exercise of the utmost care. Strict liability would only lie, however, if the activity were not something that is commonly done in that particular community. The rationale is not necessarily to discourage those activities. Rather, it is to make them pay their way—the person who blasts trees with dynamite must pay for the damage that invariably results from blasting trees. The newer rule for determining whether strict liability will lie is a balancing test contained in the Restatement (Second) of Torts. Factors to consider in determining whether to impose strict liability include the high risk of the activity, the likelihood of great harm, whether the harm can be avoided by reasonable care, whether the activity is uncommon, and whether it is inappropriate at that particular site. Liability may be avoided if the value to the community outweighs the danger inherent in the activity. The factors, however, do not have equal weight and need not all be present in order to impose strict liability. Examples of activities that commonly invoke strict liability are the use and storage of explosives, the use and storage of toxic and poisonous substances, and keeping wild animals.

Indiana Harbor Belt R.R. Co. v. American Cyanamid Co.

(*Injured*) v. (*Tortfeasor*)

916 F.2d 1174 (7th Cir. 1990)

MANUFACTURING AND SHIPPING TOXIC CHEMICALS IS NOT ABNORMALLY DANGEROUS

■ **INSTANT FACTS** American Cyanamid (D) loaded a railway car with toxic chemicals. At Indiana Harbor's (P) railroad yard, these chemicals leaked, causing Indiana Harbor (P) to incur cleanup charges.

■ **BLACK LETTER RULE** The manufacture and shipping (as opposed to carrying) of toxic chemicals is not abnormally dangerous.

■ **PROCEDURAL BASIS**

Appeal from judgment in action for damages.

■ **FACTS**

American Cyanamid (D) loaded a railway car with Acrylonitrile, a toxic chemical, to ship to its New Jersey plant. The car stopped at Indiana Harbor's (P) railroad yard for purposes of switching to another train. While parked in Indiana Harbor's (P) yard, the car began to leak, and 4,000 of the 20,000 gallons spilled. Concerned that there was contamination of the soil, the Illinois Department of Environmental Protection ordered Indiana Harbor (P) to take decontamination measures costing $981,022.75. Indiana Harbor (P) is sung American Cyanamid (D) for this amount.

■ **ISSUE**

Is the manufacture and shipping (as opposed to carrying) of toxic chemicals an abnormally dangerous activity?

■ **DECISION AND RATIONALE**

(Posner, J.) No. Since this is a diversity case, Illinois law governs. The parties agree that the Illinois Supreme Court would look to the restatement for guidance in resolving this novel issue. According to the restatement, an abnormally dangerous activity meets the following criteria: (1) the risk of harm is great, (2) the harm that would occur if the risk materialized is great, (3) such accidents could not be prevented by the exercise of due care, (4) the activity is not a matter of common usage, (5) the activity is inappropriate to the place in which it occurs and (6) the value to the community of the activity does not outweigh the unavoidable risk. The restatement imposes strict liability in any case that meets this test because the common law doctrine of negligence is inadequate in such cases. For example, the negligence doctrine is inadequate to deter accidents if due care will not prevent such accidents. In such cases, defendants will cause accidents, but will not be made to pay for the accidents or will have no incentive to avoid the accidents. The elements of the restatement test are designed to mitigate this by imposing strict liability on defendants who, for example, fail to move such activities to less populated or more appropriate areas (element no. 5). We now look to the facts of this case. First, the district court ruled that manufacturing and shipping Acrylonitrile is abnormally dangerous merely because it was on a certain list of hazardous materials. This is too broad a definition because it would make shippers and carriers of many chemicals strictly liable. Moreover, there is no reason why a negligence test will not work here—due care would have prevented this accident. Put another way, it was not the inherent dangerousness of Acrylonitrile that caused this accident, but someone's negligence which caused a leak. Plaintiff argues that there should be strict liability because the potential harm was great—what if all 20,000 gallons were spilled? But for an activity to be deemed to be abnormally dangerous, we must examine all factors of the restatement test, and plaintiff's argument overlooks the fact that shipping chemicals is very valuable to the community. Thus, manufacturing Acrylonitrile is not abnormally dangerous. Judgment reversed.

Analysis:

Compare this case to *Rylands v. Fletcher* and other cases involving dangerous substances. In those cases, there was liability because there was indeed an abnormally dangerous activity. In this case, Indiana Harbor (P) attempted to hold American Cyanamid (D) liable not for the dangerous activity of storage of Acrylonitrile, but for the manufacturer of Acrylonitrile. The manufacture of Acrylonitrile may be an abnormally dangerous activity (which the court did not decide), but American Cyanamid (D) was not manufacturing Acrylonitrile when this accident occurred. And hauling Acrylonitrile may be an abnormally dangerous activity, but American Cyanamid (D) was not the hauler in this case.

■ CASE VOCABULARY

CARRIER: A person or entity who hauls a product to an intermediate or final destination.

MANUFACTURER: A person or entity who creates a product for sale.

SHIPPER: A person or entity who prepares a product for hauling.

CHAPTER EIGHT

Liability for Defective Products

MacPherson v. Buick Motor Co.

Instant Facts: MacPherson (P), a purchaser of a car, was permitted to sue the manufacturer for negligence in spite of the lack of privity of contract.

Black Letter Rule: A manufacturer owes a duty to the user of the product even though the user did not purchase the product directly from the manufacturer.

Escola v. Coca Cola Bottling Co. of Fresno

Instant Facts: Bottling Co. was sued for negligence by Escola (P) for injuries sustained due to exploding bottle, and concurring opinion advocated strict liability for manufacturer.

Black Letter Rule: A non-manufacturer bottling company, which has exclusive control over bottles, can be held liable in negligence for an exploding bottle, even though it is not clear why the bottle exploded, based upon the doctrine of res ipsa loquitur.

Soule v. General Motors Corporation

Instant Facts: Soule (P) injured in car accident sued GM (D) for design defect, and jury was erroneously instructed on "consumer expectation" test, rather than "risk-benefit" test.

Black Letter Rule: Use of the consumer expectations test is not appropriate where the evidence does not permit an inference that the product's performance did not meet the minimum safety expectations of its ordinary users, and the jury should therefore be instructed on the alternative risk-benefit test of design defect.

Camacho v. Honda Motor Co. Ltd.

Instant Facts: Camacho (P), injured while riding his motorcycle, sued Honda (D) the manufacturer for design defect in not providing crash bars on the motorcycle.

Black Letter Rule: Where the danger of the product is open and obvious, the danger-utility test is the appropriate design defect test to use rather than the consumer expectation test.

Hood v. Ryobi America Corporation

Instant Facts: Hood (P), injured while using saw without a guard, argued that manufacturer's warnings were not specific enough concerning blade detachment if used without guards.

Black Letter Rule: A manufacturer of a product need not warn the user of every mishap or source of injury that could possibly flow from the product; rather, the warning need only be one that is reasonable under the circumstances.

Edwards v. Basel Pharmaceuticals

Instant Facts: Wife sued for husband's wrongful death after he died from smoking while wearing a nicotine patch, and contended that the manufacturer should have warned her husband of risk, not just the doctor who prescribed the patch.

Black Letter Rule: When the FDA requires warnings be given directly to the patient with a prescribed drug, an exception to the "learned intermediary doctrine" occurs, and the manufacturer is not automatically shielded from liability by properly warning the prescribing physician.

Vassallo v. Baxter Healthcare Corporation

Instant Facts: Breast implant manufacturer, Baxter Healthcare Corporation (D) challenged state's law concerning the duty to warn even though the risk was not known at the time of sale.

Black Letter Rule: A manufacturer need only warn of risks that were reasonably foreseeable when the product was sold, or that could have been discovered through testing prior to marketing the product.

General Motors Corporation v. Sanchez

Instant Facts: Manufacturer, General Motors Corp. (D), sought to defend wrongful death action based upon deceased's failure to properly park vehicle in "Park," which caused it to slip out of gear and crush him.

Black Letter Rule: A consumer has no duty to discover or guard against a product defect, but a consumer's conduct other than the mere failure to discover or guard against a product defect is subject to comparative responsibility.

Jones v. Ryobi, Ltd.

Instant Facts: Employee Jones (P) was denied recovery in product liability action where the product was modified by a third party after it was sold.

Black Letter Rule: When a third party's modification makes a safe product unsafe, the seller is relieved of liability even if the modification is foreseeable.

Liriano v. Hobart Corp.

Instant Facts: Liriano (P) sued Hobart Corp. (D), the manufacturer of a meat grinder, for failure to warn, although the grinder had been modified post-sale by a third party who removed its safety guard.

Black Letter Rule: Manufacturer liability for failure to warn may exist in cases where the substantial modification defense would preclude liability on a design defect theory.

Royer v. Catholic Medical Center

Instant Facts: Patient who received a defective prosthetic knee sued the hospital for strict product design liability and hospital argued that it was not engaged in the business of selling goods

Black Letter Rule: A health care provider, who in the course of rendering health care services supplies a prosthetic device to be implanted into a patient, is not "engaged in the business of selling" prostheses for purposes of strict products liability.

East River Steamship Corp. v. Transamerica Delaval Inc.

Instant Facts: East River (P) sued in tort to recover cost of repair and lost income from defective turbine on supertanker.

Black Letter Rule: A cause of action in tort may not be stated when a defective product purchased in a commercial transaction malfunctions, injuring only the product itself and causing purely economic loss.

MacPherson v. Buick Motor Co.

(*Consumer*) v. (*Auto Manufacturer*)

217 N.Y. 382, 111 N.E. 1050 (1916)

PRIVITY OF CONTRACT NO LONGER REQUIRED IN ORDER FOR CONSUMER TO SUE MANUFAC-
TURER OF DEFECTIVE PRODUCT

■ **INSTANT FACTS** MacPherson (P), a purchaser of a car, was permitted to sue the manufacturer for negligence in spite of the lack of privity of contract.

■ **BLACK LETTER RULE** A manufacturer owes a duty to the user of the product even though the user did not purchase the product directly from the manufacturer.

■ **PROCEDURAL BASIS**

Appeal to state's highest court from affirming of judgment following jury trial in action for negligence for personal injuries.

■ **FACTS**

MacPherson (P) bought an automobile from a retail dealer, who had bought it from Buick Motor Co. (D), the manufacturer. While MacPherson (P) was in the car, it suddenly collapsed, throwing him from the car and causing him [and the car] injuries. One of the wheels was made of defective wood, but Buick (D) did not make the wheel and purchased it from another manufacturer. The evidence disclosed that the wheel's defects could have been discovered by reasonable inspection, but no inspection had occurred. MacPherson (P) sued Buick (D) for negligence.

■ **ISSUE**

Does a manufacturer owe a duty to the user of its product when the user did not purchase the product directly from the manufacturer?

■ **DECISION AND RATIONALE**

(Cardozo, J.) Yes. We hold that a manufacturer owes a duty to the user of a product even though the user did not purchase the product directly from the manufacturer. In *Thomas v. Winchester* we held that a consumer who consumed falsely labeled poison sold first to a druggist and then to the consumer by the druggist could recover damages from the original seller because the defendant's negligence put human life in imminent danger. In *Devlin v. Smith,* a contractor built a scaffold for a painter. The painter's servants were injured by the scaffold and were allowed to sue the contractor because he knew that if improperly constructed, the scaffold was a most dangerous trap, and thus he owed them a duty. In *Statler v. George A. Ray Mfg. Co.,* the manufacturer of a large coffee urn, installed in a restaurant, was held liable when it exploded and injured customers, because it was inherently dangerous if not properly constructed. We hold that the principle of *Thomas v. Winchester* is not limited to poisons, explosives, and things of like nature. We hold that if the nature of a thing is such that it is reasonably certain to place life and limb in peril when negligently made, it is then a thing of danger. Its nature gives warning of the consequences to be expected. If to the element of danger there is added knowledge that the things will be used by persons other than the purchaser, and used without new tests, then, irrespective of contract, the manufacturer of this thing of danger is under a duty to make it carefully. We turn to the facts of this case. The nature of an automobile gives warning of probable danger if its construction is defective. Unless its wheels were sound and strong, injury was almost certain. [That's a fact.] Buick (D) knew the danger, and it knew also that persons other than the buyer would use the car. Buick (D) would have us say that the dealer to whom it sold the car was the one person to whom it was under a legal duty to protect. In England, the limits of the rule are still unsettled. *Winterbottom v. Wright* is often cited. The defendant provided a mail coach to carry mail bags. The coach broke down from latent defects in its construction. The defendant was not the manufacturer and the court held that he was not liable for the passenger's injuries. We find that there is nothing anomalous in a rule which imposes upon A, who has contracted with B, a duty to C and D and others according as he knows or does not know that the subject-matter of the contract is intended for their use. Finally, we do not think that Buick (D) was absolved from a duty of inspection because it bought the wheels from a reputable manufacturer. It, as the manufacturer of automobiles, was responsible for the finished product. It was not at liberty to put the finished product on the market without subjecting the component parts to ordinary and simple tests. [Buick (D) has run out of defenses.] Judgment is affirmed.

Analysis:

This landmark case establishes liability in negligence cases even though there is an absence of privity of contract. MacPherson (P) did not have a contract with Buick (D), the manufacturer, because he purchased the car from the retail dealer. Nevertheless, MacPherson (P) was able to recover against Buick (D) for his injuries because (1) Buick (D) negligently failed to inspect, (2) it knew that a defectively constructed automobile was a probable danger, and (3) it knew that its cars would be used by persons other than the buyer. As Justice Cardozo noted, there were some earlier American cases that permitted suits by those not in privity of contract, but they were often limited to products that were imminently dangerous to life such as poisons, explosives, and deadly weapons. This decision was accepted throughout the United States.

■ CASE VOCABULARY

CHARGE: Referring to "charge the jury" where the judge instructs the jury on the law.

Escola v. Coca Cola Bottling Co. of Fresno

(*Injured Waitress*) v. (*Bottling Company*)
24 Cal.2d 453, 150 P.2d 436 (1944)

MANUFACTURER'S STRICT LIABILITY IS URGED FOR DEFECTIVE PRODUCTS

■ **INSTANT FACTS** Bottling Co. was sued for negligence by Escola (P) for injuries sustained due to exploding bottle, and concurring opinion advocated strict liability for manufacturer.

■ **BLACK LETTER RULE** A non-manufacturer bottling company, which has exclusive control over bottles, can be held liable in negligence for an exploding bottle, even though it is not clear why the bottle exploded, based upon the doctrine of res ipsa loquitur.

■ **PROCEDURAL BASIS**

Appeal to State Supreme Court from affirming of a judgment in a negligence action for personal injuries.

■ **FACTS**

Escola (P), a waitress, was injured when a soda bottle broke in her hand as she moved it from the case to the refrigerator, although she had handled it carefully. Coca Cola Bottling Co. of Fresno (Bottling Co.) (D) had used pressure to bottle carbonated beverages. An engineer from the bottle manufacturer testified at trial about how bottles are tested and referred to the tests as "pretty near" infallible. Escola (P) sued Bottling Co. (D) for negligence and obtained a judgment, benefiting from res ipsa loquitur. The matter was appealed to the California's Supreme Court [and it took the opportunity to talk about holding the manufacturer liable even though it was not sued].

■ **ISSUE**

Can a non-manufacturer bottling company, which has exclusive control over bottles, be held liable in negligence for an exploding bottle, even though it is not clear why the bottle exploded?

■ **DECISION AND RATIONALE**

(Justice Not Named) Yes. We hold that a non-manufacturer bottling company, which has exclusive control over bottles, can be held liable in negligence for an exploding bottle, based upon the doctrine of res ipsa loquitur, even though it is not clear why the bottle exploded. Because of the almost infallible tests that the bottles are subjected to by the manufacturer, it is not likely that they contain defects when delivered to the bottler that are not discoverable by visual inspection. Both new and used bottles are filled and distributed by Bottling Co. (D). The used bottles are not again subjected to tests, and it may be inferred that defects not discoverable by visual inspection do not develop in bottles after they are manufactured. If such defects do occur in used bottles there is a duty upon the bottler to make appropriate tests before they are refilled. Although it is not clear in this case whether the explosion was caused by an excessive charge or a defect in the glass, there is a sufficient showing that neither cause would ordinarily have been present if due care had been used. Further, Bottling Co. (D) had exclusive control over both the charging and inspection of the bottles. Thus, all the requirements necessary to entitled Escola (P) to rely on the doctrine of res ipsa loquitur to supply an inference of negligence are present. [After reading the concurring opinion that follows, it's too bad that Escola (P) did not sue the manufacturer as well.]

■ CONCURRENCE

(Traynor, J.) I believe that the manufacturer's negligence should no longer be singled out as the basis of a plaintiff's right to recover in cases like the present one. In my opinion, it should now be recognized that a manufacturer incurs an absolute liability when an article that he had placed on the market, knowing that it is to be used without inspection, proves to have a defect that causes injury to human beings. *MacPherson v. Buick Motor Co.* established the principle that, irrespective of privity of contract, the manufacturer is responsible for an injury caused by such an article to any person who comes in lawful contact with it. It is to the public interest to discourage the marketing of products having defects that are a menace to the public. If such products nevertheless find their way into the market it is to the public interest to place the responsibility for whatever injury they may cause upon the manufacturer, who, even if he is not negligent in the manufacture of the product, is responsible for its reaching the market. The injury from a defective product does not become a matter of indifference because the defect arises from causes other than the negligence of the manufacturer, such as negligence of a submanufacturer of a component part whose defects could not be revealed by inspection or unknown causes that even by the device of res ipsa loquitur cannot be classified as negligence of the manufacturer. Justice Cardozo's reasoning in *MacPherson* recognized the injured person as the real party in interest and disposed of the theory that the manufacturer's liability should apply only to the immediate purchaser. It thus paves the way for a standard of liability that would make the manufacturer guarantee the safety of his product even when there is no negligence. This standard of liability has been extended to consumers of food products, because the right of a consumer injured by unwholesome food does not depend upon the intricacies of the law of sales and that the warranty of the manufacturer to the consumer in absence of privity of contract rests on public policy. There is no reason to differentiate the dangers in defective consumers' goods from the dangers of defective food products. The manufacturer's obligation to the consumer cannot be escaped because the marketing of a product has become so complicated that intermediaries are required. There is greater reason to impose liability on the manufacturer than on the retailer who is but a conduit of a product that he is not himself able to test.

Analysis:

This case is important for its concurring opinion by Justice Traynor. He advocates strict liability for manufacturers of defective products. However, the majority affirmed the judgment for Escola (P) against the Bottling Co. (D) based upon a theory of negligence, supported by the doctrine of res ipsa loquitur. Justice Traynor suggests that absolute liability should be imposed in tort, not as a matter of warranty, which implies a contractual liability with privity limitations. As the *Notes and Questions* section following this case indicates, nineteen years after this case was decided, Justice Traynor, writing for a unanimous court in *Greenman v. Yuba Power Products, Inc.*, concluded that a "manufacturer is strictly liable in tort when an article he places on the market, knowing that it is to be used without inspection for defects, proves to have a defect that causes injury to a human being." In other words, manufacturers are strictly liable for their defective products based upon tort law, rather than an implied warranty based on contract law.

■ CASE VOCABULARY

ABSOLUTE LIABILITY: Also called strict liability, which means liability without fault, and not dependent upon negligence or intent to injure.

RES IPSA LOQUITUR: Latin for, "the thing speaks for itself," and a doctrine used in tort providing that the mere fact that something happened establishes an inference of negligence.

Soule v. General Motors Corporation

(Injured Driver) v. *(Auto Manufacturer)*

8 Cal.4th 548, 882 P.2d 298, 34 Cal.Rptr.2d 607 (1994)

THE "CONSUMER EXPECTATIONS" TEST AND THE "RISK-BENEFIT" TEST ARE ALTERNATIVE TESTS FOR THE JURY TO USE IN DETERMINING DESIGN DEFECTS

■ **INSTANT FACTS** Soule (P) injured in car accident sued GM (D) for design defect, and jury was erroneously instructed on "consumer expectation" test, rather than "risk-benefit" test.

■ **BLACK LETTER RULE** Use of the consumer expectations test is not appropriate where the evidence does not permit an inference that the product's performance did not meet the minimum safety expectations of its ordinary users, and the jury should therefore be instructed on the alternative risk-benefit test of design defect.

■ **PROCEDURAL BASIS**

Petition to State Supreme Court following affirming of judgment in action for strict liability seeking damages for personal injuries.

■ **FACTS**

Soule's (P) ankles were badly injured in an accident involving her Camaro automobile, built by General Motors. She sued General Motors Corporation (GM) (D) asserting strict liability in tort for, among other things, a defectively designed product—the wheel bracket and configuration of the frame—which caused the wheel to break free, collapse rearward, and smashed the floorboard into her feet. [Did Soule (P) believe that her ankles should not have been injured in the crash?] GM (D) denied any design defect and asserted that the force of the collision was the sole cause of Soule's (P) injuries. At trial, the court instructed the jury on an "ordinary consumer expectations" test. The jury found that the Camaro contained a "defect (of unspecified nature), which was a legal cause of Soule's enhanced injury. It found that she was at fault for not wearing a seat belt, but it was not a legal cause of her enhanced injuries. The jury awarded Soule (P) $1.65 million. [The jury too felt GM (D) should have protected Soule's (P) ankles.] The court of appeal affirmed, and GM petitioned the California Supreme Court for review.

■ **ISSUE**

Is use of the consumer expectations test appropriate where the evidence does not permit an inference that the product's performance did not meet the minimum safety expectations of its ordinary users?

■ **DECISION AND RATIONALE**

(Baxter, J.) No. Use of the consumer expectations test is not appropriate where the evidence does not permit an inference that the product's performance did not meet the minimum safety expectations of its ordinary users, and the jury should therefore be instructed on the alternative risk-benefit test of design defect. We hold that the trial court erred by giving an "ordinary consumer expectations" instruction in this case. However, the error was harmless and does not warrant reversal. In *Barker v. Lull Engineering Co., Inc.*, we offered two alternative ways to prove a design defect: The purposes, behaviors, and dangers of certain products are commonly understood by those who ordinarily use them, and the ordinary users or consumers of a product may have reasonable, widely accepted minimum expectations about the circumstances under which it should perform safely. In some cases, the ordinary knowledge as to the product's characteristics may permit an inference that the product did not perform as safely as it should. (Under *Barker's* alternative test,) a product is defective if its design embodies excessive preventable danger, that is, unless the benefits of the design outweigh the risk of danger inherent in such design. The consumer expectations test is thus reserved for cases in which the everyday experience of the product's users permits a conclusion that the product's design violated minimum safety assumptions, and is defective regardless of expert opinion about the merits of the design. It follows that where the minimum safety of a product is within the common knowledge of lay jurors, expert witnesses may not be used to demonstrate what an ordinary consumer would or should expect. Accordingly, jury instructions are misleading and incorrect if they allow a jury to avoid this risk-benefit analysis in a case where it is required. Instructions based on the ordinary consumer expectations prong of *Barker* are not appropriate where, as a matter of law, the evidence would not support a jury verdict on that theory. Whenever that is so, the jury must be instructed solely on the alternative risk-benefit theory of design defect. We reject GM's (D) assertion that the consumer expectations tests should be abolished. [Not in California anyway.] We agree that the jury in this case should not have been instructed on ordinary consumer expectations because Soule's (P) theory of design defect was one of technical and mechanical detail. An ordinary consumer cannot reasonably expect that a car's frame, suspension, or interior will be designed to remain intact in any and all accidents. Nor would ordinary experience and understanding inform such a consumer how safely an automobile's design should perform under the esoteric circumstances of the collision at issue here. Both parties assumed expert testimony was necessary to illuminate how the car's design should perform under the circumstances of the collision that occurred. Therefore, the ordinary consumer expectations test to determine design defect was improper. Nevertheless, we hold that the error was harmless because it is not reasonably probable GM (D) would have obtained a more favorable result in its absence. The consumer expectations theory was never emphasized during the trial, and the case was tried on the assumption that the design defect was a matter of technical debate, focusing on expert opinions. [In other words, there was more to the theory than just protecting Soule's (P) ankles.] The error in instructions did not cause actual prejudice. Accordingly, the judgement is affirmed.

Analysis:

The court's opinion demonstrates why there is a need for an alternative design defect test beyond the consumer expectations test. However, the court was unwilling to abolish the consumer expectations test entirely as suggested by GM (D). (Under the alternative risk-benefit test, the injured person would be able to show a defective product if its design embodies excessive preventable danger, unless the benefits of the design outweigh the risk of danger inherent in such design. The court relied upon its decision in *Barker v. Lull Engineering Co., Inc.* in rendering its opinion in this case.

■ CASE VOCABULARY

AMICUS CURIAE BRIEF: A "friend of the court" brief submitted by interested non-parties.

CONSUMER EXPECTATIONS TEST: A product may be found defective in design if it can be shown that the product failed to perform as safely as an ordinary consumer would expect when used in an intended or reasonably foreseeable manner.

RISK-BENEFIT TEST: A product may be found defective if its design embodies excessive preventable danger, that is, unless the benefits of the design outweigh the risk of danger inherent in such design.

SPECIAL INSTRUCTION: An instruction given to the jury, the content of which is proposed by a party, rather than a standard instruction previously approved by a judicial council.

Camacho v. Honda Motor Co., Ltd.

(Motorcycle Rider) v. *(Manufacturer)*

741 P.2d 1240 (Colo. 1987), cert. dismissed, 485 U.S. 901, 108 S.Ct. 1067 (1988)

COURT REJECTS CONSUMER EXPECTATION DESIGN DEFECT TEST IN FAVOR OF DANGER-UTILITY TEST

■ **INSTANT FACTS** Camacho (P), injured while riding his motorcycle, sued Honda (D) the manufacturer for design defect in not providing crash bars on the motorcycle.

■ **BLACK LETTER RULE** Where the danger of the product is open and obvious, the danger-utility test is the appropriate design defect test to use rather than the consumer expectation test.

■ **PROCEDURAL BASIS**

Appeal to State's Supreme Court from court of appeal's affirming of summary judgment in product liability suit seeking damages for personal injuries.

■ **FACTS**

Camacho (P) sued Honda Motor Co. Ltd. (D) and others in the chain of distribution under a defective product strict liability theory for injuries sustained in a motorcycle collision, alleging that Honda (D) failed to make "crash bars" available on its motorcycles. The evidence showed that effective leg protection devices were available and in use by other manufacturers at the time Camacho (P) purchased his motorcycle, and would have reduced or completely avoided Camacho's (P) injuries had they been installed on his motorcycle. The trial court granted Honda (D) summary judgment, and the court of appeal affirmed on the ground that the danger would have been fully anticipated by or within the contemplation of the ordinary user or consumer. [In other words, Camacho (P) should have expected to eat it on a motorcycle.] Camacho (P) appealed to the State's Supreme Court.

■ **ISSUE**

Is the danger-utility test the appropriate design defect test to use if the danger of the product is open and obvious?

■ **DECISION AND RATIONALE**

(Kirshbaum, J.) Yes. We hold that where the danger of the product is open and obvious, the danger-utility test is the appropriate design defect test to use rather than the consumer expectation test. We begin our analysis by adopting the crashworthiness doctrine, which provides that a motor vehicle manufacturer may be liable in negligence or strict liability for injuries sustained in a motor vehicle accident where a manufacturing or design defect, though not the cause of the accident, caused or enhanced the injuries. The landmark case that first recognized this doctrine, *Larsen v. General Motors Corp.*, held that the automobile manufacturer had a duty of reasonable care in the design and manufacture of its product, including a duty to use reasonable care to minimize the injurious effects of a foreseeable collision by employing commonsense safety features. Honda (D) argues that motorcycles are inherently dangerous motor vehicles that cannot be made perfectly crashworthy and, therefore, motorcycle manufacturers should be free of liability for injuries not actually caused by a defect in the design or manufacture of the motorcycle. [But cars are inherently dangerous as well and they are subject to the crashworthiness doctrine.] In view of the important goal of encouraging maximum development of reasonable, cost-efficient safety features in the manufacture of all products, the argument that motorcycle manufacturers should be exempt from liability under the crashworthiness doctrine because serious injury to users of that product is foreseeable must be rejected. This court has adopted the strict products liability doctrine set forth in the Restatement of Torts (Second) § 402A. The trial court and court of appeals applied the consumer contemplation test in dismissing Camacho's (P) claim. Honda (D) asserted that a motorcycle designed without leg protection devices cannot be deemed "in a defective condition unreasonably dangerous to the user" because the risk of motorcycle accidents is foreseeable to every ordinary consumer and because it is obvious that motorcycles do not generally offer leg protection devices as a standard item. Honda (D) relies upon comment *i* to section 402A, which provides that, "[t]he article sold must be dangerous to an extent beyond that which would be contemplated by the ordinary consumer who purchases it, with the ordinary knowledge common to the community as to its characteristics." The consumer contemplation concept embodied in this comment, while illustrative of a particular problem, does not provide a satisfactory test for determining whether particular products are in a defective condition unreasonably dangerous to the user or consumer. A rejection of design defect claims in all cases wherein the danger may be open and obvious thus contravenes sound public policy by encouraging design strategies that perpetuate the manufacture of dangerous products. We have previously recognized that exclusive reliance upon consumer expectations is an inappropriate means of determining whether a product is unreasonably dangerous under section 402A where both the unreasonableness of the danger in the design defect and the efficiency of alternative designs in achieving a reasonable degree of safety must be defined primarily by technical, scientific information. We noted that the following factors are of value in balancing the attendant risks and benefits of a product to determine whether a product design is unreasonably dangerous: (1) The usefulness and desirability of the product—its utility to the user and to the public as a whole; (2) The safety aspects of the product—the likelihood that it will cause injury and the probable seriousness of the injury; (3) The availability of a substitute product which would meet the same need and not be as unsafe; (4) The manufacturer's ability to eliminate the unsafe character of the product without impairing its usefulness or making it too expensive to maintain its utility; (5) The user's ability to avoid danger by the exercise of care in the use of the product; (6) The user's anticipated awareness of the dangers inherent in the product and their avoidability because of general public knowledge of the obvious condition of the product, or of the existence of suitable warnings or instructions; and, (7) The feasibility, on the part of the manufacturer, of spreading the loss by setting the price of the product or carrying liability insurance. The question in this case is whether, under the crashworthiness doctrine, the degree of inherent dangerousness could or should have been significantly reduced. The evidences shows that Honda (D) could have provided crash bars at an acceptable cost without impairing the motorcycle's utility or substantially altering its nature and Honda's (D) failure to do so rendered the vehicles unreasonably dangerous under the applicable danger-utility test. Because the factual conclusions reached by the expert witnesses are in dispute, summary judgment as to whether the design strategies of Honda (D) were reasonable was improper. Judgment reversed and case remanded.

■ **DISSENT**

(Vollack, J.) I believe that the consumer contemplation test is the appropriate test for determining whether a product has a design defect causing it to be in a defective condition that is unreasonably dangerous. An ordinary consumer is necessarily aware that motorcycles can be dangerous. Camacho (P) had the choice to purchase other motorcycles by other manufacturers, which carried additional safety features, and instead elected to purchase this particular motorcycle and ride it without leg protection devices. I also believe that the risk benefit test is not the appropriate test to use in this case.

Analysis:

The court here adopted the danger-utility (or risk-utility) test. Under this test, the risks of the product as designed are balanced against the costs of making the product safer. The seven factors cited by the court to assist in balancing the risks and benefits of a product are taken from an article written by Dean John W. Wade, and are often used by courts as guidance for determining whether a product design is unreasonably dangerous. Note that the court is not making a finding that the motorcycle's design was unreasonably dangerous. Rather, the court reversed summary judgment in favor of Honda (D) in order for the matter to be returned to the trial court for further consideration consistent with the court's views. The court commented that the question to be determined in this case is whether the degree of inherent dangerousness of a motorcycle could or should have been significantly reduced by a leg protection device.

■ CASE VOCABULARY

CRASHWORTHINESS DOCTRINE: Liability may be imposed upon manufacturer where a manufacturing or design defect, though not the cause of the accident, caused or enhanced the injuries.

Hood v. Ryobi America Corporation

(User of Saw) v. *(Manufacturer)*

181 F.3d 608 (4th Cir. 1999)

MULTIPLE WARNINGS IN THE OWNER'S MANUAL AND AFFIXED TO THE PRODUCT ARE ADEQUATE, IN SPITE OF NO SPECIFIC WARNING ADVISING HOW AN INJURY CAN OCCUR

■ **INSTANT FACTS** Hood (P), injured while using saw without a guard, argued that manufacturer's warnings were not specific enough concerning blade detachment if used without guards.

■ **BLACK LETTER RULE** A manufacturer of a product need not warn the user of every mishap or source of injury that could possibly flow from the product; rather, the warning need only be one that is reasonable under the circumstances.

■ **PROCEDURAL BASIS**

Appeal from summary judgment in product liability suit for damages for personal injuries.

■ **FACTS**

Hood (P) purchased a miter saw manufactured by Ryobi America Corporation (Ryobi) (D). The operator's manual and the saw itself contained a number of warnings stating that the user should operate the saw only with the blade guards in place. Hood (P), realizing that the blade guards prevented the saw blade from passing completely through the piece of wood, removed the blade guards. He continued to work the saw with the blade exposed, when in the middle of a cut, the spinning saw blade flew off the saw and back toward Hood (P), partially amputating his thumb and lacerating his leg. Hood (P) admitted that he read the warning labels. [Why did he remove the guard you ask?] He claims, however, that he believed that the blade guards were intended solely to prevent a user's clothing or fingers from coming into contact with the saw blade. He contends that he was unaware that removing the blade guards would permit the spinning blade to detach from the saw. He sued Ryobi (D) for failure to warn and defective design under theories of strict liability, negligence, and breach of warranty. The district court granted Ryobi's (D) motion for summary judgment, finding that in the face of adequate warnings, Hood (P) had altered the saw and caused his own injury. Hood (P) appealed.

■ **ISSUE**

Must a manufacturer of a product warn the user of every mishap or source of injury that could possibly flow from the product?

■ **DECISION AND RATIONALE**

(Wilkinson, J.) No. A manufacturer may be liable for placing a product on the market that bears inadequate instructions and warnings. Hood (P) contends that the warnings were insufficiently specific, in that they were inadequate in failing to explain that removing the guards would lead to blade detachment. The law of our State does not require an encyclopedic warning. A warning need only be one that is reasonable under the circumstances. The manufacturer need not warn of every mishap or source of injury that the mind can imagine flowing from the product. Moreover, some commentators have observed that the proliferation of label detail threatens to undermine the effectiveness of warnings

---

altogether. Well-meaning attempts to warn of every possible accident lead over time to voluminous yet impenetrable labels—too prolix to read and too technical to understand. Ryobi's (D) warnings are clear and unequivocal. Most of them direct the user not to operate the saw with the blade guards removed, and two of them declare that "serious injury" could result from doing so. [But why not mention flying blades as well?] In addition, most consumers do not detach the safety feature before using the saw—Hood (P) could only identify one 15-year old incident similar to his. We hold that the warnings are adequate as a matter of law. Finally, we reject Hood's (P) claim of design defect as well. Affirmed.

Analysis:

In this case, the issue was not whether a warning was required, but whether the multiple warnings in the owner's manual and affixed to the saw were adequate. The court held that because there were multiple warnings informing the user not to operate the saw without the guards in place, use of the saw without the guard could be expected to result in serious injury. Hood (P) made a good argument that he believed that the blade guards were intended to prevent the user's clothing or fingers from coming into contact with the blade, and that he was unaware that removal of the guards could cause the blade to detach from the saw and "fly off." In other words, Hood (P) was willing to take the risk that operating the saw without the guard could cause injury if his fingers or clothing came into contact with the blade, but he was not adequately warned about the possibility of a flying blade. The court rejected Hood's (P) theory, finding that the warnings were clear, unmistakable, and prominent, and were sufficient to accomplish their purpose—i.e. remove the guard and injury will occur. Many courts hold that the adequacy of the warning is an issue for the jury, but this court felt that it was a clear case that could be ruled upon as a matter of law by way of summary judgment.

■ CASE VOCABULARY

DIVERSITY: Federal court jurisdiction based upon diversity of citizenship, where case between citizens of different states forms the basis of federal court jurisdiction.

Edwards v. Basel Pharmaceuticals

(Wife of Deceased Smoker) v. *(Nicotine Patch Manufacturer)*

933 P.2d 298 (Okla. 1997)

EXCEPT IN LIMITED CIRCUMSTANCES, MANUFACTURERS OF PRESCRIPTION DRUGS DO NOT HAVE A DUTY TO DIRECTLY WARN USERS, SINCE THE USERS MUST OBTAIN THE DRUGS FROM THEIR DOCTORS

■ **INSTANT FACTS** Wife sued for husband's wrongful death after he died from smoking while wearing a nicotine patch, and contended that the manufacturer should have warned her husband of risk, not just the doctor who prescribed the patch.

■ **BLACK LETTER RULE** When the FDA requires warnings be given directly to the patient with a prescribed drug, an exception to the "learned intermediary doctrine" occurs, and the manufacturer is not automatically shielded from liability by properly warning the prescribing physician.

■ **PROCEDURAL BASIS**

Federal court of appeals certified a question to the State Supreme Court in action for wrongful death.

■ **FACTS**

Mrs. Edwards (P) brought a wrongful death action for the death of her husband who died of a nicotine-induced heart attack as a result of smoking while wearing two nicotine patches manufactured by Basel Pharmaceuticals (D). [In other words, he OD'd on nicotine.] Edwards (P) asserted that the warnings concerning the patches were inadequate because they warned only the doctor who prescribed the patches of the risk of death due to nicotine overdose, and not Mr. Edwards, the user of the patch. Basel (D) contends that the "learned intermediary doctrine" [exception to manufacturer's duty to warn the ultimate consumer concerning prescription drugs] bars liability because the prescribing physicians were given complete warnings regarding the patches. The Food and Drug Administration (FDA) required consumer warnings but Basel (D) asserts that the learned intermediary doctrine should be controlling.

■ **ISSUE**

Is there an exception to the "learned intermediary doctrine" when the FDA requires warnings be given directly to the patient with a prescribed drug, so that the manufacturer is not automatically shielded from liability by properly warning the prescribing physician?

■ **DECISION AND RATIONALE**

(Summers, J.) Yes. The "learned intermediary doctrine", applicable in prescription drug and prosthetic implant cases, is an exception to the manufacturer's duty to warn the ultimate consumer. Under this doctrine, the manufacturer is shielded from liability if it adequately warns the prescribing physicians of the dangers of the drug. The doctor acts as a learned intermediary between the patient and the prescription drug manufacturer. There are two exceptions to the learned intermediary doctrine. One involves mass immunizations. Because there may be no physician-patient relationship, and the drug is not administered as a prescription drug, the manufacturer must therefore warn the patient. The second exception arises when the FDA mandates that a warning be given directly to the consumer. Most cases falling within this second exception involve contraceptive drugs and devices. We see no reason why this second exception should not apply to nicotine patches available by prescription. The FDA requires that prescriptions for nicotine patches be accompanied by warnings to the ultimate consumer as well as to the physician. [So do you think that Basel (D) did not warn Mr. Edwards because it was confident it could rely upon some legal doctrine to shield itself from liability?] Thus, we hold that when the FDA requires warnings be given directly to the patient with a prescribed drug, an exception to the "learned intermediary doctrine" has occurred, and the manufacturer is not automatically shielded from liability by properly warning the prescribing physician. Question Answered.

Analysis:

The learned intermediary doctrine is an exception to the general rule that manufacturers must warn consumers of the dangers associated with the use of their products. Prescription drugs are not capable of being made entirely safe, but they are of great benefit to the public in spite of the risks. However, the benefits depend upon adequate warnings. The doctrine allows the manufacturers to provide the adequate warnings to the doctors who prescribe drugs, and they in turn use the information to make an informed decision on how best to treat their patients. This case is an example of an exception to the exception. In other words, if there is a safety regulation that mandates direct warnings to the consumers by the manufacturers, such as the FDA did in this case, then an exception to the learned intermediary doctrine exists, thereby requiring warning to the patient.

■ CASE VOCABULARY

CERTIFIED QUESTION: Where federal appellate courts seeks to have the U.S. Supreme Court or state supreme court answer a question concerning a point of law.

Vassallo v. Baxter Healthcare Corporation

(Breast Implant Victim) v. *(Manufacturer)*

428 Mass. 1, 696 N.E.2d 909 (1998)

MASSACHUSETTS CHANGES ITS LAW—NO LONGER MUST A MANUFACTURER WARN ABOUT A PRODUCT'S RISKS THAT WERE UNKNOWN AT THE TIME OF SALE

■ **INSTANT FACTS** Breast implant manufacturer, Baxter Healthcare Corporation (D) challenged state's law concerning the duty to warn even though the risk was not known at the time of sale.

■ **BLACK LETTER RULE** A manufacturer need only warn of risks that were reasonably foreseeable when the product was sold, or that could have been discovered through testing prior to marketing the product.

■ **PROCEDURAL BASIS**

Direct appeal to State Supreme Court after judgment entered on jury verdict for negligence and breach of warranty.

■ **FACTS**

Vassallo (P) alleged that her silicone breast implants—manufactured by company since bought by Baxter Healthcare Corporation (Baxter) (D)—had been accompanied by negligent product warnings, plus other theories of product liability. A jury returned verdicts on negligence and breach of warranty claims. Baxter (D) took a direct appeal to the State Supreme Court. Baxter (D) asserts that the judge should not have denied its request to instruct the jury that a manufacturer need only warn of risks known or reasonably knowable in light of the generally accepted scientific knowledge available at the time of the manufacture and distribution of the device. [Baxter (D) should have known that new law is not created at the trial court level.]

■ **ISSUE**

Must a manufacturer warn of risks that were not reasonably foreseeable when the product was sold?

■ **DECISION AND RATIONALE**

(Greaney, J.) No. A manufacturer need only warn of risks that were reasonably foreseeable when the product was sold, or that could have been discovered through testing prior to marketing the product. Baxter (D) seeks to have us change our products liability law so as to adopt a "state of the art" standard that conditions a manufacturer's liability on actual or constructive knowledge of the risks. Our current state law, which follows the minority "hindsight analysis" view of the duty to warn, presumes that a manufacturer was fully informed of all risks associated with the product at issue, regardless of the state of the art at the time of the sale, and amounts to strict liability for failure to warn of these risks. The trial judge in this case gave the correct statement of our law. We, however, hereby revise our law to come within the view adopted by the majority of states, following the Restatement (Second) of Torts § 402A and the Products Restatement § 2(c). Thus, a defendant will not be held liable under an implied warranty of merchantability for failure to warn or provide instructions about risks that were not reasonably foreseeable at the time of sale or could not have been discovered by way of reasonable testing prior to marketing the product. A manufacturer will be held to the standard of knowledge of an

---

expert in the appropriate field, and will remain subject to a continuing duty to warn (at least purchasers) of risks discovered following the sale of the product at issue. In accordance with the usual rules governing retroactivity, the standard just expressed will apply to all claims in which a final judgment has not been entered, or as to which an appeal is pending or the appeal has not expired, and to all claims on which an action is commenced after the release of this opinion. The jury's sustainable verdict on negligence in failing to warn of known risks precludes Baxter (D) from taking advantage of the change in law. Judgment affirmed. [Poor Baxter (D), it was successful in getting the law changed, but it still lost.]

Analysis:

No longer is a manufacturer subjected to a "hindsight" approach duty to warn, amounting to strict liability for failure to warn of all risks associated with the product regardless of the state of the art at the time of the sale. The Restatement's duty to warn of risks reasonably foreseeable at the time of sale, or that could have been discovered by reasonable testing, is based on the goal of the law to induce conduct that is capable of being performed. This goal is not advanced by imposing liability for failure to warn of risks that were not capable of being known.

■ CASE VOCABULARY

LOSS OF CONSORTIUM: A claim by the spouse of an injured or deceased victim seeking damages for loss of companionship, cooperation, aid, affection, and sexual relations.

RETROACTIVITY: Applying a new rule of law to a transaction that occurred before the rule was adopted.

STATE OF THE ART: Industry custom or practice; safest existing technology that has been adopted for use; cutting edge technology.

General Motors Corporation v. Sanchez

(*Manufacturer*) v. (*Family of Deceased*)

997 S.W.2d 584 (Tex. 1999)

FAILURE TO DISCOVER A PRODUCT DEFECT DOES NOT REDUCE PLAINTIFF'S RECOVERY

■ **INSTANT FACTS** Manufacturer, General Motors Corp. (D), sought to defend wrongful death action based upon deceased's failure to properly park vehicle in "Park," which caused it to slip out of gear and crush him.

■ **BLACK LETTER RULE** A consumer has no duty to discover or guard against a product defect, but a consumer's conduct other than the mere failure to discover or guard against a product defect is subject to comparative responsibility.

■ **PROCEDURAL BASIS**

Appeal to State Supreme Court following court of appeal affirming judgment rendered following jury trial in products liability action for wrongful death damages.

■ **FACTS**

Mr. Sanchez was killed after he exited his pickup truck, manufactured by General Motors Corporation (GM) (D), when it rolled backward, pinning him against a gate and causing injuries from which he bled to death. His family (P) sued GM (D) for negligence, products liability and gross negligence based upon a defect in the truck's transmission and transmission-control linkage. The circumstantial evidence presented at trial showed that the accident probably occurred when he mis-shifted into what he though was Park, but which was actually an intermediate, "perched" position between Park and Reverse where the transmission was in "hydraulic neutral." The gear shift slipped from the perched position of hydraulic neutral into Reverse and the truck rolled backwards. The jury found that GM (D) was negligent, the transmission was defectively designed and the warning was inadequate. The jury also found that Mr. Sanchez was fifty percent responsible for the accident, but the trial court disregarded this finding [because it didn't think it was a proper defense]. The trial court rendered judgment for actual and punitive damages of $8.5 million for Mr. Sanchez's family (P). The court of appeals affirmed. GM (D) appealed to the State Supreme Court.

■ **ISSUE**

Does a consumer have a duty to discover or guard against a product defect?

■ **DECISION AND RATIONALE**

(Gonzales, J.) No. We hold that a consumer has no duty to discover or guard against a product defect, but a consumer's conduct other than the mere failure to discover or guard against a product defect is subject to comparative responsibility. GM (D) challenges, among other things, the trial court's refusal to apply the comparative responsibility statute. It argues that its liability for damages should be reduced due to Mr. Sanchez' fifty percent responsibility for the accident. The Sanchez family (P) asserts that Mr. Sanchez's negligence was nothing more than a failure to discover or guard against a product defect, and that comparative responsibility does not apply as a defense to strict liability. In

---

Keen v. Ashot Ashkelon we held that a failure to discover or guard against a defect is no defense to a strict liability claim. Our state statute was revised by the Legislature changing the law from a comparative *negligence* to a comparative *responsibility* standard. Under comparative *responsibility*, a court reduces a claimant's damages recovery by the percentage of responsibility attributed to him by the trier of fact. It expressly included suits based upon strict liability. The new statute applies to a claimant's conduct that violated the duty to use ordinary care or some other applicable legal standard. GM (D) contends that the revision to the statute effectively overruled the *Keen* decision. Implicit in the ruling was that a consumer has no duty to discover or guard against a product defect. The legislative revisions to the statute, which apportion responsibility based on a breach of legal duty or other applicable legal standard, do not impose a new duty on plaintiffs. The statute merely says that if a claimant breaches an existing duty, then comparative responsibility shall apply. Accordingly, if a plaintiff's failure to discover or guard against a product defect breaches no duty, the statute does not apply. Our holding in this case reflects that a consumer is not relieved of the responsibility to act reasonably nor may a consumer fail to take reasonable precautions regardless of a known or unknown product defect. We thus disapprove of *Keen* to the extent it supports that the failure to discover or guard against a product defect is a broad category that includes all conduct except the assumption of a known risk. The evidence at trial established Mr. Sanchez failed to perform any of the safety measures described in the owner's manual and that performing any one of them would have prevented the accident. [Too bad Mr. Sanchez was not around to tell what really happened.] This is sufficient to support the negligence finding. A driver has a duty to take reasonable precautions to secure his vehicle before exiting it. Sanchez had a responsibility to operate his truck in a safe manner. The fact that the precautions demanded of a driver generally would have prevented this accident does not make Sanchez's negligence a mere failure to discover or guard against a mis-shift. Sanchez's actions amounted to conduct other than a mere failure to discover or guard against a product defect, and is subject to comparative responsibility. Reversed and remanded for entry of the award for actual damages reduced by 50 percent and reversed as to the punitive damage award.

Analysis:

This case looks at the "failure to discover" rule, which provides that no comparative fault reductions should be made when the plaintiff's only fault is a failure to discover the product's defect. In other words, a plaintiff should not be held at fault for trusting a product. The court acknowledged that this was the proper rule to apply However, it also held that Mr. Sanchez was at fault for parking his truck unsafely, which was independent of any alleged defect.

■ CASE VOCABULARY

CIRCUMSTANTIAL EVIDENCE: Indirect evidence from which inferences from the facts are drawn.

EN BANC: Where all members of the reviewing court for a particular district or circuit hear a case on review, rather than just the limited quorum members initially assigned to hear the case.

Jones v. Ryobi, Ltd.

(Injured Printing Press Employee) v. *(Manufacturer)*

37 F.3d 423 (8th Cir. 1994)

EMPLOYEE IS NOT PROHIBITED FROM SUING MANUFACTURER OF EQUIPMENT PURCHASED BY EMPLOYER

■ **INSTANT FACTS** Employee Jones (P) was denied recovery in product liability action where the product was modified by a third party after it was sold.

■ **BLACK LETTER RULE** When a third party's modification makes a safe product unsafe, the seller is relieved of liability even if the modification is foreseeable.

■ **PROCEDURAL BASIS**

Appeal from the granting of motions for judgment as a matter of law in suit for negligence and strict product liability.

■ **FACTS**

Jones (P) was employed at Business Cards Tomorrow as an operator of a printing press known as an offset duplicator. She was seriously injured when her hand was caught in the moving parts of the press. She sued Ryobi, Ltd. (D), the manufacturer and A.B. Dick Corporation (D2), the distributor, for negligence and strict product liability for defective design. The evidence at trial established that a third party had modified the printing press and the safety guard had been removed. Jones (P) knew that the guard was missing and knew it was dangerous to have her hands near the unguarded moving parts, but her supervisor allegedly pressured her to save time by adjusting the eject wheels while the press was running. Jones (P) testified that she feared she would be fired if she took the time to stop the press. While she was adjusting the eject wheels on the running press, [Can you guess what happens next?] her hand was caught in the moving parts and was crushed. The district court, at the close of Jones's (P) case, granted Ryobi (D) and A.B. Dick's (D2) motions for judgment as a matter law, relying upon the open and obvious nature of the asserted danger of operating the press without a guard. The court also denied Jones's (P) motion to amend her complaint to reassert the negligence claim against the distributor (D2), which she had previously dismissed.

■ **ISSUE**

Is the seller of a product relieved of liability when a third party's modification makes a safe product unsafe, even if the modification is foreseeable?

■ **DECISION AND RATIONALE**

(Fagg, J.) Yes. When a third party's modification makes a safe product unsafe, the seller is relieved of liability even if the modification is foreseeable. We conclude that the granting of the motions for judgment as a matter of law was proper, but on an alternate ground than that relied upon by the district court in reaching its decision. To recover on a theory of strict liability for defective design, Jones (P) must prove she was injured as a direct result of a defect that existed when the press was sold. She had the burden to show that the press had not been modified to create a defect that could have proximately caused her injury. Jones (P) failed to meet this burden. The evidence showed that removing the safety guard had substantially modified the press. Although the evidence did not show who modified the press, it clearly showed that a third party, not the manufacturer or the distributor, was responsible for the modification. We do not believe that Ryobi (D), the manufacturer, is responsible even though it provided tools for general maintenance that could be used to remove the guard. Nor did the employer follow the distributor's (D2) advice to repair the disabled safety features. We believe that the press was safe before the modification because it would not run without the safety guard. [That's logical.] Thus, Jones's (P) strict product liability claim for defective design fails as a matter of law. Nor do we believe that there was error in refusing to allow Jones (P) to amend her complaint since the evidence did not show colorable grounds for a negligence theory. Affirmed.

■ DISSENT

(Heaney, J.) I cannot subscribe to the majority's opinion that the printing press was safe as originally manufactured. Jones's (P) expert witness' testimony is sufficient to support the inference that it was not safe as originally designed. He testified that the guard, in addition to not being fail-safe, was made of readily breakable material, did not allow for proper ventilation, and invited removal. He also testified that the design of the eject wheels was absolutely not safe. Moreover, the fact that an overwhelming majority of machines had their guards removed after their delivery is evidence that the printing press was incapable of operating efficiently according to industry standards. Nearly 98% of all machines that the expert witness came in contact with had their safety covers removed. Thus, there was sufficient evidence to support the inference that the press was unreasonably dangerous and thus was defectively designed.

Analysis:

Note that the trial court's basis for denying Jones relief was on different grounds than those relied upon by the court of appeals. The trial court relied on the open and obvious nature of the asserted danger to deny relief. The court of appeals held that Jones (P) was unable to prove that she was injured as a direct result of a defect that existed when the press was sold. The court of appeals held that the third party's modification of the machine relieved the manufacturer (D) and distributor (D2) of liability, even if the modification was foreseeable. The dissenting justice felt that there was sufficient evidence to infer that the machine was not safe as originally designed. He opined that the fact that so many of the machines had their guards removed should have been sufficient evidence that the press was incapable of operating efficiently. This decision is hard to reconcile with the general principle that a manufacturer has a duty to market a reasonably safe product. If unsafe modifications are foreseeable, it would seem that there was a failure to market a reasonably safe product.

■ CASE VOCABULARY

DE NOVO: As used by courts of appeal to denote reviewing the entire record and making its decision anew, and without regard to lower court's decision.

MOTION FOR JUDGMENT AS A MATTER OF LAW: Requesting judge to enter judgment in favor of one party before case is submitted to the jury (formerly called motion for directed verdict), or after a jury verdict (formerly known as motion for judgment notwithstanding the verdict).

Liriano v. Hobart Corp.

(Injured Meat-Grinding Employee) v. *(Manufacturer)*

92 N.Y.2d 232, 700 N.E.2d 303, 677 N.Y.S.2d 764 (1998)

COURT EXTENDS MANUFACTURER'S DUTY TO WARN OF POST-SALE THIRD PARTY MODIFICATIONS THAT MAKE PRODUCT UNSAFE

■ **INSTANT FACTS** Liriano (P) sued Hobart Corp. (D), the manufacturer of a meat grinder, for failure to warn, although the grinder had been modified post-sale by a third party who removed its safety guard.

■ **BLACK LETTER RULE** Manufacturer liability for failure to warn may exist in cases where the substantial modification defense would preclude liability on a design defect theory.

■ **PROCEDURAL BASIS**

Certified question to State's highest court after appeal from judgment following jury trial in product liability action.

■ **FACTS**

Liriano (P), a meat department employee of a grocery store, lost his right hand and lower forearm in a meat grinder manufactured and sold by Hobart Corp. (D) more than 30 years earlier. The safety guard had been removed from the grinder while in the store's possession and there was no warning on the grinder about the danger of using it without a guard. Within one year following the grinder's manufacture and sale, Hobart Corp. (D) became aware that a significant number of purchasers of its meat grinders had removed the safety guards, and it thus began issuing warnings on its grinders concerning the removal of the safety guard. [It now wishes it had sent a warning to the store!] Liriano (P) sued Hobart Corp. (D) under theories of negligence and strict products liability for defective product design and failure to warn, among other things. Hobart Corp. (D) impleaded the store. At trial, the jury apportioned liability 5% to Hobart (D) and 95% to the store. It then allocated 33 1/3% of the total responsibility to Liriano (P). Judgment was entered accordingly.

■ **ISSUE**

Can a manufacturer liability exist under a failure to warn theory in cases in which the substantial modification defense would preclude liability under a design defect theory?

■ **DECISION AND RATIONALE**

(Ciparick, J.) Yes. We hold that manufacturer liability can exist under a failure to warn theory in cases in which the substantial modification defense would preclude liability under a design defect theory. In *Robinson v. Reed-Prentice Div. of Package Mach. Co.* we held that a manufacturer is not responsible for injuries resulting from substantial alterations or modifications of a product by a third party that render the product defective or otherwise unsafe. Thus, a manufacturer is not required to insure that subsequent owners and users will not adapt the product to their own unique uses. However, *Robinson* did not resolve the issue of whether preclusion of a claim for defective design because of substantial alteration by a third party should also bar a claim for failure to warn. Although it is virtually impossible to design a product to forestall all future risk-enhancing modifications that could occur after the sale, it is neither infeasible nor onerous, in some cases, to warn of the dangers of foreseeable modifications that pose the risk of injury. We have previously held that a manufacturer may be liable for failing to warn against the dangers of foreseeable misuse of its product. There should be no material distinction between foreseeable misuse and foreseeable alteration of a product. Moreover, we have also previously held that a manufacturer may have a duty to warn of dangers associated with the use of its product even after it has been sold, such as where a defect or danger is revealed post-sale. The manufacturer's ability to learn of post-sale modifications is no less than its ability to learn of post-sale misuse of a product. Thus, we conclude that manufacturer liability can exist under a failure to warn theory in cases in which the substantial modification defense might otherwise preclude a design defect claim. However, if an injured party was fully aware of the product's hazard through general knowledge, observation or common sense, or participated in the removal of the safety device whose purpose is obvious, lack of a warning about that danger may well obviate the failure to warn as a legal cause of an injury resulting from that danger. In addition, there is a limited class of hazards that need not be warned of as a matter of law because they are patently dangerous or pose open and obvious risks. In these cases, there should be no liability for failing to warn someone of a risk or hazard that he or she appreciated to the same extent as a warning would have provided. [You can bet that Hobart (D) will be making these arguments if the matter is retried.] Thus, the certified question should be answered as follows: manufacturer liability for failure to warn may exist in cases where the substantial modification defense would preclude liability on a design defect theory.

Analysis:

The primary issue in this case is whether a manufacturer has a duty to warn about the dangers of its product if a substantial modification occurs. The court held that such a duty could exist. The general rule is that there is no manufacturer liability when the substantial alterations or modifications render the product defective or otherwise unsafe. Thus, Linano (P) would not have been successful in suing Hobart (D) for defective *design* if the safety guard was capable of being removed and/or the grinder was capable of running without the guard in place. However, the court held that a duty to *warn* did exist. Recall that Hobart (D) had received knowledge about a significant number of users removing the guard within a short time after it manufactured and sold the grinder to the store. Based upon this information, it began issuing warnings about the dangers associated with removal of the guard. The court correctly held that there should be no reason to distinguish between the duty to warn where post-sale defects are discovered and the duty to warn where post-sale modifications are discovered. The exceptions to the rule laid down by this case involve those hazards that are so obvious based upon the safety device built into the product that a warning is not required.

■ **CASE VOCABULARY**

IMPLEADED: Bringing a new party into the lawsuit.

PRECLUSION OF A CLAIM: When litigation of one claim forecloses litigation of a later claim.

Royer v. Catholic Medical Center

(Prosthetic Knee Patient) v. *(Hospital)*

144 N.H. 330, 741 A.2d 74 (1999)

STRICT LIABILITY IS NOT EXTENDED TO PROVIDING SERVICES, EVEN WHEN PRODUCTS ARE SOLD AS PART OF THE SERVICE

■ **INSTANT FACTS** Patient who received a defective prosthetic knee sued the hospital for strict product design liability and hospital argued that it was not engaged in the business of selling goods

■ **BLACK LETTER RULE** A health care provider, who in the course of rendering health care services supplies a prosthetic device to be implanted into a patient, is not "engaged in the business of selling" prostheses for purposes of strict products liability.

■ **PROCEDURAL BASIS**

Appeal from dismissal of complaint in action for products liability.

■ **FACTS**

Royer (P) underwent a total knee replacement at Catholic Medical Center (CMC) (D), during which a prosthetic knee was surgically implanted. After discovering that the prosthesis was defective, Royer (P) underwent a second operation to replace the defective one. Royer (P) [being an unhappy camper after having not one, but two surgeries] sued CMC (D) for strict product design liability. CMC (D) moved to dismiss asserting that it was not a "seller of goods" for purposes of strict products liability. The trial court granted the motion to dismiss the complaint and Royer (P) appealed.

■ **ISSUE**

Is a health care provider that supplies a defective prosthesis in the course of delivering health care services a "seller" of prosthetic devices in order to be held liable for strict products liability?

■ **DECISION AND RATIONALE**

(Brock, J.) No. We hold that a health care provider, who in the course of rendering health care services supplies a prosthetic device to be implanted into a patient, is not "engaged in the business of selling" prostheses for purposes of strict products liability. In this State, one who sells any product in a defective condition unreasonably dangerous to the user or consumer or to his property is subject to strict liability for physical harm thereby caused if the seller is engaged in the business of selling such a product. If the defendant merely provides a service, however, there is no liability, absent proof of a violation of a legal duty. In another case, we previously rejected an argument that strict liability should extend to architects and building contractors who allegedly designed and manufactured a defective building, concluding that they are engaged primarily in the rendition of services. Other jurisdictions have declined to extend strict liability to health care providers who supply defective prostheses reasoning that they primarily render services, and the prosthetic device is merely incidental to the services. Royer (P) argues [with merit] that CMC (D) acted both as a seller of a prosthetic knee and as a provider of professional services, charging separately for and earning a profit on the sale of the prosthesis. The dispositive issue however is whether CMC (D) was an entity "engaged in the business of selling" prosthetic knees. In looking at the relationship of the parties, a patient does not enter a hospital to purchase a prosthesis, but to obtain treatment, which includes the implantation of the knee, with the overall objective of restoring his health. This is not analogous to a situation where a plaintiff purchases a defective tire from a retail tire distributor and has the distributor install the tire. Medical services are distinguished by factors that make them significantly different in kind from the retail marketing enterprise at which the Restatement is directed. Affirmed.

Analysis:

The court acknowledges that strict liability may be imposed under certain circumstances where a defendant provides both a service and a product as part of the same transaction, but concludes that this case is not one of those circumstances. The court looked at the entire transaction between Royer (P) and CMC (D) and found that the primary purpose of going to CMC (D) was not to purchase the prosthesis, but to obtain health care with the overall objective of restoring good health. Apparently, Royer (P) did not sue the manufacturer of the prosthesis because it had filed for bankruptcy. Royer (P) made a unique argument, though rejected by the court, that the medical center sold the prosthesis and the surgeon performed the services of the surgery. Nevertheless, the court distinguished the relationship between the patient and the medical center from that of a retail buyer and seller. The primary issue involved whether CMC (D) was "engaged in the business of selling," not whether it "sold" the product to Royer (P). Thus, the theory of strict liability was not extended to providing services.

■ CASE VOCABULARY

INTER ALIA: Latin for among other things.

MOTION TO DISMISS COMPLAINT: Challenging the right of the court to entertain the lawsuit based on various legal theories.

East River Steamship Corp. v. Transamerica Delaval Inc.

(Supertanker Charterer) v. *(Turbine Manufacturer)*
476 U.S. 858, 106 S.Ct. 2295, 90 L.Ed.2d 865 (1986)

TORT CLAIM NOT PERMITTED FOR INJURY TO DEFECTIVE PRODUCT ONLY

■ **INSTANT FACTS** East River (P) sued in tort to recover cost of repair and lost income from defective turbine on supertanker.

■ **BLACK LETTER RULE** A cause of action in tort may not be stated when a defective product purchased in a commercial transaction malfunctions, injuring only the product itself and causing purely economic loss.

■ **PROCEDURAL BASIS**

Certiorari granted by United States Supreme Court following the affirming of summary judgment to resolve conflict among lower courts sitting in admiralty concerning tort actions for product-related economic harm.

■ **FACTS**

East River Steamship Corp. (East River) (P) was in the business of chartering supertankers from the ships' owners for 20–22 years, and assumed responsibility for the cost of any repairs. Transamerica Delaval Inc. (Delaval) (D) made turbines for 4 supertankers chartered by East River (P). Some of the turbines malfunctioned and inspections of others revealed similar problems. Satisfactory repairs were eventually made. East River (P) sued Delaval (D) in tort for the cost of repairing the ships and for income lost while the ships were out of service. The trial court granted Delaval (D) summary judgment and the court of appeals affirmed. The Supreme Court granted certiorari to resolve a conflict among the courts of appeal sitting in admiralty concerning whether a tort action may be stated when a defective product injures only the product itself and causes only economic loss. [Things would be different had someone been injured by the malfunctioning turbines.]

■ **ISSUE**

May a cause of action in tort be stated when a defective product purchased in a commercial transaction malfunctions, injuring only the product itself and causing purely economic loss?

■ **DECISION AND RATIONALE**

(Blackmun, J.) No. We hold that a cause of action in tort may not be stated when a defective product purchased in a commercial transaction malfunctions, injuring only the product itself and causing purely economic loss. In this case, the damage from the defective product is not to other property, but only to the defective turbine itself. We conclude that a manufacturer in a commercial relationship has no duty under either a negligence or strict products-liability theory to prevent a product from injuring itself. When a product injures only itself the reasons for imposing a tort duty are weak and those for leaving the party to its contractual remedies are strong. A claim of a nonworking product can be brought as a breach of warranty action or, if the customer prefers, it can reject the product or revoke its acceptance and sue for breach of contract. Warranty law sufficiently protects the purchaser by allowing it to obtain the benefit of its bargain. Recovery on a warranty theory would give the charterers their repair costs and lost profits, and would place them in the position they would have been in had the turbines functioned properly. A warranty action also has a built-in limitation on liability, whereas a tort action could subject the manufacturer to damages of an indefinite amount. The limitation in a contract action comes from the agreement of the parties and the requirement that consequential damages, such as lost profits, be a foreseeable result of the breach. In a warranty action where the loss is purely economic, the limitation derives from the requirements of foreseeability and of privity, which is still generally enforced for such claims. In products liability law, where there is a duty to the public generally, forseeability is an inadequate brake. [It won't hold back the floodgates] Permitting recovery for all foreseeable claims for purely economic loss could make a manufacturer liable for vast sums. It would be difficult for a manufacturer to take into account the expectations of persons downstream who may encounter its product. For example, in this case, East (P)—already one step removed from the transaction—would be permitted to recover its economic losses, and the companies that subchartered the ships might also claim economic losses from the delays, as could the customers of the charterers. The law does not spread its protection so far. Thus, whether stated in negligence or strict liability, no products liability claim lies in admiralty when the only injury claimed is economic loss. Affirmed.

Analysis:

This case concerns purely economic harm and whether recovery therefor may be had based upon tort law. The defective product in this case caused an injury to itself, which resulted in economic harm to East River (P.) in the form of the cost of repairs and lost income. The court concluded that the proper basis for recovery was not in tort, but rather a breach of warranty or breach of contract action. The court explained its reasoning by noting that warranty law adequately protects the purchaser, whereas a tort action could subject the manufacturer to indefinite damages, including allegedly foreseeable claims by persons downstream who may encounter the product. The court's decision followed the majority approach, which held that preserving a proper role for the law of warranty precluded imposing tort liability if a defective product causes purely monetary harm. At the other end of the conflicting spectrum was the minority approach, which held that a manufacturer's duty to make nondefective products encompassed injury to the product itself, whether or not the defect created an unreasonable risk of harm.

■ CASE VOCABULARY

SITTING IN ADMIRALTY: A court hearing maritime cases.

CHAPTER NINE

Trespass and Nuisance

Martin v. Reynolds Metals Co.

Instant Facts: A metals company is held liable for damages in trespass, after their aluminum reduction plant emitted fluoride compounds, damaging nearby farm land, despite the metal company's contention that the action should have been brought under nuisance.

Black Letter Rule: A trespass is any intrusion which invades the possessor's protected interest in exclusive possession, whether that intrusion is by visible or invisible pieces of matter or energy.

Boomer v. Atlantic Cement Co., Inc.

Instant Facts: A land owner sought an injunction and damages for the air pollution emitted from a neighboring cement plant, and the trial court denied the injunction while allowing continuing actions for damages.

Black Letter Rule: A continuing nuisance may be remedied by the payment of permanent damages, allowing the interfering activity to continue.

Martin v. Reynolds Metals Co.

(Farmer) v. *(Neighboring Aluminum Plant)*

221 Or. 86, 342 P.2d 790 (1959), cert. denied, 362 U.S. 918, 80 S.Ct. 672 (1960)

INTRUSIONS BY INTANGIBLE OBJECTS MAY CONSTITUTE A TRESPASS

■ **INSTANT FACTS** A metals company is held liable for damages in trespass, after their aluminum reduction plant emitted fluoride compounds, damaging nearby farm land, despite the metal company's contention that the action should have been brought under nuisance.

■ **BLACK LETTER RULE** A trespass is any intrusion which invades the possessor's protected interest in exclusive possession, whether that intrusion is by visible or invisible pieces of matter or energy.

■ **PROCEDURAL BASIS**

Certification to the Supreme Court of Oregon, of a judgment by the trial court awarding damages for the trespass of fluoride compounds from a nearby aluminum plant.

■ **FACTS**

Martin (P) sued Reynolds Metals Co. (Reynolds) (D), claiming that their farm land had been damaged from the operation of Reynolds' (D) nearby aluminum reduction plant. Reynolds' (D) plant emanated an average of 800 pounds of fluorides. The trial judge awarded Martin (P) $71,500 for damages to their land, which could no longer be used to raise livestock due to cattle poisoning from the fluoride compounds that became airborne from the plant. The trial judge also awarded $20,000 for the deterioration of the land through growth of bush and weeds resulting from the lack of grazing, but rejected punitive damages. The damages covered the period from August 1951 through the end of 1955. If the action was properly brought in trespass, which has a six-year statute of limitations, the award was permissible. However, if the action were one of nuisance, which has a two-year statue of limitations, then damages were recoverable for only 1954 and 1955. Reynolds (D) appeals.

■ **ISSUE**

Do intrusions by intangible or microscopic entities constitute a trespass?

■ **DECISION AND RATIONALE**

(O'Connell, J.) Yes. A trespass is any intrusion which invades the possessor's protected interest in exclusive possession, whether that intrusion is by visible or invisible pieces of matter or energy. Reynolds (D) argues that an action for trespass arises only when there has been a breaking and entering upon real property, constituting a direct rather than consequential invasion of the possessor's interest in land. They then further argue that fluoride compounds, consisting of gas, fumes, and particles, are not sufficient to satisfy these requirements. Trespass and private nuisance are separate fields of tort liability which relate to actionable interference with the possession of land. While a "trespass" is an actionable invasion of a possessor's interest in the exclusive possession of land, "nuisance" is an actionable invasion of a possessor's interest in the use and enjoyment of his land. Conduct such as Reynolds' (D) may and often does result in the actionable invasion of both of these interests, in which case the choice between the two remedies is, in most cases, a matter of little consequence. In some of the cases relied upon by Reynolds (D), the courts are not called upon to determine the issue of trespass, because the action is brought on the theory of nuisance alone. However, there are cases which have held that the defendant's interference with the plaintiff's possession, resulting from the settling upon his land of effluents emanating from the defendant's operation is exclusively nontrespassory. Although in such cases, the separate particles which collectively cause the invasion are minute, the deposit of each of the particles constitutes a physical intrusion and would clearly give rise to an action of trespass if not for the size of the particle. Reynolds' (D) asks us to differentiate between the sizes of the objects which constitute the intrusion, and to regulate entirely to the field of nuisance law certain invasions which do not pass this test of size. However, Reynolds' (D) must admit that there are cases which have held that a trespass results from the movement or deposit of rather small objects over or upon the surface of the possessor's land. Moreover, liability for trespass has been recognized where the harm was produced by the vibration of the soil or by the concussion of the air which is nothing more than the movement of molecules. Recognizing a trespassory invasion where there is no "thing" which can be seen with the naked eye undoubtedly runs counter to the definition of trespass. It is quite possible that in an earlier day when science had not yet peered into the molecular and atomic world of small particles, the courts could not fit an invasion through unseen physical instrumentalities into requirements that a trespass can result only from a direct invasion. But in this atomic age even the uneducated know the great and awful force contained in the atom and what it can do to a man's property if it is released. Therefore, we must look to the character of the instrumentality which is used in making an intrusion upon another's land, and emphasize the object's energy or force rather than its size. Viewed in this way, we may define trespass as any intrusion which invades the possessor's protected interest in exclusive possession, whether that intrusion is by visible or invisible pieces of matter or energy. Originally all types of trespass were punishable under the criminal law because the conduct was regarded as a breach of the peace. A civil action for trespass was colored by its past, and the idea that the peace of the community was put in danger by the trespasser's conduct influenced the court's ideas of the character of the tort. Therefore, relief was granted even where there was no actual damage, partly as a means of discouraging disruptive influences in the community. Yet, probably the most important factor which describes the nature of the interest protected under the law of trespass is nothing more than a feeling which a possessor has with respect to land which he holds. Thus, it is understandable why actual damage is not an essential ingredient in the law of trespass. With these considerations in mind, we think a possessor's interest in land could be violated by a ray of light, an atomic particle, or by a particulate of fluoride. On the other hand, if such interest circumscribed by these considerations is not violated or endangered, the defendant's conduct will not render him liable in an action for trespass, even though it may result in a physical intrusion. Reynolds (D) contends that trespass will not lie in this case because the injury was indirect and consequential and that the requirement that the injury must be direct and immediate to constitute a trespass was not met. However, we find that the intrusion was direct and that consequential damage may be proven in an action for trespass. Although the distinction between direct and indirect invasions has been abandoned by some courts, it is not necessary for us to decide whether the distinction is recognized in this state because the invasion in this case was direct. As to the issue raised concerning the character of Reynolds' (D) conduct in making the intrusion upon Martin's (P) land, we find that this would be material only with respect to the claim for punitive damages which was rejected by the trial court. Since we hold that the intrusion in this case constituted a trespass, it is immaterial whether Reynolds' (D) conduct was careless, wanton and willful or entirely free from fault. Therefore, the trial court's refusal to enter a special finding on this issue was not error, even though trial court had elected to enter special rather than general findings. Affirmed.

Analysis:

Strict liability has been a dominant feature of trespass. Because this action was for a *direct* trespass, Reynolds's (D) negligence was held an irrelevant issue, and a showing of actual damages was not required. While this case illustrates the importance of distinguishing between conduct that constitutes a trespass rather than a nuisance, the court seems to blur the distinction with its overarching definition of trespass. Entering into or depositing garbage onto another's property without the owner's consent can easily be categorized as interfering with the owner's possession of the land. However, non-visible particles that, in this case, prevented a land owner from the "use and enjoyment" of his land traditionally constituted a nuisance. By extending "trespass" to invasions by non-visible particles, this case leaves little conduct to be considered exclusively under the nuisance doctrine.

■ **CASE VOCABULARY**

PRIVATE NUISANCE: A condition or activity that interferes with a possessor's use and enjoyment of his or her land.

TRESPASS: Any willful or voluntary unauthorized entry by a person or object onto another's land, which interferes with the land owner's possession of the land.

Boomer v. Atlantic Cement Co., Inc.

(Land Owner) v. *(Cement Manufacturer)*

26 N.Y.2d 219, 257 N.E.2d 870, 309 N.Y.S.2d 312 (1970)

GENERALLY, COURTS SHOULD RESOLVE NUISANCE DISPUTES BETWEEN THE PARTIES RATHER THAN ATTEMPT TO ELIMINATE PERVASIVE PROBLEMS SUCH AS AIR POLLUTION

■ **INSTANT FACTS** A land owner sought an injunction and damages for the air pollution emitted from a neighboring cement plant, and the trial court denied the injunction while allowing continuing actions for damages.

■ **BLACK LETTER RULE** A continuing nuisance may be remedied by the payment of permanent damages, allowing the interfering activity to continue.

■ **PROCEDURAL BASIS**

Appeal from judgment denying an injunction but allowing continued actions for damages for nuisance.

■ **FACTS**

Boomer (P), a private land owner, brought an action for damages and an injunction against Atlantic Cement Co., Inc. (D), operators of a large cement plant that allegedly injured neighbors by emitting dirt, smoke and vibrations. The trial court found that Atlantic Cement (D) was causing a nuisance, but the court declined to impose a permanent injunction. The effect of this ruling was that Atlantic Cement (D) could continue to pollute the environment, but that Boomer (P) could maintain successive actions for damages for as long as it continued suffering damages from Atlantic Cement's (D) activities. Atlantic Cement (D) appealed the availability of continuing actions for nuisance.

■ **ISSUE**

Must an injunction be granted where a nuisance results in substantial continuing damage?

■ **DECISION AND RATIONALE**

(Bergan, J.) No. An injunction is not necessarily required, even where a nuisance results in substantial continuing damage. In arriving at this conclusion, we overrule long-established and consistently-followed precedent. However, our decision is equitable in terms of the large disparity in economic consequences of the nuisance and of the injunction. In prior cases, we held that an injunction should be granted even though it would be of slight advantage to the injured party and would cause great loss to the enjoined party. This harsh result can be avoided by following one of two alternatives. One option would be to grant the injunction against Atlantic Cement (D) but postpone its effect for, say, 18 months. If Atlantic Cement (D) failed to abate the nuisance during this time by using improved methods of cement manufacturing, a permanent injunction would be entered. The problem with this option is its dependence on research and technological advances which are beyond the control of Atlantic Cement (D). There is a very real possibility that the cement industry would not find a solution to the pollution problems within the time period, and irreparable harm to Atlantic Cement (D) would result. A second option is more reasonable, as it redresses the economic losses suffered by Boomer (P) without unjustly harming Atlantic Cement (D). Under this option, which we now adopt, the injunction will be granted until Atlantic Cement (D) pays permanent damages to Boomer (P) which would compensate Boomer (P) for the total present and future economic loss to his property caused by Atlantic Cement's (D) operations. This option limits the relief to the particular parties before us, and it does not involve the court in attempting to achieve public objectives that are beyond the scope of the court's function. In addition, the requirement to pay damages may spur Atlantic Cement (D) and other manufacturers to pursue research into improved techniques. Furthermore, the damages award is consistent with the "servitude" imposed onto Boomer's (P) land by Atlantic Cement's (D) nuisance. Finally, the damages award is consistent with the notion that there can be but one recovery for permanent and unabatable nuisance; the award would preclude future recovery by Boomer (P). Reversed and remitted for injunction which shall be vacated upon payment of such permanent damages as shall be determined by the lower court.

■ DISSENT

(Jasen, J.) I see grave dangers in refusing to grant an injunction where a nuisance results in substantial continuing damage. The majority opinion provides no incentive for Atlantic Cement (D) to rectify its pollution, because once the damages are paid there is no incentive for the manufacturer to abate its air pollution. The inverse condemnation allowed by the trial court should only be permitted when the public is served by the impairment of private property. However, in the instant action the public does not benefit from the continued existence of the cement company. Finally, it is impermissible to impose a servitude upon Boomer's (P) land without the consent of the private property owner.

Analysis:

It is interesting to compare this case to *Carpenter v. The Double R Cattle Company, Inc.*. Both cases involve a balancing of the equities when determining whether an injunction should be granted. Since the utility of the interfering activities was great in both cases in relation to the degree of harm caused, both courts held that an injunction was improper. However, in the instant case, the interference was deemed to be so substantial that compensation was warranted for the private land owner. Perhaps another alternative—based on the theory of continuing nuisance—would have been a better option. Under this approach, the land owner would receive compensation on an ongoing basis for as long as the nuisance continued. This would serve the three goals of compensating the private party for the wrong, providing an incentive to the manufacturer to abate the nuisance, and allowing the useful manufacturing to continue if the business was willing to pay continuing damages.

■ CASE VOCABULARY

INVERSE CONDEMNATION: The impairment of private property that causes the property to lose much of its value, for which compensation must be paid to the owner.

CHAPTER TEN

Damages and Insurance

Seffert v. Los Angeles Transit Lines

Instant Facts: A bus passenger who was permanently and severely injured when the bus dragged her for several blocks while her arm and foot were caught in the bus door was awarded a large amount for pain and suffering.

Black Letter Rule: A jury's award of damages for pain and suffering will not be disturbed unless it is so large as to shock the conscience of the court.

McDougald v. Garber

Instant Facts: A doctor's malpractice left the patient permanently comatose, so the patient (through a representative) sued for the loss of enjoyment of life as well as pain and suffering.

Black Letter Rule: The loss of enjoyment of life is an element of pain and suffering and cannot be calculated separately.

Arambula v. Wells

Instant Facts: Arambula (P) was injured in a car accident and unable to work, but his employer (who was also his brother) continued to pay his weekly salary.

Black Letter Rule: Payment of an element of tort damages (such as lost wages) by an outside source (such as an employer) will not excuse the tortfeasor from having to pay for those damages as well.

Taylor v. Superior Court

Instant Facts: An accident victim sued a drunk driver that caused the accident for compensatory and punitive damages, but the court threw out the claim for punitive damages.

Black Letter Rule: Drunk driving is well known to cause lethal accidents and as such drunk drivers exhibit the kind of conscious disregard for the safety of others upon which an award of punitive damages may be based.

State Farm Mutual Automobile Insurance Co. v. Campbell

Instant Facts: After State Farm (D) failed to settle claims against Campbell (P) for its policy limits, Campbell obtained a judgment for $1 million in compensatory damages and $145 million in punitive damages.

Black Letter Rule: In evaluating the appropriateness of a punitive damages award, a court must weigh the reprehensibility of the defendant's conduct, the disparity between the actual harm caused and the amount of the punitive damages awarded, and the difference between the punitive damages awarded and the civil penalties imposed under state law.

Frost v. Porter Leasing Corp.

Instant Facts: An insurance company paid for some of the medical expenses of an insured accident victim, and then the insurance company tried to get repaid from the proceeds of the victim's settlement with the tortfeasor.

Black Letter Rule: Unless there is a specific contractual provision in the insurance agreement, insurers do not have a right of subrogation for medical expenses.

Lalomia v. Bankers & Shippers Ins. Co.

Instant Facts: A motor-driven bicycle collided with a car causing the death of both drivers. The parties seek a declaratory judgment to determine which of several insurance policies will cover the damage.

Black Letter Rule: Absent a specific provision to the contrary, automobile insurance does not cover vehicles that cannot be properly considered automobiles.

Pavia v. State Farm Mutual Automobile Ins. Co.

Instant Facts: An insured and his assignee sued the insurance company for failing to settle a claim for the policy limits upon demand.

Black Letter Rule: When the insurer's investigation into the merits of a claim is not yet completed, the insurer by refusing to settle the claim does not evidence bad faith, which requires a conscious and knowing indifference to the probability that the insured will be held personally accountable for a large judgment.

Seffert v. Los Angeles Transit Lines

(Injured Woman) v. *(Bus Company)*

56 Cal.2d 498, 364 P.2d 337, 15 Cal.Rptr. 161 (1961)

A JURY'S DETERMINATION OF DAMAGES SHOULD NOT BE DISTURBED UNLESS IT WAS THE PRODUCT OF PASSION, PREJUDICE, WHIM OR CAPRICE

■ **INSTANT FACTS** A bus passenger who was permanently and severely injured when the bus dragged her for several blocks while her arm and foot were caught in the bus door was awarded a large amount for pain and suffering.

■ **BLACK LETTER RULE** A jury's award of damages for pain and suffering will not be disturbed unless it is so large as to shock the conscience of the court.

■ **PROCEDURAL BASIS**

Appeal from jury verdict on the basis of excessive damages.

■ **FACTS**

Seffert (P) was entering a bus owned by Los Angeles Transit Lines ("Bus Co.") (D) when the doors closed suddenly. The bus doors caught her right hand and left foot. The bus started moving [someone was in a hurry], dragged her some distance, and then threw her to the pavement. Prior to the accident Seffert (P) was in good health and had suffered no prior serious injuries. She was single and had been self-supporting for the past 20 years. Seffert's (P) injuries were serious, painful, disabling and permanent. Most of the injuries were to her left foot, which is now permanently raised about two inches above floor level. Seffert (P) is crippled and will suffer pain for life. She has already undergone nine operations and has spent eight months in various hospitals and rehabilitation centers. These operations involved skin grafting and other painful procedures. She has a persistent open ulcer on her heel that could at any time become infected, which always leaves open the possibility that the foot will have to be amputated. At trial, Seffert (P) was able to prove $53,903.75 in pecuniary or actual damages: past and future medical expenses and lost wages. The jury awarded the total amount of pecuniary damages plus an additional $134,000.00 for pain and suffering. [Is that all?!] Seffert's (P) attorneys suggested that figure using the following formula: $100 per day from the time of the accident to the time of trial (660 days) plus $2,000 per year for the remainder of her life expectancy (34 years). Bus Co. (D) now claims that these damages are excessive.

■ **ISSUE**

Was the amount of damages for pain and suffering, which was several times greater than the pecuniary damages and was based on a mathematical formula suggested by plaintiff's attorney, excessive?

■ **DECISION AND RATIONALE**

(Peters, J.) No. It must be remembered that the jury fixed these damages and that the trial judge denied a motion for a new trial. These determinations are entitled to great weight. The jury sees and hears the witnesses and frequently, as in this case, see the injury and the impairment that has resulted therefrom. An appellate court can interfere and declare the judgment to be excessive only if the verdict is so large that, at first blush, it shocks the conscience and suggests passion, prejudice, or corruption on the part of the jury. In making this determination, the appellate court may consider the amounts awarded prior cases for similar injuries, but each case must be decided on its own facts and circumstances—injuries are seldom identical and the amount of pain and suffering in each case will vary greatly. In the present case, non-pecuniary damages include pain and suffering, humiliation as a result of being disfigured and permanently crippled, and constant anxiety and fear that the leg will have to be amputated. Considering these factors, we cannot say as a matter of law that the jury's award, though high, is so high that it shocks the conscience and gives rise to the presumption that it was the result of passion or prejudice on the part of the jurors. Affirmed.

■ DISSENT

(Traynor, J.) I believe that the award of $134,000 for pain and suffering is so excessive as to indicate that it was prompted by passion, prejudice, whim or caprice. [Inflation sure does change the value of money.] It would hardly ever be possible to compensate a person fully for pain and suffering. Translating pain and anguish into dollars can, at best, be only an arbitrary allowance best left to the jury's discretion. The award in this case exceeds not only the pecuniary losses but any such award heretofore sustained in this state even in cases involving injuries far more serious than those suffered by Seffert (P). To say that passion or prejudice has influenced a verdict is but another way of saying that the verdict exceeds any amount justified by the evidence. The excessive award in this case was undoubtedly the result of the improper argument of Seffert's (P) counsel to the jury. Counsel urged the jury to award $100 a day for pain and suffering from the time of the accident to the time of trial and $2,000 a year for pain and suffering for the remainder of Seffert's (P) life. The reason usually advanced for not allowing such an argument is that since there is no way of translating pain and suffering into monetary terms, counsel's proposal of a particular sum for each day of suffering represents an opinion and conclusion on matters not disclosed by the evidence. Counsel may argue all legitimate inferences from the evidence. However, a specified sum for pain and suffering for any particular period is bound to be conjectural—it cannot be supported by any evidence presented. I would reverse the judgment and remand the cause for a new trial on the issue of damages.

Analysis:

Unlike a product or a service that has some quantifiable value in the marketplace, pain and suffering cannot be measured in monetary terms. Yet, if compensation is the goal of the tort system, then there should be some sort of compensation for the pain and suffering that flow from a defendant's negligence. Courts are most concerned that a victim will be over-compensated, especially in modern times, when most sophisticated jurors will be aware that insurance policies are likely to pay all or part of the award. The majority's approach seems to be to accept the per diem method ($100 per day for the first two years and $2,000 per year for the rest of the plaintiff's life), because it is as good as any other method. It also seems to at least add some structure to the determination of the award, compared to the alternative, which is to just have the jury pick some lump sum out of a hat.

■ CASE VOCABULARY

NONPECUNIARY DAMAGES: Damages that were not in the form of a monetary expense to the plaintiff, but still deserve compensation; e.g. pain and suffering, embarrassment, humiliation, emotional distress.

PECUNIARY DAMAGES: Also known as actual damages or out-of-pocket damages, these damages are the amount that the plaintiff has actually paid or will pay as a result of defendant's conduct; e.g., medical bills, lost wages, replacing destroyed property.

McDougald v. Garber

(Patient) v. *(Doctor)*

73 N.Y.2d 246, 536 N.E.2d 372, 538 N.Y.S.2d 937 (1989)

NONPECUNIARY TORT DAMAGE AWARDS SHOULD FULLY COMPENSATE BUT NOT OVERCOMPENSATE THE TORT VICTIM

■ **INSTANT FACTS** A doctor's malpractice left the patient permanently comatose, so the patient (through a representative) sued for the loss of enjoyment of life as well as pain and suffering.

■ **BLACK LETTER RULE** The loss of enjoyment of life is an element of pain and suffering and cannot be calculated separately.

■ **PROCEDURAL BASIS**

Appeal from jury's award of non-pecuniary damages.

■ **FACTS**

Garber's (D) malpractice left McDougald (P) in a permanently comatose condition. The parties agreed that if liability were established, McDougald (P) would be entitled to the usual pecuniary damage items—loss of earning capacity and medical expenses. The parties also agreed that McDougald (P) would be entitled to damages for pain and suffering only if she were conscious and aware of the pain and suffering. At trial, Garber (D) argued that McDougald (P) was so severely injured that she was incapable of either experiencing pain or appreciating her condition. McDougald (P) introduced evidence that she responded to certain stimuli to a sufficient extent to indicate that she was aware of her circumstances. In addition to pain and suffering, the judge also instructed the jury that it could award damages for McDougald's (P) loss of the enjoyment of life, regardless of whether she was conscious or not. Damages for loss of the enjoyment of life relate not to what McDougald (P) is aware of, but rather to what she has lost. What her life was prior to her injury and what it has been since Garber's (D) malpractice and what it will be for as long as she lives. Over and above the award for pecuniary damages, the jury awarded $1 million for conscious pain and suffering and $3.5 million for loss of enjoyment of life. The judge reduced these amounts to a single award of $2 million. Garber (D) appeals the award of non-pecuniary damages.

■ **ISSUE**

Is the damage caused by loss of enjoyment of life a separate element of damage that is distinct from the damage caused by pain and suffering?

■ **DECISION AND RATIONALE**

(Wachtler, J.) No. An award of damages to a person injured by the negligence of another is to compensate the victim, not to punish the wrongdoer. Punitive damages are only allowed if the harmful conduct was intentional, malicious, outrageous, or otherwise aggravated beyond mere negligence. Recovery for non-economic losses such as pain and suffering and loss of enjoyment of life rests on the legal fiction that money damages can compensate for a victim's injury. We accept this fiction knowing that although money will neither ease the pain nor restore the victim's abilities, this devise is as close as the law can come in its effort to right the wrong. Our willingness to indulge this fiction comes to an end, however, when it ceases to serve the compensatory goals of tort recovery. When a person is unaware of the loss of enjoyment of life, the award of money damages has no meaning or utility to the injured person. It cannot provide the victim with any consolation or ease any burden resting on him. He cannot spend it on necessities or pleasures. Cognitive awareness is a prerequisite to recovery for loss of enjoyment of life. With respect to pain and suffering, the trial court instructed the jury simply that there must be some level of awareness in order for McDougald (P) to recover. We think that this is an appropriate standard for all aspects of non-pecuniary loss. In assessing non-pecuniary damages, the finder of fact may consider the effect of the injuries on McDougald's (P) capacity to lead a normal life. The inability of a plaintiff to enjoy life to its fullest should be one type of suffering to be factored into a general award for non-pecuniary damages, commonly known as pain and suffering. The concept of pain and suffering has broad meaning and application and is broad enough to encompass the frustration and anguish caused by the inability to participate in activities that once brought pleasure. Some would contend that because pain and suffering and loss of enjoyment of life can be distinguished, they must be treated separately if a plaintiff is to be compensated fully for each distinct injury. Such an approach may have its place when the subject is pecuniary damages, which can be calculated with precision. However, non-pecuniary damages are not calculable with such precision. We are not persuaded that any purpose would be served by having the jury make separate awards for pain and suffering and for loss of enjoyment of life. We are confident in counsel's ability to guarantee that none of their clients' injuries will be ignored by the jury. A new trial is ordered on the matter of non-pecuniary damages. Reversed.

■ DISSENT

(Titone, J.) The majority's holding neither comports with the fundamental principles of tort compensation nor does it furnish a logically consistent framework for compensating non-pecuniary loss. It is elementary that the purpose of awarding tort damages is to compensate the wronged party for the actual loss he or she has sustained. The capacity to enjoy life is an attribute of an ordinary, healthy individual. Loss of that capacity is at least as serious as the permanent destruction of a physical function, which has always been treated as a compensable item under traditional tort principles. Pain and suffering are subjective concepts, requiring cognitive capacity in order to experience them. The destruction of an individual's capacity to enjoy life, however, is an objective fact that does not differ from the permanent loss of an eye or limb. In both cases, an essential characteristic of a healthy human life has been wrongfully taken, and, consequently, the injured party is entitled to a monetary award as a substitute. Moreover, the impairment exists independently of the victim's ability to comprehend it. The majority would add the additional requirement that, aside from being compensatory, the award must have meaning or utility to the injured person. This additional requirement has no foundation in law or logic. Meaning and utility are subjective value judgments that have no place in the law of tort recovery, where the primary goal is to find ways of quantifying, to the extent possible, the worth of various forms of human tragedy. The rule that the majority sets forth today is an arbitrary one in that it denies or allows recovery on the basis of a criterion that is not truly related to its stated goal. In my view, it is fundamentally unsound, as well as grossly unfair, to deny recovery to those who are completely without cognitive capacity while permitting it for those with a mere spark of awareness, regardless of the latter's ability to appreciate either the loss sustained or the benefits of the monetary award offered in compensation. I would conclude that the loss of enjoyment of life is a distinct damage item that is recoverable separate and apart from the award for conscious pain and suffering.

Analysis:

Some damages are easy to determine and calculate. For example, past monetary damages, including medical bills and lost wages, are relatively easy to calculate and are relatively certain. There are other damages that are more difficult to calculate, but are still undisputedly valid. For example, future losses, such as future medical expenses and future lost wages, present some difficulty. It is difficult to know whether the plaintiff will live to a full life expectancy and whether the plaintiff would have kept the same job. However, since the actions of the defendant are the cause of the uncertainty, it seems reasonable to resolve the doubt in favor of the plaintiff. There are other damages, however, that are even more questionable. For example, damages for pain and suffering are so subjective and difficult to determine, and money is such an inadequate substitute for the ability to live a normal life, that it could be disputed whether it is sensible to compensate for pain and suffering. In addition, there is the debate over what constitutes pain and suffering. The majority agreed with the trial court's determination that pain and suffering should only be awarded if the person can experience the pain and suffering. However, this outcome is not compelled.

Arambula v. Wells

(*Accident Victim*) v. (*Negligent Driver*)

72 Cal.App.4th 1006, 85 Cal.Rptr.2d 584 (1999)

MONEY THAT A VICTIM RECEIVES TO ASSIST IN RECOVERING FROM AN ACCIDENT WILL NOT INURE TO THE BENEFIT OF THE DEFENDANT

■ **INSTANT FACTS** Arambula (P) was injured in a car accident and unable to work, but his employer (who was also his brother) continued to pay his weekly salary.

■ **BLACK LETTER RULE** Payment of an element of tort damages (such as lost wages) by an outside source (such as an employer) will not excuse the tortfeasor from having to pay for those damages as well.

■ **PROCEDURAL BASIS**

Appeal from trial court's refusal to allow lost wages as an item of damages.

■ **FACTS**

Arambula (P) was injured in a rear-end collision. He worked at the family-owned business, where he held 15% of the stock and his brother held 70%. Despite missing work because of his injuries, Arambula (P) continued to receive his $2,800 weekly salary. Wells (D) brought a motion in limine to exclude all evidence and testimony regarding Arambula's (P) claim for lost wages because he was still receiving wages from his brother. Arambula (P) testified that his brother wished to be reimbursed for Arambula's (P) salary, but there was no contract for reimbursement. The trial judge instructed the jury not to award Arambula (P) any damages for lost earnings because his employer paid for the time that he was off.

■ **ISSUE**

Will the tortfeasor be let off the hook if the victim's damages are paid by another source?

■ **DECISION AND RATIONALE**

(Crosby, J.) No. Under the collateral source rule, plaintiffs in personal injury actions can still recover full damages even though they already have received compensation for their injuries from such "collateral sources" as medical insurance. Tortfeasors should not receive a windfall from the thrift and foresight of persons who have secured insurance, pension, or disability benefits to provide for themselves and their families. A contrary rule would misallocate liability and discourage people from obtaining benefits from independent collateral sources. The leading case in this state is *Helfend v. Southern Cal. Rapid Transit Dist.* There, the court rejected defense efforts to introduce evidence that about 80% of an injured motorist's medical bills had been paid by his insurance carrier. The court there stated that the tortfeasor should not garner the benefits of his victim's providence. Wells (D), however, convinced the trial court that *Helfend* limits the collateral source rule to situations where plaintiffs have incurred an expense, obligation, or liability (such as purchasing medical insurance) in order to receive the benefit and not to situations where the payments and services are gratuitous. There are five reasons why we believe the trial court erred in its application of *Helfend.* First, case law on the collateral sources rule existing prior to *Helfend* states that the law makes no special distinction for purely gratuitous benefits.

If the supreme court meant to change the law with *Helfend,* it would have used unambiguous language to do so. Second, appellate opinions subsequent to *Helfend* rejected the reading of the case that was suggested by Wells (D). Several post-*Helfend* decisions have allowed plaintiffs to recover the costs of gratuitous medical care as an element of their damages. Third, the majority of jurisdictions and commentators hold that the collateral source rule covers gratuitous payments and services. Fourth, public policy concerns weigh heavily in favor of application of the collateral source rule to gratuitous payments and services. If we permit a tortfeasor to benefit from a third party's charitable gift, future tort victims will suffer—why would a family member or stranger give freely of his or her money or time if the wrongdoer would ultimately reap the benefits of such generosity? Any reduction in charitable giving would ultimately lead to an increase in the necessity to dip into the public coffers to help support these tort victims. Fifth, the collateral source rule partially serves to compensate for the victim's attorneys' fees and to further compensate the victim for his pain and suffering. It will serve to inspire victims to either repay their benefactors or to similar acts of charity. Thus, there is really no danger of double recovery on the part of the victim. Thus, we conclude that the collateral source rule favors sheltering gratuitous gifts of money or services intended to benefit tort victims, just as it favors insurance payments from coverage that they had arranged. As a rule of evidence, the collateral source rule prevents the introduction of evidence of the plaintiff being compensated by a collateral source unless there is a persuasive showing that such evidence is of substantial probative value for purposes other than reducing damages. For example, evidence that a plaintiff is paid wages after an accident could be used to impeach his claimed inability to work—to show that no time was lost, that the employee is capable of working, or had a motive to malinger. This case is remanded for a new trial on the amount of damages for lost wages legally caused by the negligence of Wells (D). Reversed.

Analysis:

Here, the court adheres to the traditional rule, that defendants do not get the benefit of the charitable impulses of others or of the plaintiff's foresight and investment in insurance. In the context of an award from an insurance policy, the collateral source rule acts to preserve the subrogation rights of insurers. That is, if the defendant is liable for all of the damage, and the insurer was forced to pay for some of the damage, then the insurer can recoup from the defendant. If the collateral source rule did not exist, the defendant would only be liable for the amount not covered by insurance, and therefore insurance companies, standing in the shoes of the plaintiff, would have no legal theory on which to recover. The collateral source rule also prevents the defendant from getting a windfall. After all, the plaintiff had to pay for the insurance, so it hardly seems fair that the defendant should benefit.

■ CASE VOCABULARY

COLLATERAL SOURCE RULE: The rule that when determining damages, the jury should consider evidence of the damages that a plaintiff suffered because of the tort as if all damages had been unreimbursed, even though some other source (such as insurance or family) paid for some of the damages. The defendant cannot argue that the plaintiff would be getting a double recovery.

MOTION IN LIMINE: A motion before trial and outside of the hearing of the jury in which the judge makes a preliminary determination as to the admissibility of certain contested evidence.

Taylor v. Superior Court

(*Accident Victim*) v. (*Drunk Driver*)

24 Cal.3d 890, 598 P.2d 854, 157 Cal.Rptr. 693 (1979)

PUNITIVE DAMAGES ARE AWARDED WHERE THE DEFENDANT SHOULD HAVE KNOWN THAT HE WAS ENDANGERING OTHERS

■ **INSTANT FACTS** An accident victim sued a drunk driver that caused the accident for compensatory and punitive damages, but the court threw out the claim for punitive damages.

■ **BLACK LETTER RULE** Drunk driving is well known to cause lethal accidents and as such drunk drivers exhibit the kind of conscious disregard for the safety of others upon which an award of punitive damages may be based.

■ **PROCEDURAL BASIS**

Writ of mandate to require the trial court to reinstate the plaintiff's claim for punitive damages.

■ **FACTS**

Taylor (P) sued Stille (D) for compensatory and punitive damages arising from a collision between their cars. Taylor (P) alleged that Stille (D) was an alcoholic with a long history of driving under the influence of alcohol (DUI), that he had numerous prior criminal DUI convictions, and that at the time of the accident Stille (D) had a DUI charge pending against him. Taylor (P) also alleged that at the time of the accident Stille (D) was working delivering alcoholic beverages in his car, was driving while consuming an alcoholic beverage, and was driving drunk. Stille (D) moved to dismiss the claim for punitive damages against him, and the trial court granted the motion.

■ **ISSUE**

Is the absence of an intent to harm on defendant's part fatal to the plaintiff's claim for punitive damages?

■ **DECISION AND RATIONALE**

(Richardson, J.) No. Our statutes authorize the recovery of punitive damages where the defendant has been guilty of "oppression, fraud, or malice, express or implied." *Civil Code § 3294.* "Malice" implies an act conceived in a spirit of mischief or with criminal indifference towards the obligations owed to others. Something more than the commission of a tort is always required for punitive damages. There must be circumstances of aggravation or outrage such as spite or malice, a fraudulent or evil motive, or such a conscious and deliberate disregard of the interests of others that his conduct may be called willful or wanton. Stille's (D) successful demurrer to the claim for punitive damages was based upon Taylor's (P) failure to allege any actual intent on the part of Stille (D) to harm Taylor (P) or others. We find that, regardless of intent, a conscious disregard for the safety of others is sufficient to support an award of punitive damages. The pleadings before us in this case contain sufficient allegations upon which it may be reasonably concluded that Stille (D) consciously disregarded the safety of others. It is commonly known that drunk driving may have a lethal effect, whether or not the driver had a prior history of drunk driving incidents. Punitive damages are appropriate in this context because they also serve to deter similar future conduct, the incalculable cost of which is well documented. It is crystal clear to us that courts in the formulation of rules on damage assessment and in weighing the deterrent function must recognize the severe threat to the public safety that is posed by drunk drivers. Stille (D) claims that there are many instances of simple negligent conduct not involving consumption of alcoholic beverages that could also be alleged to involve a conscious disregard of the safety of others. For example, one who willfully disobeys traffic signals or speed limit laws arguably possesses such a state of mind and culpability. However, that case is not before us and we express no opinion on it. Therefore, we overrule Stille's (D) demurrer and reinstate the claim for punitive damages. Reversed.

■ CONCURRENCE

(Bird, J.) Although I concur in the judgment of the court, I respectfully dissent from that portion of the majority opinion that allows a claim for punitive damages in every case of drunk driving. However, in this particular case Stille (D) is charged with repeatedly driving while intoxicated after his own experience made him completely aware of the possible consequences of his act. Therefore, a reasonable jury may conclude that the second time was no accident.

■ DISSENT

(Clark, J.) If today's decision would significantly reduce the number of drunk driving accidents, then the majority might be justified in changing the law relating to punitive damages. However, clearly this decision will not reduce the number of drunk drivers. There are several obvious reasons for hesitancy in awarding punitive damages. Plaintiffs are fully compensated by compensatory damages—punitive damages constitute unjust enrichment. In addition, civil law is properly concerned with vindicating rights and compensating injured persons; criminal law, which is determined by the legislature (not the courts), is the proper vehicle for punishment. When a defendant's tortious conduct also constitutes a crime, the allowance of punitive damages punishes him twice for the same crime and exposes him to a greater penalty than allowed by the Penal Code. Furthermore, punitive damage trials interfere with policies governing trial procedures. The plaintiff in a punitive damage trial can offer evidence of the financial statue of the defendant, thus turning the focus of personal injury trials from liability to the financial standing of the defendant. Moreover, deterrence in the context of drunk driving is marginal at best. In situations where compensatory damages only require a wrongdoer to give up ill-gotten gains, a punitive award may be necessary to deter. Otherwise, persons contemplating wrongful conduct have nothing to lose by their actions. On the other hand, the deterrent effect of punitive damages is minimal where, as here, the conduct of the defendant is a crime that is regularly and effectively enforced and where the wrongful conduct is as likely to result in injury to the wrongdoer as to others. These considerations convince me that we should adhere rigidly to the fundamental principle that punitive damages should be awarded with the greatest caution in accident cases.

Analysis:

This case explores the question of what type of behavior will trigger liability for punitive damages. The opinions present three different views. The majority opinion takes the position that punitive damages should be awarded when a defendant intentionally engages in an activity with a serious risk of causing injury to others (such as driving while intoxicated), even though the defendant had no intention of harming others. The majority seems to suggest that a defendant should be aware of the well-known consequences of his actions, no matter how many times in the past he has been able to escape those consequences. If the activity is dangerous enough, punitive damages are appropriate. The majority seems to take a negligence-type approach to the question of how culpable a defendant must be in order to be liable for punitive damages. So long as the defendant should have known of a great danger, that is enough. The concurrence takes an approach that requires more culpability than the majority. It relies on Stille's (D) prior history and knowledge of the consequences of his actions. The concurrence seems to suggest that liability will only arise if there is some true, practical knowledge and action in disregard of that knowledge. The concurrence takes an approach analogous to recklessness in deciding culpability. The dissent is of the opinion that because of the extreme nature of punitive damages, they should be awarded only where the defendant acted maliciously toward his victims. The dissent's approach requires intentional action to establish the proper amount of culpability.

■ CASE VOCABULARY

PUNITIVE DAMAGES: A sum awarded against a defendant in excess of any compensatory damages, the purpose of which is either to punish the defendant or to deter the defendant or others from similar actions.

State Farm Mutual Automobile Insurance Co. v. Campbell

(*Insurance Company*) v. (*Insured Automobile Driver*)

538 U.S. 408, 123 S.Ct. 1513, 155 L.Ed.2d 585 (2003)

PUNITIVE DAMAGES ARE SUBJECT TO REASONABLE LIMITS UNDER THE FOURTEENTH AMENDMENT

■ **INSTANT FACTS** After State Farm (D) failed to settle claims against Campbell (P) for its policy limits, Campbell obtained a judgment for $1 million in compensatory damages and $145 million in punitive damages.

■ **BLACK LETTER RULE** In evaluating the appropriateness of a punitive damages award, a court must weigh the reprehensibility of the defendant's conduct, the disparity between the actual harm caused and the amount of the punitive damages awarded, and the difference between the punitive damages awarded and the civil penalties imposed under state law.

■ **PROCEDURAL BASIS**

Certiorari to review the excessiveness of a punitive damages verdict.

■ **FACTS**

Campbell (P) held an automobile policy with State Farm Mutual Automobile Insurance Co. (D). While traveling in Utah, Campbell (P) decided to pass six vans traveling slowly in front of him. As Campbell (P) was driving in the wrong direction, Ospital was forced onto the shoulder to avoid a head-on collision. In the process, Ospital lost control of his vehicle, collided with a vehicle driven by Slusher, and died. Slusher became permanently disabled. An investigation of the incident determined that Campbell's (P) unsafe pass had caused Ospital's death and Slusher's injuries. Nonetheless, State Farm (D) decided to contest liability and declined offers from Ospital's estate and Slusher to settle both claims for its total policy limit of $50,000. At trial, a jury found Campbell (P) liable for the accident and returned a verdict for $185,849. State Farm (D) refused to pay the verdict in excess of its $50,000 policy limits and refused to post a supersedeas bond required for Campbell's (P) appeal. Campbell (P) subsequently obtained independent counsel and appealed the verdict.

During the appeal, Campbell (P) agreed to pursue a bad faith action against State Farm (D) in exchange for an agreement by Ospital's estate and Slusher not to seek satisfaction of the judgment against Campbell (P). Ospital's estate and Slusher agreed to accept ninety percent of any proceeds received from State Farm (D) in the bad faith suit. The Utah Supreme Court denied Campbell's (P) appeal from the wrongful death judgment, and State Farm (D) subsequently agreed to pay the full amount of the judgment against him. Campbell (P) then commenced his bad faith suit. A jury awarded Campbell $2.6 million in compensatory damages and $145 million in punitive damages. After the trial court reduced the compensatory damages award to $1 million and the punitive damages to $25 million, the Utah Supreme Court reinstated the $145 million punitive damages verdict. State Farm (D) sought a writ of certiorari.

■ **ISSUE**

When compensatory damages are $1 million, is an award of $145 million in punitive damages excessive, in violation of the Due Process Clause of the Fourteenth Amendment?

■ DECISION AND RATIONALE

(Kennedy, J.) Yes. Unlike compensatory damages, which compensate an injured person for the wrongful conduct of another, punitive damages are aimed at deterrence and retribution against the wrongdoer. The Due Process Clause does not permit "the imposition of grossly excessive or arbitrary punishments on a tortfeasor." Because punitive damages serve a purpose similar to criminal sanctions, but without the procedural protections accompanying criminal punishment, a court must weigh the reprehensibility of the defendant's conduct, the disparity between the actual harm caused and the amount of the punitive damages awarded, and the difference between the punitive damages awarded and the civil penalties imposed under state law. Weighing these factors, the jury's $145 million punitive damages award was excessive.

First, State Farm's (D) conduct cannot be considered so reprehensible as to justify the award. In gauging a defendant's conduct, a court should consider whether the harm caused was physical rather than economic, whether the defendant acted with reckless disregard for the health and safety of others, whether the plaintiff was financially vulnerable, whether the conduct involved a repetitive pattern or an isolated incident, and whether the conduct was intentional. Here, while State Farm's (D) handling of Campbell's (P) insurance claims is not laudable, its conduct does not justify such an excessive punitive damages award. Rather than focusing on the particular conduct of the case, the award focuses on State Farm's (D) nationwide handling of claims. A state court, however, has no authority to punish a defendant for conduct that occurred outside its territorial limits and involving parties who were directly affected by the out-of-state conduct. A defendant's dissimilar conduct, bearing no relation to the harm involved in a particular lawsuit, may not be taken into account when determining punitive damages. Due process does not permit a court to award punitive damages merely because the defendant may have caused some harm to others who were not proper parties to the litigation.

Second, although there is no bright-line ratio between the amount of punitive damages and the harm caused to a plaintiff, an award 145 times the actual harm suffered is excessive. Generally, anything over a single-digit ratio calls for close judicial scrutiny. Likewise, as the compensatory damages award increases, the appropriate proportion to the punitive damages award decreases, since a larger ratio is unnecessary to serve the purposes of deterrence and retribution. Here, the 145:1 ratio between the punitive award and the compensatory award is unreasonable given the $1 million compensatory damages award for emotional distress.

Finally, the $145 million punitive damages award is grossly in excess of the maximum civil penalty of $10,000 imposed under Utah law. Under this factor, the punitive damages award is again excessive. Because a punitive award more closely approximating the compensatory award would be an adequate and rational punishment for the defendant's conduct, the Court holds that the award is excessive. Reversed and remanded.

■ DISSENT

(Scalia, J.) The Due Process Clause affords no protections against "excessive" or "unreasonable" punitive damages awards.

■ DISSENT

(Thomas, J.) The Constitution does not "constrain the size of punitive damages awards."

■ DISSENT

(Ginsburg, J.) The field of punitive damages lies entirely within the prerogative of the states. While the punitive damages award in this case may be excessive, it should be addressed through state tort reform legislation, but the Court should not substitute its judgment for that of the state courts. The state court could have determined that State Farm's national scheme to deny benefits to its consumers had an adverse impact on Utah residents. In second-guessing the state's determination on the trial record, the Court affords no respect to the states and inappropriately threatens to create a bright-line test for determining the appropriateness of a punitive damages award.

Analysis:

The Court's fascination with the appropriate ratio between the compensatory damages and punitive damages is interesting. If punitive damages serve a separate and distinct purpose from compensatory damages, why should the amount of compensatory damages affect the amount of punitive damages? If a defendant commits intentional conduct worthy of punishment, should it matter whether the compensatory damages were substantial or not?

■ **CASE VOCABULARY:**

BAD FAITH: Dishonesty of belief or purpose.

COMPENSATORY DAMAGES: Damages sufficient in amount to indemnify the injured person for the loss suffered.

PUNITIVE DAMAGES: Damages awarded in addition to actual damages when the defendant acted with recklessness, malice, or deceit.

SUPERSEDEAS BOND: A bond that suspends a judgment creditor's power to levy execution, usually pending appeal.

Frost v. Porter Leasing Corp.

(*Car Accident Victim*) v. (*Other Driver*)

386 Mass. 425, 436 N.E.2d 387 (1982)

INSURERS HAVE AN IMPLIED RIGHT OF SUBROGATION FOR PROPERTY CLAIMS BUT ONLY A CONTRACTUAL RIGHT OF SUBROGATION FOR MEDICAL BENEFITS

■ **INSTANT FACTS** An insurance company paid for some of the medical expenses of an insured accident victim, and then the insurance company tried to get repaid from the proceeds of the victim's settlement with the tortfeasor.

■ **BLACK LETTER RULE** Unless there is a specific contractual provision in the insurance agreement, insurers do not have a right of subrogation for medical expenses.

■ **PROCEDURAL BASIS**

Appeal from trial court determination that insurer has the right of subrogation.

■ **FACTS**

Frost (P) was injured in a car accident. He sued the other driver for medical expenses, pain and suffering, impaired earning capacity, and future expenses. His wife sued for loss of consortium. While his case was pending. Frost (P) received medical expense benefits of $22,700 under an insurance plan that was paid for by his employer. The Frosts (P) settled their claim for a lump sum of $250,00. The insurance company intervened and claimed a right of subrogation as to any damages that Frost (P) recovered for medical expenses. The trial court determined that the insurance company had the right of subrogation in the settlement in the amount that it had paid out minus a share of the costs that the Frosts had incurred in obtaining a settlement.

■ **ISSUE**

Does an insurer who pays health benefits to an injured party have a non-contractual, implied right of subrogation in any damage award that the injured party recovers?

■ **DECISION AND RATIONALE**

(Hennessey, J.) No. We conclude that the insurer has no right, in the absence of a subrogation clause, to share in the insured's recovery against the tortfeasor for damages awarded for personal injury. Subrogation is an equitable adjustment of rights that operates when a creditor (such as a tort victim) is entitled to recover from two sources and one of those sources (the tortfeasor) bears primary legal responsibility. If the secondary source (the insurance company) pays the obligation, then it succeeds to the rights of the party that it paid (the insured victim) against the primarily responsible party (the tortfeasor). With certain limits, the doctrine of subrogation applies to payments made pursuant to insurance policies. The right of subrogation may arise from a contractual agreement between the insurer and the insured, or it may arise by implication in common law. In this case, there was no contractual right to subrogation, and therefore we discuss only the implied right to subrogation. The reason for implied subrogation in the context of insurance is to prevent a double recovery by the insured. Subrogation returns any excess to the insurer, who can then recycle it in the form of lower insurance costs. The right to subrogation does not arise automatically—it depends on the type of coverage involved. In cases of property damage, the insurer's right to subrogation is generally recognized. The insured can be fully compensated by the wrongdoer for the destruction of property and the actual loss can be determined with certainty. Personal insurance (medical coverage, life insurance, and accident insurance), however, is less of a contract than a form of investment. The insured's receipt of both insurance benefits and tort damages may not produce a measurably duplicative recovery. The insured is likely to have suffered intangible losses that are unsusceptible to precise measurement, and the two sources of recovery may cover different ranges of loss and be differently affected by considerations such as fault. When subrogation is based on broad principles of equity and efficiency, rather than on the contract of the parties, isolation of medical expenses is artificial, and the accident victim's position should be viewed as a whole. Subrogation played no part of the bargain between insurer and insured, and in this circumstance, the courts should not intervene to adjust the rights of the parties unless all the adverse consequences of the accident have been offset. It is unlikely that all of the losses of an accident victim will be recovered, much less duplicated, by the payment of both damages and insurance proceeds. The insured may be faced with property damage, pain and suffering, diminished earning capacity and medical bills. The costs of litigation or decision to settle may reduce his overall recovery. In the absence of a contractual agreement, an insurer that has paid medical or hospital expense benefits has no right to share in the proceeds of the insured's recovery against a tortfeasor. Reversed.

■ CONCURRENCE

(Wilkins, J.) I agree with the conclusion of the court that, in the absence of a provision for subrogation in the insurance policy, an insurer is not entitled to subrogation as to amounts paid or payable by a tortfeasor to the insured. In fairness to an insured, a policy should disclose the possibility of subrogation claims. A person or group purchasing coverage for medical costs should know the limitations of such coverage. However, I do not share the majority's belief that subrogation for payment of medical expenses presents any greater problems than for any other type of injury. Subrogation is a reasonable method of assisting in holding down the costs of health insurance. It prevents an undeserved windfall to the insured. I see no justification for denying subrogation because the claimant may not have been made whole on all elements of his damages. The claimant is made whole on his medical costs to the extent of his coverage. A health insurer should not be forced to assist in making the claimant whole on some other aspect of his damages, such as lost wages and pain and suffering, for which the insured has not purchased coverage from the health insurer.

Analysis:

This opinion focuses on the topic of subrogation, which is related to but distinct from the collateral source rule. The collateral source rule states that a defendant's award of damages is not reduced just because a third party, such as an insurance company, paid for part of the insured's medical treatment and injuries. Subrogation requires that somebody has to reimburse the insurance company for having to pay out benefits to the insured. Both the majority and minority say that, where there was a settlement agreement, the insurer is not entitled to subrogation from the settlement proceeds absent a contractual provision granting subrogation rights in the settlement proceeds. The majority reasons that personal injury insurance is an investment by the plaintiff, and that the return from the investment is the seeming double recovery when the plaintiff can collect both insurance proceeds and settlement proceeds. In addition, the court reasoned that there really was no double recovery because an injured person cannot be compensated too much for pain and suffering. The minority bases its opinion on contract grounds—everyone should get what they contracted for.

■ CASE VOCABULARY

SUBROGATION: When the insurance company stands in the shoes of the insured and may collect from the defendant or settlement proceeds a partial or full reimbursement for the benefits that the insurer was required to pay to the insured.

Lalomia v. Bankers & Shippers Ins. Co.

(Accident Victim) v. *(Insurer)*

35 A.D.2d 114, 312 N.Y.S.2d 1018 (1970)

DEPENDING ON THE THEORY OF LIABILITY, SEVERAL DIFFERENT INSURANCE POLICIES MAY COVER THE SAME CLAIM

■ **INSTANT FACTS** A motor-driven bicycle collided with a car causing the death of both drivers. The parties seek a declaratory judgment to determine which of several insurance policies will cover the damage.

■ **BLACK LETTER RULE** Absent a specific provision to the contrary, automobile insurance does not cover vehicles that cannot be properly considered automobiles

■ **PROCEDURAL BASIS**

Declaratory judgment to determine coverage under various insurance policies.

■ **FACTS**

Twelve-year-old Michael Maddock was operating a motorized bicycle—a bicycle from which various operational parts (such as the pedals) had been removed and to which a gasoline powered lawn mower engine had been added. Maddock collided with an automobile driven by Jean Lalomia (P), a wife and mother of four children. Both Maddock and Lalomia (P) were killed in the collision. On Maddock's side, Bankers and Shippers Insurance Company (B&S) (D) had issued two automobile insurance policies to Maddock's father, each covering a different family automobile. The policies would provide coverage to any after-acquired "private passenger automobile." Maddock's father also carried a homeowner's insurance policy that would pay for damages due to personal injury or property damage, but excluded from coverage injuries due to the operation of an "automobile" away from the homeowner's premises. The homeowner's policy defined "automobile" as a "land motor vehicle." On Lalomia's (P) side, her automobile insurance policy had an uninsured motorist endorsement, which is deemed to cover the damage caused by all uninsured motor vehicles. This court's job is to sort out which policies, if any, will cover the damage suffered by Lalomia (P).

■ **ISSUE**

Is the coverage by an insured's automobile insurance policy broad enough to make the insurance company liable for damage done by a motorized vehicle of the insured that is not an automobile?

■ **DECISION AND RATIONALE**

(Benjamin, J.) No. We first consider the Maddocks' automobile insurance policies. The coverage of the B&S (D) insurance policy, extending coverage to after-acquired private passenger vehicles, was not intended to alter the nature of the risk involved in insuring private passenger vehicles. It would be unfair to compel an insurer to extend coverage to higher-risk vehicles such as motorized bicycles, motorcycles, or racing cars. We next consider the Maddocks' homeowner's insurance. The policy exempts damage caused by the maintenance, operation, or use of motor vehicles outside of the insured's premises. We find that the motor-driven bicycle in this case is a "motor vehicle" under the homeowner's policy. The accident occurred several blocks away from the Maddocks' premises.

Therefore, the homeowner's insurer is not liable for damage caused by Maddock's (P) maintenance, operation, or use of the bicycle. However, Lalomia (P) is also alleging negligence on the part of Maddock's father in placing a dangerous instrumentality in the possession of and at the disposal of a 12-year-old boy. We hold that the common-law negligent entrustment claim against the father is distinct from the claim against the son for his operation of the vehicle. Therefore, the homeowner's insurer is liable for damages due to the negligent entrustment. Finally, we turn to the automobile insurance policy maintained by Lalomia (P), which contained an uninsured motorist endorsement. Such an endorsement covers all uninsured motor vehicles. Since the motor-driven bicycle was an uninsured motor vehicle, the Lalomias' (P) automobile insurance also covers damage caused by the accident. In summary, liability imposed on the insurer that issued the Maddocks' homeowner's insurance policy is limited to the theory of negligently permitting the operation of a dangerous mechanism. As there is no policy in force with respect to the operation of the motor-driven bicycle, the Lalomia's (P) uninsured motorist endorsement is applicable.

Analysis:

Here there were several insurance policies that could potentially cover the same type of claim. Therefore, the parties and insurance companies asked the court to sort out who would be responsible to pay the claim if Lalomia (P) were able to make his case. Such a determination is important to an insurer not only to determine if it may ultimately be liable, but also because the insurer whose policy provides coverage has a duty to defend against the claim. An insurance company that does not defend because of an erroneous belief that there was no coverage under its policy could be liable to the defendant for not adequately defending the claim. Conversely, an insurer that did defend in the erroneous belief that there was coverage under its policy would have to bear the expense of an unnecessary lawsuit.

■ CASE VOCABULARY

DECLARATORY JUDGMENT: One type of relief that may be sought in court where the plaintiff is not asking for money damages but for the court to determine the rights of the parties.

Pavia v. State Farm Mutual Automobile Ins. Co.

(Accident Victim) v. *(Insurer)*

82 N.Y.2d 445, 626 N.E.2d 24, 605 N.Y.S.2d 208 (1993)

INSURERS WHO DO NOT AGREE TO SETTLE FOR THE POLICY LIMITS OPEN THEMSELVES UP TO LIABILITY FOR ANY JURY AWARD IN EXCESS OF POLICY LIMITS

■ **INSTANT FACTS** An insured and his assignee sued the insurance company for failing to settle a claim for the policy limits upon demand.

■ **BLACK LETTER RULE** When the insurer's investigation into the merits of a claim is not yet completed, the insurer by refusing to settle the claim does not evidence bad faith, which requires a conscious and knowing indifference to the probability that the insured will be held personally accountable for a large judgment.

■ **PROCEDURAL BASIS**

Appeal of jury determination that the insurer acted in bad faith.

■ **FACTS**

One night in April 1985, Carmine Rosato was driving his mother's car with Pavia (P) and another youth as passengers. Rosato was 16 years old and only had a learner's permit that did not authorize driving at night. The car was insured by State Farm Mutual Automobile Insurance Company (State Farm) (D) with a $100,000 liability limit. As he swerved to avoid a double-parked car, Rosato collided with a car driven by Amerosa. On October 1985, Pavia (P) brought a personal injury suit against Rosato. In March 1986, a preliminary investigation done by State Farm (D) indicated that Rosato was 100% responsible for the accident. In August 1986, State Farm (D) had medical reports indicating the severity of Pavia's (P) injuries. In April 1987, State Farm's (D) physicians confirmed those medical reports. On June 9, 1987, Rosato was deposed. Rosato testified that the double-parked car may have been backing up, that there were witnesses to the accident that were previously unknown to State Farm (D), that Pavia (P) was not wearing a seatbelt, and that drugs were being used in the car that night. This testimony gave State Farm (D) the possibility of two extra defenses—an emergency defense and an assumption of the risk defense. The day after the deposition counsel for Rosato, which had been retained by State Farm (D), indicated that their chances to win the case were extremely unfavorable, but recommended further investigation in light of the new information obtained in the deposition. On June 26, 1987, Pavia's (P) counsel wrote to State Farm (D) demanding $100,000 (the policy limit) to settle the case. The letter gave State Farm (D) 30 days to accept to offer. State Farm (D) did not respond to the offer, but instead conducted a thorough investigation of the accident based on the new information learned in Rosato's deposition. In November 1987, the investigation was abandoned as fruitless. In December 1987, State Farm (D) authorized settlement for the policy limits. In January 1988, this offer was conveyed to Pavia (P), but was rejected as too late. A trial was held in March 1988, wherein the jury awarded Pavia (P) $6,322,000 and attributed 85% of the fault to Rosato and 15% of the fault to Amerosa. The trial court reduced the amount to $5 million, and the appellate court reduced it even further to $3,880,000. Rosato then assigned any claim that it might have against State Farm (D) to Pavia (P) in consideration for an agreement by Pavia (P) that he would not seek to collect from Rosato any money in excess of what was collected from State Farm (D). Rosato and Pavia (P) then sued State

Farm (D), alleging that it had acted in bad faith by failing to accept Pavia's (P) offer to settle for the policy limits despite clear liability and obvious damages in excess of the policy limits.

■ ISSUE

Does an insurance company act in bad faith when it refuses early settlement of a claim that the insured is likely to lose if litigated?

■ DECISION AND RATIONALE

(Titone, J.) No. It is well settled that an insurer may be held liable to its insured for the breach of the insurer's duty of good faith in defending and settling claims over which the insurer exercises exclusive control on behalf of the insured. Whenever an offer to settle is presented that is within policy limits, the insurer faces a conflict between its desire to minimize payments and the insured's interest in avoiding liability beyond policy limits. The bad faith doctrine rests on the fact that insurers typically exercise complete control over the settlement of claims against their insureds, and they are therefore required to act in the best interests of the insured. On the other hand, courts are understandably reluctant to expose insurers to liability in excess of the policy limits for failure to settle that is merely the product of bad judgment or lack of foresight. Faced with these conflicting interests of insurer and insured, we hold that in order for an insured to establish a prima facie case of bad faith against an insurer in failing to settle a claim, the insured must establish conduct that amounts to a gross disregard of the insured's interests. The insurer must place the interest of the insured on an equal footing with the insurer's own interests when considering a settlement offer. The insured must establish that the insurer engaged in a pattern of behavior evincing a conscious or knowing indifference to the probability that an insured would be held personally accountable for a large judgment if a settlement offer within the policy limits were not accepted. The gross disregard strikes a fair balance between an ordinary negligence standard, which would too greatly restrict the latitude that insurers need to investigate and resist unfounded claims, and a standard that requires the showing of dishonest motives, which is all but impossible to satisfy and would effectively insulate insurers from conduct that would severely prejudice the rights of the insured. In the present case, it is true that the insurer turned down a settlement offer. However, in considering all of the relevant facts and circumstances—including the early settlement demand, the unilateral and arbitrary 30-day time limit, several significant questions about the insured's liability at the time of the demand, and the insurer's duty to make a full and adequate investigation of all reasonable defenses—we conclude that this record lacks any indicia of recklessness or conscious disregard for the insured's rights upon which to base a finding of bad faith. Reversed.

Analysis:

The insurer has a duty to defend in a suit against the insured if the insurer's policy will cover the loss. Therefore, it is usually the insurer that hires the lawyers to defend the claim (though the lawyers still owe their professional responsibilities to the insured as the client). However, insurance policies contain clauses that require the insured to cooperate fully with the insurer. The insured agrees that he will not settle a case without the insured's permission, which means that usually the insurance company has full discretion over when to settle a claim. This creates the conflict that arises in the present case. If the plaintiff makes a demand for the policy limits, the insurance company has nothing to lose by going to trial: if the defendant wins, the insurance company has no liability; if the plaintiff wins, there is still the possibility that the jury will come in with an award that is less than the policy maximum, and even if the jury does come back with a number in excess of the policy limits, the insurer is only liable up to the amount of the policy limits. Since the insured is personally liable for any award above the policy maximum, the insured would rather settle for the policy limits. Thus the conflict is between the insurance company's willingness to go for broke and the insured's desire to settle. The answer to this conflict, as in the present case, is to impose upon the insurer a duty of good faith settlement if liability is clear and the insured will be faced with the likelihood of being stuck with an award greatly in excess of the policy limits.

CHAPTER TWELVE

Intentional Harm

Garratt v. Dailey

Instant Facts: A woman brought suit against a young boy when she was injured in a fall that resulted from his pulling a chair out from underneath her.

Black Letter Rule: When a person has knowledge to a substantial certainty that harmful or offensive contact will result from a certain action, a battery occurs if that action is taken, even if there is no intent to cause harm to another.

Picard v. Barry Pontiac–Buick, Inc.

Instant Facts: After Picard (P) took a picture of Barry Pontiac–Buick, Inc.'s (Barry Pontiac) (D) service worker inspecting her brakes, the service worker (D) became angry, moved toward her, put his finger on the camera she was holding, and said, "Who gave you permission to take my picture?"

Black Letter Rule: (1) An assault requires an act which puts a person in reasonable fear of imminent bodily harm. (2) A battery occurs when a person intentionally causes an offensive bodily contact with another person, which includes contact with an object connected with that person.

Wishnatsky v. Huey

Instant Facts: While Huey (D) was conversing with attorney Crary in Crary's office, Wishnatsky (P), Crary's paralegal, tried to enter without knocking, and Huey (D) closed the door pushing Wishnatsky (P) back into the hall.

Black Letter Rule: A person commits an offensive contact battery if he acts with an intent to cause a harmful or offensive contact with another person, and his act directly or indirectly causes a contact with another person which would offend a reasonable sense of personal dignity.

Lopez v. Winchell's Donut House

Instant Facts: A donut shop clerk voluntarily joined two other employees in a back room where they accused her of theft and questioned her.

Black Letter Rule: False imprisonment requires confinement against a person's will, which may be effected by physical force, a threat of force, or the assertion of authority, but not by moral pressure or a threat of future action.

Womack v. Eldridge

Instant Facts: An investigator took Womack's (P) picture for an attorney to use in a child molesting case, thus involving Womack (P) in the case and causing him severe emotional distress.

Black Letter Rule: A person may recover for emotional distress absent physical injury if the distress was severe and resulted from conduct which was outrageous and intolerable and either intentional or reckless.

McDermott v. Reynolds

Instant Facts: Reynolds (D) had an adulterous affair with McDermott's (P) wife and continued to do so after McDermott (P) confronted him and asked him to stop, causing him severe emotional distress.

Black Letter Rule: A statutory bar of actions for alienation of affection also bars an action for intentional infliction of emotional distress where the alleged conduct would support an action for alienation of affection.

Hustler Magazine v. Falwell

Instant Facts: Jerry Falwell (P) sued Hustler Magazine (D) for intentional infliction of emotional distress for publishing a parody of Falwell (P) engaged in incestuous acts with his mother.

Black Letter Rule: In order to recover for intentional infliction of emotional distress, public figures must show that a false statement of fact was made with actual malice.

Hart v. Geysel

Instant Facts: Cartwright (P) died as a result of a blow he received in an illegal prize fight he engaged in with Geysel (D).

Black Letter Rule: One who consents to particular conduct has no right to recover damages for an injury he sustains when another acts on that consent.

Courvoisier v. Raymond

Instant Facts: After being attacked by rioters and unsuccessfully trying to scare them away, Courvoisier (D) saw Raymond (P) approach him, mistakenly believed he was a rioter, and, fearing for his life, shot him.

Black Letter Rule: A person is privileged to act in self-defense if the surrounding circumstances would lead a reasonable man to believe that he was in danger of losing his life or of receiving great bodily harm, and the person does so believe.

Katko v. Briney

Instant Facts: Briney (D) set a spring gun in his unoccupied farm house, and the gun seriously injured Katko (P) when he broke into the house to steal old bottles and fruit jars.

Black Letter Rule: An owner has a privilege to use reasonable force to protect his property, but this privilege does not allow him to use a deadly trap in an unoccupied building to protect his property against trespassers and thieves.

Vincent v. Lake Erie Transportation Co.

Instant Facts: During a fierce storm, a steamship was repeatedly thrown against a dock, causing damage to the dock.

Black Letter Rule: Damage caused to another's property due to necessity requires compensation for the actual harm caused.

Wilson v. Layne

Instant Facts: Officers (D) permitted the media to ride along and enter Wilson's (P) home with them as they executed an arrest warrant, but the media did not assist the officers (D) in executing the warrant.

Black Letter Rule: The defense of qualified immunity shields an officer from liability for prohibited conduct only if the unlawfulness of the conduct was not "clearly established" when the conduct occurred.

Garratt v. Dailey

(Young Boy) v. (Older Woman)
46 Wash.2d 197, 279 P.2d 1091 (1955)

WHEN A MINOR COMMITS A TORT WITH FORCE HE IS LIABLE AS ANY OTHER PERSON WOULD BE

■ **INSTANT FACTS** A woman brought suit against a young boy when she was injured in a fall that resulted from his pulling a chair out from underneath her.

■ **BLACK LETTER RULE** When a person has knowledge to a substantial certainty that harmful or offensive contact will result from a certain action, a battery occurs if that action is taken, even if there is no intent to cause harm to another.

■ **PROCEDURAL BASIS**

Certification to the Supreme Court of Washington of a trial court finding that there was no battery in a suit brought by an adult woman against a young boy.

■ **FACTS**

Ruth Garratt (P) suffered a fractured hip and other serious and painful injuries when, on July 16, 1951, she fell to the ground while trying to sit down in a lawn chair. How she came to fall was the subject of dispute. Garratt's (P) sister, who was present during the fall, testified that Brian Dailey (D), a five year-old boy, deliberately pulled the chair out from under Garratt (P) as she was about to sit in it. Dailey (D) testified that he had moved the chair and was about to sit in it when he saw Garratt (P) sitting down (with nothing underneath her). At that time, he jumped up and tried to move the chair to a position underneath her so as to prevent injury. Garratt (P) brought suit against Dailey (D) for the injuries. The trial court found in favor of Dailey (D), stressing that he did not have any intent to injure Garratt (P) when he moved the chair, and therefore did not commit a battery. Garratt (P) appealed.

■ **ISSUE**

Can a battery occur if there is no intent to injure another but there is a knowledge that a certain action will result in harmful contact and that action is taken?

■ **DECISION AND RATIONALE**

(Hill, J.) Yes. Brian (D), whether 5 or 55, must have committed a wrongful act before he can be held liable for Garratt's (P) injuries. Garratt (P) argues that the act of moving the chair constituted a battery, which is defined as the intentional infliction of a harmful bodily contact upon another. The rule used in determining liability for battery is found in 29 Restatement (First) of Torts § 13, which states: "An act which, directly or indirectly, is the legal cause of a harmful contact with another's person makes the actor liable to the other, if (a) the act is done with the intention of bringing about a harmful or offensive contact." The comments to this section further state that in order for an act to be done "with the intention of bringing about a harmful or offensive contact . . . . [it] must be done for the purpose of causing the contact . . . or with knowledge on the part of the actor that such contact . . . is substantially certain to be produced." Had Garratt (P) proved to the satisfaction of the trial court that Brian (D) moved the chair while she was in the act of sitting down, his action would have been with the intent of causing her injury, and she would be entitled to a judgment against him. The trial court did not so find, but accepted Brian's (D) version of the facts. It then considered whether a battery was established under the facts as it found them. In this connection, we quote another section of the comments to the Restatement: "It is not enough that the act itself is intentionally done and this, even though the actor realizes or should realize that it contains a ... risk of bringing about the contact or apprehension. Such realization may make the actor's conduct negligent or even reckless but unless he realizes that to a substantial certainty, the contact or apprehension will result, the actor has not that intention which is necessary to make him liable under the rule stated in this section." Thus, a battery would be established if, in addition to Garratt's (P) fall, it was proved that, when Brian (D) moved the chair, he knew with substantial certainty that she would attempt to sit down where the chair had been. The mere absence of any intent to injure Garratt (P) or to play a prank on her or to embarrass her, or to commit an assault and battery on her would not absolve him from liability if in fact he had such knowledge. Without such a knowledge, however, there would be no wrongful act and thus no liability. We believe that before Garratt's (P) case can be dismissed, there should be no question but that the trial court addresses this issue; hence, the case should be remanded for clarifications of the findings to specifically cover the question of Brian's (D) knowledge, because intent could be inferred therefrom. If the court finds that he had such knowledge the necessary intent will be established and Garratt (P) will be entitled to recover, even though there was no purpose to injure or embarrass her. The only circumstance where Brian's (D) age is of any consequence is in determining what he knew, and there his experience, capacity, and understanding are material. Remanded.

Analysis:

Under *Garratt,* a battery will occur despite a lack of an offensive intentional touching when a person has knowledge to a substantial certainty that harmful or offensive contact will result from a certain action. Thus, in this case, it was found that Brian (D) might have committed a battery even though he never touched Garratt (P); the fact that he knew pulling the chair away might cause her harm was enough for the court. Some jurisdictions accept the Washington view of battery laid out in *Garratt,* but many others still require an actual touching of the battery victim. On remand, the trial court found that Garratt (P) was actually in the act of seating herself when the chair was moved, and that Brian (D) knew what she was doing. On that ground, the trial court ruled in favor of Garratt (P).

Picard v. Barry Pontiac-Buick, Inc.

(*Customer*) v. (*Brake Inspector*)

654 A.2d 690 (R.I. 1995)

THE INTENTIONAL TORTS OF ASSAULT AND BATTERY ARE SEPARATE BUT RELATED TORTS WITH SOME OVERLAP OF THEIR ELEMENTS

■ **INSTANT FACTS** After Picard (P) took a picture of Barry Pontiac-Buick, Inc.'s (Barry Pontiac) (D) service worker inspecting her brakes, the service worker (D) became angry, moved toward her, put his finger on the camera she was holding, and said, "Who gave you permission to take my picture?"

■ **BLACK LETTER RULE** (1) An assault requires an act which puts a person in reasonable fear of imminent bodily harm. (2) A battery occurs when a person intentionally causes an offensive bodily contact with another person, which includes contact with an object connected with that person.

■ PROCEDURAL BASIS

Appeal of judgment entered after trial of assault and battery action for damages.

■ FACTS

Picard (P), unhappy with Barry Pontiac's (D) brake inspection, photographed Barry Pontiac's service worker (D) inspecting her brakes. Picard (P) alleges that the service worker (D) lunged at her and spun her around. The service worker (D) claims that he only placed his finger on the camera she was holding and did not grab or threaten her. Picard (P) prevailed at trial, and Barry Pontiac (D) appeals. Barry Pontiac (D) argues that Picard (P) failed to prove an assault because she did not prove that the service worker (D) placed her in reasonable fear of imminent bodily harm. Barry Pontiac (D) further argues that Picard (P) failed to prove a battery because she did not prove that the service worker (D) intended to inflict an unconsented touching of her person.

■ ISSUE

(1) Does an assault generally require a person's fear of imminent bodily harm to be reasonable? (2) Can touching an object a person is holding satisfy the contact element of battery?

■ DECISION AND RATIONALE

(Lederberg, J.) (1) Yes. Assault and battery are separate acts. An assault is a threatening physical act or an offer of corporal injury which puts a person in reasonable fear of imminent bodily harm. The harm of the assault is the person's apprehension of injury, and the recoverable damages are therefore for this mental disturbance, including fright, humiliation, and the like, and for any physical illness which the disturbance may cause. However, the apprehension must be the type of fear a reasonable person would normally experience from such an incident. Picard (P) testified that the service worker's (D) actions frightened her, and under the circumstances such a reaction was reasonable. The service worker (D) admitted approaching Picard (P), and the photograph Picard (P) took that day showed the service worker (D) pointing his finger at her as he approached her. Because Picard's (P) fear of imminent bodily harm was reasonable, she has established a prima facie case of assault. (2) Yes. A battery is an act that a person intended to cause, and which did cause, an offensive contact with or unconsented touching of another person. However, battery does not require the intent to injure the other person if the actor wilfully set in motion a force which in its ordinary course would cause injury. Here, Barry Pontiac (D) argues that a battery did not occur because the service worker (D) did not intend to touch or injure Picard (P). Barry Pontiac (D) contends that the service worker (D) only intended to touch Picard's (P) camera, not her person, and that this contact was insufficient to prove battery. We disagree. Even if the service worker (D) did only intend to touch Picard's (P) camera, a battery occurred. Barry Pontiac (D) did not prove that the service worker's (D) actions were accidental or involuntary. As comment c to the *Restatement (Second) of Torts § 18* [battery by offensive contact] explains, "[u]npermitted and intentional contacts with anything so connected with the body as to be customarily regarded as part of the other's person and therefore as partaking of its inviolability is actionable as an offensive contact with his person." The Restatement further explains that such things might include clothing, a cane, or anything directly grasped by the hand. Because the camera Picard (P) was holding was an object connected with Picard's (P) person, the service worker's (D) contact with it sufficed to constitute a battery. On the issues of assault and battery, the judgment is affirmed.

Analysis:

This case discusses the torts of assault and battery. An assault requires an act that causes another to have a reasonable apprehension of an imminent battery, and the intent to cause either a battery or the apprehension of a battery. Under Restatement (Second) of Torts § 21, an assault occurs when the actor intended his act to cause either a battery or the imminent apprehension of a battery, or knew with substantial certainty that it would cause an apprehension of a battery. If the actor does not have the requisite intent, he will not be liable for assault even if he recklessly or negligently causes a person to apprehend a battery. An assault requires only the apprehension of a battery, and the actor is subject to liability even if the battery does not occur. It is also not necessary for the person to act out of hostility. If a person intends his act to cause the apprehension as a practical joke, or even to be helpful, his conduct can still constitute an assault. Similarly, there may be an assault even if a person recognizes that the actor intends only an assault and not a battery, as long as the person still apprehends a possible battery. Because apprehension is the essence of an assault, a person must become aware of the threatening act before the actor terminates it. The person must also believe that the actor has the intent and the ability to cause the contact immediately, and that the act will cause an imminent contact unless some defensive or intervening act prevents it.

■ CASE VOCABULARY

APPREHENSION: A perception, understanding or awareness.

ASSAULT: A tort which occurs when a person acts with the intent to cause either a harmful or offensive bodily contact or the imminent apprehension of such a contact, and his act does cause another to apprehend an imminent harmful or offensive bodily contact.

BATTERY: A tort which occurs when a person acts with the intent to cause either a harmful or offensive bodily contact or the imminent apprehension of such a contact, and his act does inflict a harmful or offensive bodily contact upon another.

Wishnatsky v. Huey

(*Sensitive Paralegal*) v. (*Rude Assistant Attorney General*)

584 N.W.2d 859 (N.D. App. 1998)

A CONTACT WHICH WOULD NOT OFFEND AN ORDINARY PERSON CANNOT SUBJECT A PERSON TO LIABILITY FOR AN OFFENSIVE CONTACT BATTERY

■ **INSTANT FACTS** While Huey (D) was conversing with attorney Crary in Crary's office, Wishnatsky (P), Crary's paralegal, tried to enter without knocking, and Huey (D) closed the door pushing Wishnatsky (P) back into the hall.

■ **BLACK LETTER RULE** A person commits an offensive contact battery if he acts with an intent to cause a harmful or offensive contact with another person, and his act directly or indirectly causes a contact with another person which would offend a reasonable sense of personal dignity.

■ **PROCEDURAL BASIS**

Appeal of summary judgment dismissing battery action for damages.

■ **FACTS**

Huey (D), an assistant attorney general, was having a private meeting with attorney Crary in Crary's office when Wishnatsky (P), Crary's paralegal, attempted to enter the room without first knocking or announcing his entry. Huey (D) pushed the door closed, pushing Wishnatsky (P) back into the hall. Wishnatsky (P) states that he became fearful, his blood pressure rose, his heartbeat accelerated, his hands began to shake and his body trembled. Wishnatsky (P) brought this action for damages, and the trial court granted Huey's (D) motion for summary judgment and dismissed the claim. Wishnatsky (P) appeals, insisting that the evidence he submitted satisfies the elements of a battery claim.

■ **ISSUE**

Must the offense a person takes at another's intentional contact with his body be reasonable for the act to subject the other to liability for an offensive contact battery?

■ **DECISION AND RATIONALE**

(Per Curiam) Yes. Originally, a battery claim required the infliction of actual physical injury, but by the eighteenth century the courts eliminated this requirement. As one early court explains, the least touching of another in anger is a battery. If two meet in a narrow passage and one touches the other gently with no harmful intent, there is no battery, but if he uses violence to force his way in a rude inordinate matter, there is a battery. Similarly, Blackstone states that the least touching of another's person willfully or in anger is a battery. He explains that the law does not draw the line between different degrees of violence, but prohibits the lowest stage of it, because every man's person is sacred and no one has a right to meddle with it even slightly. On the other hand, Prosser and Keeton note that in a crowded world, we must accept a certain amount of inevitable personal contact. The *Restatement (Second) of Torts §§ 18, 19* [battery by offensive contacts] strikes a balance between the interest in unwanted contacts and the contacts which are inevitable in a crowded world. Section 18 explains that a person commits a battery if he acts with an intent to cause a harmful or offensive contact

---

with another person or a third person, or with an intent to cause an imminent apprehension of such a contact, and his act directly or indirectly causes an offensive contact with the other person. Section 18 makes clear that intent is necessary, and that negligently or recklessly causing an offensive contact will not render a person liable for battery. The essence of an offensive contact battery is not physical harm, but the offense to a person's dignity involved in the unpermitted and intentional invasion of the inviolability of his person. Section 19 explains that a contact is offensive if it "offends a reasonable sense of personal dignity." An offensive contact thus would offend an ordinary person who is not unduly sensitive, and would be unwarranted under the social usages of the time and place. While Huey (D) apparently reacted to Wishnatsky's (P) attempt to enter the room in a rude and abrupt manner, his conduct did not rise to the level of battery. [Ordinary people expect lawyers to be rude.] The evidence demonstrates that Wishnatsky (P) is unduly sensitive as to his personal dignity. Without knocking or announcing his intentions, Wishnatsky (P) attempted to enter the office where Huey (D) and Crary were having a private conversation. Huey (D) closed the door, stopping him from entering and pushing Wishnatsky (P) back into the hall. The bodily contact was momentary, indirect, and incidental. Because an ordinary person, not unduly sensitive as to his personal dignity, intruding upon a private conversation, would not have been offended by Huey's (D) response to the intrusion, this conduct did not constitute an offensive contact battery as a matter of law. Affirmed.

Analysis:

This case further discusses the offensive contact battery. Under Restatement (Second) of Torts § 19, "[a] bodily contact is offensive if it offends a reasonable sense of personal dignity." A person might inflict an offensive contact upon another by being hostile, insulting, or unduly personal, such as by grabbing another's clothing or by kissing a stranger. However, as with assault and harmful contact battery, the actor may be subject to liability for an offensive contact battery even if he is not motivated by hostility or a desire to injure, and even if his desire is to help. It is what the actor intends to do, not why he intends to do it, that is important, and whether his act would offend a reasonable sense of personal dignity. Unlike an assault, an offensive contact battery may also subject the actor to liability even if the other person does not know of the offensive contact until a later time. The basis of the offensive contact battery is the invasion of the person's dignity, and this invasion will affect the person when he learns of it, whether it is as the invasion happens or at a later time. The basis of an assault, on the other hand, is the imminent apprehension of a bodily contact. If the person does not learn about the actor's conduct until later, it cannot cause an imminent apprehension.

■ CASE VOCABULARY

OFFENSIVE CONTACT: A contact which, under the circumstances, would offend an ordinary person who is not unduly sensitive as to his personal dignity.

Lopez v. Winchell's Donut House

(*Thieving Employee*) v. (*Employer*)

126 Ill.App.3d 46, 466 N.E.2d 1309 (1984)

A FALSE IMPRISONMENT CLAIM REQUIRES INVOLUNTARY CONFINEMENT, BUT MORAL OR SO-CIAL PRESSURE DOES NOT SUFFICE

■ **INSTANT FACTS** A donut shop clerk voluntarily joined two other employees in a back room where they accused her of theft and questioned her.

■ **BLACK LETTER RULE** False imprisonment requires confinement against a person's will, which may be effected by physical force, a threat of force, or the assertion of authority, but not by moral pressure or a threat of future action.

■ **PROCEDURAL BASIS**

Appeal from summary judgment granted in false imprisonment action for damages.

■ **FACTS**

Winchell's Donut House (Winchell's) (D) employed Lopez (P) as a clerk. Lopez (P) alleged that Winchell's (D) agents accused her of theft and falsely detained and imprisoned her against her will in a room on Winchell's (D) premises, with force and without probable or reasonable cause. In defense, Winchell's (D) answered that it had reasonable grounds to believe Lopez (P) was guilty of retail theft and that it conducted its inquiry into this matter in a reasonable manner and for a reasonable length of time. Lopez (P) testified in her deposition that Winchell's (D) agents called her at home one afternoon and asked her to come to the shop, without explaining why. Lopez (P) walked to the shop, and one of Winchell's (D) agents asked her to come with him to the baking room, where she found another agent (D) waiting. Lopez (P) sat down and the agents (D) closed the door and locked it with a "little latch." The agents (D) told Lopez (P) that spotters had bought donuts from her, but her register did not record the sale, and questioned her about how long she had been "shorting" the cash register. The agents (D) refused Lopez's (P) request for "proof." Lopez (P) stated that during the questioning, the agents (D) never made any threat to fire her or to do anything else and never prevented her from leaving, and that she never feared for her safety. Lopez (P) stated that she left the room after she began to shake and feel ill, and that Winchell's (D) later fired her. In her appeal, Lopez (P) argues that she felt compelled to remain in the room to protect her reputation by protesting her innocence, and that she only left the room when she began to feel ill. Lopez (P) claims that she suffered "serious emotional upset" as a result of Winchell's agents' (D) intimidating actions, including sitting next to her during questioning with a pad and pencil in hand, using a raised voice, and repeatedly stating that they had proof of her guilt.

■ **ISSUE**

Can false imprisonment occur where a person is confined only by moral pressure or a threat of future action?

■ **DECISION AND RATIONALE**

(Lorenz, J.) No. The common law defines the tort of false imprisonment as the unlawful restraint of an individual's personal liberty or freedom of locomotion. Imprisonment is any unlawful exercise or show of force which compels a person to remain where he does not wish to remain or to go where he does not wish to go. False imprisonment requires an actual or legal intent to restrain. A person may unlawfully restrain another by words, acts, or both; force is not necessary. The *Restatement (Second) of Torts §§ 38–41* [methods of confinement] explains that the confinement element of false imprisonment may be effected by (1) actual or apparent physical barriers; (2) physical force; (3) threats of physical force; (4) other duress; and (5) asserted legal authority. Whatever the method, it is essential that the confinement be against the person's will. If a person voluntarily consents to the confinement, there is no false imprisonment. Moral pressure, as where a person remains in a place to clear himself of suspicion of theft, does not suffice, nor does any threat of future action. Such wrongs lie instead within the tort of intentional infliction of mental distress. Lopez (P) relied upon *Marcus v. Liebman* [no confinement by threat of future action], but this case does not support her position. In *Marcus,* the court examined the concept that threats of future action do not suffice to constitute confinement, but found a present threat in that case. All of the other cases Lopez (P) cited are distinguishable as well, because they all involved either physical restraint or a present threat of physical restraint. [Her attorney won't be citing this case in his brochure!] Here, Lopez (P) testified that she voluntarily went to Winchell's (D) baking room; she stayed there to protect her reputation; Winchell's agents (D) never threatened her with the loss of her job; she was never in fear for her safety; and Winchell's agents (D) never prevented her from leaving the room. Lopez's (P) statement that she only left the room after she began to feel ill does not raise any issue of material fact. Lopez (P) testified in her deposition that she "got up and left" when Winchell's agent (D) asked her how long her theft had been going on. It is not sufficient for a claim of false imprisonment that a person feels "compelled" to remain in a place to protect her reputation. False imprisonment requires restraint against a person's will, as where a person yields to force, a threat of force, or the assertion of authority. In this case, there is no evidence that Lopez (P) went to the baking room against her will or that she yielded to any threat or physical force. Affirmed.

Analysis:

Under Restatement (Second) of Torts § 35, false imprisonment occurs when an actor intends to confine a person within certain boundaries, his act directly or indirectly causes the confinement of a person within those boundaries, and the confined person either is aware of the confinement or is harmed by it. The actor is subject to liability if he acts with the purpose of confining a person or with knowledge that such confinement is substantially certain to result from his act. Acting with knowledge of a likelihood of confinement short of substantial certainty does not suffice. As with assault and battery, the intent to confine may be directed at the person confined or at a third person, and therefore a mistake of identity does not excuse the confinement. Also like assault and battery, no hostility or desire to injure is necessary. Thus, a good faith belief that the confinement is justified is no excuse. As *Lopez* explains, the person may accomplish confinement by several means, including actual or apparent physical barriers; physical force or the threat of physical force; some other duress, such as a threat to harm some valuable property or another person; or the color of legal authority. However, as *Lopez* demonstrates, moral or social pressure, such as to protect the person's reputation or to avoid humiliation, does not satisfy the element of confinement. To confine a person the actor need only prevent him from leaving a particular area, and the area may be quite broad. A person may also confine another by forcing him to go where he does not wish to go. In such a case the place of confinement is constantly changing, but it still restricts the person's freedom of locomotion and is therefore actionable. False arrest is a special category of false imprisonment. If a person confines another by making an arrest, but is not privileged to do so, he is subject to liability for false arrest. False imprisonment and false arrest are distinct from the tort of malicious prosecution, which involves making an arrest without probable cause and for an improper purpose. If there was no proper basis for the arrest, there may be a malicious prosecution claim even if there is no basis for a false arrest claim because the legal forms were proper and the arrest was valid.

■ CASE VOCABULARY

FALSE IMPRISONMENT: A tort which occurs when a person intentionally confines another person or restricts his freedom of locomotion against his will and without a lawful privilege or authority.

IMPRISONMENT: The coercive restraint of a person's freedom of locomotion to force him to remain where he does not wish to remain or to go where he does not wish to go.

Womack v. Eldridge

(Innocent Bystander) v. *(Attorney's Investigator)*
215 Va. 338, 210 S.E.2d 145 (1974)

ONLY EXTREMELY OUTRAGEOUS CONDUCT WILL SUBJECT A PERSON TO LIABILITY FOR INTENTIONALLY CAUSING EMOTIONAL DISTRESS WHERE THERE IS NO BODILY HARM

■ **INSTANT FACTS** An investigator took Womack's (P) picture for an attorney to use in a child molesting case, thus involving Womack (P) in the case and causing him severe emotional distress.

■ **BLACK LETTER RULE** A person may recover for emotional distress absent physical injury if the distress was severe and resulted from conduct which was outrageous and intolerable and either intentional or reckless.

■ **PROCEDURAL BASIS**

Writ of error granted on order setting aside jury verdict after trial of intentional infliction of emotional distress action for damages.

■ **FACTS**

Seifert and his attorney hired Eldridge (D) to obtain a photograph of Womack (P) as evidence for Seifert's trial for sexually molesting two young boys. Eldridge (D) went to Womack's (P) home, told him she worked for a newspaper and was writing an article on Skateland, where Womack (P) worked, and asked if she could take his picture for the article. Womack (P) consented. At trial, Seifert's attorney showed Womack's (P) picture to the two boys and asked if he was the man who molested them. They said he was not. [Whew!] However, the prosecutor asked for additional information about Womack (P), and Eldridge (D) testified as to his name and address. The only excuse Eldridge (D) offered for the use of Womack's (P) picture was that he was at Skateland when Seifert was arrested. The alleged offenses did not occur at Skateland. The prosecutor sent a detective to Womack's (P) home to bring him to court. The detective told Womack (P) that his picture was presented at the trial and that the prosecutor wanted him to appear, and that if he did not go voluntarily he would be summoned. Womack (P) went voluntarily. Womack (P) testified about how Eldridge (D) obtained his picture, and that he had not molested any children and knew nothing about the charges against Seifert. The police questioned Womack (P) several times, and the grand jury summoned him as a witness, but did not call on him to testify. Womack (P) was also summoned to appear several more times at Seifert's trial due to continuances. Womack (P) testified that he suffered great shock, distress and nervousness as a result of Eldridge's (D) fraudulently and maliciously obtaining his photograph and turning it over to Seifert's attorney for Seifert's trial. He suffered great anxiety as to his reputation and feared that he would be accused of molesting the boys. He suffered from loss of sleep and mental depression, and became emotional and incoherent while testifying in this case. The jury returned a verdict of $45,000 for Womack (P), but the trial court set the verdict aside, holding that damages for emotional distress were not recoverable in the absence of physical harm.

■ **ISSUE**

Can a person who by extreme and outrageous conduct intentionally or recklessly causes severe emotional distress to another be subject to liability for the emotional distress if there is no physical injury?

■ DECISION AND RATIONALE

(l'Anson, J.) Yes. Other jurisdictions disagree on this issue, but most courts that have addressed it recently have held that there may be recovery for severe emotional distress in the absence of physical injury where another intentionally or recklessly causes the distress by extreme and outrageous conduct. Under the *Restatement (Second) of Torts § 46* [elements of intentional infliction of emotional distress], a person who by extreme and outrageous conduct intentionally or recklessly causes severe emotional distress to another is subject to liability for that distress, and if bodily harm results from it, also for that bodily harm. Comment i to this section explains that this rule applies where the person knows that distress is certain or substantially certain to result from his conduct. Most courts that allow recovery do so when the act was intentional and the actor desired the emotional distress or knew or should have known that it was likely to result. We hold that a cause of action will lie for emotional distress absent physical injury if: (1) the actor's conduct was intentional or reckless; (2) the conduct was outrageous and intolerable; (3) the conduct caused the emotional distress; and (4) the emotional distress was severe. The intent element is satisfied where the actor's specific purpose was to inflict emotional distress or where he intended his conduct and knew or should have known that it would likely cause emotional distress. Conduct is outrageous and intolerable if it offends against generally accepted standards of decency and morality. The purpose of this element is to limit frivolous suits. Bad manners and hurt feelings do not suffice. Whether the conduct is sufficiently extreme and outrageous is initially for the court, and only for the jury if reasonable men may differ on this issue. In this case, reasonable men could differ on this issue and the question was thus for the jury. The jury could conclude that Eldridge (D) intentionally or recklessly obtained Womack's (P) photograph for use in Seifert's trial without considering the effect it would have on Womack (P). A reasonable person should have recognized the likelihood that involving an innocent person in a child molesting case would cause that person serious mental distress. Judgment reversed and jury verdict reinstated.

Analysis:

A person may recover for emotional distress absent physical injury if the distress was severe and resulted from conduct that was outrageous and intolerable and either intentional or reckless. Thus, unlike the torts of assault, battery, and false imprisonment, the tort of intentional infliction of emotional distress does not clearly define the conduct it prohibits, but rather requires an evaluation of behavior as outrageous or not outrageous. To subject the actor to liability, his conduct must be extreme, and not merely insulting, annoying, or even threatening. However, if the actor is aware of a person's special sensitivity, he may be subject to liability for conduct that is extreme in light of that sensitivity. Like the actor's conduct, the emotional distress it causes must also be extreme. A person cannot recover for mild unhappiness or humiliation. In addition, the emotional distress must generally be the type of distress that a reasonable person of ordinary sensitivity would experience as a result of the actor's conduct. To the extent the person's response is beyond the bounds of normal human reactions to the conduct, the person will not be able to recover.

■ CASE VOCABULARY

EMOTIONAL DISTRESS: Any highly unpleasant mental suffering, including fright, horror, grief, humiliation, anger, disappointment, and worry.

OUTRAGEOUS: Atrocious, exceeding all bounds of decency and utterly intolerable in civilized society.

McDermott v. Reynolds

(*Husband*) v. (*Wife's Boyfriend*)

260 Va. 98, 530 S.E.2d 902 (2000)

MOST COURTS NO LONGER ALLOW ACTIONS FOR INTENTIONAL INFLICTION OF EMOTIONAL DISTRESS FOR INTERFERENCE WITH A HUSBAND-WIFE RELATIONSHIP, BUT MAY ALLOW THEM AS TO PARENT-CHILD RELATIONSHIPS

■ **INSTANT FACTS** Reynolds (D) had an adulterous affair with McDermott's (P) wife and continued to do so after McDermott (P) confronted him and asked him to stop, causing him severe emotional distress.

■ **BLACK LETTER RULE** A statutory bar of actions for alienation of affection also bars an action for intentional infliction of emotional distress where the alleged conduct would support an action for alienation of affection.

■ PROCEDURAL BASIS

Appeal of dismissal of intentional infliction of emotional distress action for damages.

■ FACTS

McDermott (P) sued Reynolds (D) for intentional infliction of emotional distress based on Reynolds' (D) maintaining an adulterous relationship with McDermott's (P) wife. When McDermott (P) learned of his wife's relationship with Reynolds (D), they had been married for 18 years and had three children. McDermott (P) demanded that Reynolds (D) end the relationship, but instead Reynolds (D) "flaunted it outwardly." McDermott (P) argues that in continuing to "flaunt" the relationship Reynolds (D) acted with the intent to cause McDermott (P) severe emotional distress, and succeeded in doing so. McDermott (P) suffered sleeplessness, loss of weight, and interference with the performance of his duties, and he and his children both experienced severe embarrassment and humiliation. Reynolds' (D) conduct also caused the break up of McDermott's (P) family and required McDermott (P) and his children to seek counseling. Reynolds (D) moved to dismiss, arguing that the action was essentially one for alienation of affection, which was prohibited by statute, and the trial court granted his motion. On appeal McDermott (P) argues that the statutory bar does not apply to this action simply because the conduct at issue has overtones of alienation of affection. Rather, McDermott (P) argues that his action for intentional infliction of emotional distress is separate and distinct from an action for alienation of affection, and that his damages arose from Reynolds' (D) intentional infliction of emotional distress and not from his alienation of the affection of McDermott's (P) wife.

■ ISSUE

Does a statutory bar of actions for alienation of affection also bar an action for intentional infliction of emotional distress where the alleged conduct would support an action for alienation of affection?

■ DECISION AND RATIONALE

(Keenan, J.) Yes. In *Womack v. Eldridge* [intentional infliction of emotional distress] we held that a person may recover for emotional distress absent physical injury if he alleges and proves by clear and convincing evidence that (1) the wrongdoer's conduct was intentional or reckless, (2) outrageous and intolerable, and (3) caused the emotional distress, and (4) the emotional distress was severe. The statute at issue in this case prohibits actions for alienation of affection and related actions. The statute does not refer to the tort of intentional infliction of emotional distress, but that does not affect our analysis because this tort covers many types of conduct unrelated to the prohibited actions. In enacting this statute, the legislature manifested its intent to abolish actions seeking damages for a particular type of conduct. We must therefore consider the conduct alleged to decide this case. The basis of McDermott's (P) claim is that Reynolds (D) had an adulterous relationship with McDermott's (P) wife, and continued that relationship in an open and notorious manner after McDermott (P) confronted him. Because this is precisely the type of conduct that the legislature intended to exclude from civil liability, the fact that McDermott (P) labels it the intentional infliction of emotional distress and recites the elements of that tort does not shield his action from the statutory bar. We must consider the nature of the action, not merely its form. Our conclusion and our rationale are in accord with most jurisdictions that have addressed this issue. We disagree with the Fourth Circuit's decision and analysis in *Raftery v. Scott* [intentional infliction of emotional distress based on the alienation of affection between a parent and child]. In *Raftery,* the court reasoned that the torts of intentional infliction of emotional distress and alienation of affection have different characteristics and require different proof. Thus focusing on the elements of the torts rather than on the alleged conduct, the court allowed the claim of intentional infliction of emotional distress even though the conduct had overtones of alienation of affection. We instead base our analysis on the conduct at issue because that method allows us to give effect to the legislative intent behind the statutory bar of the claim for alienation of affection. [The decide-where-you-want-to-go-and-then-how-to-get-there approach.] Affirmed.

Analysis:

This case discusses the relationship between the tort of intentional infliction of emotional distress and the tort of alienation of affection. In *McDermott,* the court focuses on the conduct at issue and finds that because it is the same type of conduct that would support an action for alienation of affection, the statutory bar to that action applies, whatever the name given to the wrong. The Fourth Circuit addressed the same statutory bar in *Raftery,* which involved conduct that would have supported a claim for the alienation of affection between a parent and child. Like Reynolds (D), the mother in *Raftery* essentially argued that "even as the rose, alienation of affection by any other name is still the same," and that the statutory bar to the alienation of affection claim should therefore also apply to the intentional infliction of emotional distress claim. However, by analyzing the elements of both torts rather than focusing on the fact that the conduct at issue could support either claim, the Fourth Circuit permitted the action for intentional infliction of emotional distress. The court explained that to establish the intentional infliction of emotional distress, a person must show that the conduct was intentional or reckless, that it was outrageous and intolerable, that it caused the emotional distress, and that the emotional distress was severe. On the other hand, to establish the tort of alienation of affection, it was not necessary to show outrageous and intolerable conduct or severe emotional distress. Instead, the person must only show a "malicious" or unjustifiable interference, or an intention that such interference cause the loss of affection. Further, unlike the tort of intentional infliction of emotional distress, alienation of affection also requires an existing family relationship. Thus, the court explains that the elements of the two torts are not only different, but the tort of intentional infliction of emotional distress requires a higher burden of proof than the tort of alienation of affection.

■ CASE VOCABULARY

ALIENATION OF AFFECTION: A largely abolished tort which occurred when a person intentionally interfered with the relationship between a husband and wife, but which survives in its application to parent-child relationships.

CRIMINAL CONVERSATION: A largely abolished tort which occurred when a person had sexual intercourse with another's spouse.

SEDUCTION: A largely abolished tort which occurred when a person enticed another to have sexual intercourse outside marriage, without force or intimidation.

Hustler Magazine v. Falwell

(*Publisher*) v. (*Minister*)
485 U.S. 46, 108 S.Ct. 876 (1988)

ACTUAL MALICE STANDARD APPLIES TO ACTIONS FOR EMOTION DISTRESS AS WELL AS FALSE LIGHT

■ **INSTANT FACTS** Jerry Falwell (P) sued Hustler Magazine (D) for intentional infliction of emotional distress for publishing a parody of Falwell (P) engaged in incestuous acts with his mother.

■ **BLACK LETTER RULE** In order to recover for intentional infliction of emotional distress, public figures must show that a false statement of fact was made with actual malice.

■ **PROCEDURAL BASIS**

Writ of certiorari reviewing affirmation of verdict for damages for intentional infliction of emotional distress.

■ **FACTS**

Hustler Magazine (D) published a parody of Reverend Jerry Falwell (P). The drawing and text stated that Falwell's (P) "first time" was during a drunken incestuous rendezvous with his mother in an outhouse. Beneath the parody, in small print, is a disclaimer stating "ad parody—not to be taken seriously." Falwell (P) sued for invasion of privacy, libel, and intentional infliction of emotional distress. The District Court directed a verdict for Hustler (D) on the privacy claim, and the jury awarded Falwell (P) $200,000 in damages for the intentional infliction of emotional distress claim. The Court of Appeals affirmed, rejecting Hustler's (D) argument that *New York Times* actual malice must be proven before emotional damages can be recovered. Hustler (D) also claimed that because the jury found that the parody did not describe actual events about Falwell (P), the parody was an opinion that was protected by the First Amendment. The Court of Appeals held that this was irrelevant on the issue of whether the conduct was sufficiently outrageous to allow recovery for intentional infliction of emotional distress. The Supreme Court granted certiorari.

■ **ISSUE**

Must actual malice be proven in order for a public figure to recover for intentional infliction of emotional distress?

■ **DECISION AND RATIONALE**

(Rehnquist, J.) Yes. Actual malice must be proven in order for a public figure to recover for intentional infliction of emotional distress. Falwell (P) argues that the State's interest in protecting public figures from emotional distress is sufficient to deny First Amendment protection for the speech at issue. We disagree. The First Amendment recognizes the fundamental importance of the free flow of ideas on matters of public interest, and this is bound to produce speech that is critical of public figures. While the First Amendment does not protect *any* type of speech about public figures, these figures must meet a high burden in order to recover. The mere presence of a bad motive, or of the "outrageous" nature of the speech, is not sufficient to recover for intentional infliction of emotional distress. Rather, public figures must prove that the publication contains a false statement of fact which was made with actual malice. In the case at hand, Falwell (P) was a public figure. The jury already found that the caricature did not contain a statement of fact. Thus, Falwell (P) cannot recover. Reversed.

■ CONCURRENCE

(White, J.) I see little reason for the majority's reference to *New York Times v. Sullivan.* However, I agree with the holding because the jury did find that the ad contained no assertion of fact.

Analysis:

This case presents an excellent application of the tort of intentional infliction of emotional distress in the context of public figures. However, the case barely mentions privacy at all. The tort of false light requires some intentional or reckless publication of material that places a person in a false light in the eyes of the public. This standard is nearly identical to that laid down by the Supreme Court in the instant action. In fact, the two torts seem virtually indistinguishable. Both involve the same overriding constitutional restraints, requiring actual malice to be proven.

Hart v. Geysel

(*Deceased's Administrator*) v. (*Other Fighter*)

159 Wash. 632, 294 P. 570 (1930)

LANDMARK CASE FOLLOWS MINORITY RULE THAT CONSENT TO CRIMINAL CONDUCT IS EFFECTIVE BAR TO RECOVERY IN TORT

■ **INSTANT FACTS** Cartwright (P) died as a result of a blow he received in an illegal prize fight he engaged in with Geysel (D).

■ **BLACK LETTER RULE** One who consents to particular conduct has no right to recover damages for an injury he sustains when another acts on that consent.

■ **PROCEDURAL BASIS**

Appeal of judgment dismissing wrongful death action for damages.

■ **FACTS**

Cartwright (P) and Geysel (D) engaged in an illegal prize fight, and a blow Cartwright (P) received in the fight caused his death. There is no claim that the mutual combat involved anger, a malicious intent to seriously injure, or excessive force. Hart (P), the administrator of Cartwright's (P) estate, brought this action for wrongful death. The trial court sustained Geysel's (D) demurrer and dismissed the action.

■ **ISSUE**

Does one who consents to particular conduct have a right to recover damages for an injury he sustains when another acts on that consent?

■ **DECISION AND RATIONALE**

(Main, J.) No. The majority rule is that when parties engage in mutual combat in anger, each is civilly liable to the other for any physical injury he causes during the fight, and the fact that the parties voluntarily engaged in the fight is no defense. The minority rule, on the other hand, is that when parties engage in mutual combat in anger, both of them act unlawfully and therefore cannot recover damages in a civil action unless they can show excessive force or a malicious intent to cause serious injury. Neither rule applies to the facts of this case because there was no anger, malicious intent to injure, or excessive force. It is unnecessary, therefore, to adopt either rule here. However, in our opinion, one who consents to and engages in prize fighting, despite its being prohibited by law, should not have a right to recover damages for any injury he sustains in the fight. Enforcement of the criminal statute against prize fighting does not require rewarding the loser at the expense of the winner. This view is supported by the rule tentatively adopted in a draft of the Restatement of Torts. Although the majority of jurisdictions hold otherwise, the drafters of the Restatement prefer the minority rule based on two fundamental principles. One principle is that one who expresses his willingness to suffer a particular invasion has no right to complain when another acts on that consent. Another principle is that no man shall profit by his own wrongdoing. The majority view is an exception to both principles. If a person consents to being struck in a brawl, his right to determine how his person shall be touched is not invaded. Further, if the person's consent to the blow would ordinarily bar liability, he would profit from his illegal conduct if his breach of the peace would give him a cause of action he would not otherwise have. Affirmed.

Analysis:

This landmark case introduces the defense of consent and illustrates its application to criminal conduct. Consent is a common defense to intentional torts and is analogous to the defense of assumption of risk in negligence and strict liability cases. If a person actually consents to certain conduct, he suffers no wrong when that conduct occurs, even if the actor was unaware of the consent. A person can manifest consent by words or by conduct, and even by silence or inaction if a reasonable person would usually speak or move if he did not consent. A person may also infer consent from prior dealings or a relationship with the other person, or from custom and usage. A person can control the scope of his consent by limiting its time, place, duration, purpose, and extent. However, once a person does consent to certain conduct, he cannot recover damages for the results of that conduct, whether foreseen or unforeseen. A person's consent to the conduct will be effective even if he is substantially mistaken about the nature of the invasion it would cause or the extent of harm that would result, unless the person asserting the privilege of consent knew of the mistake or fraudulently induced it.

■ CASE VOCABULARY

CONSENT: A defense to intentional torts which arises when a person is actually or apparently willing for particular conduct to occur.

Courvoisier v. Raymond

(*Defensive Shooter*) v. (*Police Officer*)

23 Colo. 113, 47 P. 284 (1896)

A PERSON HAS A PRIVILEGE TO USE FORCE IN SELF-DEFENSE WHEN HE ERRONEOUSLY, BUT REASONABLY, BELIEVES ANOTHER IS ABOUT TO ATTACK HIM

■ **INSTANT FACTS** After being attacked by rioters and unsuccessfully trying to scare them away, Courvoisier (D) saw Raymond (P) approach him, mistakenly believed he was a rioter, and, fearing for his life, shot him.

■ **BLACK LETTER RULE** A person is privileged to act in self-defense if the surrounding circumstances would lead a reasonable man to believe that he was in danger of losing his life or of receiving great bodily harm, and the person does so believe.

■ **PROCEDURAL BASIS**

Appeal of judgment entered after trial of battery action for damages.

■ **FACTS**

Two rowdy men entered Courvoisier's (D) building after midnight without permission. Supposing the men to be burglars, Courvoisier (D) took out his gun and ejected them. The men gathered outside with a few other men while Courvoisier (D) stood on the steps of his building. Courvoisier (D) fired a shot in the air to scare them away. Instead of retreating they started throwing stones and brickbats at him, so Courvoisier (D) fired again. Raymond (P), a police officer, and two other officers nearby heard the first shot and started toward Courvoisier (D) as he continued to shoot. The two other officers stopped when they reached the men to arrest them. Raymond (P) proceeded toward Courvoisier (D), calling out that he was an officer and to stop shooting. Courvoisier (D) did not hear Raymond (P), but saw him come out of the crowd toward him and put his hand to his hip pocket. Thinking he was one of the rioters and that he did not have time to jump aside, Courvoisier (D) shaded his eyes, aimed, and shot him. Courvoisier (D) had bad eyesight and required glasses, but was without them at the time of the shooting and could not see clearly. He did not know that Raymond (P) was an officer until after he shot him. Rather, Courvoisier (D) felt certain that Raymond (P) was coming to rob him because someone robbed the store next door a few weeks earlier. Raymond (P) obtained a judgment against Courvoisier (D). Raymond (P) argues that Courvoisier (D) was committing a breach of the peace and, knowing Raymond (P) was a police officer, recklessly shot at him. Courvoisier (D) argues that the surrounding circumstances were such that a reasonable man would believe that his life was in danger and that it was necessary to shoot in self-defense, and that this was what he believed when he fired the shot. Courvoisier (D) also objects to the trial court's instruction to the jury that if they believed that Raymond (P) was not assaulting Courvoisier (D) when Courvoisier (D) shot him, their verdict should be for Raymond (P).

■ **ISSUE**

Is a person privileged to act in self-defense if the surrounding circumstances would lead a reasonable man to believe that he was in danger of losing his life or of receiving great bodily harm, and the person does so believe?

■ DECISION AND RATIONALE

(Hayt, J.) Yes. The court's instruction to the jury was clearly erroneous because it did not include a full consideration of the justification of self-defense. The evidence for Raymond (P) tends to show that the shooting, even if not malicious, was reckless. On the other hand, the evidence for Courvoisier (D) tends to show that the surrounding circumstances at the time would lead a reasonable man to believe that he was in danger of losing his life or of receiving great bodily harm at Raymond's (P) hands, and that this was what Courvoisier (D) believed. The evidence raises two issues: first, whether Raymond (P) was assaulting Courvoisier (D) when Courvoisier (D) shot him; and second, if Raymond (P) was not assaulting Courvoisier (D), whether there was sufficient evidence of justification for consideration of the jury. The trial court's instruction to the jury included the first issue, but improperly excluded the second. Courvoisier's (D) justification did not rest entirely on proof of assault. Also meriting the jury's consideration was the evidence that a riot was in progress, that the rioters attacked Courvoisier (D) with stones and brickbats, and that Courvoisier (D) shot Raymond (P) supposing him to be one of the rioters. If the jury believed from the evidence that Courvoisier (D) would have been justified in shooting one of the rioters if one of them approached him as Raymond (P) did, then it was important to determine whether Courvoisier (D) mistook Raymond (P) for one of the rioters, and if so, whether such a mistake was excusable under the circumstances. If the jury decided these questions in Courvoisier's (D) favor, he would have been entitled to judgment. In *Morris v. Platt* [act in self-defense injured third person], a man who shot a bystander at a riot while intending to shoot one of the rioters pleaded self-defense. The court held that if the man would have been justified in shooting his antagonist, then he was not liable to the bystander because his act of shooting was lawful under the circumstances. Thus if a person attempts to justify his conduct by necessary self-defense, he must satisfy the jury not only that he acted honestly in using force, but also that his fears were reasonable under the circumstances and that his means were reasonable. The verdict might have been different had the trial court properly instructed the jury. Reversed.

Analysis:

This is one of the few cases that address the issue of whether a person has a privilege to use force against another to defend himself when he erroneously, but reasonably, believes the other is about to attack him. The privilege of self-defense allows a person to use as much force as reasonably appears to be immediately necessary to defend himself from harm by another's intentional or negligent conduct. The privilege usually applies to cases in which a person faces a threat of bodily harm, but it may also apply to threats of offensive bodily contact and false imprisonment. A person can claim the privilege of self-defense only if he subjectively believes that his conduct is necessary to defend himself against an imminent threat of harm, and that belief is objectively reasonable under the circumstances, based on the facts known to the person. If the threatened harm is intentional, the person need not retreat or abandon any right or privilege to avoid the harm rather than defend himself, at least as long as his act in self-defense does not involve deadly force or force that might inflict serious bodily injury. On the other hand, if the threatened harm is only the result of negligence, the person must retreat or abandon any right or privilege that would allow him to avoid the threatened harm, and may use force in self-defense only as a last resort. The amount of force a person uses in self-defense must also be objectively reasonable in light of the apparent need. If the person uses more force than reasonably appears to be necessary, he is subject to liability for any harm that results to the extent it results from the excess force. The privilege of self-defense may allow a person to threaten more force than it allows him to use. Provocation does not justify the use of force in self-defense at all, especially when it is only verbal. The timing of acts in self-defense is also important. The privilege allows a person to defend himself against imminent harm, but not to retaliate for harm that he has already suffered. If harm reasonably appears to be imminent, the person can use force to avoid the harm and need not actually suffer some harm before invoking the privilege. However, the privilege does not justify a preemptive strike against someone who does not threaten imminent harm but who might attack in the future. A person generally may defend a third person under the same rules that would apply if he were defending himself.

■ CASE VOCABULARY

BRICKBAT: A piece of brick used as a weapon or missile.

SELF-DEFENSE: The privilege a person has to use reasonable force which he reasonably believes is immediately necessary to defend himself from harm.

Katko v. Briney

(Petty Thief) v. *(Violent Landowner)*

183 N.W.2d 657 (Iowa 1971)

THE PRIVILEGE TO USE FORCE IN DEFENSE OF PROPERTY PERMITS A PERSON TO USE ONLY AS MUCH FORCE IN HIS ABSENCE AS HE COULD USE WHEN PRESENT

■ **INSTANT FACTS** Briney (D) set a spring gun in his unoccupied farm house, and the gun seriously injured Katko (P) when he broke into the house to steal old bottles and fruit jars.

■ **BLACK LETTER RULE** An owner has a privilege to use reasonable force to protect his property, but this privilege does (not) allow him to use a deadly trap in an unoccupied building to protect his property against trespassers and thieves.

■ **PROCEDURAL BASIS**

Appeal of judgment entered in battery action for damages.

■ **FACTS**

Briney's wife (D) inherited a farmhouse in which her grandparents and parents had lived. No one occupied the house after her parents died, and over the next ten years a series of trespasses, break-ins and thefts occurred. Briney (D) boarded up the windows and doors and posted "no trespass" signs, but the break-ins continued. Briney (D) then set up a spring shotgun trap in a bedroom of the house with the barrel of the gun pointed at the bedroom door. At first Briney (D) set up the gun so that it would fire at an intruder's stomach when he opened the door, but lowered it at his wife's suggestion so that it would hit the person's legs. Briney (D) admitted that he did this because he was "mad and tired of being tormented," but stated that he "did not intend to injure anyone." Briney (D) did not explain why he used a loaded shell and set the gun to hit a person already in the house. Tin covered the bedroom window, and the gun was not visible from outside. Briney (D) posted no warning of the gun's presence. Katko (P) had observed Briney's (D) farmhouse for several years while hunting, knew it had long been uninhabited, and considered it abandoned. Before Briney (D) had set the spring gun trap, Katko (P) and a companion had been on the premises and found old bottles and fruit jars which they considered antiques. After Briney (D) set the trap they returned to look for more. As Katko (P) opened the bedroom door the shotgun went off and struck him in leg, blowing much of it away. Katko (P) was only able to leave the house with his companion's help. Katko (P) was in the hospital for 40 days, wore a cast for one year and a brace for another year. The shotgun blast permanently deformed and shortened his leg. The trial court instructed the jury that the law prohibited the use of spring guns except to prevent the commission of felonies of violence and where human life is in danger. The court explained that Katko (P) did commit a felony when he broke into Briney's (D) farmhouse, but not a felony of violence. The court further instructed the jury that a person may use reasonable force to protect his property, but not such force that would take human life or inflict great bodily injury. The court explained that the law prohibited owners of premises from using such deadly force to intentionally injure a trespasser, and therefore prohibited them from setting spring guns and other deadly devices for that purpose. The court instructed the jury that the only time setting a device such as a spring gun would be justified would be where the trespasser was committing a felony of violence or a felony punishable by death, or where the trespasser was endangering human life. The jury returned a verdict for Katko (P), and the trial court denied Briney's (D) motion for judgment notwithstanding the verdict and for a new trial. Briney (D) argues on appeal, as he did at trial, that the law permits the use of a spring gun in a dwelling or warehouse for the purpose of preventing unlawful entry and theft.

■ ISSUE

May an owner use a deadly trap in an unoccupied building to protect personal property against trespassers and thieves?

■ DECISION AND RATIONALE

(Moore, J.) No. The overwhelming weight of authority supports the trial court's statement of the law. As Prosser and the *Restatement (Second) of Torts § 85* [use of deadly mechanical device to defend property] explain, the law places a higher value on human safety than on property rights. A person has no privilege to use force calculated to cause death or serious bodily injury to defend land or chattels unless there is also a threat to his personal safety which would justify his use of such force in self-defense. The use of spring guns and other deadly traps is not justifiable against mere trespassers or petty thieves. A landowner may only use such deadly devices when he would be privileged to use deadly force if he were present, and a mere trespass against property other than a dwelling does not justify the use of a deadly weapon in its defense. If death results in such a case it would be murder, even if the killing were necessary to prevent the trespass. Landowners may not inflict trespassers and other inconsiderable violators with inhuman bodily injuries. Punitive damages are allowable in this state when a person has acted with malice or with wanton and reckless disregard of others' rights. However, we express no opinion about whether punitive damages are allowable in this type of case because Briney's (D) attorney did not raise the issue. [Hint hint.] Affirmed.

■ DISSENT

(Larson, J.) The majority oversimplifies the impact of this case. I see no compelling reason why use of a spring gun to protect a person's life's accumulations, tools, and treasured antiques should create liability as a matter of law where the evidence could sustain a finding that the person installed the device only as a warning to deter thieves. The trial court's jury instructions erred in that they failed to recognize a defense if Briney (D) did not intend to cause death or serious harm. I also object to awarding punitive damages to a criminal.

Analysis:

This case addresses the privilege a person has to use force to defend his property. A possessor may use reasonable force to defend his possession of land or chattels against intrusion, taking, or harm by another person or chattel. However, the possessor must first ask the intruder to cease his intrusion, unless such a request would be futile or substantial harm would occur before the possessor could make the request. For example, if an intruder enters forcibly, it may be reasonable for a possessor to resist immediately with no request to desist. Once a possessor does ask an intruder to desist, if the intruder refuses or disregards the request, the possessor may use such force as reasonably appears to be adapted, proportioned, and minimally necessary to defend his property. Unless the intruder presents a danger to those on the premises, a possessor may not put an intruder in an unreasonably risky situation by ejecting him. The intruder's privilege to enter or remain when necessary to save himself from death or serious bodily harm negates the possessor's privilege for a reasonable period of time. As with the privilege of self-defense, if the possessor uses excess force, he will exceed his privilege and will be subject to liability for harm that results from the excess force. As the court explained in *Katko,* deadly force is justifiable against a trespasser when the trespasser is committing a felony of violence or a felony punishable by death, or when the trespasser is endangering human life. Thus, if a possessor uses a spring gun, a concealed trap, a vicious animal, or some other unattended device to defend his property, he will be subject to liability if the device causes harm to an intruder unless he would have been privileged to inflict that harm if he were present.

■ CASE VOCABULARY

CHATTELS: Movable personal property, as opposed to land and buildings.

DWELLING: A house or other structure where a person lives, and in particular, sleeps regularly.

Vincent v. Lake Erie Transportation Co.

(Dock Owner) v. *(Ship Owner)*
109 Minn. 456, 124 N.W. 221 (1910)

DAMAGE TO ANOTHER'S PROPERTY DUE TO NECESSITY REQUIRES COMPENSATION

■ **INSTANT FACTS** During a fierce storm, a steamship was repeatedly thrown against a dock, causing damage to the dock.

■ **BLACK LETTER RULE** Damage caused to another's property due to necessity requires compensation for the actual harm caused.

■ **PROCEDURAL BASIS**

Appeal of tort action for damages.

■ **FACTS**

The steamship Reynolds, owned by the Lake Erie Transportation Co. ("Lake Erie") (D), was moored to Vincent's (P) dock to unload its cargo. A violent storm developed. During the storm, the Reynolds was unable to safely leave the dock. Lake Erie (D) kept the ship tied tightly to the dock and replaced the ropes used to attach it as they became worn. The fierce wind and waves caused the Reynolds to be thrown against the dock, causing damage to it.

■ **ISSUE**

Does damage to another's property due to a private necessity require compensation?

■ **DECISION AND RATIONALE**

(O'Brien, J.) Yes. Necessity may require one to take or damage another's property, but compensation is still required. If the Reynolds had entered the harbor during the storm and then been thrown against Vincent's (P) dock, Vincent (P) could not have recovered. However, here, Lake Erie (D) deliberately kept the Reynolds in a position that would damage the dock. Although this was the prudent thing to do, Lake Erie (D) is liable for the damage. Affirmed.

■ **DISSENT**

(Lewis, J.) One who constructs a dock and contracts with ship owners for docking assumes the risk of damage caused by storms. Therefore, Vincent (P) assumed the risk of damage and Lake Erie (D) is not liable to him.

Analysis:

This is the leading case on the private necessity privilege. Under this privilege, Lake Erie (D) would not be liable for damages if it did not cause any harm, Lake Erie (D) is not liable for trespassing, Vincent (P) would not have been justified in untying the Reynolds and casting it into the lake, and Lake Erie (D) is still liable for the actual harm it caused. However, if the emergency or necessity had been caused by Lake Erie (D), it likely would have lost its immunity from liability for trespass. To invoke the private necessity privilege, a defendant must have been actually threatened or must have reasonably believed that he was threatened with serious and imminent harm. The private necessity privilege differs from the public necessity privilege in that, under the private necessity privilege, the defendant is still liable for any actual harm caused.

Wilson v. Layne

(Innocent Homeowner) v. *(Federal Marshal)*
526 U.S. 603, 119 S.Ct. 1692, 143 L.Ed.2d 818 (1999)

POLICE OFFICERS ENJOY QUALIFIED IMMUNITY AS LONG AS THEIR CONDUCT DOES NOT VIOLATE CLEARLY ESTABLISHED RIGHTS OF WHICH A REASONABLE PERSON WOULD HAVE KNOWN

■ **INSTANT FACTS** Officers (D) permitted the media to ride along and enter Wilson's (P) home with them as they executed an arrest warrant, but the media did not assist the officers (D) in executing the warrant.

■ **BLACK LETTER RULE** The defense of qualified immunity shields an officer from liability for prohibited conduct only if the unlawfulness of the conduct was not "clearly established" when the conduct occurred.

■ **PROCEDURAL BASIS**

Certiorari granted after court of appeals reversed denial of summary judgment in civil rights action for damages.

■ **FACTS**

As part of their ride-along policy, a team of police officers and federal marshals (D) invited members of the media to accompany them to Wilson's (P) home where they intended to execute an arrest warrant for Wilson's (P) son. The warrant did not mention media presence or assistance. The members of the media observed the officers' (D) attempt to execute the warrant and took photographs of Wilson (P) and his wife during the incident. The media never became involved in the execution of the warrant, and did not publish its photographs. Wilson (P) sued the officers (D) in their personal capacity under *Bivens v. Six Unknown Fed. Narcotics Agents* [permits civil rights actions against federal officials] and *14 U.S.C. § 1983* [permits civil rights actions against state officials]. Wilson (P) argued that the officers (D) violated their *Fourth Amendment* [search and seizure] rights by bringing members of the media to observe and record their attempt to execute the warrant. The officers (D) asserted the defense of qualified immunity.

■ **ISSUE**

Does the defense of qualified immunity shield an officer from liability for prohibited conduct if the unlawfulness of the conduct was not "clearly established" when the conduct occurred?

■ **DECISION AND RATIONALE**

(Rehnquist, J.) Yes. Both *Bivens* and § 1983 allow a person to seek damages from government officials who have violated his Fourth Amendment rights. However, government officials performing discretionary functions generally have qualified immunity which shields them from liability insofar as their conduct does not violate clearly established statutory or constitutional rights of which a reasonable person would have known. To evaluate a claim of qualified immunity, a court must first determine whether there is an allegation of the deprivation of a constitutional right, and if so, whether that right was clearly established at the time of the alleged violation. Deciding the constitutional question before the qualified immunity question protects officials from unwarranted liability and litigation demands, and promotes clarity in the legal standards for official conduct. Here, the officers (D) had a warrant which entitled them to enter Wilson's (P) home. However, this did not necessarily entitle the officers (D) to bring the media with them. The Fourth Amendment requires that police (D) actions in execution of a warrant be related to the objectives of the intrusion the warrant authorizes. The presence of the media inside Wilson's (P) home was not related to the objectives of the authorized intrusion. The objective of the intrusion was to apprehend Wilson's (P) son. The reporters did not assist in this task. The officers (D) argue that the presence of the media served several legitimate law enforcement purposes, but none of these purposes trumps the constitutional right to privacy which the Fourth Amendment protects. We hold that it is a violation of the Fourth Amendment for police to bring members of the media or other third parties into a home during the execution of a warrant when their presence is not to aid the execution of the warrant. In this case the officers (D) violated Wilson's (P) Fourth Amendment right. Next we must decide whether this right was a clearly established right of which a reasonable person would have known at the time of the violation. In practice, whether an official's qualified immunity shields him from personal liability for his unlawful conduct generally turns on whether the conduct was reasonable in light of the legal rules that were clearly established when the conduct occurred. For purposes of qualified immunity, "clearly established" means that the contours of the right must be sufficiently clear that a reasonable official would understand that his conduct violates that right. A previous declaration that the conduct is unlawful is not necessary to satisfy this requirement, but the unlawfulness of the conduct must be apparent in light of pre-existing law. Whether the unlawfulness of an act is clearly established depends largely on the level of generality at which the relevant legal rule must be established. One might argue that any violation of the Fourth Amendment is clearly established because it is clearly established that the Fourth Amendment applies to the actions of police. However, the right allegedly violated must be defined at the appropriate level of specificity before a court can determine if it was clearly established at a particular time. Here the question is whether a reasonable officer (D) could have believed that bringing members of the media into a home during the execution of an arrest warrant was lawful in light of clearly established law and the information the officers (D) possessed. Such a belief was not unreasonable for the officers (D) in this case when they entered Wilson's (P) home. At that time the constitutional issue this case presents was not yet clearly decided. It is not obvious from the general principles of the Fourth Amendment that the conduct of the officers (D) violated the Amendment. Although media ride-alongs had become common police practice, there were not yet any judicial opinions holding that this practice was unlawful if it entered a home. There were a few cases that touched on the issue, but these cases do not clearly establish that media entry into homes during a police ride-along violates the Fourth Amendment. Wilson (P) has not produced any cases of controlling authority at the time of the incident which clearly established the rule on which they seek to rely, nor has he identified a consensus of cases of persuasive authority such that a reasonable officer (D) could not have believed that his actions were lawful. The marshals (D) here relied upon a Marshal's Service ride-along policy which explicitly permitted media on a ride-along to enter a private home. The local sheriff's department also had a ride-along program at that time that did not expressly prohibit media entry into private homes. Such policy could not make reasonable a belief that was contrary to a decided body of case law. However, because here the law was so undeveloped, it was not unreasonable for the officers (D) to rely on their formal ride-along policies. Affirmed.

■ CONCURRENCE

(Stevens, J.) I believe the homeowner's right to protection against this type of trespass was clearly established long before this incident occurred. The absence of judicial opinions expressly holding that police violate the Fourth Amendment if they bring the media into a private home provides little support for the conclusion that a competent officer (D) could reasonably believe that such conduct would be lawful. The easiest cases don't even arise.

Analysis:

The last two cases, *Courvoisier v. Raymond* [self-defense] and *Katko v. Briney* [defense of property], addressed privileges which permit a person to use force in self-defense and in defense of property, respectively. This case addresses the privilege of qualified immunity, which gives government officials a limited privilege to commit acts which would otherwise be tortious, including the use of force. The scope of different officials' immunity varies with the nature of their authority and other factors. In

Wilson, the Supreme Court explained that a police officer's conduct is privileged if it does not violate clearly established statutory or constitutional rights of which a reasonable person should know. In general, an official's discretionary acts are privileged if the official acts in good faith. In contrast, an official's ministerial acts are not privileged if done improperly, regardless of good faith. The *Restatement (Second) of Torts § 895D* [immunities of public officers] explains that courts have traditionally granted officials some degree of immunity because if they did not, the officials would be "unduly hampered, deterred and intimidated in the discharge of their duties" by the threat of personal liability. In addition, it would be unfair to require a person to exercise his judgment, and then to subject him to liability based on the judgment of others, particularly others who may be much less qualified than he to pass judgment or who may be acting on the basis of hindsight [i.e., those pesky jurors]. Officials performing judicial and legislative functions traditionally enjoy absolute immunity. Again, this immunity allows judicial and legislative officers to avoid the deterrence and impaired effectiveness they would otherwise face if their purposes, motives and beliefs were subjected to the uncertain appraisal of juries or judges.

■ CASE VOCABULARY

APPREHEND: In this context, to arrest.

QUALIFIED IMMUNITY: Limited immunity which shields public officials from civil liability if they do not violate clearly established rights.

CHAPTER THIRTEEN

Defamation

Romaine v. Kallinger

Instant Facts: A woman is suing the author and publisher of a book claiming that a passage in the book suggesting that the woman knew a criminal was defamatory as a matter of law.

Black Letter Rule: A statement is defamatory as a matter of law only if no reasonable person could disagree on the defamatory nature of the statement.

Matherson v. Marchello

Instant Facts: A man is suing members of a band for defamation after a band member broadcast over the radio a suggestion that the man was a homosexual.

Black Letter Rule: A statement which may appear to be objectively inoffensive, may nevertheless be defamatory if the statement could be reasonably expected to be found offensive by at least a segment of the audience to whom it was made.

Matherson v. Marchello

Instant Facts: A man is claiming that members of a band committed libel when they made defamatory statements about him over the radio.

Black Letter Rule: The issue of whether or not a defamatory statement is libel turns not on the question of whether the statement is written or spoken, but on how widely the statement is disseminated.

Liberman v. Gelstein

Instant Facts: A tenant stated to another tenant that the landlord had been bribing police officers and the landlord sued for slander.

Black Letter Rule: Certain types of allegations are considered slander per se, in such instances, damages are presumed and do not need to be alleged with specificity.

Liberman v. Gelstein

Instant Facts: A tenant being sued for defamation claimed that the defamatory statement he made was privileged and therefore could not be sued upon.

Black Letter Rule: A person cannot be sued for making a defamatory statement without malice and under conditions of privilege.

Medico v. Time, Inc.

Instant Facts: A Time magazine article about a congressman stated that an acquaintance of the congressman was a mafia figure; the accused mafia figure sued for defamation.

Black Letter Rule: A publisher which accurately reports on information taken from an official report or proceeding cannot be held liable for defamation.

Burnett v. National Enquirer, Inc.

Instant Facts: A person sued a publisher for punitive damages for publishing a defamatory article even though the publisher had printed a timely retraction of the article.

Black Letter Rule: A newspaper is not liable for punitive damages if it publishes a timely retraction or correction of a defamatory article.

Carafano v. Metrosplash.com, Inc.

Instant Facts: After an unknown user posted a personal profile of Carafano (P) on Matchmaker.com, Carafano (P) sued the website host.

Black Letter Rule: A provider or user of an interactive web-based service is not considered the publisher or speaker of any information provided by another information provider.

New York Times Co. v. Sullivan

Instant Facts: A police chief sued the New York Times for defamation for an ad the newspaper ran implying that the chief had violated people's civil rights in the South.

Black Letter Rule: A public official cannot recover damages for defamation unless the official can prove that the defamatory statement was made with actual malice.

Gertz v. Robert Welch, Inc.

Instant Facts: A lawyer sued the publisher of a magazine for defamatory statements the magazine made when it accused the lawyer of being a communist who was involved in a conspiracy against the police.

Black Letter Rule: A private citizen does not need to prove actual malice in order to recover actual damages for defamation.

Wells v. Liddy

Instant Facts: A secretary who was peripherally involved in the Watergate scandal sued Gordon Liddy for defamation when he suggested that she had helped to run a prostitution ring for the Democratic National Committee.

Black Letter Rule: An involuntary public figure, who must prove defamation by actual malice, is a person who engages in conduct that a reasonable person would foresee could result in a significant controversy and who then becomes a central figure in that controversy.

Milkovich v. Lorain Journal Co.

Instant Facts: A wrestling coach sued a newspaper for defamation after the paper published a column stating that the coach had committed perjury.

Black Letter Rule: A statement on a matter of public concern must be provable as false before there can be liability for defamation.

Flamm v. American Association of University Women

Instant Facts: A Lawyer sued the publisher of a directory for defamation after the directory described him as an ambulance chaser.

Black Letter Rule: Whenever a statement involves a matter of public concern, the statement must be provable as false in order for a defamation suit to proceed, regardless of whether the defendant is a member of the media.

Khawar v. Globe International, Inc.

Instant Facts: A man sued The Globe, a tabloid, for publishing an accurate summary of a book which had concluded that the man had been the true assassin of Robert Kennedy.

Black Letter Rule: A private figure may recover damages for defamation from a media source which has done no more than accurately report on another's defamatory statements regarding a matter of public concern.

Romaine v. Kallinger

(*Libeled Citizen*) v. (*Author*)

109 N.J. 282, 537 A.2d 284 (1988)

AS A MATTER OF LAW, A STATEMENT CANNOT BE DEFAMATORY IF NO REASONABLE PERSON COULD FIND THAT THE STATEMENT IS SUSCEPTIBLE OF A DEFAMATORY MEANING

■ **INSTANT FACTS** A woman is suing the author and publisher of a book claiming that a passage in the book suggesting that the woman knew a criminal was defamatory as a matter of law.

■ **BLACK LETTER RULE** A statement is defamatory as a matter of law only if no reasonable person could disagree on the defamatory nature of the statement.

■ **PROCEDURAL BASIS**

Appeal to New Jersey Supreme Court from trial court and then appellate court's decision to uphold summary judgment for failure to state a claim.

■ **FACTS**

Randi Romaine (P) filed a libel claim against the author and the publisher (D) of a book entitled "The Shoemaker." The book, a non-fiction account of a man who went on a killing spree, contained a passage about a woman named Maria Fashing. The author (D) wrote about an episode where Ms. Fasching, described as a caring person who liked to help people down on their luck, visited Ms. Romaine (P) at her home. In connection with the visit, the author (D) wrote that, among other things, "Maria was eager for news from Randi [Ms. Romaine] (P) about a junkie they knew who was doing time in prison." Ms. Romaine (P) sued claiming that the passage mentioning her in connection with a "junkie" was defamatory. The trial court granted summary judgment for the author and publisher (D) and the appellate court affirmed the trial court's ruling. On appeal to the Supreme Court of New Jersey, Ms. Romaine (P) argued that the statement in question was defamatory as a matter of law or, in the alternative, that the statement's defamatory content was at least a question for a jury. The New Jersey Supreme Court upheld the lower courts' grant of summary judgment.

■ **ISSUE**

Are there instances where a court can find that a statement cannot be defamatory as a matter of law?

■ **DECISION AND RATIONALE**

(Handler, J.) Yes. The threshold question in any defamation case is whether the statement at issue is reasonably susceptible of a defamatory interpretation. In determining whether a statement could be interpreted as defamatory, a court should consider the statement according to its everyday meaning and in the context it was made. If the statement lends itself only to a defamatory interpretation, then the statement is defamatory as a matter of law. If, on the other hand, the statement can only be ascribed a non-defamatory interpretation, then a court must dismiss an action for defamation. It is only when a statement is capable of being interpreted as both defamatory and non-defamatory that a claim of libel should go to a jury. Ms. Romaine (P) argues that the statement in question paints her as a criminal or, at least one who associates with criminals. Because the statement can be viewed in only a negative light, Ms. Romaine (P) argues that the statement is libelous *per se*. We do not agree. In this instance, we do not believe that any reasonable person could ascribe a defamatory meaning to the statement about which Ms. Romaine (P) complains. At most, the sentence could be read to suggest that Ms. Romaine (P) knew a junkie. Even if we make the assumption that a junkie is a criminal, the mere allegation that a person knows a criminal is not defamatory as a matter of law. Furthermore, in the context of the passage in which the statement was made—a context which suggests that Ms. Romaine (P) knew the junkie not as a peer or fellow criminal but rather as someone who may have been inclined to help the less fortunate—no reasonable person could have interpreted the statement as defamatory. We therefore find that the lower courts properly granted summary judgment on the complaint of libel. The statement was not defamatory as a matter of law.

■ DISSENT

(O'Hern, J.) I believe that a reasonable person could have interpreted the passage complained of as defamatory. The issue of libel should therefore have been submitted to a jury.

Analysis:

The first issue for any court to decide in a defamation case is whether any reasonable person could view the statement at issue as defamatory. Statements that can be viewed as none other than defamatory are libelous as a matter of law. In such instances, presumably, a court will direct a verdict for the plaintiff. Where no reasonable person could view a statement as defamatory however, a court must grant a summary judgment for the defendant. As the court notes, the question of whether or not a statement can be interpreted as defamatory depends upon not only the statement itself, but also upon the context in which the statement was made. The final determination of whether or not a statement could be viewed as defamatory however, has to rest with the subjective interpretation of the audience receiving it.

Matherson v. Marchello

(Libeled Person) v. *(Band Member)*
100 A.D.2d 233, 473 N.Y.S.2d 998 (App. Div. 2 Dept. 1984)

THE QUESTION OF WHETHER OR NOT A STATEMENT IS DEFAMATORY DEPENDS, IN PART, ON THE PERCEPTIONS OF THE AUDIENCE RECEIVING THE STATEMENT

■ **INSTANT FACTS** A man is suing members of a band for defamation after a band member broadcast over the radio a suggestion that the man was a homosexual.

■ **BLACK LETTER RULE** A statement which may appear to be objectively inoffensive, may nevertheless be defamatory if the statement could be reasonably expected to be found offensive by at least a segment of the audience to whom it was made.

■ **PROCEDURAL BASIS**

Appeal to New York Appellate division after dismissal of defamation suit by trial court.

■ **FACTS**

Mr. Matherson (P) sued the members of a band called "The Good Rats" (Rats) (D) for defamation after the band stated during a radio interview that a band member had "fooled around" with Matherson's (P) wife and another band member stated, "I think it was when somebody started messing around with his (Matherson's) boyfriend that he really freaked out." Mr. Matherson (P) claimed that both statements were defamatory and had caused him humiliation, mental anguish, loss of reputation, and injury to his marriage and business. The trial court dismissed Mr. Matherson's (P) suit for defamation and he appealed to the New York Appellate division.

■ **ISSUE**

Are statements, which may appear to be objectively inoffensive, but which are considered offensive by at least some, defamatory as a matter of law?

■ **DECISION AND RATIONALE**

(Titone, J.P.) Yes. The issue for this court on appeal is whether or not the statements Mr. Matherson (P) complains of were or were not defamatory as a matter of law. If the statements were not defamatory as a matter of law, the trial court clearly acted properly when it dismissed Mr. Matherson's (P) claims. If, on the other hand, the statements could have been interpreted as defamatory, that question should have been submitted to a jury. We first consider the statement alleging that a band member had "fooled around" with Mr. Matherson's (P) wife and find that, according to the standards of contemporary usage, this statement was clearly libelous. We next turn to the more tricky question of whether the suggestion that Mr. Matherson (P) is a homosexual could have been interpreted as defamatory and whether that issue should have therefore gone to the jury. The Rats (D) argue that many public figures are homosexual and that an allegation that one is a homosexual cannot be said to be defamatory. We disagree. Unfortunately, in our society many individuals still view homosexuality as immoral and shameful. In addition to the social opprobrium that comes with being a homosexual, this court also recognizes that the law discriminates against homosexuals. Legal sanctions are imposed on homosexuals in areas ranging from immigration to military service. Thus, while this court does not need to pass judgment on the morality of homosexual behavior, it is compelled to acknowledge that homosexuality carries a stigma in this society and consequences for the homosexual. Because the imputation of homosexuality is "reasonably susceptible of a defamatory connotation," we find that the trial court erred when it declined to submit the issue to a jury. Reversed.

Analysis:

Defamation cannot take place in a vacuum. The question of whether or not a statement is defamatory turns not only on the content of the statement and the context in which it was made, but also on the audience to whom the statement was addressed. In this case, the court does not focus on the question of whether homosexuality itself is immoral or wrong; rather, the court focuses its analysis on the issue of how homosexuality is viewed in society. The court notes that, regardless of whether homosexual behavior is right or wrong, the fact remains that a significant segment of society views homosexuality in a negative light. Of particular significance, the court points out, is that in some areas, such as military service and immigration, discrimination against homosexuals has the imprimatur of law. Thus, the question of whether or not a statement is defamatory cannot be answered by simply considering the statement alone. A statement that, standing alone, may not appear offensive, may nevertheless be defamatory if it could reasonably be expected to be viewed as such by the audience to whom it was addressed.

Matherson v. Marchello

(Libeled Person) v. *(Band Member)*
100 A.D.2d 233, 473 N.Y.S.2d 998 (App. Div. 2 Dept. 1984)

DEFAMATORY STATEMENTS BROADCAST OVER RADIO OR TELEVISION QUALIFY AS LIBEL BE-
CAUSE THEY ARE AT LEAST AS HARMFUL AS DEFAMATORY WRITTEN STATEMENTS

■ **INSTANT FACTS** A man is claiming that members of a band committed libel when they made
defamatory statements about him over the radio.

■ **BLACK LETTER RULE** The issue of whether
or not a defamatory statement is libel turns not
on the question of whether the statement is
written or spoken, but on how widely the statement is disseminated.

■ **PROCEDURAL BASIS**

Appeal to the Appellate Division from trial court's grant of defendant's motion to dismiss.

■ **FACTS**

[Note: This opinion is a continuation of the opinion in an earlier portion of the casebook, supra.
Though the facts are the same, this opinion addresses a different aspect of the law on defamation.] Mr.
Matherson (P) sued members of a band called "The Good Rats" (Rats) (D) for defamation. During a
radio interview, band members had suggested that they were carrying on an affair with Mr. Matherson's
(P) wife and also suggested that Mr. Matherson (P) was a homosexual. Mr. Matherson (P) sued the
Rats (D) and sought compensatory and punitive damages for humiliation, mental anguish, loss of
reputation and injury to his marital relationship as well as for the loss of customers to his business and
loss of business opportunities. Mr. Matherson (P) did not claim "special damages." Special damages
are specific losses which flow directly from the injury to reputation caused by the alleged defamation.
The trial court ruled that a suit for defamation required a plaintiff to allege special damages; because
Mr. Matherson (P) did not claim special damages, the trial court dismissed his compliant. The court of
appeals reversed the trial court and reinstated Mr. Matherson's (P) complaint.

■ **ISSUE**

May a spoken defamatory statement qualify as libel?

■ **DECISION AND RATIONALE**

(Titone, J.P.) Yes. Traditionally, courts have considered only written defamatory statements as libel;
spoken defamatory statements fell into the category of slander. A plaintiff who alleges defamation by
slander must claim special damages or the claim will be dismissed. Special damages are damages
which flow directly from the alleged act of defamation. Special damages are not emotional damages;
they are actual economic losses suffered as a direct result of the defamation. Special damages must
be alleged with particularity and, when as here, it is alleged that the defamation led to a loss of
business, the persons who ceased to be customers must be named and the losses itemized. It is clear
to us that the lower court ruled correctly when it found that Mr. Matherson (P) failed to allege special
damages. Nevertheless, we find that the lower court erred when it dismissed Mr. Matherson's (P) claim
for defamation. Although a plaintiff who alleges defamation by slander must claim special damages
[the exceptions to this rule are discussed in the case which follows], a plaintiff alleging defamation by

libel has no such obligation. The question for this court then becomes: did the statements made by the Rats (D) constitute slander or libel? The traditional test for whether a statement constituted libel or slander rested upon a determination of whether the words were written or spoken. Written defamation (libel) was considered to be a far more serious offense, first, because the written word was considered to carry a greater ring of truth and, second, because the written word could be more broadly distributed. Today, the reasons for distinguishing between the spoken and written word have largely disappeared. Radio, television, and film, now allow the spoken word to be broadcast as widely and with as much authority as the written word. It is clear to this court that a defamatory statement disseminated by means of radio or television has the potential to do at least as much harm to a defamed person as any written statement. We therefore hold that a defamatory statement broadcast by radio or television constitutes libel. Because the Rat's (D) defamatory statements were libel, Mr. Matherson (P) did not need to allege special damages. Reversed.

Analysis:

Prior to the development of modern means for broadcasting speech, courts presumed that spoken defamation was not as harmful as written defamation and; accordingly, a person alleging slander also had to allege special damages. This case makes clear that the test for whether defamation is slander or libel depends not on whether the defamation is written or spoken, but on how many people will potentially hear the defamatory statement. The court concludes that spoken defamation broadcast by means of radio or television is presumptively libelous, but leaves open the question of how the court would regard spoken defamation broadcast by other means. For instance, how would the court view a defamatory statement broadcast over a school's P.A. system or shouted from a stage at a rally? Presumably, in order to answer these questions a court would have to consider the size of the audience receiving the statement as well as the measure of authority conferred by the medium used to broadcast the statement.

■ CASE VOCABULARY

LIBEL: Any written defamatory statement or, a spoken defamatory statement which is widely disseminated, possibly by means of radio, film, or television.

SPECIAL DAMAGES: In cases of slander damages are not presumed, therefore, a plaintiff claiming defamation by slander must allege special damages which are damages which can be quantified, itemized and otherwise specified with particularity.

Liberman v. Gelstein

(*Landlord*) v. (*Tenant*)

80 N.Y.2d 429, 605 N.E.2d 344, 590 N.Y.S.2d 857 (1992)

CERTAIN STATEMENTS ARE CONSIDERED TO BE SO OFFENSIVE THAT THEY ARE SLANDER PER SE AND DAMAGES ARE PRESUMED

■ **INSTANT FACTS** A tenant stated to another tenant that the landlord had been bribing police officers and the landlord sued for slander.

■ **BLACK LETTER RULE** Certain types of allegations are considered slander per se, in such instances, damages are presumed and do not need to be alleged with specificity.

■ **PROCEDURAL BASIS**

Appeal to Court of Appeals of New York from Appellate Division's decision to affirm trial court's order to dismiss.

■ **FACTS**

Mr. Liberman (P), a landlord, sued Mr. Gelstein (D), a member of the tenants' board of governors in Mr. Liberman's (P) building, for defamation by slander. Mr. Liberman (P) specifically complained that two statements made by Mr. Gelstein (D) were slanderous. In the first statement, Mr. Gelstein (D) advised Mr. Kohler, another member of the board of governors, that Mr. Liberman (P) had bribed police officers so that they would not issue parking tickets to vehicles parked in front of the apartment building. In the second statement, Mr. Gelstein (D) stated, in the presence of employees of the apartment building, that Mr. Liberman (P) had threatened him and his family. The trial court dismissed Mr. Liberman's (P) claims for slander as to both statements. The trial court found that the first statement, made to another member of the board of governors, was privileged and could not be sued upon. The trial court found that the second statement, where Mr. Liberman (P) was said to have threatened Mr. Gelstein (D) and his family, was not slanderous because it could only have been interpreted as rhetorical hyperbole. The appellate division affirmed the trial court's decision and Mr. Liberman (P) appealed to the Court of Appeals.

■ **ISSUE**

Must a lawsuit for defamation by slander include a claim for special damages?

■ **DECISION AND RATIONALE**

(Kaye, J.) No. Typically, a lawsuit claiming defamation by slander must include a claim for special damages. Special damages are quantifiable damages that can be specifically linked to the slander alleged. The law recognizes four specific instances where a claim for slander will not require a claim for special damages: 1) a statement which charges a person with a serious crime; 2) a statement which tends to injure another in his trade or profession; 3.) a statement alleging that a person has a loathsome disease; and 4) a statement which suggests that a woman is unchaste. Statements alleging one of the foregoing are called *slander per se* and are presumed to be so harmful that a plaintiff alleging one of them is not required to allege any special damages. In the case before us, Mr. Liberman (P) argues that both statements made by Mr. Gelstein (D) were slanderous per se because both charged him with criminal conduct. We find that Mr. Liberman's (P) argument fails because not every statement alleging that one has engaged in unlawful conduct is necessarily slanderous per se. This court recognizes that there are many shades of criminal misconduct not all of which subject a person to the opprobrium of society. For instance, while it may be unlawful to commit a minor traffic offense, this court will not find that it is slanderous per se to accuse a person of having committed such an offense. Nevertheless, we do find that Mr. Liberman (P) did sufficiently allege that Mr. Gelstein (D) committed slander per se when he accused him of bribery. The law presumes damages when there is an accusation that a person has engaged in as serious an offense as bribery. We find, however, that the second statement attributed to Mr. Gelstein (D), essentially a statement accusing Mr. Liberman (P) of harassment, was not slanderous per se; the law will not presume damages when there is an accusation of only minor misconduct. Neither are we persuaded by Mr. Liberman's (P) argument that Mr. Gelstein's (D) charge of harassment harmed him in his profession. In order to meet the "trade or profession" test for slander per se, the defamatory statement cannot be general in nature; it must relate directly to the person's ability to engage in the profession. In sum, we find that Mr. Gelstein's (D) statement alleging that Mr. Liberman (P) engaged in bribery was slander per se and, as such, did not require an allegation of special damages. The statement alleging harassment was not slander per se. The lower courts properly held that both claims of defamation should be dismissed. Affirmed.

Analysis:

This case reveals how difficult it is to formulate simple, black-letter rules of law. In almost any situation, it seems, lawyers can argue that the law is not applicable to whatever facts are presented. In this instance, while the court agreed that an allegation that one has committed a serious crime is slanderous per se, it did not agree that harassment qualified as a serious crime. Of course, in order to arrive at this conclusion, the court first had to determine that Mr. Gelstein (D) accused Mr. Liberman (P) of no more than harassment. Even the court's conclusion that Mr. Gelstein (D) was guilty of no more than harassment is open to debate. Many would consider an offer to do serious physical harm to another to be aggravated assault, a felony that would likely be considered a serious crime. Similarly, the court exercised considerable discretion when it concluded that Mr. Gelstein's (D) accusations did not tend to harm Mr. Liberman (P) in his profession. The court stated that in order to meet this exception, the accusation must relate directly to the plaintiff's ability to engage in his profession.

■ CASE VOCABULARY

SLANDER PER SE: The law considers the following four types of defamatory statement to be so offensive that they are considered slander per se and damages are presumed: 1) A statement accusing one of a serious crime; 2) a statement which would tend to injure another in his trade or profession; 3) a statement alleging that one has a loathsome disease; and 4) a statement alleging that a woman is unchaste.

Liberman v. Gelstein

(Landlord) v. *(Tenant)*

80 N.Y.2d 429, 605 N.E.2d 344, 590 N.Y.S.2d 857 (1992)

ONE CANNOT BE HELD LIABLE FOR A DEFAMTORY STATEMENT MADE UNDER A CONDITION OF PRIVILEGE AND WITHOUT MALICE

■ **INSTANT FACTS** A tenant being sued for defamation claimed that the defamatory statement he made was privileged and therefore could not be sued upon.

■ **BLACK LETTER RULE** A person cannot be sued for making a defamatory statement without malice and under conditions of privilege.

■ **PROCEDURAL BASIS**

Appeal to Court of Appeals of New York from Appellate Division's decision to affirm trial court's order to dismiss.

■ **FACTS**

[Note: This case is a continuation of the same case found *supra* of the casebook.] Mr. Liberman (P), the landlord of an apartment building, sued Mr. Gelstein (D), a member of the tenants' board of governors, for defamation. Mr. Liberman (P) claimed that two statements made by Mr. Gelstein (D) were slanderous per se. In the first statement, Mr. Gelstein (D) told Mr. Kohler, another member of the board of governors, that Mr. Liberman (P) had been bribing police officers so they would not issue parking tickets to cars parked in front of the building. In the second statement, Mr. Gelstein (D) stated in the presence of employees of the building that Mr. Liberman (P) had threatened him and his family. The lower court found that the second statement was not slanderous per se because it did not accuse Mr. Liberman (P) of a serious crime and it did not tend to injure him in the conduct of his profession. Because the statement was not slanderous per se and Mr. Liberman (P) had not alleged special damages, the court dismissed the claim for defamation as to that statement. The court did find that Mr. Gelstein (D) had accused Mr. Liberman (P) of a serious crime when he alleged that he had engaged in bribery and that that statement did therefore qualify as slander per se. Nevertheless, Mr. Gelstein (D) argued that he could not be held liable for the accusation of bribery because it was made to another member of the tenants' board of governors and was therefore conditionally privileged. The trial court dismissed the claim for defamation based on the accusation of bribery finding that the statement was qualifiedly privileged and the appellate court affirmed. Mr. Liberman (P) appealed to the Court of Appeals.

■ **ISSUE**

Does a finding that a statement is slander per se automatically entitle the victim of the slander to recover damages?

■ **DECISION AND RATIONALE**

(Kaye, J.) No. Though we have found that Mr. Gelstein's (D) allegation that Mr. Liberman (P) engaged in bribery was slanderous per se and that therefore Mr. Liberman (P) was not required to allege special damages, that is not the end of the matter. A finding that a statement was slanderous per se does not automatically entitle a plaintiff to recovery; there are several defenses to a charge of slander, in this instance, Mr. Gelstein (D) has asserted the defense of conditional privilege. Mr. Gelstein (D) claims that even if his statement regarding Mr. Liberman (P) was slanderous per se, he cannot be held liable because he made the statement to a fellow member of the tenants' board of governors and the statement concerned a matter of common interest to both. Courts have long recognized that certain statements, though defamatory, should be shielded against litigation if they serve public interest. Public policy requires that certain statements, such as statements made by legislators during debate, should be entirely immune from suit while other statements which serve a less compelling public interest, should be only conditionally privileged. One conditional, or qualified, privilege is the "common interest" privilege. The common interest privilege allows parties with a common interest to make defamatory statements without fear of a lawsuit so long as they do not abuse the privilege. In this instance, we agree that Mr. Gelstein (D) and Mr. Kohler, the fellow board member, had a common interest: both were members of the tenants' board of governors and, as such, both had an interest in whether Mr. Liberman (P) was bribing police so that his cars could occupy parking spaces in front of the building. Nevertheless, a finding that a statement is conditionally privileged does not render the statement immune from a lawsuit. A plaintiff who can demonstrate that a statement was made with malice can recover damages even if the statement was conditionally privileged. Under common law, malice is defined as spite or ill will, however, in the context of defamation cases, the most commonly applied definition of malice is that set forth in the U.S Supreme Court case of *New York Times, Co. v. Sullivan*. The *Times* case requires that a plaintiff show that the statements complained of were made with "a high degree of awareness of their probable falsity" or with a reckless disregard of their truth, in order to prove malice. In this case, Mr. Liberman (P) has not sufficiently alleged malice under the *Times* standard because he has offered no proof that Mr. Gelstein (D) believed that his accusations concerning bribery were false. Neither has Mr. Liberman (P) alleged malice under the common law standard. Mere ill will between two parties does not establish malice, the common law requires a plaintiff to show that the defamatory statements were motivated by malice rather that some other, more constructive, purpose. Mr. Liberman (P) has made no such showing in this case. We therefore find that, because the statements concerning bribery were conditionally privileged and Mr. Liberman (P) has presented no triable issues on malice, the lower courts properly dismissed the claim for defamation. Affirmed.

■ DISSENT

(Smith, J.) Mr. Gelstein's (D) statements to his fellow board members raise legitimate questions on the issue of malice. Consequently, I believe the issue of malice should have been resolved by a jury.

Analysis:

The common interest exception is meant to promote a free exchange of relevant information among those in pursuit of a common goal or interest. It seems that in the instant case, the court properly found that Mr. Gelstein's (D) statement concerning Mr. Liberman (P) should have been protected by the common interest privilege. Plainly, Mr. Gelstein (D) and Mr. Kohler, the recipient of the statement, were members of a defined group, the tenant's board of governors. Equally clear was the fact that the statement alleging bribery on the part of Mr. Liberman (P) related to the group's interests, namely, preserving the quality of life in the apartment complex. The court rightly found that, in an instance such as the one presented, public policy requires that people be able to speak freely and without fear of suit. One can, however, imagine circumstances where the common interest privilege would not so clearly apply to a defamatory statement. For instance, though it is clear that members of an organization such as a tenants' board have a common interest, would the court find the same for two people who just happen to live in the same apartment building? How formal must an organization be before its members will be deemed to have a common interests? And, assuming that a common interest exists, how directly must a defamatory statement relate to the interest in order to qualify as privileged?

■ CASE VOCABULARY

QUALIFIED PRIVILEGE: The law recognizes several areas of qualified privilege where, for public policy reasons such as the advancement of a greater public good, people are allowed to make defamatory statements without fear of being sued.

Medico v. Time, Inc.

(Mobster) v. *(Magazine)*
643 F.2d 134 (3d Cir. 1981)

A PUBLISHER WHICH ACCURATELY REPORTS A DEFAMATORY STATEMENT MADE IN AN OFFICIAL DOCUMENT OR PROCEEDING MAY NOT BE HELD LIABLE FOR DEFAMMTION

■ **INSTANT FACTS** A Time magazine article about a congressman stated that an acquaintance of the congressman was a mafia figure; the accused mafia figure sued for defamation.

■ **BLACK LETTER RULE** A publisher which accurately reports on information taken from an official report or proceeding cannot be held liable for defamation.

■ **PROCEDURAL BASIS**

Appeal to United States Court of Appeal from District Court's grant of summary judgment in favor of the defendant.

■ **FACTS**

Time Magazine (D) published an article describing the suspected criminal activities of a U.S. Congressman. The article summarized FBI documents that named Phillip Medico (P) as an intermediary between the congressman and an organized crime family. Mr. Medico (P) sued Time (D) for defamation. Time (D) moved for summary judgment based on the claim that its assertions were substantially true. The district court, however, dismissed Mr. Medico's (P) claim on the grounds that the Time (P) article fell within the common law privilege allowing the press to report on official proceedings or documents. Mr. Medico (P) appealed and argued that, because the Time (D) article relied on internal FBI documents that were not public record, the subsequent publication of the documents was not privileged. The United States Court of Appeal heard the case.

■ **ISSUE**

Does the Fair Report Privilege shield from liability a publisher who prints or summarizes documents that are not public record?

■ **DECISION AND RATIONALE**

(Adams, C.J.) Yes. In order to promote full and complete media coverage of newsworthy events, the law has long recognized a "fair report privilege" which allows the press to publish accounts of official proceedings or reports without fear of being sued for defamation. The fair report privilege can be overcome however if it is proven either, that the publisher did not fairly and accurately summarize the report or proceedings, or that the publisher acted for the sole purpose of harming the person defamed. In this instance, Mr. Medico (P) argues that the fair report privilege does not apply at all because Time (D) published summaries of internal reports that were not "official" in that they expressed only tentative and preliminary conclusions which the FBI never adopted as accurate. In support of his argument, Mr. Medico (P) points to the title page of the report which states that the document "contains neither recommendations nor conclusions of the FBI." We find that a report does not have to be a matter of public record before the fair report privilege applies. We are guided to this conclusion by an earlier decision where a court found that the fair report privilege shielded from liability a publisher who

---

summarized a civil complaint. If publishers enjoy a privilege when publishing details of civil complaints, we believe that they should enjoy the same privilege when summarizing police reports: the danger that a civil litigant would insert defamatory statements in a civil complaint is at least as great as the danger that law enforcement would falsify a police report. Furthermore, the policies underlying the fair report privilege support our conclusion that it applies to the publication of police reports. There are three rationales for the fair report privilege: the agency theory which argues that a reporter merely acts as an agent for members of the public who could have attended the official proceeding had they wanted; the public interest theory which holds that the privilege promotes and protects the public's interest in learning about important matters; and finally, the public supervision theory which holds that society has an interest in seeing that the acts of its public officials are open to scrutiny. The public interest theory supports our conclusions today. If citizens are to discharge their obligation to effectively monitor and supervise their government, then there can be no penalty for exposing to the general view the misconduct of government officials. The Time (D) article that implicated Mr. Medico (P), largely concerned the activities of a U.S. congressman. Clearly, the public has an interest in monitoring the activities of such a high ranking elected official and also in knowing with whom the official associates. To allow Time (D) to be held liable for publishing information of such considerable public interest would be contrary to the rationale behind the fair report privilege. Having found then that the Time (D) article was privileged, our only remaining consideration is whether Mr. Medico (P) has offered evidence to overcome the privilege. In order to overcome the fair report privilege, Mr. Medico (P) would have to show either that Time (D) published its article with the sole purpose of causing him harm or that it did not fairly and accurately summarize the reports relied on. The record does not reflect evidence of either circumstance. The district court is affirmed.

Analysis:

The public supervision rationale holds that the public's interest in knowing the affairs of its public officials requires that publishers be allowed to disseminate information about those officials without fear of being sued for defamation. Naturally, the public's interest in information about a public official would include information about people with whom the official associated. In this case, the court found that the public supervision rationale should protect Time (D) from liability because its article concerned the affairs of a congressman. Though Mr. Medico (P) was not a public official, it seems that the court nevertheless found that the public had an interest in knowing his affairs because he associated with a public official. The court could have found a different rationale for holding that the Fair Report Privilege protected Time (D) had less prominent people been involved in this case. The Fair Report Privilege is intended to protect publishers who print or summarize official documents. The rationale behind the policy is that official documents are inherently trustworthy as well as newsworthy.

■ CASE VOCABULARY

FAIR REPORT PRIVILEGE: The Fair Report Privilege provides that one who accurately publishes the details of an official report or proceeding cannot be held liable for defamation.

Burnett v. National Enquirer, Inc.

(Comedian) v. *(Tabloid)*

144 Cal.App.3d 991, 193 Cal.Rptr. 206 (1983)

A PUBLICATION THAT PRINTS DEFAMATORY NEWS ITEMS WHICH ARE NOT OF A TIME-SENSITIVE NATURE MAY BE HELD LIABLE FOR PUNITIVE DAMAGES EVEN IF IT PRINTS A TIMELY RETRACTION OR CORRECTION

■ **INSTANT FACTS** A person sued a publisher for punitive damages for publishing a defamatory article even though the publisher had printed a timely retraction of the article.

■ **BLACK LETTER RULE** A newspaper is not liable for punitive damages if it publishes a timely retraction or correction of a defamatory article.

■ **PROCEDURAL BASIS**

Appeal from trial court to Court of Appeal of California.

■ **FACTS**

The National Enquirer (Enquirer) (D) published an article stating that Carol Burnett (P) had been in a Washington restaurant where she had had a loud argument with Henry Kissinger and had then spilled wine on another patron. Ms. Burnett (P), stating that no such incident had occurred, demanded that the Enquirer (D) publish a retraction of the article. California law provided that, in cases of slander or libel, a newspaper could not be sued for anything other than special damages if the newspaper published a retraction of the defamatory statements in a timely fashion. Subsequently, the Enquirer (D) did print a retraction of the article and stated that the facts alleged by the article never occurred. Nonetheless, Ms. Burnett (P) chose to file suit against the Enquirer (D) and a jury awarded her $300,000 in compensatory damages and $1.3 million in punitive damages. The trial court reduced the damages to $50,000 and $750,000 respectively. The Enquirer (D) appealed claiming that, because it printed a retraction of the libelous article as allowed by law, it could not be liable to Ms. Burnett (P) for anything more than special damages. The Court of Appeal of California heard the case.

■ **ISSUE**

May the publisher of a defamatory article be liable for punitive damages even if it publishes a timely retraction of the defamatory piece?

■ **DECISION AND RATIONALE**

(Roth, P.J.) Yes. The law clearly provides that when a newspaper publishes an article which proves to be false or defamatory, the newspaper can nevertheless be held liable for no more than special damages if it publishes a correction or retraction of the defamatory piece upon timely notice. In this case, we are satisfied that the Enquirer (D) did publish an adequate retraction of the defamatory piece; however, the concern for this court is whether or not the Enquirer (D) is a newspaper within the meaning of the law. Though the Enquirer (D) argues that it is a newspaper and is able to provide evidence to support its assertion, we find that it is not a newspaper for the purposes of the statute. In coming to this conclusion, we must examine the rationale behind the law protecting newspapers from all but special damages in cases of defamation. The law provides special protections for newspapers in defamation cases because it recognizes that newspapers are under time constraints not shared by other publications. The nature of the newspaper business requires papers to disseminate news almost as they receive it. Most news articles are published no later that a day after an event takes place. Courts have recognized that newspapers do not always have time to check stories for accuracy and that errors do take place. Because of the public's interest in seeing news disseminated in a timely fashion however, courts and legislatures have provided that newspapers should not be liable for punitive damages in the event a publication mistake does take place. We find that the rationale for shielding newspapers from liability in cases of defamation does not apply to the Enquirer (D). The Enquirer (D) is not a publication that publishes items concerning current events or anything else of a time sensitive nature. Mainly, the Enquirer (D) publishes celebrity pieces, gossip and personal improvement articles. There is no pressing need to publish items of this nature to the public without first taking the time to verify their accuracy. Accordingly, we find that Enquirer (D) is not a newspaper for purposes of the law and that, therefore, damages against the Enquirer (D) should not be limited to special damages. The trial court is affirmed.

Analysis:

The court here recognized that newspapers must frequently publish news items on short notice and without time to verify their accuracy. The public's interest in having news disseminated quickly, the court stated, justified protecting newspapers form liability in the event of a mistake. Because the Enquirer (D) was not a publication that typically published breaking news, the court found that it should not enjoy the protection the law affords some publications accused of defamation. Implicit in the court's finding was the conclusion that a more traditional newspaper that published breaking news would have been protected from punitive damages in this case. But, such a result would be contrary to the logic of the court's opinion. Rather than finding that the Enquirer (D) was not a newspaper because it typically published stories that did not concern current affairs, it seems that the court could have considered the nature of the defamatory article itself. It is a fact that in the modem media, many traditional newspapers publish human interest stories thatare not time sensitive, while tabloids such as the Enquirer (D) occasionally publish breaking news.

Carafano v. Metrosplash.com, Inc.

(*Actress*) v. (*Online Dating Service Host*)

339 F.3d 1119 (9th Cir. 2003)

A WEBSITE HOST IS NOT LIABLE FOR FALSE INFORMATION POSTED BY A VISITOR

I have it all...
Youth, speed, and immunity
from defamation suits.

stus.com

■ **INSTANT FACTS** After an unknown user posted a personal profile of Carafano (P) on Matchmaker.com, Carafano (P) sued the website host.

■ **BLACK LETTER RULE** A provider or user of an interactive web-based service is not considered the publisher or speaker of any information provided by another information provider.

■ **PROCEDURAL BASIS**

On appeal to review a district court's entry of summary judgment for the defendant.

■ **FACTS**

Metrosplash.com, Inc. (D) hosts an online dating service entitled Matchmaker.com. To use its service, users are asked to complete a questionnaire, which is used to generate a personal profile. An unknown user posted a sexually suggestive profile for Carafano (P), an actress, without her consent. The profile contained pictures of Carafano (P), and e-mailers to the account received responses containing her home address and telephone number. After Carafano (P) received sexually explicit messages and faxes threatening her son, she contacted the police. Carafano's (P) representative contacted the defendant, and the profile was deleted. Carafano (P) sued the defendant in state court for invasion of privacy, misappropriation of the right of publicity, defamation, and negligence. After the action was removed to federal court, summary judgment was granted for the defendant, but the court held that the defendant was not immune from liability under 47 U.S.C. § 230(c)(1). Both parties appealed.

■ **ISSUE**

Is a computer matchmaking service legally responsible for false content in a dating profile provided by someone posing as another?

■ **DECISION AND RATIONALE**

(Thomas, J.) No. Under 47 U.S.C. § 230(c)(1), "[n]o provider or user of an interactive computer service shall be treated as the publisher or speaker of any information provided by another information content provider." This section affords Internet providers immunity from suit related to content published over the Internet and treats them differently than publishers of print media. The statute was designed to promote the free exchange of information over the Internet and to encourage voluntary monitoring of offensive or obscene material. Due to the policies underlying the statute, courts have applied it broadly to all interactive computer services that are not also the information content provider.

Here, although the defendant provided the questionnaire from which the profile was created, all information was provided completely by the user. Matchmaker.com (D) is not the information content provider, nor is Matchmaker.com (D) a developer of the underlying information by its categorization of user responses. The information Matchmaker.com (D) collects is designed to provide its users with

---

features necessary to enhance the value of the website. As such, it facilitates the free exchange of information within the intent of the immunity statute. Affirmed.

Analysis:

Carafano represents one of the challenges the Internet has brought to American jurisprudence. By enacting the Communications Decency Act, Congress sought to protect website hosts from liability for content added to their sites by others. In so doing, Congress distinguished the host from publishers of traditional print media. This distinction is necessary because of the ease of entering a website and anonymously posting information without the host's knowledge, unlike with newspapers and magazines.

■ CASE VOCABULARY:

DEFAMATION: The act of harming the reputation of another by making a false statement to a third person.

INVASION OF PRIVACY: An unjustified exploitation of one's personality or intrusion into one's personal activity, actionable under tort law and sometimes under constitutional law.

RIGHT OF PUBLICITY: The right to control the use of one's own name, picture, or likeness and to prevent another from using it for commercial benefit without one's consent.

New York Times Co. v. Sullivan

(*Newspaper*) v. (*Police Chief*)

376 U.S. 254, 84 S.Ct. 710 (1964)

A PUBLIC OFFICIAL MUST PROVE ACTUAL MALICE IN ORDER TO RECOVER DAMAGES FOR DEFAMATION

■ **INSTANT FACTS** A police chief sued the New York Times for defamation for an ad the newspaper ran implying that the chief had violated people's civil rights in the South.

■ **BLACK LETTER RULE** A public official cannot recover damages for defamation unless the official can prove that the defamatory statement was made with actual malice.

■ **PROCEDURAL BASIS**

Appeal to U.S. Supreme Court from Alabama Supreme Court's decision to affirm trial court's jury verdict.

■ **FACTS**

In the early 1960s, the New York Times (Times) (D) published a full-page advertisement detailing civil rights abuses against blacks in the South. Mr. Sullivan (P), a Montgomery, Alabama city commissioner who was also in charge of the city's police force demanded that the Times (D) print a retraction of the advertisement. The Times (D) refused to print a retraction and Mr. Sullivan (P) then sued the Times (D) for defamation. Specifically, Mr. Sullivan (P) claimed that he had been defamed because he was in charge of the police and the advertisement implied that police had falsely arrested people and otherwise abused their civil rights; the advertisement did not personally refer to Mr. Sullivan (P). The trial court found that the advertisement had contained several errors of fact and also found that statements contained in the advertisement were *libel per se* and that damages should therefore be presumed. A jury found that the libelous statements did refer to Mr. Sullivan (P) and returned a verdict of $500,000 for actual and punitive damages. Pursuant to the trial court's instructions, the jury issued its verdict in a lump sum and did not note which portion of the $500,00 was for punitive damages. The Alabama Supreme Court upheld the trial court's verdict and the Times (D) appealed to the United States Supreme Court.

■ **ISSUE**

Are defamatory statements about public figures protected by the Constitution's guarantee of freedom of speech?

■ **DECISION AND RATIONALE**

(Brennan, J.) Yes. Under Alabama law, when a statement is determined to be *libel per se* the only defense available to a person accused of defamation is to prove that the statements made were true. Unless an accused person can meet the burden of proving the truth of the statements made, the court will presume that general damages are owed, punitive damages may be ordered only upon a showing of *actual malice*. The issue for this Court is whether the Alabama rule of liability which places the burden of proof on the person accused of defamation, violates the U.S. Constitution's First Amendment guarantees of freedom of speech and of the press. Mr. Sullivan (P) argues that the Constitution's guarantee of the right to free speech does not apply to defamatory statements. Nothing could be further from the truth; as with any other speech in this country, limitations on defamatory speech must be measured against the First Amendment. Of particular concern in this case is the fact that the libel complained of referred, allegedly at least, to a public official. This country has always been committed to the notion that a healthy a democracy must promote a wide-open, vigorous and robust debate on public issues. A robust debate may well include vehement, caustic and sometimes unpleasantly sharp attack on government and public officials. Criticism of government officials or government policy may at times include exaggerations or even inadvertent false statements of fact; a simple inadvertent false statement of fact, however, will not cause a statement to lose its Constitutional protections. To place the burden of proving a critical statement's truth on the person making the statement, as Alabama law does here, would greatly reduce the vigor of public debate. Persons wishing to make criticisms of public officials would be reluctant to step forward if they faced the threat of having to go through the time and expense of proving the truth of their statements in court. Because the Alabama rule dampens the vigor and limits the variety of public debate, it is inconsistent with the First and Fourteenth Amendments. We find today that constitutional guarantees of free speech prohibit a public official from recovering damages for a defamatory falsehood relating to official conduct unless it is proven that the statement was made with "actual malice"—that is, with knowledge that it was false or with reckless disregard of whether it was false or not. On the facts presented here, we find that Mr. Sullivan (P) did not present evidence of "actual malice" sufficient to satisfy the requirements of the Constitution nor did he offer sufficient proof that the alleged defamatory statements even referred to him. The judgment of the Supreme Court of Alabama is reversed.

■ CONCURRENCE

(Black, J.) I believe that the "actual malice" standard set forth by the court today does not offer enough protection to those who wish to criticize their public officials. The term "actual malice" even as defined by the court here today is a vague and elusive one. I fear that the threat and uncertainty of being found liable for actual malice will impair the freedom and flow of debate on important issues. I believe that there is an absolute and unconditional constitutional right to criticize government officials and this right should not be limited by the actual malice standard.

■ CONCURRENCE

(Goldberg, J.) Like Justice Black, I believe that there should be no limitation on speech which criticizes a public official acting in his official capacity. If individual citizens may be held liable in damages for strong words, which a jury finds false and maliciously motivated, there can be little doubt that public debate and advocacy will be constrained.

Analysis:

The First Amendments guarantee of freedom of speech and of the press is one of the cornerstones of the Constitution. The rights guaranteed by the First Amendment are meant, among other things, to promote public debate and to ensure a healthy democracy. The Court found that Alabama's law requiring that a person making a defamatory statement concerning a public official be required to prove the truth of that statement in a suit for defamation was contrary to the Constitution. Such a rule would make people reluctant to share negative statements even if they were certain the statements were true. Rather than the Alabama rule, the Court espoused a rule that would place the burden of proving defamation on the public official. Under the Court's rule, a public official claiming damages for defamation must prove "actual damages." The Court felt that the actual damages rule was a fair compromise between the public's interest in unfettered speech and the public official's desire not to be defamed.

■ CASE VOCABULARY

ACTUAL MALICE: A public official must prove actual malice—that a statement was made with knowledge that it was false or with reckless disregard of whether it was false or not—before the official can recover for defamation.

Gertz v. Robert Welch, Inc.

(*Private Citizen*) v. (*Magazine Publisher*)

418 U.S. 323, 94 S.Ct. 2997 (1974)

UNLIKE A PUBLIC FIGURE, A PRIVATE CITIZEN DOES NOT NEED TO SHOW ACTUAL MALICE IN ORDER TO RECOVER ACTUAL DAMAGES FOR DEFAMATION

■ **INSTANT FACTS** A lawyer sued the publisher of a magazine for defamatory statements the magazine made when it accused the lawyer of being a communist who was involved in a conspiracy against the police.

■ **BLACK LETTER RULE** A private citizen does not need to prove actual malice in order to recover actual damages for defamation.

■ **PROCEDURAL BASIS**

Appeal to United States Supreme Court from court of appeal's decision to affirm trial court's grant of judgment notwithstanding verdict.

■ **FACTS**

Mr. Gertz (P), an attorney, was hired to represent the family of a youth killed by Nuccio, a Chicago policeman. As part of his representation of the youth's family, Mr. Gertz (P) filed a civil suit and attended a coroner's inquest; Mr. Gertz (P) played no role in a criminal trial where Nuccio was convicted of second-degree murder. Nevertheless, subsequent to Nuccio's trial, Robert Welch (D) published an article which claimed that Mr. Gertz (P) was part of a nation wide conspiracy to discredit police. The article was published in American Opinion magazine and it charged that Mr. Gertz (P) was a communist who played a major role in framing Nuccio. Mr. Gertz (P) sued for defamation. The trial court ruled that Mr. Gertz (P) was not a public official and did not have to prove actual malice; a jury returned a verdict of $50,000. Upon further consideration however, the trial court found that because the American Opinion article concerned a matter of public concern, the *New York Times* (*Times*) standard of actual malice should apply regardless of Mr. Gertz's (P) stature as a private citizen. Accordingly, the trial court set aside the jury's verdict for Mr. Gertz (P). On appeal, the court of appeal relied on *Rosenbloom v. Metromedia, Inc.* (*Rosenbloom*) in finding that the trial court had acted properly. *Rosenbloom*, not decided by the U.S. Supreme Court until after the jury rendered its verdict, held that the *Times* standard of actual malice should be extended to "all discussion and communication involving matters of public or general concern, without regard to whether the persons involved are famous or anonymous." Because Mr. Gertz (P) had not offered proof that Mr. Welch (D) had shown reckless disregard for the truth, the court of appeal upheld the lower court's decision to set aside the jury verdict. Mr. Gertz (P) appealed to the United States Supreme Court.

■ **ISSUE**

Does a private citizen have to show actual malice in order to recover actual damages for defamation?

■ **DECISION AND RATIONALE**

(Powell, J.) No. We hold today the *New York Times* standard which requires a public official to prove actual malice in a claim for defamation cannot apply to private citizens. The Court decided the *Times* case by balancing society's interest in a free press against states' interests in compensating individuals for harm inflicted upon them by a defamatory falsehood. In the *Times* case, we decided that society's interest in having the press report on the affairs of its public officials was so great that a public official should not recover for defamation unless the official could show that the defamatory statement was made with "actual malice." The Court held that the actual malice standard would protect against the danger of censorship of the press while it would also address the states' need to protect their officials from deliberate falsehoods. When it comes to the defamation of private citizens however, we conclude that the actual malice standard should not apply. We distinguish between public and private citizens for several reasons. First, as we have stated, the public has a greater interest in knowing the affairs of its public officials and a corresponding interest in having the press freely report on the affairs of these individuals. The actual malice standard protects against the danger of the press censoring itself when reporting on the affairs of public officials. Second, public figures generally have greater access to the press and other channels of communication than do private citizens and they may therefore more easily correct false or injurious statements. Because a private citizen is more vulnerable to injury than a public figure, the state has a greater interest in protecting them from defamation. Third, people who become public figures generally do so by choice and with that choice comes the risk of closer public scrutiny than might otherwise be the case. Public figures, by choosing their role in society, invite the public to scrutinize and comment on their honesty and character; private citizens do not volunteer for similar scrutiny. In sum, private citizens are not only more vulnerable to injury from defamation than are public figures, they are also more deserving of recovery. For these reasons, we reject any suggestion made in the *Rosenbloom* case to extend the *Times* actual malice test to cases involving private citizens. We hold that, so long as they do not impose liability without fault, the States may define for themselves the appropriate standard of liability for a publisher or broadcaster of defamatory falsehood injurious to a private individual. We caution however, that the States may not impose punitive or presumed damages for a defamatory statement unless there is proof of actual malice. To allow punitive or presumed damages absent a showing of actual malice would allow the risk that courts or juries would punish people for expressing unpopular views rather than for the actual damage that their statements caused. Consequently, we limit our decision today to hold that states may set their own standard by which private citizens may recover for defamation only to the extent that the private citizen is seeking to recover *actual* damages; private citizens seeking to recover general or punitive damages must prove actual malice. Finally, we reject the argument that Mr. Gertz (P) was a public figure. Absent clear evidence of general fame or notoriety in the community, and pervasive involvement in the affairs of society, an individual should not be deemed a public figure. Accordingly, the court of appeal is reversed.

■ CONCURRENCE

(Blackmun, J.) Although I joined the plurality in the *Rosenbloom* decision, I concur with the Court's opinion today for two reasons: First, I believe that the Court's requirement that actual malice be proven before general or punitive damages may be recovered will sufficiently protect against the danger of self-censorship on the part of the press; second, I believe that it is important to set forth a clearly defined majority position in the area of defamation. Were my vote not needed to form a majority, I would hold to my position in *Rosenbloom*.

■ DISSENT

(Burger, C.J.) I believe that the Court is making law which is not based on precedent. Rather than create law from whole cloth, I would prefer to see the law evolve in this area. In this case, Mr. Gertz (P) was performing as an attorney and an advocate. Society has a great interest in seeing these functions performed well and a corresponding interest in seeing that advocates are not wrongly defamed. I would not require Mr. Gertz (P) to prove actual malice to recover punitive or general damages and I would re-instate the entire jury verdict.

■ DISSENT

(Douglas, J.) The Court today leaves states free to apply the simple negligence standard in cases where private citizens sue for defamation. I feel that the negligence standard is far too low a hurdle to overcome and that, by allowing such a low standard, the Court's decision threatens free speech.

■ DISSENT

(Brennan, J.) I must continue to adhere to the views I expressed in *Rosenbloom.* I continue to believe that the public's interest in a vigorous public debate and discourse is such that it strongly outweighs the states' interests in allowing private individuals to recover for defamation. The *Times* standard of actual malice is appropriate because it reflects the fact that the interest in free speech is no less significant when private, rather than public, figures are involved in issues of public concern. While the Court today set forth a number of valid reasons to distinguish between private and public citizens, these reasons do not convince me that the actual malice standard should not apply in situations where matters of general or public interest are being discussed.

■ DISSENT

(White. J.) I believe that the Court's decision today violates states' rights to protect their own citizens and also imposes upon the states an unwieldy and burdensome federally created rule of liability. Moreover, I believe that the Court's decision today is intellectually dishonest. The press today is vigorous and robust; it is to me incredible to suggest that the threat of lawsuits from private citizens will cause the press to refrain from publishing the truth. Private citizens should not bear the burden of proving actual malice in order to recover punitive or general damages for a defamatory statement. I would reverse the court of appeal and re-instate the jury's verdict in its full amount.

Analysis:

The Court listed a number of reasons for offering the private citizen greater protections than the public one: public citizens have a greater ability to fight back and set the record straight; public citizens, unlike private citizens, choose to be in the public eye; and, the public has a greater interest in learning about the affairs of its public officials. Arguably, the reasons the Court provides for distinguishing between public and private citizens are not very strong ones; today almost anyone can gain access to the media and private citizens are frequently involved in matters of public concern. Nevertheless, as Justice Brennan pointed out, the Court's opinion did not really do much to strengthen the position of the private citizen. Even under the rules the Court issued, private citizens are still required to prove actual malice if they hope to recover anything beyond actual damages.

■ CASE VOCABULARY

ACTUAL DAMAGES: The type of damages which a private citizen suing for defamation may recover with less than a showing of actual malice, they include: damages for harm to reputation and standing in the community; loss of business; mental anguish; and out of pocket expenses.

Wells v. Liddy

(*Secretary*) v. (*Burglar*)

186 F.3d 505 (4th Cir. 1999)

INVOLVEMENT IN A PUBLIC CONTORVERSY DOES NOT NECESSARILY RENDER A PERSON AN INVOLUNTARY PUBLIC FIGURE WHO MUST PROVE ACTUAL MALICE IN ORDER TO RECOVER FOR DEFAMATION

■ **INSTANT FACTS** A secretary who was peripherally involved in the Watergate scandal sued Gordon Liddy for defamation when he suggested that she had helped to run a prostitution ring for the Democratic National Committee.

■ **BLACK LETTER RULE** An involuntary public figure, who must prove defamation by actual malice, is a person who engages in conduct that a reasonable person would foresee could result in a significant controversy and who then becomes a central figure in that controversy.

■ **PROCEDURAL BASIS**

Appeal to Court of Appeal from trial court's order of summary judgment.

■ **FACTS**

In the 1970's, Maxine Wells (P) worked as a secretary for Spencer Oliver, the Executive Director of State Democratic Chairmen. In the Watergate burglary of 1972, burglars broke into Wells' desk. Later, Gordon Liddy (D) claimed that the burglars had been searching for a list and photographs of various prostitutes. Liddy (D) based his claims on material contained in a book entitled "Silent Coup: The Removal of a President." "Silent Coup" asserted that John Dean had ordered the Watergate break-in in order to obtain evidence that the Democratic National Committee was arranging to have call girls visit various dignitaries. According to Liddy (D), Dean hoped to find evidence of the prostitution ring in Wells' (P) desk. Wells (P) sued Liddy (D) claiming that he had defamed her by repeating his assertions on four different occasions: 1. in a speech at James Madison University; 2.) in a speech on a cruise ship; 3.) on a nationally broadcast radio talk show; and, 4.) on the internet. The trial court found that Wells (P) was an "involuntary public figure" and, as such, had to prove actual malice before she could recover for actual damages sustained as a result of defamation. Because Wells (P) had failed to prove actual malice, the trial court granted summary judgment on all four claims. Wells (P) appealed to the United Sates Court of Appeals. The Court of Appeals reversed the trial court's summary judgment on two claims, finding that the speech at James Madison University and the speech on the cruise ship were defamatory because listeners could have taken them to mean that Wells (P) was a participant in a scheme to procure prostitutes. The court upheld the trial court's grant of summary judgment on the two remaining claims. The court addressed the issue of whether Wells (P) was an involuntary public figure and thus had to prove actual malice in the body of its opinion.

■ **ISSUE**

Is a person an involuntary public figure simply because, by virtue of misfortune, the person became involved in a significant public controversy?

■ DECISION AND RATIONALE

(Williams, J.) No. On appeal Liddy (D) argues that the trial court was correct when it ruled that Wells (P) was an involuntary public figure who would have to prove actual malice in order to recover even actual damages for defamation. In the alternative, Liddy (D) argues that even if Wells (P) is not an involuntary public figure, her participation in Watergate related dialogue qualifies her as a "voluntary limited-purpose public figure," a status which would also require her to prove actual malice in order to prevail in her suit. We will consider Liddy's (D) arguments one at a time. First, we conclude that the trial court was correct when it ruled that Wells (P) was not a voluntary limited-purpose public figure. In order to classify Wells (P) as a limited-purpose public figure, it must be shown that: 1) she had access to effective channels of communication; 2) she voluntarily assumed a role of prominence in a public controversy; 3) she sought to influence the outcome of the controversy; 4) the controversy in which she was involved existed prior to the publication of Liddy's (D) defamatory statements; and, 5) she retained public figure status at the time Liddy (D) made his statements. Like the trial court, we conclude that Wells (P) is not a limited-purpose public figure because she did not voluntarily insert herself into the Watergate controversy. Wells (P) first became involved in the controversy as a victim of the burglary, her subsequent involvement in the controversy mainly involved her speaking with FBI investigators and answering Senate subpoenas. We cannot find that participation of this sort is voluntary by any definition of the word. We further reject Liddy's (D) assertion that Wells (P) voluntarily inserted herself into the controversy by speaking with the media. Media contact does not *per se* indicate that a person has thrust herself into a public controversy; when a person has contact with the media, the proper question to ask is whether the media contact was intended to influence the outcome of the controversy, clearly, this was not Well's (P) intention. Next, we turn our attention to Liddy's (D) claim that Wells (P) is an involuntary public figure. The trial court concluded that Wells (P) was an involuntary public figure because she had had the "misfortune" of having herself drawn into the Watergate controversy. We are reluctant to find that someone is an involuntary public figure on the mere basis of misfortune. Misfortune is, unfortunately, a common occurrence in the world and the Supreme Court has told us in *Gertz v. Robert Welch, Inc.* that cases involving involuntary public figures must be "exceedingly rare." If misfortune alone were enough to classify a person as an involuntary public figure it seems to us that the class of person who qualified for involuntary public figure status would be so broad as to be without distinction. We cannot therefore find that Wells (P) is an involuntary public figure on the basis of her misfortune alone. Rather, we prefer to fashion a test that will ensure that people falling into the class of involuntary public figures will be exceedingly rare and that will also address concerns the Supreme Court expressed in *Gertz.* In *Gertz,* Justice Powell wrote there were two primary reasons which justified treating public figures differently than private ones: 1) a public figure has greater access to the media and is thus better able to defend himself; 2) a public figure has taken actions through which he has voluntarily assumed the risk of publicity. With *Gertz'* two supporting rationales and the need for a narrow class of involuntary public figure in mind, we have developed our own test for when a person will be considered an involuntary public figure. First, to prove that a person is an involuntary public figure, a defendant must show that the person has become a *central* figure in a *significant* public controversy and that the allegedly defamatory statement was made in the course of discourse regarding the public matter. Secondly, a person cannot be considered an involuntary public figure unless it is first shown that the person took some action from which it was reasonably foreseeable that public interest would arise. Finally, the controversy must have existed prior to the alleged defamatory statement was made and the plaintiff must have retained public figure status at the time of the defamation. We believe that this test captures the "exceedingly rare" individual who, though remaining silent during public discussion of the results of her action, nevertheless has become a principal in an important public matter. Because Wells (P) does not fit the criteria set forth today, the trial court erred when it found that she was an involuntary public figure. This case is reversed and remanded.

Analysis:

A person becomes an involuntary public figure when she engages in conduct of the sort a reasonable person would anticipate might result in controversy and then, in fact, becomes a central figure in a significant controversy. The consequence of being deemed an involuntary public figure is, of course, that the person has to prove actual malice in order to recover actual damages for defamation. The court felt that the test it devised adequately addressed the *Gertz* Court's rationales for treating public figures differently. Essentially, the *Gertz* Court stated that public figures could be treated differently because they enjoy greater access to the media than do private figures and also because, by their actions, they expose themselves to public scrutiny. Combined with the greater First Amendment interest in having the media freely report on the actions of public figures, the *Gertz* Court felt that it was justified in treating them differently by requiring them to prove actual malice before they could recover actual damages in a defamation case. Considering the *Gertz* Court's constitutional concerns and the rationales it provided for treating public figures differently, it seems that the test devised by the court in this case was a good one.

■ CASE VOCABULARY

INVOLUNTARY PUBLIC FIGURE: An involuntary public figure, one who must prove actual malice in order to recover actual damages in a claim for defamation, is a person who engages in some conduct a reasonable person would foresee might result in significant public controversy and then in fact becomes a central figure in that controversy.

LIMITED PURPOSE PUBLIC FIGURE: In order to prove that a plaintiff is a limited purpose public figure who must prove actual malice in order to recover actual damages for defamation, a defendant must show the following: 1) The plaintiff had access to effective channels of communication; 2) The plaintiff voluntarily assumed a role in a public controversy; 3) The plaintiff sought to influence the resolution or outcome of the controversy; 4) The controversy existed prior to the publication of the defamatory statement; and, 5) The plaintiff retained public figure status at the time of the alleged defamation.

Milkovich v. Lorain Journal Co.

(Coach) v. *(Newspaper)*

497 U.S. 1, 110 S.Ct. 2695 (1990)

WHETHER OR NOT IT IS LABELED AS OPINION, A STATEMENT WHICH IS PROVABLE AS FALSE IS ACTIONABLE FOR DEFAMATION

■ **INSTANT FACTS** A wrestling coach sued a newspaper for defamation after the paper published a column stating that the coach had committed perjury.

■ **BLACK LETTER RULE** A statement on a matter of public concern must be provable as false before there can be liability for defamation.

■ **PROCEDURAL BASIS**

Appeal to U.S. Supreme Court from Ohio Court of Court of Appeal's grant of summary judgment.

■ **FACTS**

The Ohio High School Athletic Association (OHSAA) censored Mr. Milkovich (P), a wrestling coach at Maple Heights High School, and placed his wrestling team on probation after the team had become involved in a brawl with a competing team. The parents of some of the wrestlers sued to enjoin the OHSAA from enforcing the probation and at a subsequent hearing, Milkovich (P) testified that he had done nothing to incite the brawl between the two teams. The hearing judge subsequently granted the restraining order sought by the parents. The following day, the Lorain Journal Company (Lorain) (D) published a column by a sports writer who had attended the wrestling match but not the hearing. The column, entitled "Maple beat the law with a 'big lie,'" asserted that Milkovich (P) had committed perjury at the judicial hearing. Milkovich (P) sued the paper for defamation claiming that its charge of perjury was libelous per se. After 15 years of litigation, the Ohio Court of Appeals finally held that the column was constitutionally protected opinion and granted the newspapers motion for summary judgment. The United States Supreme Court reversed.

■ **ISSUE**

Is every statement of opinion entitled to constitutional protection from claims for defamation?

■ **DECISION AND RATIONALE**

(Rehnquist, C.J.) No. Lorain (D) argues that the trial court properly granted summary judgment because the First Amendment protects defamatory statements which are classified as opinion. As support for its argument, Lorain (D) cites to dictum in the case of *Gertz v. Robert Welch, Inc.* In *Gertz*, Justice Powell wrote that, "under the First Amendment, there is no such thing as a false idea." We believe that Lorain's (D) reliance on *Gertz* is misplaced. *Gertz* did not intend to create a defamation exemption for anything that might be labeled "opinion." The fact is, many so-called expressions of "opinion" often strongly imply an assertion of objective fact. For instance, the statement, "In my opinion, Jones is a liar," implies that the speaker has a knowledge of facts to support the statement, as such, the statement has every bit the potential to injure Jones' reputation as the more direct statement "Jones is a liar." The First Amendment does not protect false statements of fact whether expressly stated or implied from an expression of opinion. We wish to make clear that there is not, at present, a judicial doctrine which distinguishes between fact and opinion in defamation cases. Moreover, we do not feel the need to create an "opinion exception" in defamation cases today because there is already judicial doctrine in place which sufficiently safeguards the right to freedom of expression. In *Philadelphia Newspapers, Inc. v. Hepps,* the Court held that one cannot be held liable for defamation unless the alleged defamatory statement is "provable" as false. For example, the statement "Jones is a liar," is provable as false because theoretically one could offer evidence that Jones tells the truth. The statement, "Jones made a poor decision, " would not however be provable as false. The *Hepps* case therefore ensures that a statement of opinion relating to matters of public concern which does not contain a provably false factual connotation, will receive full constitutional protection. It is clear to this Court, that whether the column which asserted that Milkovich committed perjury is labeled "opinion" or not, the accusation of perjury is provable as false. We also reject any argument that the column's charge of perjury could not reasonably have been interpreted as stating actual facts about Milkovich and is therefore not actionable. The accusation of perjury is actionable because it was clearly not a joke or parody made with the sort of loose, figurative, or hyperbolic language which would have suggested to a reasonable person that it was not a serious charge. To summarize, we find that a person who makes a defamatory statement which is provable as false may be held liable for damages. Accordingly, we reverse the court of appeal and remand this case for further proceedings consistent with this opinion.

■ DISSENT

(Brennan, J.) While I agree with the Court's legal conclusion that there is no "opinion exception" for defamation, I disagree with its factual conclusion that the challenged statements could have been reasonably interpreted as asserting defamatory facts about Miklovich. The allegation that Miklovich committed perjury was conjecture and, as such, it is deserving of constitutional protection.

Analysis:

The Court seemed eager to clarify that *Gertz* had not created a special "opinion" privilege in the area of defamation law and it stated in no uncertain terms that it was not prepared to create such an exception in this case. Nevertheless, if one defines an opinion as a statement that can neither be proved nor disproved, it seems that by holding that a statement that does not contain a provably false statement or connotation is protected by the First Amendment, the Court simply recognized an opinion exception by another name. The Court, of course, adopted this rule from *Hepps,* a case which the Court had already ensured that statements of opinion not containing provable falsehoods would receive constitutional protection.

Flamm v. American Association of University Women

(Lawyer) v. *(Directory Publisher)*

201 F.3d 144 (2d Cir. 2000)

WHETHER MADE BY A MEDIA DEFENDANT OR NOT, STATEMENTS INVOLVING MATTERS OF PUBLIC CONCERN MUST BE PROVABLE AS FALSE IN ORDER FOR A SUIT FOR DEFAMATION TO PROCEED

■ **INSTANT FACTS** A lawyer sued the publisher of a directory for defamation after the directory described him as an ambulance chaser.

■ **BLACK LETTER RULE** Whenever a statement involves a matter of public concern, the statement must be provable as false in order for a defamation suit to proceed, regardless of whether the defendant is a member of the media..

■ **PROCEDURAL BASIS**

Appeal to United States Court of Appeal from district court's grant of defendant's motion to dismiss.

■ **FACTS**

The American Association of University Women (AAUW) (D) published a directory of attorneys willing to consult with women who were considering bringing a gender discrimination action against a university. The directory, which was mailed to members of the AAUW (D) as well as to members of the bar, contained contact information as well as a short blurb about each attorney listed. The blurb on attorney Lionel Flamm (P) stated that "At least one plaintiff has described Flamm (P) as an 'ambulance chaser' with interest only in 'slam dunk' cases." Flamm (P) filed suit in state court, alleging that the description of him as an "ambulance chaser" interested only in "slam dunk" cases constituted libel per se. The AAUW (D) removed the case to federal court and the district court then granted AAUW's (D) motion to dismiss after it determined that the statement challenged by Flamm could not have reasonably been construed as a statement of objective fact. Flamm (P) appealed to the United States Court of Appeals.

■ **ISSUE**

In a defamation suit involving a matter of public concern, does it matter whether the defendant is a member of the media?

■ **DECISION AND RATIONALE**

(Meskill, J.) No. While courts of New York have found that the state's constitution protects statements of opinion, the United States Supreme Court stated in *Milkovich v. Lorain Journal Co.* that there is no constitutionally required protection for statements of opinion which assert or imply statements of provable fact. Though we must, therefore, review this case under both the state and federal constitutions, we believe that the dispositive inquiry in either analysis is the same, namely, whether a reasonable person could have construed the challenged statements to be statements of fact. In *Milkovich,* the Court held that, in a suit against a media defendant, an allegedly defamatory statement which involves a matter of public concern must be provable as false before liability can be established. *Milkovich* did not, however, state whether the same rule applies to claims against non-media defendants. We believe that it does. The Supreme Court has held that, in the law of defamation, it is necessary to differentiate between matters of public and private concern, between media and non-media defendants, and between public and private figures, because the resolution of each issue depends on a balancing of the state's interest in compensating its citizen for injury against the First Amendment interest in protecting expression. The Supreme Court has never ruled explicitly on the issue of whether the Constitution requires us to treat media and non-media defendants differently. In his concurring opinion in *Dun & Bradstreet v. Greenmoss Builders*, however, Justice White wrote that a distinction between media and non-media defendants would be "irreconcilable with the fundamental First Amendment principle that 'the inherent worth of . . . speech . . . does not depend upon the identity of its source.'" We agree with Justice White's position that a distinction drawn according to whether the defendant is a member of the media is untenable. Accordingly, we hold that, in order to proceed on a claim for defamation in a matter involving public concern, a private plaintiff must demonstrate only that a statement is provable as false. The issue in applying this rule is not whether the person who made the alleged defamatory statement was a member of the media but, rather, whether the statement was made to a public audience with an interest in the matter concerned. We believe that this approach appropriately balances the state's interests in protecting its citizens from defamation with the First Amendment interest in seeing that ideas can be freely disseminated to an audience. Turning to the instant case, we find that the statements made regarding Flamm's (P) ethics as a gender discrimination lawyer do involve matters of public concern because gender discrimination is a problem of constitutional dimensions. We further find that the statement accusing Flamm (P) of being an "ambulance chaser" reasonably implies that he engaged in unethical behavior. The statement was published in a directory which in all other respects contained facts such as names, addresses and phone numbers of attorneys. In the context of a fact-laden directory, we think it possible that a reasonable reader would take the statement as one of fact. In that the challenged statement reasonably implies a defamatory fact capable of being proven false, we find that the First Amendment does not entitle AAUW (D) to a dismissal in this case. We also find that the district court erred when it found that New York law required a dismissal of Flamm's (P) claim. Though New York law protects opinion from claims for defamation, for the reasons we have already stated we do not believe that the statement that Flamm (P) is an ambulance chaser was a statement of opinion. The district court is reversed and this case is remanded.

Analysis:

The court in this case found that the Supreme Court had expressed in *New York Times v. Sullivan* and *Gertz v. Robert Welch, Inc.* to find that there was no reason to distinguish between media and non-media defendants in a defamation case. The First Amendment concerns that the Supreme Court has cited as a reason for distinguishing between public and private matters, compelled it to find that a plaintiff in a defamation suit involving a matter of public concern should have to demonstrate that the challenged statement was probably false in order to proceed. Furthermore, the court found, the party alleging defamation bears the burden of proving that the challenged statement was false. The court felt that this approach sufficiently balanced the state's interests in allowing its citizens to recover for defamation against the First Amendment interest in seeing that ideas are freely disseminated. The court could find no logical basis to justify a distinction between media and non-media defendants. If it is the First Amendment that requires us to differentiate between public and private matters and, if our ultimate objective is to have ideas concerning public matters disseminated as freely as possible, then why, the court asked, should we differentiate between media and non-media defendants?

Khawar v. Globe International, Inc.

(Alleged Assassin) v. *(Tabloid)*

19 Cal.4th 254, 965 P.2d 696, 79 Cal.Rptr.2d 178 (1998)

THERE IS NO "NEUTRAL REPORT PRIVILEGE" WHICH WOULD PREVENT A PRIVATE FIGURE FROM RECOVERING DAMAGES FROM ONE WHO REPORTS ON ANOTHER'S DEFAMATORY STATEMENT REGARDING A PUBLIC MATTER

■ **INSTANT FACTS** A man sued The Globe, a tabloid, for publishing an accurate summary of a book which had concluded that the man had been the true assassin of Robert Kennedy.

■ **BLACK LETTER RULE** A private figure may recover damages for defamation from a media source which has done no more than accurately report on another's defamatory statements regarding a matter of public concern.

■ **PROCEDURAL BASIS**

Appeal to Supreme Court of California from court of appeal's decision to affirm trial court's jury verdict.

■ **FACTS**

Globe International, Inc. (Globe) (D) published an article entitled "Iranians Killed Bobby Kennedy for the Mafia" in its weekly tabloid newspaper "Globe." The article was an abbreviated and uncritical summary of a book which alleged that the Iranian secret police carried out the assassination of Robert Kennedy rather than, as the FBI had concluded, Sirhan Sirhan. The Globe (D) article identified a man named Ali Ahmand as the true killer. The Globe (D) article also included a photograph taken of a group of people standing around Kennedy at the time of the assassination. To the photograph, the Globe (D) added an arrow pointing to a person it identified as the assassin, Ali Ahamand. In fact, the arrow pointed to the image of Khalid Khawar (P). As a result of the article and the accompanying photograph, Khawar (P) received a number of death threats and became very frightened. Khawar (P) sued the Globe (D) for defamation and a jury, finding that the Globe (D) article was published with actual malice, awarded him $1,175,000 in actual and punitive damages. Globe (D) appealed the judgment claiming that it could not be held liable because it had simply published an accurate summary of a book on the Kennedy assassination. The First Amendment, argued the Globe (D), mandates a "neutral reportage privilege" when a media defendant publishes a neutral and accurate report on a controversial book's allegations regarding a matter of public concern. The court of appeal concluded that there was no neutral report privilege when an article makes claims about a private figure. Finding that Khawar (P) was a private figure, the court did not address the issue of whether there is a neutral report privilege when an article concerns a public figure. Accordingly, the court of appeal upheld the jury verdict. Globe (D) appealed to the Supreme Court of California.

■ **ISSUE**

Is there an neutral report privilege which prevents a private figure from recovering damages for defamation from a media source which has done no more than accurately report on another person's defamatory statements regarding a public matter?

■ **DECISION AND RATIONALE**

(Kennard, J.) No. To support its argument that a "neutral reportage privilege" shields it from liability in this case, Globe (D) points to a federal appellate court decision which held that "when a responsible, prominent organization ... makes serious charges against a public figure, the First Amendment protects the accurate and disinterested reporting of those charges." First, we conclude that, for purposes of this litigation, Khawar (P) was not a public figure, consequently, the case cited by Globe (D) is not persuasive. We will however, consider the issue of whether there is a neutral reportage privilege when a media source summarizes a defamatory statement involving a private figure. Courts are split on the issue of whether there should be a neutral reportage privilege. Proponents of the privilege argue that there is a First Amendment interest in having defamatory allegations relating to an existing public controversy reported to the public regardless of the truth of the allegations. The First Amendment interests in having the details of an argument published, so the argument goes, outweigh the state's interest in allowing defamed citizens to recover damages for defamation. Critics of the privilege however, argue that U.S. Supreme Court jurisprudence in this area does not support a neutral report privilege. Because the Supreme Court has never decided whether the First Amendment mandates a neutral reportage privilege, we are left to decide the issue for ourselves. Globe (D) argues that there should be a neutral report privilege to allow newspapers such as itself to accurately report on defamatory statements made by public figures if the statements regard matters of public concern. Globe (D) argues that this privilege should apply even if the defamation concerns a private figure because the public has a greater interest in knowing what its public figures are saying than the state has in protecting private figures from accusations by public figures. In essence, the Globe (D) argues that the public is better able to analyze and judge the character of a public figure if it knows what the official is saying about an issue. This rationale holds true regardless of whether the statements made by the public are true and regardless of whether the statements relate to a private figure. Consequently, the Globe (D) would have us hold that, even though it reported a false and defamatory statement against a private figure, the neutral report privilege protects it from liability as long as the statement reported was initially made by a public figure. We reject this argument categorically. Rather, we find that there is *never* a neutral report privilege no matter the private or public status of figures involved in a controversy. Although we recognize that the public has a legitimate interest in knowing that public figures have made charges, perhaps unfounded, against a private figure, recognition of an *absolute* privilege would be inconsistent with the United States Supreme Court's jurisprudence. The Supreme Court has long held that the resolution of defamation cases depends on a balancing of the First Amendment interest in promoting the broad dissemination of information relevant to public controversies against the reputation interests of private figures. To hold that there is an absolute privilege which allows one to report on defamatory statements would be to dispense with any balancing of First Amendment and private interests. Because there is no fair report privilege for statements involving private figures, we find that the trial court properly required Khawar (P), a private figure, to prove only negligence to recover actual damages and actual malice to recover punitive damages. We further find that Khawar (P) did prove actual malice because the Globe (D) had obvious reason (namely, the fact that an exhaustive state and FBI investigation concluded that Sirhan Sirhan was Kennedy's assassin) to doubt the veracity of the statements it reported. The judgment of the Court of Appeal is affirmed.

Analysis:

This court determined that private figures' interests are such that there can never be an absolute privilege where they are involved. While public figures have a weaker privacy interest than do private figures, the court's decision leads to the conclusion that they too might be entitled to a balancing of interests when a court is determining whether or not to allow a defamation suit against a media defendant to proceed. Consequently, a media source that is sued for reporting a defamatory statement made by a public figure may have to defend in court a claim that it reported the statement with actual malice. In this case, the court found that the Globe (D) had acted with actual malice because it acted with disregard for the truth. While the Globe (D) probably could not have avoided the court's conclusion that it acted with actual malice even if it had investigated the statements it reported, it seems that the Globe (D) might nevertheless have avoided liability had its article made clear that the statements were no more than the speculative conclusions of a an author, not conclusions of fact.

CHAPTER FOURTEEN

Protecting Privacy

Haynes v. Alfred A. Knopf, Inc.

Instant Facts: Following publication of certain embarrassing but true facts about his relationship with his first wife as part of a social history book examining the migration of African Americans from the South to the North from 1940 through 1970, a man sued the book's author and publisher for invasion of privacy.

Black Letter Rule: A person will not be liable for publicizing embarrassing but true facts about another person if the facts are of legitimate concern to the public.

The Florida Star v. B.J.F.

Instant Facts: A rape victim sued a newspaper for civil damages after her name and an account of her rape was published by the newspaper in violation of a state law making it unlawful to print, publish, or broadcast in any instrument of mass communication, the name of a victim of a sexual offense.

Black Letter Rule: If a newspaper lawfully obtains truthful information about a matter of public significance, then state officials may not constitutionally punish publication of the information, unless there is a need to further a compelling state interest.

Humphers v. First Interstate Bank of Oregon

Instant Facts: A mother who had given up her daughter for adoption many years earlier sued the estate of the doctor who had delivered the daughter for invasion of privacy and breach of a confidential relationship after the doctor, who had since died, helped the daughter locate the mother.

Black Letter Rule: The disclosure of confidential facts about a patient in violation of a state statute imposing a duty of confidentiality on doctors and without a valid statutory defense or privilege, can constitute an actionable tort for which damages may be recovered by the patient.

Cantrell v. Forest City Publishing Co.

Instant Facts: Margaret Cantrell (P) and her children sued for the publication of a newspaper article depicting their family as living in abject poverty.

Black Letter Rule: Actual malice must be proven in order to recover under a "false light" theory.

Nader v. General Motors Corp.

Instant Facts: A consumer advocate, who was about to publish a book critical of a car manufacturer, sued the car manufacturer for invasion of privacy, alleging the manufacturer had inquired into his social and political views, kept him under surveillance in public places, had women attempt to entrap him into illicit relationships, made harassing telephone calls to him, and wiretapped his telephone.

Black Letter Rule: To be liable for invasion of privacy on the theory of unlawful intrusion, a person must be seeking confidential information about another and his conduct in seeking the information must be unreasonably intrusive.

Galella v. Onassis

Instant Facts: A former first lady sued a photographer for invasion of privacy, seeking injunctive relief limiting the photographer's contact with her and her children, after the photographer endangered their safety.

Black Letter Rule: While social needs such as news gathering may justify some intrusion despite a person's reasonable expectation of privacy, the interference allowed may be no greater than that necessary to protect the overriding public interest and may not be unreasonably intrusive.

Desnick v. American Broadcasting Companies, Inc.

Instant Facts: An eye clinic sued a television network for trespass, invasion of privacy, and illegal electronic surveillance after the network broadcast a news segment using hidden cameras on people posing as clinic patients.

Black Letter Rule: The recording of a professional conversation between an undercover journalist seeking to uncover wrongdoing and a physician in an office open to the public does not constitute an invasion of privacy.

Shulman v. Group W Productions Inc., et al.

Instant Facts: A victim of a car accident sued a television production company for invasion of privacy after the company broadcast footage it recorded of her being rescued from the accident scene and her comments to rescue personnel while being transported to the hospital.

Black Letter Rule: A person who intentionally intrudes into a private place, conversation, or matter in a manner highly offensive to a reasonable person, without consent or a privilege to do so, is subject to liability for invasion of privacy.

Bartnicki v. Vopper

Instant Facts: Bartnicki's (P) cell phone conversation with a union representative was intercepted and played on the radio by Vopper (D); Bartnicki (P) sued Vopper (D) for violation of a federal anti-wiretapping statute.

Black Letter Rule: If a media outlet lawfully obtains truthful information about a matter of public significance, publication of that information may not be sanctioned absent a need "of the highest order."

Zacchini v. Scripps–Howard Broadcasting Co.

Instant Facts: A daredevil performer sued a television station for appropriation after the station broadcast footage of his 15 second human cannonball act on its nightly news program, without the performer's consent.

Black Letter Rule: A state may, consistent with the First and Fourteenth Amendments of the U.S. Constitution, impose liability for the appropriation of a performer's entire public performance.

Winter v. DC Comics

Instant Facts: Winter (P) claimed that characters in a comic book published by DC Comics (D) so closely resembled him as to be an appropriation of his likeness.

Black Letter Rule: An artist faced with a right of publicity claim has an affirmative defense based on the First Amendment if the artist's work has significant transformative elements or if the value of the work does not derive primarily from the celebrity's fame.

Haynes v. Alfred A. Knopf, Inc.

(Ex-Husband) v. *(Book Publisher)*

8 F.3d 1222 (7th Cir. 1993)

FEDERAL APPEALS COURT FINDS NO INVASION OF PRIVACY WHERE EMBARRASSING BUT TRUE FACTS WERE OF LEGITIMATE CONCERN TO THE PUBLIC

■ **INSTANT FACTS** Following publication of certain embarrassing but true facts about his relationship with his first wife as part of a social history book examining the migration of African Americans from the South to the North from 1940 through 1970, a man sued the book's author and publisher for invasion of privacy.

■ **BLACK LETTER RULE** A person will not be liable for publicizing embarrassing but true facts about another person if the facts are of legitimate concern to the public.

■ FACTS

Nicholas Lemann ("Lemann") (D1) wrote a best-selling book, *The Great Migration,* about the social, political, and economic effects of the movement of African Americans from the rural South to the cities of the North between 1940 and 1970. Part of the book detailed the life of Ruby Lee Daniels ("Ruby"), a Mississippi sharecropper who later moved to Chicago. Lemann (D1) wrote about Ruby's ex-husband, Luther Haynes ("Haynes") (P), depicted by Ruby as a heavy drinker, neglectful of his children, unfaithful, and unable to keep a job during their marriage. While Haynes (P) admitted many of the incidents in the book were true, he claimed that they had occurred many years earlier and that he had since reformed, remarried, and lived an exemplary life, becoming a deacon in his church. Haynes (P) sued Lemann (D1) and the book's publisher, Alfred A. Knopf, Inc. ("Knopf") (D2) in federal court under diversity jurisdiction for invasion of privacy. The trial court granted summary judgment in favor of Lemann (D1) and Knopf (D2). Haynes (P) appealed.

■ ISSUE

Will a person be liable for publicizing embarrassing but true facts about another person if the facts are of legitimate concern to the public?

■ DECISION AND RATIONALE

(Posner, C.J.) No. People who do not desire the limelight and do not deliberately choose a way of life or course of conduct calculated to thrust them into it nevertheless have no legal right to extinguish it if the experiences that have befallen them are newsworthy, even if they would prefer that those experiences be kept private. This branch of the privacy tort requires not only that the private facts publicized be such as would deeply offend a reasonable person who had such facts exposed, but also that they be facts in which the public has no legitimate interest. The two criteria, offensiveness and newsworthiness, are related. An individual is most offended by the publication of intimate personal facts when the community has no interest in them beyond the voyeuristic thrill of penetrating the wall of privacy that surrounds a stranger. The reader of a book about the black migration to the North would have no legitimate interest in the details of Haynes's (P) sex life; but no such details are disclosed. Such a reader does have a legitimate interest in the aspects of Haynes's (P) conduct that the book reveals. No detail in the book claimed to invade Haynes's (P) privacy is not relevant to the story the author wanted to tell, a story of legitimate public interest, detailing the interaction of a transferred sharecropper mentality with governmental programs meant to alleviate poverty, which discouraged Ruby and Haynes (P) from living together and precipitated a marriage doomed to fail. Haynes (P) argues that the book could have been written differently, changing names and other details, for example. Lemann (D1) would no longer have been writing history, however. He would have been writing fiction. Reporting the true facts about real people was necessary to obviate the impression that the problems raised in the book were remote or hypothetical. Surely a composite portrait of ghetto residents would be attacked as racial stereotyping. The public needs the information conveyed in the book, including the information about Haynes (P), in order to evaluate the profound social and political questions raised by the author. Affirmed.

Analysis:

Under Restatement (Second) of Torts § 652(D), a person who gives publicity to a matter concerning the private life of another is subject to liability to the other for invasion of privacy, if the matter is one that would be highly offensive to a reasonable person and is not of legitimate concern to the public. Applying Illinois case law, which was substantially similar to the Restatement formulation, the U.S. Court of Appeals for the Seventh Circuit here concludes that, even if the published material could be found highly offensive, it was of legitimate interest to the public reading Lemann's (D1) book. The court balances Haynes's (P) right to keep even true details of his life private against the public's interest in knowing those details and finds the public's interest paramount in this case. The court indicates that historical accuracy and the need to avoid claims of racial stereotyping justified publication.

■ CASE VOCABULARY

INVASION OF PRIVACY: Here, a tort action involving the public disclosure of private facts about a person. It can also include tort actions for the appropriation of a person's name or likeness for profit, intrusion upon a person's solitude, and for publicity that portrays a person in a false light.

The Florida Star v. B.J.F.

(Newspaper) v. *(Rape Victim)*

491 U.S. 524, 109 S.Ct. 2603 (1989)

U.S. SUPREME COURT FINDS FLORIDA LAW PROHIBITING MASS PUBLICATION OF THE NAME OF A RAPE VICTIM TO VIOLATE THE FIRST AMENDMENT

■ **INSTANT FACTS** A rape victim sued a newspaper for civil damages after her name and an account of her rape was published by the newspaper in violation of a state law making it unlawful to print, publish, or broadcast in any instrument of mass communication, the name of a victim of a sexual offense.

■ **BLACK LETTER RULE** If a newspaper lawfully obtains truthful information about a matter of public significance, then state officials may not constitutionally punish publication of the information, unless there is a need to further a compelling state interest.

■ PROCEDURAL BASIS

Appeal to the U.S. Supreme Court of a from a denial of review by the Florida Supreme Court of an appellate court affirmance of a state trial court's grant of a directed verdict of negligence.

■ FACTS

A woman, B.J.F. (P), reported to the sheriff's department of Duval County, Florida that she had been robbed and raped by an unknown assailant. The sheriff's department prepared a report on the incident, which identified B.J.F. (P) by her full name, and placed the report in its press room where it was made available to reporters. A reporter for the Florida Star (D) prepared a one paragraph article about the incident derived from the police report and identified B.J.F. (P) by her full name. Following the article's publication, B.J.F. (P) sued the Florida Star (D) in state court for negligence, claiming that the publication of the article violated a Florida law making it unlawful to print, publish, or broadcast in any instrument of mass communication, the name of a victim of a sexual offense, and that this violation of the law constituted negligence per se, for which she was entitled to damages. At the close of B.J.F.'s (P) case, the Florida Star (D) moved for a directed verdict, asserting that the Florida law at issue was an unconstitutional violation of the First Amendment. The trial judge denied the newspaper's motion and at the close of the evidence granted a directed verdict on the issue of negligence in favor of B.J.F. (P). The jury awarded damages. On appeal, the state appellate court affirmed the trial court and the Florida Supreme Court denied review. The Florida Star (D) then appealed to the U.S. Supreme Court.

■ ISSUE

Where a newspaper lawfully obtains truthful information about a matter of public significance, may state officials constitutionally punish publication of the information, in the absence of a need to further a compelling state interest?

■ DECISION AND RATIONALE

(Marshall, J.) No. We conclude that imposing damages on the Florida Star (D) for publishing B.J.F.'s (P) name violates the First Amendment. Our prior cases have established that, if a newspaper lawfully obtains truthful information about a matter of public significance, then state officials may not constitutionally punish publication of the information, unless there is a need to further a state interest of the highest order. Here, the news article describing the assault was accurate and the Florida Star (D) lawfully obtained B.J.F.'s (P) name. B.J.F. (P) argues that a rule punishing publication furthers three closely related interests: the privacy of victims of sexual offenses; the physical safety of such victims, who may be targeted for retaliation if their names become known; and the goal of encouraging victims to report offenses without fear of exposure. While we do not rule out the possibility that, in a proper case, a civil sanction for publication of the name of a rape victim might be so overwhelmingly necessary to advance these significant interests, we believe that imposing liability here is too weak a means of advancing these interests to convince us there is a need to take this extreme step. The government itself provided the information to the media and could have used a far more limited means of guarding against the dissemination of the victim's name than the extreme step of punishing truthful speech. It could have blacked out the victim's name from the report it gave to the press, for example. Moreover, the government's issuance of this information was in the form of a routine news release. If the newspaper had simply copied the news release prepared by the sheriff's department, imposing civil damages would surely violate the First Amendment. The fact that the newspaper converted the news release into full sentences cannot change this result. Additionally, we see a problem with the broad sweep of the negligence per se standard applied in this case. Unlike claims based on the common law tort of invasion of privacy, civil actions based on the statute at issue here require no case-by-case findings that the disclosure of a fact would be highly offensive to a reasonable person. Under the negligence per se theory adopted by the Florida courts, liability is automatic upon publication, regardless of whether the identity of the victim is already known in the community or even if the victim, herself, had voluntarily called public attention to the offense. Such categorical prohibitions on media access are impermissible. Finally, the statute at issue punishes publication of information in an "instrument of mass communication," but does not prohibit the spread by other means of such information. When a state attempts the extraordinary measure of punishing truthful publication in the name of privacy, it must demonstrate its commitment to advancing this interest by applying its prohibition evenhandedly, to the small time disseminator as well as to the media giant. Reversed.

■ CONCURRENCE

(Scalia, J.) I think it enough to decide this case on the last ground mentioned by the court that the statute at issue is facially under-inclusive. I would anticipate that the rape victim's discomfort at the dissemination of the news of her misfortune among friends and acquaintances would be at least as great as her discomfort at its publication by the media to people to whom she is only a name. The statute in question, however, does not prohibit the dissemination of the news to friends and relatives, either in oral or written form. This law has every appearance of a prohibition that society is prepared to impose on the press but not on itself. I agree that the judgment below should be reversed.

■ DISSENT

(White, J.) Yes. The government's release of the information was inadvertent. They made a mistake. When the state makes a mistake in its efforts to protect privacy, it is not too much to ask the press, in instances such as this, to respect simple standards of decency and refrain from publishing a victim's name, address, and/or phone number. As to the issue that the statute is facially under-inclusive, I am willing to accept the apparent legislative conclusion that neighborhood gossips do not pose the danger and intrusion to rape victims that instruments of mass communication do. Simply put, Florida wanted to prevent the widespread distribution of rape victims' names, and therefore enacted a statute tailored almost as precisely as possible to achieving that end. There was no public interest in identifying the victim here and no public interest in immunizing the press from liability in the rare cases where a state's efforts to protect a victim's privacy have failed. I would affirm.

Analysis:

In attempting to strike a fair balance between the rights given to the press under the First Amendment and the rights of individuals to personal privacy, the Court adopts the principle that, if the press lawfully obtains truthful information about a matter of public significance, a state may not constitutionally punish publication of that information in the absence of a need to further a state interest of "the highest order." In this particular case, the information was lawfully obtained, and the Court finds that any interest Florida has in safeguarding information about the identity of a rape victim does not rise high enough to justify impeding on the First Amendment rights of the press. The Court does indicate, however, that there could be instances that do rise to the level of importance necessary to justify a limit on publication.

■ CASE VOCABULARY

DIRECTED VERDICT: A verdict ordered by a trial court judge as a matter of law following a finding that the party having the burden of proof has failed to present evidence sufficient for a reasonable jury to find for that party on the disputed issue.

NEGLIGENCE PER SE: An automatic finding of negligence based on a showing that a party violated a statute without sufficient excuse or privilege to do so.

Humphers v. First Interstate Bank of Oregon

(*Birth Mother*) v. (*Personal Representative of an Estate*)

298 Or. 706, 696 P.2d 527 (1985)

OREGON SUPREME COURT FINDS THAT A DOCTOR'S UNAUTHORIZED AND UNPRIVILEGED DISCLOSURE OF CONFIDENTIAL INFORMATION ABOUT A PATIENT CAN GIVE RISE TO TORT DAMAGES

■ **INSTANT FACTS** A mother who had given up her daughter for adoption many years earlier sued the estate of the doctor who had delivered the daughter for invasion of privacy and breach of a confidential relationship after the doctor, who had since died, helped the daughter locate the mother.

■ **BLACK LETTER RULE** The disclosure of confidential facts about a patient in violation of a state statute imposing a duty of confidentiality on doctors and without a valid statutory defense or privilege, can constitute an actionable tort for which damages may be recovered by the patient.

■ **PROCEDURAL BASIS**

Appeal from a state appellate court's reversal of a trial court's dismissal of a tort claim for damages for invasion of privacy and breach of a confidential relationship.

■ **FACTS**

Ramona Humphers ("Ramona") (P), an unmarried woman, gave birth to a daughter, Dawn, in 1959, who she immediately gave up for adoption. Ramona (P) later married. Her mother, new husband, and Dr. Mackey, who had delivered the baby, were the only ones who knew of the birth and adoption. In 1980, seeking to meet her birth mother and unable to get access to confidential court files from the adoption, Dawn found Dr. Mackey and asked for his help. Dr. Mackey gave Dawn a letter that falsely stated that Ramona (P) had taken a dangerous drug during pregnancy and that it was therefore important for Dawn to learn about her mother's medical history. Relying on the letter, hospital personnel identified Ramona (P) for Dawn. Ramona (P) suffered emotional distress, sleeplessness, and embarrassment. Dr. Mackey had died, so Ramona (P) sued the personal representative of his estate, First Interstate Bank of Oregon ("Estate") (D) for damages, asserting, among other things, that the disclosure constituted an invasion of privacy and breached an obligation of secrecy to Ramona (P). The trial court granted the Estate's (D) motion to dismiss the complaint, finding that the facts did not justify relief under the theories asserted. On appeal by Ramona (P), the state Court of Appeals found a breach of a confidential relationship and an invasion of privacy. The Estate (D) then appealed to the Oregon Supreme Court, which granted review.

■ **ISSUE**

Can the disclosure of confidential facts about a patient in violation of a state statute imposing a duty of confidentiality on doctors and without a valid statutory defense or privilege, constitute an actionable tort for which damages may be recovered by the patient?

■ **DECISION AND RATIONALE**

(Linde, J.) Yes. The Court of Appeals found that a tort claim could be made under the facts of this case for both an invasion of privacy and a breach of confidence. We hold that, if Ramona (P) has a claim, it arose from Dr. Mackey's breach of a professional duty to keep Ramona's (P) secret rather than from a violation of her privacy. Dr. Mackey himself did not approach Ramona (P) or pry into any personal facts that he did not know. The point of the claim against Dr. Mackey is not that he pried into a confidence, but that he failed to keep one. Dr. Mackey has a legal duty imposed as a condition of engaging in the professional practice of medicine. A physician's duty to keep medical and related information about a patient in confidence is imposed by statute. Oregon statutory law provides for disqualifying or otherwise disciplining a doctor for willfully or negligently divulging a professional secret. While there are circumstances in which a privilege might exist for a doctor to legally violate the confidence of a patient, no privilege exists in this case. If Dawn had really needed information about her mother for medical reasons, as Dr. Mackey here pretended, the state medical board might have found his action privileged against a charge of breach of confidence. Given the existence of other statutes that specifically mandate the secrecy of adoption records, however, there is no privilege to disregard the professional duty of confidentiality solely in order to satisfy the curiosity of a person given up for adoption. Thus, we reverse the appellate court's finding that a claim may lie for an invasion of privacy, but agree that the claim may proceed on the grounds of a breach of confidentiality. Reversed in part and affirmed in part.

Analysis:

The court of appeals had found two potential causes of action; a tort action based on invasion of privacy and a tort action based on breach of confidence. The Oregon Supreme Court notes that an invasion of privacy can be committed by anyone, but a breach of confidence can only occur where a person has either a contractual or statutory duty to maintain a person's confidence. Here, Dr. Mackey did not invade Ramona's (P) privacy in the sense of making an unauthorized intrusion upon her seclusion, solitude, or private affairs. As the Oregon Supreme Court recognizes, the real problem with what Dr. Mackey did in this case was that he violated his statutory duty to keep patient information confidential. This case essentially follows in the tradition of the negligence per se cases, finding that civil damages can be recovered for an unprivileged violation of a statute.

■ CASE VOCABULARY

BREACH OF CONFIDENTIALITY: A tort based on a person's disclosure of confidential information about another in violation of a statutory or contractual obligation of disclosure.

Cantrell v. Forest City Publishing Co.

(Widow and Children) v. *(Publisher)*
419 U.S. 245, 95 S.Ct. 465 (1974)

ACTUAL MALICE MUST BE SHOWN TO RECOVER FOR "FALSE LIGHT" IN THE PUBLIC EYE

■ **INSTANT FACTS** Margaret Cantrell (P) and her children sued for the publication of a newspaper article depicting their family as living in abject poverty.

■ **BLACK LETTER RULE** Actual malice must be proven in order to recover under a "false light" theory.

■ **PROCEDURAL BASIS**

Writ of certiorari reviewing reversal of verdict for compensatory damages for false light.

■ **FACTS**

In 1967, Melvin Cantrell was one of 43 people who died when a bridge collapsed. Forest City Publishing Co. (D) published two stories focusing on the impact of Mr. Cantrell's death on the Cantrell family. For the second story, a reporter and photographer visited the Cantrell's home, taking several pictures and interviewing the Cantrell children. Margaret Cantrell (P) was not home at the time. The article focused on the family's abject poverty, including pictures and text of the poor living conditions. Mrs. Cantrell (P) and her children (P) sued for damages. They alleged that the story was inaccurate and portrayed the family in a false light, which made the Cantrells (P) the subject of ridicule and caused mental distress, shame and humiliation. Forest City Publishing (D) conceded that the story contained a number of inaccuracies regarding Mrs. Cantrell (P) and the conditions of the family residence. The District Court instructed the jury that liability could be imposed only if it concluded that Forest City Publishing (D) had actual knowledge of the falsity or reckless disregard of the truth. The District Judge also struck the demand for punitive damages, finding that the evidence did not show legal malice. The jury returned a verdict awarding compulsory damages for Mrs. Cantrell (P) and William Cantrell (P). The Court of Appeals reversed, holding that the requisite malice was not shown. The Supreme Court granted certiorari.

■ **ISSUE**

In order to recover for "false light," must knowledge of falsity or reckless disregard of the truth be proven?

■ **DECISION AND RATIONALE**

(Stewart, J.) Yes. In order to recover for "false light," *New York Times* malice—i.e., knowledge of falsity or reckless disregard of the truth—must be proven. The Court of Appeals held that such knowledge or recklessness had not been shown, interpreting the District Judge's striking of punitive damages as a finding that there was no evidence of knowledge of falsity or reckless disregard of the truth. However, the actual malice required for a false light action is very different from the common-law standard of malice generally required to support an award of punitive damages. In order to recover punitives, the Cantrells (P) would have to show some personal ill-will or wanton disregard of the Cantrells' (P) rights. This malice standard would focus on Forest City Publishing's (D) attitude toward the Cantrells' (P) privacy, not towards the truth or falsity of the material published. We conclude, contrary to the appellate court, that the District Judge was referring to the punitive standard of malice, not the actual malice standard of *New York Times*. Furthermore, in denying Forest City Publishing's (D) motion for a new trial, the District Judge necessarily and correctly found that the evidence was sufficient to support a finding that Forest City Publishing (D) had published knowing or reckless falsehoods. The knowledge of the reporter and photographer are imputed to Forest City Publishing (D), who is vicariously liable under the theory of *respondeat superior* for portraying the Cantrells (P) in a false light. Reversed and remanded with directions to enter a judgment affirming the District Court's judgment.

■ DISSENT

(Douglas, J.) No. The Cantrells' accident was newsworthy. To make the First Amendment freedom to report the news turn on subtle differences between common-law malice and actual malice stands the Amendment on its head. News reporters deal in fast-moving events and the need for "spot" reporting. Under the majority's approach, the jury now sits as a censor, with broad powers to lay heavy damages on the press. The press is "free" only if the jury is sufficiently disenchanted with the Cantrells to let the press be free of the damages claim. Some may view this system of supervising the press as better than no system at all. I believe it requires an amendment of our Constitution. The press should not be frightened into playing a more minor role than the Framers of the Constitution imagined. I would affirm.

Analysis:

This case essentially restates the requirements for a cause of action for false light. The main import of the case is the requirement that actual malice, as defined in *New York Times Co. v. Sullivan*, be proven in order to recover damages. Thus, a publisher may be liable for knowingly or recklessly publishing falsities. Note that the false light need not necessarily be a defamatory one, although it very often is. Thus, actions for defamation and false light may be brought concurrently. However, false light typically requires that the publication be offensive to a reasonable person. In addition, defamation differs from false light in that the former protects a person's reputation, whereas the latter protects a person's interest in being left alone. The privileges available in defamation actions, including those regarding public figures, are also available in false light actions.

■ CASE VOCABULARY

RESPONDEAT SUPERIOR: A theory of liability in which an employer can be held vicariously liable for the torts of its employees.

Nader v. General Motors Corp.

(*Consumer Advocate*) v. (*Car Manufacturer*)

25 N.Y.2d 560, 255 N.E.2d 765, 307 N.Y.S.2d 647 (1970)

INTRUSION OCCURS ONLY WHERE THE INFORMATION SOUGHT ABOUT ANOTHER IS OF A CONFIDENTIAL NATURE

■ **INSTANT FACTS** A consumer advocate, who was about to publish a book critical of a car manufacturer, sued the car manufacturer for invasion of privacy, alleging the manufacturer had inquired into his social and political views, kept him under surveillance in public places, had women attempt to entrap him into illicit relationships, made harassing telephone calls to him, and wiretapped his telephone.

■ **BLACK LETTER RULE** To be liable for invasion of privacy on the theory of unlawful intrusion, a person must be seeking confidential information about another and his conduct in seeking the information must be unreasonably intrusive.

■ **PROCEDURAL BASIS**

Appeal to the New York Court of Appeals of a state appellate court's affirmance of a trial court denial of a motion to dismiss two counts of a complaint alleging invasion of privacy.

■ **FACTS**

Consumer advocate, Ralph Nader ("Nader") (P), who was about to publish a book severely critical of car manufacturers, filed suit in New York state court against General Motors Corporation ("GM") (D) for invasion of privacy, intentional infliction of emotional distress, and interference with his economic advantage, alleging that GM (D) had made an effort to intimidate him in order to get him to suppress his criticism of the company. Nader (P) claimed that GM (D) had: unlawfully inquired into his political, social, racial, and religious views, his integrity, and his sexual behavior, casting aspersions on his character; kept him under surveillance in public places; had women attempt to entrap him into illicit relationships; made threatening and harassing telephone calls to him; and wiretapped his telephone, eavesdropping on private conversations. The acts allegedly occurred in Washington, D.C. ("D.C.") and the parties agreed that D.C. law controlled the case. GM (D) moved to dismiss the invasion of privacy claim and the trial court denied the motion. The appellate division affirmed and GM (D) then appealed to the New York Court of Appeals, the state's highest court.

■ **ISSUE**

In order to be liable for invasion of privacy on the theory of unlawful intrusion, must the person charged have been seeking information of a confidential nature?

■ **DECISION AND RATIONALE**

(Fuld, C.J.) Yes. D.C. courts have broadened the traditional scope of the common-law action for invasion of privacy to include instances of intrusion into areas from which an ordinary person could reasonably expect that other persons should be excluded. Obviously, some intrusions into a person's private sphere are inevitable in an industrial and densely populated society and the law does not provide a remedy for every annoyance that occurs in everyday life. We must predict how the D.C. courts would react to the intrusion claims at issue in this case. Would they, as Nader (P) insists, find a right to be protected against any interference whatsoever with a person's seclusion and solitude? Or would they adopt the more restrictive approach, urged by GM (D), merely protecting individuals from intrusion into something secret? The case law we have reviewed suggests that D.C. courts would find that the interest protected is the right to prevent the obtaining of *private* information by improperly intrusive means. The mere gathering of information about an individual does not give rise to a cause of action under this theory. Privacy is invaded only if the information sought is confidential and the seeker's conduct was unreasonably intrusive. Here, the appellate division found that *all* of the activities complained of by Nader (P) constituted actionable invasions of privacy under D.C. law. We disagree with that sweeping determination. Nader (P) alleges that GM (D) interviewed persons who knew Nader (P), asking personal questions and casting aspersions on his character. While the questions may have uncovered personal information, it is difficult to see how they invaded Nader's (P) privacy. Information about Nader (P) that was already known to others could hardly be regarded as private to him. By previously revealing the information to others, Nader (P) assumed the risk they might breach his confidence. If a question disparaged his character, Nader's (P) remedy is an action for defamation, rather than a claim of breach of his right of privacy. Additionally, we find no actionable invasion of privacy in the claims that GM (D) caused Nader (P) to be accosted by women with illicit proposals, or that GM (D) made harassing telephone calls. However offensive, neither activity involved intrusion for the purpose of gathering private information. Nader (P) may, however, have a claim for intentional infliction of emotional distress from these actions. Nader's (P) allegations that GM (D) engaged in unauthorized wiretapping of his calls do satisfy the requirements for actionable invasion of privacy. Nader's (P) claim that he was kept under surveillance may also amount to an actionable invasion of privacy, depending on the circumstances of the surveillance. While observation in a public place does not usually amount to invasion of privacy, under certain circumstances, it could. The mere fact that Nader (P) was in a bank, for example, does not give anyone the right to try to discover the amount of money he was withdrawing. On the other hand, if he acted in a way that would reveal that fact to a casual observer, there would be no intrusion. Since Nader's causes of action do contain allegations adequate to state a cause of action for invasion of privacy under D.C. law, the courts below properly denied GM's (D) motion to dismiss. Affirmed.

■ CONCURRENCE

(Breitel, J.) The court is correct that Nader's (P) allegations are sufficient to allege an invasion of privacy under D.C. law. I see no reason, however, to go further now and advance into a complicated and still changing field of law of another jurisdiction just to determine, before trial, the relevancy of projected, but not yet offered items of evidence. It is inappropriate to decide now that several of the allegations as they currently appear are referable only to the more restricted tort of intentional infliction of emotional distress rather than to the common-law right of privacy. Intentional infliction of emotional distress is harder to show, requiring demonstration that the disputed activities were designed to make plaintiff unhappy and not to discover disgraceful information about him. It is not a stretch to conceive of the systematic "public" surveillance of another as being the implementation of a plan to intrude on his privacy. I concur in the result, but not the reasoning of the court.

Analysis:

The court here emphasizes an important point regarding an invasion of privacy claim based on the theory of intrusion. Merely asking questions about a person or gathering information will generally not be actionable. Instead, to intrude on a person's solitude, a person must be seeking *confidential* information and must be using unreasonably intrusive means to obtain that information. The intrusion must be into something that is private. Here, if GM (D) tapped Nader's (P) telephone and eavesdropped on his personal conversations, that would be unreasonably intrusive and would be an attempt to obtain confidential information, permitting a cause of action. Following Nader's (P) movement on a public street and recording his actions might not be unreasonably intrusive and would probably not be an effort to seek "private" information, because he would be making his actions publicly visible.

■ **CASE VOCABULARY**

CONFIDENTIAL: Intended to be kept private or secret.

DEFAMATION: An intentionally false communication that damages a person's reputation. It includes both libel and slander.

INTENTIONAL INFLICTION OF EMOTIONAL DISTRESS: A tort cause of action permitting damages to be awarded to a person who is purposefully emotionally injured by another's extreme conduct.

INTRUSION: One type of invasion of privacy which some courts and legislatures have recognized. It involves the unreasonable gathering of private or confidential information about a person or other invasion of the person's solitude or seclusion without consent.

Galella v. Onassis

(*Paparazzo Photographer*) v. (*Former First Lady of the United States*)

487 F.2d 986 (2d Cir. 1973)

COURT BALANCES RIGHT TO GATHER NEWS AGAINST PRIVACY RIGHTS OF THE NEWSWORTHY

■ **INSTANT FACTS** A former first lady sued a photographer for invasion of privacy, seeking injunctive relief limiting the photographer's contact with her and her children, after the photographer endangered their safety.

■ **BLACK LETTER RULE** While social needs such as news gathering may justify some intrusion despite a person's reasonable expectation of privacy, the interference allowed may be no greater than that necessary to protect the overriding public interest and may not be unreasonably intrusive.

■ **PROCEDURAL BASIS**

Appeal of a dismissal of a suit in federal district court for false arrest and malicious prosecution and the grant of injunctive relief in a counterclaim for harassment and invasion of privacy.

■ **FACTS**

Ron Galella ("Galella") (P) was a paparazzo photographer, whose object was to make himself as visible to the public and annoying to his photographic subjects as possible in order to aid in the advertisement and sale of his pictures. Galella (P) took pictures of former first lady, Jacqueline Kennedy Onassis ("Onassis") (D) and her children, jumping into the path of her young son while he was riding his bike in the park, invading the children's private schools, touching Onassis (D) and her daughter, following Onassis (D) and her children too closely in a car, and coming very close in a power boat while Onassis (D) was swimming. Galella (P) sued Onassis (D) for false arrest and malicious prosecution after he was arrested by Secret Service agents protecting Onassis's (D) children. Onassis (D) counterclaimed for injunctive relief against Galella's (P) attempts to photograph her and her children. Following a trial, the trial judge dismissed Galella's (P) suit and granted injunctive relief to Onassis (D), holding Galella (P) guilty of harassment, intentional infliction of emotional distress, assault and battery, commercial exploitation of Onassis (D), and invasion of privacy. Finding a need to prevent a further invasion of privacy, the court enjoined Galella (P) from (1) keeping Onassis (D) and her children under surveillance or following any of them; (2) approaching within 100 yards of the Onassis (D) home or the children's school, within 75 yards of the Onassis (D) children, or within 50 yards of Onassis (D); (3) using the name, portrait, or picture of Onassis (D) or her children for advertising; and (4) attempting to communicate with Onassis (D) or her children, except through her attorney. Galella appealed.

■ **ISSUE**

Does the First Amendment protect newsmen from any liability for their conduct while gathering the news?

■ **DECISION AND RATIONALE**

(Smith, J.) No. Legitimate social needs may justify some intrusion despite a person's reasonable expectation of privacy and freedom from harassment. Nevertheless, the interference allowed may be

---

no greater than that necessary to protect the overriding public interest. Galella's (P) actions went far beyond the reasonable bounds of news gathering. When weighed against the minimal public importance of the daily activities of Onassis (D), Galella's (P) constant surveillance and intruding presence was unjustified and unreasonable. Galella (P) argues that the First Amendment serves as a wall of immunity protecting newsmen from any liability for their conduct while gathering the news. There is no such scope to the First Amendment right. Crimes and torts committed in news gathering are not protected. There is no threat to a free press in requiring its agents to act within the law. We find that injunctive relief is appropriate in this case. Galella (P) has stated his intent to continue covering Onassis (D) and continued harassment even while temporary restraining orders were in effect in this case. The trial court's injunction, however, is broader than is required to protect Onassis (D). Onassis's (D) protective relief must not unnecessarily infringe on reasonable efforts to gather information about her. We therefore modify the trial court's injunction to prohibit only (1) any approach within 25 feet of or touching of Onassis (D); (2) any blocking of her movement in public places; (3) any act reasonably calculated to place Onassis's (D) life or safety in danger; and (4) any conduct that would reasonably harass, alarm, or frighten Onassis (D). We modify the injunction as to the children to permit photographs within 30 feet. As modified, the relief granted allows Galella (P) the chance to photograph and report on Onassis's (P) public activities. Any restraint on news gathering is minor and fully supported by the record. Order modified.

■ DISSENT

(Timbers, J.) I dissent from the reduction of the distance limits imposed by the trial judge.

Analysis:

Galella (P) claimed that his photographic activity was news gathering and immune under the First Amendment from potential tort liability. Rejecting this assertion, the court holds that the First Amendment does not grant immunity from state tort law to those gathering the news where the tortious conduct was unwarranted and unreasonable. While judging Galella's (P) conduct to have been unreasonably intrusive, the court does indicate that some First Amendment protection exists and that a balancing test must be conducted, weighing a journalist's right to cover a newsworthy subject against that subject's privacy rights. Despite the injunction, Galella (P) continued his coverage of Onassis (D) after the opinion was published. In 1982, faced with a finding that he had violated the injunction and a potential fine of $120,000, he finally agreed never again to photograph her. Time Magazine once published a notorious picture of Galella (P) following Onassis (D) on the street with a tape measure extended to keep him outside the distance ordered by the court.

■ CASE VOCABULARY

HARASSMENT: Here, a criminal offense under New York law which could also be the basis of a private cause of action. It outlaws intentionally bothering another person by following them, inflicting physical contact, or engaging in annoying conduct towards them without legitimate cause.

PAPARAZZO: An Italian word meaning an annoying insect. It has come to be associated with celebrity photographers who will go to virtually any lengths to obtain pictures of their photographic subjects that can be sold to the press.

Desnick v. American Broadcasting Companies, Inc.

(Eye Clinic) v. *(Television Network)*

44 F.3d 1345 (7th Cir. 1995)

FEDERAL APPEALS COURT FINDS NO INVASION OF PRIVACY FROM TV NEWS SHOW'S USE OF HIDDEN CAMERAS TO INVESTIGATE CLAIMS THAT DOCTORS WERE PRESCRIBING UNNECESSARY SURGERY

■ **INSTANT FACTS** An eye clinic sued a television network for trespass, invasion of privacy, and illegal electronic surveillance after the network broadcast a news segment using hidden cameras on people posing as clinic patients.

■ **BLACK LETTER RULE** The recording of a professional conversation between an undercover journalist seeking to uncover wrongdoing and a physician in an office open to the public does not constitute an invasion of privacy.

■ **PROCEDURAL BASIS**

Appeal of a dismissal of a diversity jurisdiction suit in federal district court for trespass, invasion of privacy, illegal electronic surveillance, fraud, and defamation.

■ **FACTS**

The Desnick Eye Center ("the Center") (P) sued American Broadcasting Companies, Inc. ("ABC") (D) asserting that a segment of an ABC (D) news program, PrimeTime Live, detailing claims of unnecessary cataract surgery allegedly performed by the clinic's doctors, was defamatory and involved a trespass and invasion of privacy. The Center (D) claimed that the show's producer had told the clinic's owner that he wanted to do a segment on cataract practice that would not involve undercover surveillance and that would be fair and balanced. The Center (P) permitted ABC (D) to film an operation and to interview its Chicago clinic personnel. The Center (P) claimed that without its knowledge or consent, ABC (D) sent people to other clinics it owned in Indiana and Wisconsin to pose as patients with hidden cameras. When the program aired, it detailed an undercover investigation of the clinics, charging the Center (P) with doing unnecessary surgery to make money. The program included a professor of ophthalmology who asserted that the test patients sent by ABC (D) into the clinic who were told by clinic doctors that they needed surgery, did not actually need surgery. The show also included claims that records had been changed and machines tampered with so patients would think they had cataracts. On motion by ABC (D), the trial court dismissed the suit for failure to state a claim. The Center (P) appealed.

■ **ISSUE**

Does the recording of a professional conversation between an undercover journalist seeking to uncover wrongdoing and a physician in an office open to the public constitute an invasion of privacy?

■ **DECISION AND RATIONALE**

(Posner, C.J.) No. The Center (P) claims that ABC (D) (1) committed a trespass in placing test patients into its Indiana and Wisconsin clinics; (2) invaded the Center's (P) right of privacy and its doctors' privacy rights; and (3) violated federal and state statutes regulating electronic surveillance. There is no journalist's privilege to trespass and there can be no implied consent to enter another's land when express consent is procured by a misrepresentation or a misleading omission. The Center (P) would not have agreed to the entry of test patients had it known they wanted eye exams only in order to get material for a television expose of the Center (P) and that they were going to make secret tapes of the exams. Nevertheless, some cases deem consent effective even though it was obtained by fraud. Without this result, a restaurant critic could not conceal his identity when he ordered a meal and dinner guests would be trespassers if they were false friends who never would have been invited had the host known their true character. A consumer trying to bargain down a car dealer by falsely claiming to be able to buy the same car elsewhere for a lower price would be trespasser in the dealer's showroom. Consent to an entry is often given legal effect even though the entrant has intentions that, if known to the property owner, would cause him to revoke his consent. Here, there was no invasion of any of the specific interests that the tort of trespass seeks to protect. It was not an interference with the ownership or possession of land. The test patients entered offices that were open to anyone with a desire for ophthalmic services and taped doctors engaged in professional, not personal communications with strangers. The activities of the offices were not disrupted and there was no invasion of a person's private space. There was no eavesdropping on private conversations; the testers recorded their own conversations with the doctors, which the federal and state wiretapping statutes permit, so long as the purpose of recording the conversation is not to commit a crime or tort. No embarrassingly intimate details of anyone's private life were publicized. There is no invasion of privacy in this case. Today's ''tabloid'' style journalism conducted by networks desperate for viewers in an increasingly competitive market is still part of the vigorous market in ideas and opinions designed to be protected by the First Amendment. If the content is not defamatory and no established rights are invaded in the process of creating it, then the target has no legal remedy, even if the tactics used are surreptitious, confrontational, unscrupulous, and ungentlemanly. Affirmed in Part, Reversed in Part.

Analysis:

The court here properly recognizes the value of a free press and hard-hitting investigative journalism techniques. Vigorous news gathering helps protect society from those who seek to harm the public. The court finds no actionable trespass in this case because the offices were not disrupted and there was no interference with the ownership or possession of the premises. The court narrows the concept of invasion of privacy to exclude conversations and information gathered from a person engaged in his professional duties. The Center's (P) offices were generally open for business. No personal or private conversations were recorded. Nothing but the professional advice offered by the clinic was detailed. Since the clinics were essentially public, there was no invasion of privacy.

■ CASE VOCABULARY

EXPRESS CONSENT: Unequivocal assent to do an action, given orally, in writing, or by other manifestly clear indication.

IMPLIED CONSENT: An inference or presumption that consent has been given by a person to an action by another, arising from a relationship between the two in which there is a lack of objection under circumstances suggesting assent.

TRESPASS: Unauthorized entry of the private premises or land of another.

Shulman v. Group W Productions Inc., et al.

(*Accident Victim*) v. (*Documentary Television Producers*)

18 Cal.4th 200, 955 P.2d 469, 74 Cal.Rptr.2d 843 (1998)

CALIFORNIA SUPREME COURT SPELLS OUT THE REQUIREMENTS FOR ACTIONABLE INTRUSION

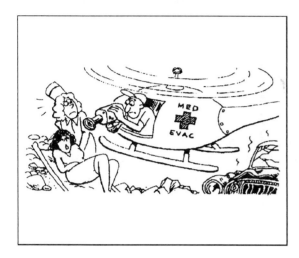

■ **INSTANT FACTS** A victim of a car accident sued a television production company for invasion of privacy after the company broadcast footage it recorded of her being rescued from the accident scene and her comments to rescue personnel while being transported to the hospital.

■ **BLACK LETTER RULE** A person who intentionally intrudes into a private place, conversation, or matter in a manner highly offensive to a reasonable person, without consent or a privilege to do so, is subject to liability for invasion of privacy.

■ **PROCEDURAL BASIS**

Appeal of a state appellate court decision affirming in part and reversing in part a trial court's dismissal of a suit for invasion of privacy.

■ **FACTS**

Ruth Shulman ("Shulman") (P) and her son were injured in a car accident. A rescue helicopter was sent to the accident scene with a nurse, a medic, and a video cameraman employed by Group W Productions, Inc. ("Group W") (D), producers of a documentary television show about emergency response units. The nurse was wearing a wireless microphone that picked up conversations with Shulman (P). The camera and microphone record Shulman (D) saying: "This is terrible. Am I dreaming?" and "I just want to die. I don't want to go through this." Shulman (D) was left paraplegic from the accident. Group W (D) broadcast the footage as part of its documentary television program. After seeing the program in her hospital room, Shulman (P) sued Group W (D) for intrusion and publication of private facts. Shulman (P) stipulated that auto accidents on public highways and publicly provided emergency rescue services were both matters of public interest. The trial court granted summary judgment in favor of Group W (D) and Shulman (P) appealed. A California appellate court affirmed part of the trial court's ruling, but reversed on the issue of intrusion. Shulman (P) appealed to the California Supreme Court, which found that the trial court had been correct on the publication of private facts claim, but not on intrusion.

■ **ISSUE**

Could a reasonable jury find that the recording and broadcast of the comments of an accident victim to her medical rescuers in a rescue helicopter constituted an intentional intrusion into a private place, conversation, or matter in a manner highly offensive to a reasonable person?

■ **DECISION AND RATIONALE**

(Werdegar, J.) Yes. We hold that triable issues exist as to whether Group W (D) invaded Shulman's (P) privacy by accompanying her in the helicopter, listening to her confidential conversations with the nurse without her consent, and that Group W (D) had no constitutional privilege to intrude on Shulman's (P) seclusion in this way. The action for intrusion has two elements: (1) intrusion into a private place, conversation or matter, (2) in a manner highly offensive to a reasonable person. Shulman (P) must show that Group W (D) penetrated some zone of physical or sensory privacy surrounding her or obtained unwanted access to data about her and that she had an objectively reasonable expectation of seclusion or solitude in the place, conversation, or data source. The cameraman's mere presence at the accident scene and filming of events there cannot be deemed a physical or sensory intrusion on Shulman's (P) seclusion. Shulman (P) had no right of ownership or possession of the property where the rescue took place, nor any actual control of the premises. Nor could she have had a reasonable expectation that journalists would not be permitted to photograph the scene. Nevertheless, a triable issue exists as to whether Shulman (P) had an objectively reasonable expectation of privacy in the inside of the rescue helicopter. While people expect reporters and photographers at accident scenes, we are aware of no law or custom allowing the press to ride in ambulances or enter hospital rooms during treatment without a patient's consent. Additionally, Shulman (P) was entitled to privacy in her conversations with the nurse and other medical rescuers at the accident scene. By placing a microphone on the nurse to record what Shulman (P) said, Group W (D) may have listened in on conversations Shulman (P) could reasonably have expected to be private. As to the offensiveness of any intrusion by Group W (D), in deciding whether a reporter's alleged intrusion into private matters is "offensive" and thus actionable as an invasion of privacy, courts must consider the extent to which the intrusion was justified by the legitimate motive of news gathering. Information collecting techniques that may be highly offensive when done for socially unprotected reasons such as harassment or blackmail, may not be offensive to a reasonable person when used by journalists to cover a socially or politically important story. Offensiveness also depends on the particular method of investigation used. Routine reporting techniques like asking questions of people with information are rarely, if ever, actionable. Trespass into a home or tapping a personal phone, on the other hand, are rarely not actionable. Between these extremes, lie difficult cases. There is no bright line and each case must be examined on its own facts. Here, we think a jury could find that the recording of Shulman's (P) comments to the nurse and filming in the air ambulance to be highly offensive to a reasonable person. Group W (D), a reasonable jury could find, took advantage of Shulman's (P) vulnerability and confusion. Arguably, the last thing an accident victim should have to worry about while being pried from her wrecked car is that a producer may be recording everything she says. A reasonable jury could also find that Group W's (D) motive—to gather material for a newsworthy story—did not privilege its intrusive conduct. A jury could conclude that a producer's desire to get footage that would convey the real feel of a rescue did not justify placing a microphone on the nurse or filming the patient inside of the helicopter. These questions should be decided by a jury. Affirmed [except for the appellate court's reversal of the trial court's dismissal of Shulman's (P) publication of private facts claim].

■ DISSENT

(Chin, J.) No. I do not believe that a reasonable trier of fact could find that Group W's (D) conduct in this case was highly offensive to a reasonable person. Shulman (P) does not allege that Group W (D) interfered with the rescue or medical efforts, elicited embarrassing or offensive information, or even tried to interrogate or interview them. The cameraman merely recorded newsworthy events of legitimate public concern as they happened. Group W's (D) apparent motive in undertaking the supposed privacy invasion was reasonable and nonmalicious: to obtain an accurate depiction of the rescue efforts from start to finish. The ultimate broadcast was dramatic and educational, rather than tawdry or embarrassing. Recording the innocuous and inoffensive conversations that occurred between Shulman (P) and the nurse and filming the helicopter ride may have *technically* invaded Shulman's (P) private space, but in my view, no "highly offensive" invasion of her privacy occurred. We are not dealing with surreptitious wiretapping of a truly private pace like a psychiatrist's examining room or priest's confessional. Instead, Shulman (P) spoke in settings where others could hear her, and the fact that she did not know she was being recorded does not transform legitimate news gathering techniques into highly offensive conduct. To turn a jury loose on Group W (D) is "highly offensive" to me. I would reverse on the issue of intrusion.

Analysis:

The California Supreme Court states that there are no bright lines in terms of judging the offensiveness of reporting techniques in cases such as this one. In the court's opinion, a reasonable jury could find that Group W's (D) conduct was highly offensive to a reasonable person. A jury might, like Shulman (P), be outraged by the idea of a reporter riding along in a rescue helicopter recording everything said during the rescue. A reasonable jury could also come to the conclusion that the dissent does and find that Group W's (D) conduct was not highly offensive. The court's point, however, is that this is a factual question for a jury to decide and that it cannot be decided as a matter of *law* by judges.

■ CASE VOCABULARY

PUBLICATION OF PRIVATE FACTS: A form of the common law tort of invasion of privacy; it involves the publicizing of details of another person's private life without their consent, in a manner that would be highly offensive to a reasonable person.

Bartnicki v. Vopper

(*Union's Chief Negotiator*) v. (*Radio Show Host*)
532 U.S. 514, 121 S.Ct. 1753 (2001)

ILLEGALLY OBTAINED INFORMATION MAY BE PUBLISHED BY A THIRD–PARTY WHO OBTAINS IT THROUGH PROPER MEANS

■ **INSTANT FACTS:** Bartnicki's (P) cell phone conversation with a union representative was intercepted and played on the radio by Vopper (D); Bartnicki (P) sued Vopper (D) for violation of a federal anti-wiretapping statute.

■ **BLACK LETTER RULE:** If a media outlet lawfully obtains truthful information about a matter of public significance, publication of that information may not be sanctioned absent a need "of the highest order."

■ **PROCEDURAL BASIS**

Certiorari to review an undisclosed appellate decision.

■ **FACTS**

Bartnicki (P) was the lead negotiator for a teacher's union. During a cell phone call with the union's president, Bartnicki (P) stated that, unless negotiations started progressing, the union would have to "blow off [the school district negotiators'] front porches." After the school district and teachers settled, Vopper (D) played a tape of the conversation between Bartnicki (P) and the union president on his local radio talk show. Bartnicki (P) sued Vopper (D) for the unlawful disclosure of the contents of the intercepted call. During discovery, it was learned that Vopper (D) received the recording from a union opponent, who claimed to have received the unsolicited recording in his mailbox. In defense of the action, Vopper (D) claimed he did not himself intercept the call and does not know who did, that the radio station legally obtained a tape of the call, and that the subject matter of the conversation was a matter of public concern.

■ **ISSUE**

May a third party publish unlawfully obtained information if the third party itself obtains the information legally?

■ **DECISION AND RATIONALE**

(Stevens, J.) Yes. Under 18 U.S.C. § 2511(1)(c), any person who "intentionally discloses, or endeavors to disclose, to any other person the contents of any wire, oral, or electronic communication, knowing or having reason to know that the information was obtained through the interception of a [protected] wire or oral communication," shall be punished. As it exists, the statute is content neutral, protecting all wire, oral, and electronic communications regardless of their content. Yet, subsection (c) does not regulate conduct, but rather prohibits one from revealing the content of a particular truthful message.

The government, as intervenor, identified two interests served by the federal statute. First, the statute removes the incentive to intercept private conversations; second, it minimizes the harm to those whose conversations have been unlawfully intercepted. The desire to deter privacy violations is a worthy goal, but punishing a disclosure of information related to the public interest by one not involved in the initial illegality does not properly serve that goal. Moreover, the fear of disclosure of private conversations may have a chilling effect on private speech. The Court cannot accept one interest as superior to the other; instead, it must balance the competing interests.

It is clear that some violations of privacy are worse than others, and, while interception alone is embarrassing, public disclosure can be even worse. Notwithstanding the legitimate access to an illegally intercepted message, there is justification for preventing disclosure. This case presents a different scenario, however. The information that was intercepted is related to an important public issue. The illegality of the interception is insufficient to overcome the lawful publication of matters of public concern. Accordingly, the broadcast was not illegal. Affirmed.

■ CONCURRENCE

(Breyer, J.) The holding of this case is strictly limited to the facts presented here: the lawful conduct on the part of the broadcasters and the fact the subject matter was of public concern. Because the statute presents the competing constitutional issues of the right of privacy and the freedom of speech, the statute must reasonably balance its speech-restricting and speech-enhancing consequences. The statute encourages private speech by protecting it from interception and future disclosure, but discourages public speech by protecting private communications from disclosure. Yet, here, the statute acts to disproportionately infringe upon the freedom of the press. Bartnicki (P) had no legitimate interest in the privacy of his inflammatory statements, and Vopper (D) acted lawfully in receiving the tape. Likewise, the speakers on the tape were limited public figures, voluntarily speaking of matters of public concern, eroding away their interests in the privacy of their communication. In cases such as this, involving a low privacy interest relating to a matter of public concern, the rights of the press must prevail.

■ DISSENT

(Rehnquist, C.J.) To prevent at least some violations of privacy, laws have been enacted prohibiting the intentional interception of communications. The majority holds that these statutes violate the First Amendment, at least in those cases where the content of the calls involves a matter a public concern. As a result, the majority must see that this holding, rather than encouraging freedom of speech, impedes it. Under the prior rulings of this Court, the statute should withstand constitutional challenge. Punishing the lawful publication of unlawfully obtained information is often the surest way to dissuade the unlawful interception by reducing demand for such information. As long as publication remains permissible, anonymous sources will continue to invade privacy rights. The Court nonetheless accepts this risk in the name of the First Amendment.

Analysis:

Just as in *Sullivan v. New York Times*, the Court here forced those that choose to venture into the public arena to suffer a certain loss of privacy. In Chief Justice Rehnquist's dissent, he reminds the Court that even public figures have the right to engage in private conversations. While the Court makes every effort to describe the radio station's access to the taped conversation as "legal," it would be difficult for the radio station to claim a belief that the conversation was lawfully intercepted.

■ CASE VOCABULARY:

CHILLING EFFECT: The result of a law or practice that seriously discourages the exercise of a constitutional right, such as the right to appeal or the right of free speech.

INTERVENOR: One who voluntarily enters a pending lawsuit because of a personal stake in it.

Zacchini v. Scripps-Howard Broadcasting Co.

(*Human Cannonball*) v. (*Television Station Owner*)

433 U.S. 562, 97 S.Ct. 2849 (1977)

U.S. SUPREME COURT FINDS FIRST AMENDMENT PROHIBITION FOR BROADCASTING OF A PERFORMER'S ENTIRE PERFORMANCE

■ **INSTANT FACTS** A daredevil performer sued a television station for appropriation after the station broadcast footage of his 15 second human cannonball act on its nightly news program, without the performer's consent.

■ **BLACK LETTER RULE** A state may, consistent with the First and Fourteenth Amendments of the U.S. Constitution, impose liability for the appropriation of a performer's entire public performance.

■ **PROCEDURAL BASIS**

Appeal, following a grant of certiorari by the United States Supreme Court, of an Ohio Supreme Court decision denying a state law claim for breach of the right of publicity.

■ **FACTS**

Entertainer Hugo Zacchini ("Zacchini") (P) performed a "human cannonball" act, in which he was shot from a cannon into a net 200 feet away [squashed Zucchini]. Zacchini was hired to perform his act at a county fair in Ohio. A freelance reporter for Scripps-Howard Broadcasting Co. ("Scripps") (D), the operator of a television station in the area videotaped the 15 second act, which was shown on the evening news, with favorable comments. Alleging that the act he performed was invented by his father and performed only by his family for the past fifty years and that the film was shown without his consent, Zacchini (P) then sued Scripps (D) for unlawful appropriation of his professional property. The trial court granted Scripps's (D) motion for summary judgment and Zacchini (P) [being in a pickle] appealed. The Ohio Supreme Court, although recognizing that Zacchini (P) had a state law cause of action on his right to the publicity value of his performance, held, relying on the U.S. Supreme Court's decision in *Time, Inc. v. Hill* [False light invasion of privacy claim rejected where plaintiff could not show that a magazine's report about a matter of public interest was knowingly false or was published with a reckless disregard for the truth] that Scripps (D) was privileged under the First Amendment to show matters of public interest that would otherwise be protected by state law rights of publicity, in the absence of an intent to injure or appropriate the broadcast for some nonprivileged purpose. Zacchini (P) appealed to the U.S. Supreme Court, which granted certiorari.

■ **ISSUE**

Consistent with the First and Fourteenth Amendments of the U.S. Constitution, may a state impose liability for the appropriation of a performer's entire public performance?

■ **DECISION AND RATIONALE**

(White, J.) Yes. The Ohio Supreme Court relied heavily on *Time, Inc. v. Hill* and concluded that federal law, as enunciated by this Court privileged Scripps (D) to televise a matter of public interest. That case, however, does not mandate a media privilege to televise a performer's entire act without his consent. *Time, Inc. v. Hill* was a claim under New York's privacy statute that Life Magazine, in reviewing a new play, had connected it with a past incident involving Hill and his family and had falsely described their experience and conduct. It involved a claim for nondefamatory false light invasion of privacy, an entirely different tort from the right of publicity recognized by the Ohio Supreme Court and at issue in this case. The differences between these two torts are important. The state interest protected in permitting recovery for placing a person in a false light is that of reputation, with the same overtones of mental distress as defamation. The state interest in permitting a right of publicity is in protecting the proprietary interest of the individual in his act, similar to the goals of patent and copyright law in focusing on the right to reap the rewards of one's own work. The torts also differ in the degree to which they hamper the dissemination of information to the public. In false light cases, the only way to protect the interest involved is to try to prevent publication. In right of publicity cases, the only issue is who gets to do the publication. Zacchini's (P) state-law right of publicity would not prevent Scripps (D) from reporting newsworthy facts about his act. Wherever the line is to be drawn between media reports that are protected by the First Amendment and those that are not, we are sure that the Constitution does not immunize the media when they broadcast a performer's entire act without his consent. Broadcasting his entire act threatens its economic value, much of which lies in the right of exclusive control over the publicity given to his performance. If the public can see the act for free on television, it will be less willing to pay to see it at the county fair. Zacchini (P) does not seek to enjoin the broadcast of his performance; he simply wants to be paid for it. We hold that Ohio may, as a matter of its own law, privilege the press under these circumstances, but the U.S. Constitution does not require it to do so. Reversed.

■ **DISSENT**

(Powell, J.) The majority reverses the Ohio Supreme Court based on its view that the First and Fourteenth Amendments do not immunize the media when they broadcast a performer's entire act without his consent. I doubt this formula provides a standard clear enough even for resolution of this case. The majority's holding that the station's ordinary news report may lead to substantial liability has disturbing implications. Now, when a news editor is unsure whether film footage may be held to portray an "entire act," he may decline coverage, even of clearly newsworthy events, or confine the broadcast to watered-down verbal reporting. The public is then the loser. This is hardly the kind of news reporting the First Amendment was meant to foster. Rather than do a quantitative analysis of whether something is a performer's "entire act," I believe we should ask of what use the station made of the film footage. When, as here, a film is used for a routine portion of a regular news program, I would hold that the First Amendment protects the station from a right of publicity/appropriation suit, absent a strong showing by a plaintiff that the news broadcast was a subterfuge or cover for private or commercial exploitation. Zacchini (P) welcomes publicity for his act, but seeks to retain control over the means and manner of it in order to maximize the money he can earn from such publication. Having made the matter public and newsworthy, however, I believe he cannot, consistent with the First Amendment, complain of routine news reporting. I would affirm.

Analysis:

The U.S. Supreme Court here balances the right of publicity with the rights of the media under the First Amendment. Here, the right of publicity won. Treating a person's right in his own identity as analogous to rights of patent and copyright, the Court holds that a state can, consistent with the Constitution, impose liability for a media broadcast of a performer's entire act without his consent. Thus, in the Court's view, a state can make its own choices about the extent to which it wants to grant performers a right to control the publication of their performance. The dissent, noting that the majority's decision is based largely on the fact that the station appropriated Zacchini's (P) entire act, suggests that the First Amendment should be viewed as presumptively protecting "routine" coverage of newsworthy events, so long as the news coverage is not a cover for what is really private or commercial exploitation of a performance. More recent lower court cases balancing the right of publicity with the rights of the media under the First Amendment have gone in favor of the media, but have usually involved far less than a performer's "entire act" and have been no serious threat to the performer's economic viability.

■ CASE VOCABULARY

APPROPRIATION: A tort in which a person is subject to liability for using the name or likeness of another for his own use or benefit.

FALSE LIGHT INVASION OF PRIVACY: A tort in which a person is subject to liability for knowingly or recklessly publicizing a matter which places another person before the public in a false light in a manner that would be highly offensive to a reasonable person.

Winter v. DC Comics

(Musician) v. *(Comics Publisher)*
30 Cal.4th 881, 69 P.3d 473, 134 Cal.Rptr.2d 634 (2003)

THE FIRST AMENDMENT PROTECTS THE APPROPRIATION OF A LIKENESS IF IT IS MORE THAN MERELY COPYING THE LIKENESS

I'm First Amendment Man. I protect other comic characters from courtroom attacks.

stus.com

■ **INSTANT FACTS** Winter (P) claimed that characters in a comic book published by DC Comics (D) so closely resembled him as to be an appropriation of his likeness.

■ **BLACK LETTER RULE** An artist faced with a right of publicity claim has an affirmative defense based on the First Amendment if the artist's work has significant transformative elements or if the value of the work does not derive primarily from the celebrity's fame.

■ **PROCEDURAL BASIS**

Appeal from an order of the court of appeal reversing an order for summary judgment.

■ **FACTS**

DC Comics (D) published a series of comic books. Winter (P) claimed that two of the characters in one of the comics were based on him and his brother, both well-known musicians (Johnny and Edgar Winter (P)). The characters were called Johnny and Edgar Autumn and were drawn with similar features and clothing as Winter (P). The comic prior to the one in which the Autumn brothers appeared referenced the new characters, and displayed the teaser, "NEXT: The Autumns of Our Discontent," which Winter (P) alleged was a reference to the Shakespeare phrase "the winter of our discontent." The Autumn brothers were portrayed as villainous half-worm, half-human creatures who were ultimately killed in a gun battle with the hero of the comic book series.

Winter (P) brought suit for, among other causes of action, misappropriation of likeness. DC (D) moved for summary judgment, relying partially on the First Amendment. The court granted summary judgment on all counts, and the court of appeal affirmed. The California Supreme Court remanded for reconsideration in light of its decision in *Comedy III Productions, Inc. v. Gary Saderup, Inc.*, 25 Cal.4th 387, 21 P.3d 797 (2001). The court reaffirmed the grant of summary judgment on all claims except for the claim of misappropriation of likeness.

■ **ISSUE**

Does the First Amendment protect DC's (D) portrayal of the characters in its comic books?

■ **DECISION AND RATIONALE**

(Chin, J.) Yes. An artist faced with a right of publicity claim has an affirmative defense based on the First Amendment if the artist's work has significant transformative elements or if the value of the work does not derive primarily from the celebrity's fame. Under California statutory law (Cal. Civ. Code § 3344), celebrities have a right of publicity that allows them to prohibit others from using their likenesses. In *Comedy III*, the Court held that some, but not all, uses of celebrity likenesses are protected by the First Amendment. If the use of a celebrity's likeness is just a literal depiction or imitation without any significant expression being added, the state's interest in protecting the interest of the person whose likeness is taken outweighs the expressive interest of the imitative artist. If, on the other hand, the work contains significant transformative elements, it is worthy of First Amendment protection and is also less likely to interfere with the economic interest protected by the right of publicity.

The test is whether the celebrity likeness is the substance of the work, or whether the likeness is one of the "raw materials" from which an original work has been synthesized. An original work is one that is the defendant's own expression of something other than the celebrity's likeness. The transformative elements that go into a new work may take many forms, including parody, factual reporting, fictionalized portrayal, or social criticism.

The right of publicity is, essentially, an economic right. A celebrity may not use that right to censor disagreeable portrayals. Furthermore, in considering whether a work is transformative, the court will not look at the quality of the artistic contribution. The inquiry is more quantitative than qualitative.

The copyright doctrine of fair use provides some guidance, but is not adopted wholesale into right of publicity inquiries. One part of the test—the effect of the use on the potential market for a copyrighted work—bears on the question. If, however, a transforming work is worthy of First Amendment protection, the question of whether the work cuts into the market for the celebrity's images is irrelevant. If the value of the work derives from some source other than the fame of the celebrity, it may be presumed that there has been a sufficient transformation to merit First Amendment protection.

In *Comedy III,* the challenged work was little more than pictures of the Three Stooges. The pictures were not transformed by the artist, and so did not merit First Amendment protection. In this case, however, the work is more than a literal depiction of Winter (P). Although the Autumn characters are less-than-subtle evocations of the Winter (P) brothers, they are distorted caricatures and cartoon characters. They are part of a larger story, which is itself expressive. The characters do not threaten the Winters' (P) right of publicity. Technically, the work is not a parody, but the exact literary genre does not matter. Likewise, the fact that the Winters' (P) reputations and likenesses were being used to market the comic books is unimportant. The advertising and marketing of a transformative work does not affect its transformative nature. Reversed.

Analysis:

The court traps itself in a minor contradiction when it considers the claim that the Winters' (P) likenesses were used to market the comic book. Important to a finding that a work is transformative is a finding that the value of the work "does not derive primarily from the celebrity's fame." Can that still be said of a work if a celebrity's likeness and reputation are used to market it? Although the marketing strategy does not change the artistic effort that went into the work, it is a reflection of what gives the work its value.

■ **CASE VOCABULARY**

FAIR USE: A reasonable and limited use if a copyrighted work without the author's permission, such as quoting from a book in a book review or using parts of it in a parody. 17 U.S.C.A. § 107.

PARODY: A transformative use of a well-known work for purposes of satirizing, ridiculing, critiquing, or commenting on the original work, as opposed to merely alluding to the original to draw attention to the later work. In constitutional law, a parody is protected as free speech. In copyright law, a work must meet the definition of a parody and be a fair use of the copyrighted material, or else it may constitute infringement.

CHAPTER FIFTEEN

Intentional Economic Harm

Ollerman v. O'Rourke Co., Inc.

Instant Facts: A "non-commercial" buyer uncapped an underground well while excavating recently purchased land.

Black Letter Rule: A seller has a duty to disclose "material facts" that are known to the vendor and not readily discernable by the purchaser.

Imperial Ice Co. v. Rossier

Instant Facts: Imperial (successor in interest to CCC) (P) purchased an ice distributing company from Coker, utilizing an agreement with a non-competition clause. Possier (D) and Matheson (D) induced Coker to sell ice for them in contravention of the non-competition agreement

Black Letter Rule: Actively, affirmatively, and intentionally inducing a breach of contract will be actionable unless sufficiently justified.

Della Penna v. Toyota Motor Sales, U.S.A., Inc.

Instant Facts: Toyota (D) attempted to prevent Della Penna (P) from buying Toyota automobiles in the U.S. and exporting them back to Japan by threatening its dealers with sanctions if they sold cars to Della Penna (P).

Black Letter Rule: A defendant's interference must be wrongful by some measure beyond the fact of the interference itself, in order to maintain an action for interference with prospective economic advantage.

All–Tech Telecom, Inc. v. Amway Corporation

Instant Facts: A company created to distribute telephones is held not to have an actionable tort claim for misrepresentation, after claiming that its supplier fraudulently lured them into and kept them in a losing venture which eventually flopped.

Black Letter Rule: The "economic loss doctrine" will prevent contracting commercial parties from escalating their contract dispute into tortious misrepresentation if the parties could have easily protected themselves from the misrepresentation of which they now complain.

Ollerman v. O'Rourke Co., Inc.

(Land Buyer) v. *(Real Estate Vendor)*
94 Wis.2d 17, 288 N.W.2d 95 (1980)

NONDISCLOSURE MAY BE ACTIONABLE AS AN INTENTIONAL MISREPRESENTATION WHEN THERE IS A DUTY TO DISCLOSE

■ **INSTANT FACTS** A "non-commercial" buyer uncapped an underground well while excavating recently purchased land.

■ **BLACK LETTER RULE** A seller has a duty to disclose "material facts" that are known to the vendor and not readily discernable by the purchaser.

■ **PROCEDURAL BASIS**

Certification to the Wisconsin Supreme Court, of a judgment by the court of appeals, reversing the trial court's dismissal of a claim for intentional and negligent misrepresentation for nondisclosure.

■ **FACTS**

Ollerman (P) bought a vacant lot from O'Rourke Co., Inc. (O'Rourke) (D), a corporation engaged in the business of developing and selling real estate, in order to build a house. While excavating for the house, a well was uncapped and water was released. Ollerman (P) was new to the area, and was inexperienced in matters of real estate transactions. O'Rourke (D), on the other hand, was experienced in matters of real estate, and was familiar with the particular area of real estate, having owned and subdivided the area where the lot is located. When Ollerman (P) purchased the lot, he did not know of the existence of the well underneath the land and hidden from view. He argues that if he had known of the well, then he would not have purchased the property, or purchased it at a lower price. He further argues that the well made the property worth less for residential purposes than he had been led to believe, that the well made the property unsuitable for building without added expense, and that he relied upon the O'Rourke's (D) failure to disclose the existence of the well and was thereby induced to buy this lot in ignorance of the well. Additional allegations included that O'Rourke (D): 1) Knew of the existence of the well and in order to induce Ollerman (P) to buy the land, "falsely and with intent to defraud," failed to disclose this fact which it had a duty to disclose and which would have had a material bearing on the construction of a residence on the property, or 2) should have known about the well, and had a duty to ascertain and disclose such information. The trial court granted O'Rourke's (D) motion to dismiss Ollerman's (P) complaint for failure to state a claim. The appellate court reversed in favor of Ollerman (P). O'Rourke (D) appeals to the Supreme Court of Wisconsin.

■ **ISSUE**

Does a seller have a duty to disclose known "material facts" of a transaction?

■ **DECISION AND RATIONALE**

(Abrahamson, J.) Yes. A seller has a duty to disclose "material facts" that are known to the vendor and not readily discernable by the purchaser. Generally, silence or failure to disclose a fact is not an intentional misrepresentation unless the seller has a duty to disclose. When there is a duty to disclose, failure to disclose will be treated as a representation of the non-existence of that fact. The traditional legal rule, that a seller of real estate dealing at arm's length with the buyer has no duty to disclose, is part of the common law doctrine of caveat emptor. It was believed that in a free market, the diligent should not be deprived of the fruits of superior skill and knowledge lawfully acquired. Over the years, however, courts have departed from or relaxed the "no duty to disclose" rule, due to society's attitudes towards good faith and fair dealing in business transactions. Thus, courts have refused to adhere to the rule when it works injustices, such as in cases where: 1) The seller has told a half-truth or has made an ambiguous statement with the intent to create a false impression, 2) where there is a fiduciary relationship, or 3) where the facts are peculiarly and exclusively within the knowledge of one party to the transaction and the other party is not in a position to discover the facts for himself. While the instant case does not appear to fall into one of these well-recognized exceptions, Dean Prosser has found that courts tend to find a duty to disclose in cases where the defendant has special knowledge or means of knowledge not open to the plaintiff, and is aware that the plaintiff is acting under a misapprehension as to material facts. Dean Keeton in *Fraud Concealment and Nondisclosure*, states that the object of the law in these cases should be to impose on parties to the transaction, a duty to speak whenever justice, equity, and fair dealing demand it. Furthermore, according to the *Restatement (Second) of Torts* § 551, there are situations in which the defendant not only knows that his bargaining adversary is acting under a mistaken belief as to a basic fact of the transaction, but also knows that the adversary is reasonably relying upon a disclosure of the unrevealed fact, due to circumstances and customs of the trade. Therefore, in an effort to formulate a rule embodying this trend to a more frequent recognition of a duty to disclose, the *Restatement* sets forth conditions under which a duty to disclose exists. It states that a party to a transaction is under a duty to exercise reasonable care to disclose to the other, facts basic to the transaction, if he knows that the other is about to enter into it under a mistake as to the facts, and that the other would reasonably expect a disclosure of those facts. The *Restatement*, defines "basic facts" as those that go to the basis, or essence, of the transaction, as opposed to "material facts" that serve important and persuasive inducements to enter into the transaction. However, it is understood that the concept of facts basic to the transaction may be expanding and that the duty to use reasonable care to disclose facts may be increasing. This court, like other courts in other states, have moved away from the rule of caveat emptor in real estate transactions. Therefore, the following elements are significant in persuading a court to impose a duty on a vendor of real estate to disclose known facts: 1) The condition is latent and not readily observable by the purchaser; 2) the purchaser acts upon the reasonable assumption that the condition does or does not exist; 3) the vendor has special knowledge or means of knowledge not available to the purchaser; and 4) the existence of the condition is material to the transaction. O'Rourke (D) argues that in abandoning the traditional rule, the court is really adopting what amounts to, "a strict policy of 'let the seller beware.'" Furthermore, O'Rourke (D) argues that a seller should not be held liable for failure to itemize every conceivable condition in and around the property, regardless of whether such a condition is dangerous, defective, or could become so by the negligence or recklessness of others. However, these arguments are not persuasive in light of the facts alleged and our narrow holding in this case. Where a vendor is in the real estate business and is skilled and knowledgeable and the purchaser is not, the purchaser is in a poor position to discover a condition which is not readily discernible, and the purchaser may justifiably rely on the knowledge and skill of the vendor. Therefore, in this case, a strong argument for imposing a duty on the seller to disclose could be made on this "reliance factor." We hold that a subdivider-vendor of a residential lot has a duty to a "non-commercial" purchaser to disclose facts which are known to the vendor, which are material to the transaction, and which are not readily discernible to the purchaser. A fact is "known," if the vendor has actual knowledge of the fact or if the vendor acted in reckless disregard as to the existence of the fact. The use of the word "know" is the same as in an action for intentional misrepresentation based on a false statement. A fact is material if a reasonable purchaser would attach importance to its existence or nonexistence in determining a choice of action in the transaction in question, or if the vendor knows or has reason to know that the purchaser regards or is likely to regard the matter as important in determining a choice of action. Whether or not the well is a material fact, and whether the buyer should have known about the existence of the well because it was well known in the community, are matters to be raised at trial, not on a motion to dismiss. Ollerman (P) must prove at trial that the existence of the well was a material fact and that his reliance was justified. After all, reliance is an important factor in determining the existence of a duty to disclose, and an element of intentional misrepresentation. As to the second cause of action for negligence based on misrepresentation, courts have been more reluctant to impose liability in negligence actions for misrepresentation causing pecuniary harm, as opposed to bodily harm or physical damage to property. Negligently supplied information is not determined by the same rules that govern liability for the negligent supply of chattels that endanger the security of persons or property. This is so because the fault of the maker of the misrepresentation is sufficiently less to justify a narrower responsibility for its consequences. There is a significant difference in the obligation of honesty and care, and in the reasonable expectations of the users of information that is supplied in connection with commercial transactions. By limiting the liability for negligence of a supplier of information to be used in commercial transactions, to cases in which he manifests an intent to supply the information for the sort of use in which the plaintiff's loss occurs, the law promotes the important social policy of encouraging the flow of commercial information, upon which the operation of the economy rests. We conclude that the allegation of the complaint states a claim upon which relief can be granted. It is for the trial court's and appellate court to determine what liability if any, attaches to O'Rourke (D) for its failure to exercise ordinary care in ascertaining or disclosing the existence of the well. Affirmed.

■ CONCURRENCE

Three concurring justices, while agreeing that the complaint set forth a claim on which relief could be granted, held that there was no need to discuss the various legal principles relating to Ollerman's (P) theories of recovery at the pleading stage, when the case has not yet been tried and the facts were not yet before the court.

Analysis:

Although, traditionally, a bargainer was not obliged to make affirmative revelations of known material facts, there is a modern trend away from the harsh rule of caveat emptor. Accordingly, this court held that a seller has a duty to disclose material facts that are known to the vendor, and that silence when there is a duty to disclose is equivalent to a misrepresentation of fact. This "duty to disclose" only pertains to material facts (facts that the seller knows or has reason to know that the purchaser regards, or is likely to regard, as important in determining his or her choice of action). "Materiality" helps insure not only that a buyer relied or would have relied on the facts, it also helps to insure that reliance is justified. Courts agree that reliance is not only an important factor in determining the existence of a duty to disclose, it is also an element of intentional representation.

■ CASE VOCABULARY

BASIC FACTS: Facts that are assumed by parties to a transaction as the basis for the transaction itself.

CAVEAT EMPTOR: "Let the buyer beware." The traditional legal doctrine which holds that buyers bear the risk of their purchases, and that parties to a transaction should be left to their own devices.

INTENTIONAL MISREPRESENTATION: (Fraud or Deceit) A knowingly false statement, made with intent to defraud, for the purpose of inducing another to act upon it, which actually causes the other to act upon it.

MATERIAL FACTS: Facts that a reasonable person would consider important in determining a course of action.

Imperial Ice Co. v. Rossier

(*Ice Distributors*) v. (*Competitor's Ice Suppliers*)

18 Cal.2d 33, 112 P.2d 631 (1941)

SECURING AN ECONOMIC ADVANTAGE IS NOT SUFFICIENT JUSTIFICATION FOR INDUCING A BREACH OF CONTRACT

■ **INSTANT FACTS** Imperial (successor in interest to CCC) (P) purchased an ice distributing company from Coker, utilizing an agreement with a non-competition clause. Possier (D) and Matheson (D) induced Coker to sell ice for them in contravention of the non-competition agreement

■ **BLACK LETTER RULE** Actively, affirmatively, and intentionally inducing a breach of contract will be actionable unless sufficiently justified.

■ **PROCEDURAL BASIS**

Certification to the Supreme Court of California, of a judgment by the trial court sustaining a demurrer for interference with contract.

■ **FACTS**

California Consumers Company (CCC), purchased an ice distributing company from S.L. Coker (Coker), located in the territory of the city of Santa Monica and the former city of Sawtelle. The purchase agreement provided that Coker, "will not engage in the business of selling and or distributing ice, either directly or indirectly,...so long as [CCC] or anyone deriving title" to the business from CCC, is engaged in a similar business. Imperial Ice Co. (Imperial) (P) then acquired from the successor in interest of the CCC, full title to this ice distributing business, including the right to enforce the covenant not to compete. After Coker began selling, in the same territory, ice supplied by Rossier (D), J.A. Matheson (D2), and Fred Matheson(D3), imperial (P) brought this action for an injunction to restrain Coker from violating the contract and to restrain Rossier (D) and the Mathesons (D2&3) from inducing Coker to violate the contract. The trial court sustained Rossier's (D) and the Mathesons' (D2&3) demurrer and gave judgments for both. Imperial (P) appeals, claiming that the complaint stated a cause of action against Rossier (D) and the Mathesons (D2&3) for inducing the breach of contract.

■ **ISSUE**

Can a party be held liable for actively, affirmatively, and intentionally inducing a breach of contract?

■ **DECISION AND RATIONALE**

(Traynor, J.) Yes. Actively, affirmatively, and intentionally inducing a breach of contract will be actionable unless sufficiently justified. Generally, an action will lie for inducing a breach of contract by unlawful means such as libel, slander, fraud, physical violence, or threats of such action. Most jurisdictions hold that an action will also lie for inducing a breach by the lawful use of moral, social, or economic pressures, unless there is sufficient justification for such inducement. Such justifications may exist in protecting an interest that has greater social value than insuring the stability of the contract. For example, inducing the breach of a contract which would be injurious to health, safety, or good morals, or inducing a breach through peaceful labor tactics in the interest of improving working conditions, is of such social importance that inducing a breach would be justified. On the other hand, inducing a breach of contract, simply because a party is in competition with one of the parties to the contract and seeks to further his own economic advantage, will not be justified. Contractual stability is generally accepted as of greater importance than competitive freedom. A person is free to carry on his business, and reduce prices, advertise, and solicit in the usual lawful manner, even if some third party may be induced thereby to breach his contract with a competitor in favor of dealing with the advertiser. Moreover, if two parties have separate contracts with a third party, each may resort to any legitimate means at his disposal to secure performance of his contract even though the necessary result will be to cause a breach of the other contract. However, a party, under the guise of competition, cannot actively and affirmatively induce the breach of a competitor's contract in order to secure an economic advantage over the competitor. Therefore, the act of inducing the breach must be an intentional one. If the actor had no knowledge of the existence of the contract or his actions were not intended to induce a breach, he cannot be held liable though an actual breach results form his lawful and proper acts. In Boyson v. Thorn [where a hotel manager induced the owner of the hotel to evict plaintiffs in violation of a contract], this court stated that an otherwise lawful act, is not rendered unlawful by the existence of malice. It was clear that the confidential relationship between the manager of the hotel and the owner justified the manager in advising the owner to violate his contract with the plaintiffs. Although, that case has been considered as establishing the proposition that no action will lie in this state for inducing a breach by lawful means, statements to that effect were not necessary to the decision and should be disregarded. The presence or absence of "malice" is immaterial, except as it indicates whether or not an interest is actually being protected. In the instant case, Rossier (D) is charged with actively inducing Coker to violate his contract with Imperial (P). Rossier (D) and the Mathesons (D2&3), by inducing Coker to violate his contract, sought to further their own economic advantage at Imperial's (P) expense. Such conduct is not justified. Had Rossier (D) merely sold ice to Coker without actively inducing him to violate his contract, Coker's distribution of ice in the forbidden territory in violation of the contract would not have rendered Rossier (D) liable. Therefore, it is necessary to prove that they intentionally and actively induced the breach. Since the complaint alleges that they did so, it states a cause of action, and the demurrer should have been overruled. Reversed.

Analysis:

When a defendant deliberately undertakes to interfere with the contractual relationship of the plaintiff and a third party, the defendant may be liable for tortious interference with contract. Generally, this action requires: 1) the existence of a contract, 2) the defendant's knowledge of it, 3) the defendant's improper interference with it, and 4) a breach. Although this case makes clear that a justification exists when the social value is great, this court holds that there is generally no privilege or justification based on motive or intention. Thus, no showing of "malicious intent" or "wrong," apart from the wrong inherent in the intentional interference itself, is necessary in order maintain an action for interference with contract.

■ CASE VOCABULARY

MALICE: Intent to commit a wrongful of malevolent act.

Della Penna v. Toyota Motor Sales, U.S.A., Inc.

(Car Exporter) v. *(Car Company)*

11 Cal.4th 376, 902 P.2d 740, 45 Cal.Rptr.2d 436 (1995)

"WRONGFULNESS" IS AN ELEMENT OF "INTERFERENCE WITH PROSPECTIVE ECONOMIC ADVANTAGE"

■ **INSTANT FACTS** Toyota (D) attempted to prevent Della Penna (P) from buying Toyota automobiles in the U.S. and exporting them back to Japan by threatening its dealers with sanctions if they sold cars to Della Penna (P).

■ **BLACK LETTER RULE** A defendant's interference must be wrongful by some measure beyond the fact of the interference itself, in order to maintain an action for interference with prospective economic advantage.

■ **PROCEDURAL BASIS**

Certification to the Supreme Court of California, of a judgment by the court of appeals, reversing a trial court ruling which required a showing of wrongfulness for interference with prospective economic advantage.

■ **FACTS**

Della Penna (Penna) (P) purchased Lexus cars in the United States and exported them to Japan for resale. Penna (P) brought a tort claim against Toyota (D), for interference with prospective economic advantage. In an effort to prevent Lexus autos, imported into the United States, from being re-exported to Japan, Toyota Motor Sales, U.S.A., Inc. (Toyota) (D), compiled a list of "offenders" and warned its dealers that those who did business with such offenders faced possible sanctions. Over objection, the trial judge charged Penna (P) with the burden of showing that Toyota's (D) interference was "wrongful." Penna (P) then framed the definition of "wrongful," that the trial judge read to the jury, as including conduct outside the realm of legitimate business transactions and lying in "methods used or by virtue of improper motive." The jury found for Toyota (D) and the court of appeals reversed on the ground that the judge erred by placing the burden of proof on the plaintiff. Toyota (D) appeals the judgment of the court of appeals.

■ **ISSUE**

Must a plaintiff prove that an interference was wrongful in order to maintain an action for interference with prospective economic advantage?

■ **DECISION AND RATIONALE**

(Arabian, J.) Yes. The origin of the two torts, interference with contract and interference with prospective economic advantage, is generally thought to be Lumley v. Gye [which dealt with conduct intended to induce the breach of an existing contract]. In Temperton v. Russell [which involved a suit against a labor union which demanded that the builders' suppliers cease furnishing material, and threatened to bring pressure on those who supplied the suppliers for failure to comply], it was held that there was no tangible distinction between a claim against those who induce persons to break existing contracts, and a claim against those who induce persons not to enter into contracts. Some courts and commentators have found the keystone of liability in these cases, to be the "malicious" intent of the defendant. Others have doubted whether "malicious" amounted to anything more than an intent to commit the act, knowing it would harm the plaintiff. Traditionally, the plaintiff need only allege a so-called "prima facie tort" by showing the defendant's awareness of economic relation, a deliberate interference with it, and resulting injury. It was then the defendant's burden to demonstrate that his or her conduct was privileged or justified. Since the nature and features of the economic relations tort seemed to many, unduly vague, inviting suit and hampering the presentation of coherent defenses, requirements surrounding its proof and defenses led to calls for reexamination and reform as early as the 1920's. Thus, while the American Law Institute was discarding the prima facie tort requirement, an increasing number of state high courts had already reformed the elements of the economic relations tort, and the burdens surrounding its proof and defenses. Recognizing the difficulties of defining the elements so as not to sweep within its terms a wide variety of socially very different conduct, courts have held that a claim of interference with economic relations exists when interference resulting in injury to another is wrongful by some measure beyond the fact of the interference itself. Defendant's liability may arise from improper motives or means, or by reason of statute, a recognized rule of common law, or even an established standard of a trade or profession. No question of privileges arises therefore, unless the interference would be wrongful but for the privilege. Over the past decade or so, close to a majority of the high courts have explicitly approved a rule that requires the plaintiff in such a suit to plead and prove that the alleged interference was either wrongful, improper, illegal, independently tortious, or some variant on these formulations. Accordingly, development of the economic relations tort in California, has paralleled its evolution in other jurisdictions. We have held that an action will lie for unjustifiably inducing a breach of contract. However, there is a need to distinguish between claims for the tortious disruption of an existing contract and claims that a prospective contractual or economic relationship has been interfered with. These two torts are not analytically unitary nor of equal dignity. Although the exchange of promises resulting in a formally cemented economic relationship is worthy of protection, economic relationships short of contractual should stand on a different legal footing. Our culture is firmly wedged to the social rewards of commercial contests. Thus the law takes care to draw lines of legal liability in a way that maximizes areas of competition free of legal penalties. We hold that a plaintiff seeking to recover for alleged interference with prospective economic relations has the burden of pleading and proving that the defendant's interference was wrongful by some measure beyond the fact of the interference itself. But beyond that, we need not tread today. We conclude that the trial court did not commit error in requiring the jury to find that Toyota's (D)conduct was wrongful. Since the definition of "wrongful conduct" was supplied by Penna (P), we have no occasion to review its sufficiency. Reversed.

■ CONCURRENCE

(Mosk, J.) The confusion caused by such terms as "malice," "justification," and "privilege," is causing the tort of intentional interference with prospective economic advantage to rapidly approach incoherence. One reason for this may be discovered in its doctrinal basis. When developing what has become known as the "prima facie tort doctrine" the analytical object was a framework capable of assisting comprehension and guiding an internal systematic development of the subject matter, to the end that principle and not precedent might govern. The idea is that "intentional infliction of harm" is a prima facie tort that covers a multitude of desirable acts as well as a multitude of sins. Although this may have resulted in a kind of "internal systematic development of the subject," it has sacrificed an external connection to society. This rule is a philosophical effort to state all or much of tort law in a single sentence, rather than an effort to state a meaningful principle. A second reason for the near-incoherence may also be discovered within the law itself. Tort's "protectionist" premise is at war with itself. A man should not only be protected by the law in the enjoyment of his property once it is acquired, a man should also be protected in his efforts to acquire it. However, even the interfering party deserves protection. The policy of the common law has always been in favor of free competition. So long as the plaintiff's contractual relations are merely contemplated or potential, it is considered to be in the interest of the public that any competitor should be free to divert them to himself by all fair and reasonable means. A third reason for the near-incoherence may be discovered in its focus on the interfering party's motive and on his moral character as revealed thereby. In *Boyson v. Thorn*, it was held that a legal act, would not be made illegal due to the existence of a bad motive. *Imperial Ice* erred when it rejected *Boyson's* assertion that motive was irrelevant. In cases where the trier of fact believes it has discerned good motives or at least persuades itself that it has, bad conduct and bad consequences may evade liability. Furthermore, parties which have neither engaged in bad conduct nor produced bad consequences may be made to pay for damages without wrongful act. With all this said, the only reasonable choice is reformulation. Although harm is generally directed at the plaintiff, this should not be a requirement. The tort may also be satisfied by a showing of restraint of trade, including monopolization, as well as by independently tortious means. Under the tort as reformulated, it is clear that the Court of Appeals erred. Although I agree with most of the majorities opinion, I disagree on two major points. First, I would not adopt the inherently ambiguous standard of "wrongfulness." Second, if I were to adopt such a standard, I would not allow it to remain undefined. Any definition of "standard," of course, should avoid suggesting that the interfering party's motive might be material for present purposes. As stated, a position of this sort would result in the imposition of no liability on a person who acts, to quote Justice Holmes in *American Bank & Trust Co. v. Federal Bank*, with "disinterested malevolence."

Analysis:

Claims for "interference with contract" and "interference with prospective economic advantage" are similar but distinct, and stand on different legal footing. Understanding that these two torts are distinct, this court, like other jurisdictions, required proof that the interference was wrongful, aside from the "wrongfulness" inherent in the interference itself. Thus the appellate court had erred when it shifted the burden to Toyota (D) to prove that the interference was privileged or justified. More importantly, however, the majority refused to define the specific scope of "wrongfulness." According to Penna's (P) and other jurisdictions' definition, "wrongfulness" could lie in the method used or by virtue of an improper motive. Herein lies the crux of Justice Mosk's concurrence. He argues that the standard adopted should embody a requirement that the means used to interfere with a prospective economic advantage be independently tortious, or in other words be sufficient to constitute a tort in and of itself.

■ CASE VOCABULARY

DISINTERESTED MALEVOLENCE: Conduct that causes injury or damage to another party, but is not intended or exclusively directed to causing harm.

PRIMA FACIE TORT: The intentional infliction of injury or damage to another by otherwise proper and lawful acts.

All-Tech Telecom, Inc. v. Amway Corporation

(*Telephone Distributor*) v. (*Telephone Supplier*)

174 F.3d 862 (7th Cir. 1999)

A COMMERCIAL CONTRACTING PARTY'S CLAIMS OF MISREPRESENTATION MAY BE DISMISSED IF THERE IS NO SEPARATE PHYSICAL HARM

■ **INSTANT FACTS** A company created to distribute telephones is held not to have an actionable tort claim for misrepresentation, after claiming that its supplier fraudulently lured them into and kept them in a losing venture which eventually flopped.

■ **BLACK LETTER RULE** The "economic loss doctrine" will prevent contracting commercial parties from escalating their contract dispute into tortious misrepresentation if the parties could have easily protected themselves from the misrepresentation of which they now complain.

■ **PROCEDURAL BASIS**

Appeal to the United States Court of Appeal of a judgment dismissing claims of misrepresentation on the basis of the economic loss doctrine.

■ **FACTS**

In 1988 All-Tech Telecom, Inc. (All-Tech) (P), created for the purpose of being a distributor for Amway Company's (Amway) (D) recently created "TeleCharge" phone and the associated service, bought a large number of the phones. The phone was intended for the use of customers of hotels and restaurants. In 1992, TeleCharge flopped and Amway withdrew it form the market, due to, among other things, equipment problems, regulatory impediments, and eventually the obsolescence of the phones. All-Tech (P) claims that they were lured into and kept in this losing venture by a series of misrepresentations, including Amway's assertion that it had done extensive research before offering the service, that the service would be the "best" in the nation, that any business telephone line could be used with the phone, that the service had been approved by all 50 states and did not require approval from any telephone company, that each phone could be expected to generate $750 annual revenue, that the carrier retained by Amway to handle calls and billing was the largest company of its kind in the nation (International Tele-Charge, Inc. (ITI)), and that the purchaser of the phone would have to deal with ITI because the phones could not be reprogrammed. The district court dismissed all of All-Tech's (P) claims of misrepresentation based on the "economic loss" doctrine of the common law [doctrine which asserts that when economic harm results from harm to person or property, ordinary negligence rules apply; but, when commercial or economic harm stands alone (no harm to person or property), courts will not impose a general duty of reasonable care]. All-Tech (P) appeals.

■ **ISSUE**

Can commercial contracting parties seek liability for misrepresentation in tort, if the parties could have easily protected themselves from the misrepresentation?

■ **DECISION AND RATIONALE**

(Posner, J.) No. Originally the economic loss doctrine was merely a limitation, allowing only the injured person himself, rather than employees or suppliers of a merchant, to recover for the consequences of a personal injury or damage to property. Since damage to property or persons is a real cost and hence "economic," the doctrine would be better named the "commercial loss" doctrine. One reason for this is that a tort may be both indirectly beneficial, for instance advantageous to competitors, and harmful. Thus, since a tortfeasor may not sue for the benefits, neither should he have to pay for the losses. Another reason is the desirability of confining remedies for contract-losses to contract law. Suppliers can protect themselves from loss through buying insurance, charging higher prices, or by including in their contract with the retailer, a requirement that he buy a minimum quantity of goods from the supplier. Therefore, a tort remedy is not necessary. This point has implications for commercial fraud as well as for business losses that are secondary to physical harms. Where there are well-developed contractual remedies, such as those provided by the Uniform Commercial Code, there is no need to provide tort remedies for misrepresentation. Such remedies would duplicate and undermine contract law. For example, doctrines of contract law, such as the parol evidence and "four corners" rules, are designed to limit the scope of jury trials. Tort law does not have these screens against vagaries of the jury. Parties must be able to rely on the written word and not be exposed to the unpredictable reactions of lay fact-finders to witnesses who testify that the contract means something different from what it says. Thus, the "economic loss" doctrine forbids commercial contracting parties from escalating their contract dispute into a charge of tortious misrepresentation when they could have easily have protected themselves through contractual methods such as warranty. On the other hand, if commercial fraud were to go completely by the boards, as a literal reading of some economic-loss cases might suggest, the prospective parties to contracts would be able to obtain legal protection against fraud only by insisting that the other party to the contract reduce all representations to writing, increasing contract writings and transaction costs. Furthermore, fraud tort does come with safeguards against false claims, including the requirement of pleading with particularity and in many jurisdictions, a heightened burden of proof. The claims in the instant case however, are in the nature of warranties and do not press against the boundaries of the economic—loss doctrine. All-Tech (P) has failed to present any evidence of actionable misrepresentation. Some of the alleged misrepresentations were corrected before All-Tech (P) bought its first phone. Thus All-Tech (P) cannot complain about misrepresentations not relied upon. Moreover, some misrepresentations were made by Amway distributors and not by Amway (D) itself, in describing their experiences in selling the phones. These distributors are independent contractors, not employees, whose representations may not bind their employees through the doctrine of respondeat superior. Many of Amway's (D) alleged misrepresentations were mere "puffing" or meaningless sales patter that no reasonable person would rely upon. The TeleCharge service was new. As problems surfaced, Amway (D) would notify its distributors, including All-Tech (P). Despite this, All-Tech (P) continued to purchase these phones. Some of the misrepresentations were not material, such as those concerning ITI's size as the largest in the nation, which true or not, did change the fact that ITI was capable of providing necessary service. Some were hypothetical, such as those concerning expected annual revenue. Some, such as the representation that the phones could not be reprogrammed, were not made at all. Furthermore, All-Tech's (P) alternative claim of promissory estoppel, has no basis. Promissory estoppel provides an alternative basis for consideration by treating a promise as a contractual undertaking. The promise that All-Tech (P) stresses as the basis for its claim, that Amway had thoroughly researched the TeleCharge program before offering it to distributors, is not a promise to do something in the future. It warrants a past or existing condition. Although a warranty of this type, can be considered a promise to pay for the consequences should the research turn out to be not thorough after all, a warranty which induces reasonable reliance may only form the basis of a promissory estoppel claim in limited circumstances. Promissory estoppel is meant for cases in which a promise, not being supported by consideration, would be unenforceable under conventional principles of contract law. But when there is an express contract governing the relationship out of which the promise emerged, and no issue of consideration, there is no gap in the remedial system for promissory estoppel to fill. In this case, the parties had a contract governing the relationship in the course and within the scope of which the alleged warranty of thorough research was made. This was either one of the warranties within the contract or it was not. There is no need to invoke the doctrine of promissory estoppel in this case. Affirmed.

Analysis:

Some courts have said that the plaintiff, or at least a sophisticated plaintiff, may not pursue a negligent misrepresentation claim for commercial harm against a defendant with whom he has a contractual relationship. In that view, if the claim cannot be made on grounds of intentional misrepresentation, it must be made as a contract claim or not at all. The idea is that, between contracting parties, the contract's provisions should control, and also that if a point covered by a misrepresentation is important to the plaintiff, he should have it expressed in the contract or suffer the risk of the trier's conclusion that it was not so important as he now claims. This case deals specifically with the "economic loss doctrine." As stated in the beginning of the opinion, it may be helpful in clarifying the nature of this doctrine, if it is thought of as the "commercial loss doctrine." The doctrine generally prevents contracting "commercial" parties, as opposed to consumers or other individuals not engaged in business, from escalating their contract dispute. It is this distinction that differentiates this "misrepresentation" case from those analyzed in the beginning of the chapter. Commercial parties generally stand on equal footing with the parties they are contracting with.

■ CASE VOCABULARY

ECONOMIC LOSS DOCTRINE: When commercial or economic harm stands alone (divorced from injury to person or property), courts have not imposed a general duty of reasonable care. They have instead imposed a duty of reasonable care in commercial harm cases mainly when the parties are in a special relationship and the defendant has implicitly undertaken such a duty.

PROMISSORY ESTOPPEL: The doctrine by which promises become binding, despite lack of consideration, because the promisor intended or should have reasonably expected the promise to induce reliance, and the promisee does rely on the promise.